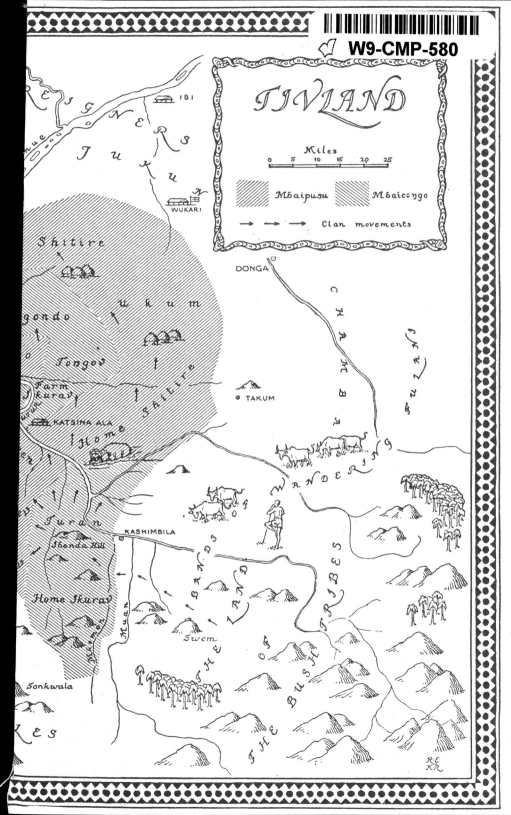

TIVLAND

Miles

0   5   10   15   20   25

Mbaipuru   Mbaicongo

→ → → Clan movements

IBI

J U K U N

WUKARI

DONGA

Shitire

U k u m

gondo

Tongov

Shitire

Farm Ikurav

KATSINA ALA

Home

TAKUM

C H A M B A

W A N D E R I N G

F U L A N I

Ikurav

Ikurav

KASHIMBILA

Ibenda Hill

Home Ikurav

Muen

Swem

Sonkwala

B A N D S   O F

T H E   L A N D

O F   T H E   B U S H   T R I B E S

R E
K R

AKIGA'S STORY

Akiga

AKIGA'S STORY

THE TIV TRIBE AS SEEN BY
ONE OF ITS MEMBERS

Translated and annotated by

RUPERT EAST
M.A., D.Litt. (Oxon.)

Published for the
INTERNATIONAL AFRICAN INSTITUTE
by the
OXFORD UNIVERSITY PRESS
LONDON   NEW YORK   TORONTO

Oxford University Press, Amen House, London E.C.4

GLASGOW   NEW YORK   TORONTO   MELBOURNE   WELLINGTON
BOMBAY   CALCUTTA   MADRAS   KARACHI   LAHORE   DACCA
CAPE TOWN   SALISBURY   NAIROBI   IBADAN   ACCRA
KUALA LUMPUR   HONG KONG

First published 1939
Reprinted (*with Bibliography and new Preface*) 1965

SET IN GREAT BRITAIN BY THE CAMELOT PRESS
AND REPRINTED LITHOGRAPHICALLY BY
THE UNIVERSITY PRESS, OXFORD

FOREWORD

THIS book, an annotated English translation by Dr. Rupert East of the major part of a work in Tiv by Akiga on the history and institutions of his people, was one of the studies recommended to the Institute in its early years. But, since it appeared just as a world war was breaking out and before the present widespread interest in the peoples of Africa and the work of African writers had begun to develop, the small first edition of *Akiga's Story* cannot be said to have exerted any great influence at the time. Its publication was, nevertheless, more than justified by the later and increasing appreciation of this remarkably vivid and penetrating account of Tiv traditions and institutions and of initial responses to the arrival of missionaries and administrators. It is engrossing as a self-portrait of the energetic, disputatious life—at once intensely practical and strongly mystical—in the multitude of hamlets of Tivland in the Benue valley. Today it is also a valuable historical document for its portrayal of an early phase of 'culture contact' and social change, and for its invaluable contextual accounts of traditional rituals and beliefs.

The publications of Drs. Paul and Laura Bohannan, who in their field studies in the fifties explored more deeply the ethnographic field opened up by R. M. Downes (*The Tiv Tribe*, 1933) and R. C. Abraham (*The Tiv People*, 1933), have stimulated interest both in Tiv ethnography and in the theoretical problems that it has presented, and so directed many students to *Akiga's Story*. Meanwhile, with greatly increased attention being given to all aspects of African studies, it had become a scarce book, often difficult to find. And it is to meet what is hoped will be a considerable demand for this work, as literature and as a scholarly source, that the Institute has arranged for this reprinted edition to which Dr. East has contributed a new preface. He, Professor Bohannan, and others, have been good enough to assist us in preparing a bibliography of writings on the Tiv for inclusion in this edition. Dr. East and the Institute have also agreed to the publication by the Oxford University Press of a smaller inexpensive book of extracts from this work to help to make Akiga's work more widely known, especially in Nigeria.

The original Tiv text is still extant. Professor Paul Bohannan found the manuscript in safe keeping at the Mkar mission of the Dutch Reformed Church in 1952 and was able to have it copied. A portion on 'The "Descent" of the Tiv from Ibenda Hill', which had not been included in this volume, he subsequently translated for inclusion in *Africa*, xxiv 1954, pp. 295–310.

In his Preface to the first edition, written in April 1939, the late Professor D. Westermann felt obliged to stress the many impediments that then existed to both the reading and the writing of literature by Africans, whether in their own or in European languages. Developments since then have probably exceeded Professor Westermann's expectations at that time, and we hope that as a further step arrangements will be made for Akiga's text to be printed in Tiv.

It should be noted that throughout the book the text in larger print is direct translation from Akiga and the smaller print the introductory notes and commentaries by Dr. East.

DARYLL FORDE

February 1965

PREFACE

IT is nearly thirty years since Akiga and I worked together on the manuscript of his book and walked the length and breadth of Tivland, discussing the material which he had spent so many years of his life collecting. A lot of water has flowed into the Benue since then. The old men's belief that the White Man would soon be leaving, which seemed so laughable at the time, has proved right after all. Nigeria has now to find the solution to her own problems, not least of which is the problem of Akiga's own countrymen, unhappily torn by internal dissension. Akiga himself, I am sorry to say, has joined the company of his ancestors, but in the intervening years until his death in May 1959 he served his people well, first in Gaskiya Corporation as editor of a Tiv news-sheet, then for five years as member of the Northern House of Assembly, and afterwards with the Tiv Native Authority in the field of literature and adult education. In politics he was a conservative and moderating influence.

Most of those whose names are mentioned in these pages, and many others whom we knew, are dead too. 'The old mushroom rots . . . but the Tribe lives on.' It lives indeed—and grows. At the time when this book was first published the Tiv were said to number 530,000; recent estimates put the figure at 800,000, and the tribe is still expanding. From being an unconsidered pocket of non-conformity in a predominantly Muslim sphere of influence, it has come in the last thirty to forty years much into prominence, even beyond the boundaries of Nigeria, as a result not only of its own forceful and sometimes embarrassing activity, but also of the valuable work of others, as will be seen from the bibliography which is included at the end of this edition.

The story of these people told by Akiga has also attracted much wider interest in recent years than when it was first written, and we should both be grateful—I know that I can speak on his behalf—to those whose support has made a second edition possible, after so many years, when his work might well have passed into oblivion. He himself, a man without vanity or pretension, would have found this also surprising. It was for his own people that he wrote, but to the modern generation, more sophisticated than their fathers, the old lore and tradition may already appear outmoded. Indeed, Akiga's declared object was to record this for posterity before it was too late. The events too that he described, which seemed so important at the time and gave rise to such violent emotions, are probably long forgotten. But the book will be valued not so much for its brave attempt to preserve tribal memories, far less for its topical appeal, but for the sympathetic and vivid image he draws of the life and character of his own people.

RUPERT EAST

Shrivenham
January 1965

CONTENTS

ix

ILLUSTRATIONS

(between pages 176 and 177)

INTRODUCTION

⟪ In May, 1911, only a few years after the arrival of the first Europeans, a small station was started by an outpost of the Sudan United and Dutch Reformed Church Missions on the edge of Tiv country. The place chosen was the village of Sai, the senior elder of a sub-section of the Shitire clan, who lived by the side of the main trade route from Wukari to Takum. Sai was a man of considerable prestige amongst his own people. He was acknowledged by every one to possess great supernatural powers, as befitted a prominent leader of tribal society, and was also famous for his skill in the magic craft of blacksmithing.

Sai had a small son called Akiga (more correctly A-kighir-ga), whose mother had left him when he was a child, and who followed him about wherever he went. He sat beside him while he worked at the forge, and was present when he carried out the magic rites or talked with the old people. This unusual friendship between father and son, particularly in view of the former's reputation in the practice of magic, led his family to suspect that Sai's son was not quite normal, and this suspicion was borne out, according to his own account, by certain ominous events which seemed clearly to indicate the presence of occult powers, manifest at an early age. It is probable, also, that the loss of an eye and a deformed foot gave Akiga a somewhat odd appearance, which in itself would have been enough to suggest to the Tiv that there was something uncanny about the child.

Whenever Sai sat and talked with the missionary who had come to live in his village, the young Akiga was at his side, and in this way he was brought to the notice of the white man. Soon after his arrival the missionary was deserted by his servants, who came from more civilized parts, and had no intention of staying to test whether there was any truth in the popular belief that the Tiv made a practice of eating all strangers that came into their country. Thereupon he persuaded Sai, after much difficulty, to allow his favourite son to come and work in his house, while he lived in the village. Akiga was thus the first of his tribe to come directly under European influence. How he subsequently grew up as a staunch adherent of the Mission, and eventually came to write the following pages, is best told in his own words:

B   I

I T is now nearly twenty years ago that I began to set my
  heart on writing this book. For at the time when the
missionaries first brought the Word of God to Tiv
country, and came to settle at my father's house, my
father took me and gave me to them, and I remained with
them in the care of Mr. Zimmerman, of the Dutch
Reformed Church Mission, who was the first to come and
live amongst the Tiv. This was in the year 1911, and I
was about thirteen years old at the time. After some years
I also believed, and became a Christian. So they taught
me the knowledge of God and of the World. And it was
while I was wandering round through every part of
Tivland, preaching the Gospel of Jesus Christ, and at the
same time seeing and hearing the things of Tiv, that the
idea of this 'History' took shape in my mind. So I began
to ask, and to look, and to delve into everything concerning
the Tiv people. Whenever I sat talking with my father,
or with the other elders, it was always about these things
that I questioned them, for my father, Sai, was a man well
known amongst the Tiv.

So it has been my constant prayer that God would help
me to write this book, in order that the new generation of
Tiv, which is beginning to learn this New Knowledge,
should know the things of the fathers as well as those of
the present generation. For everything that belongs to
Tiv is passing away, and the old people, who should tell us
about these things, will soon all be dead. It makes me sad
to think that our heritage is being lost, and that there will
be none to remember it.

¶ Here he acknowledges the encouragement given to him by
the European members of the Mission, particularly Mr. W. A.
Malherbe, and by those in government service. After this follows
a list of all the elders who have supplied the information recorded
in the book. With regard to these latter he says:

I T is not every elder who is well versed in Tiv lore.
  Some know, others do not. It is the men of mature
years who know best; of the very old men only one

or two are wise, the ignorant are in the majority. More-over, if you wish to ask them about something, and do not go about it in the right way, you will never get the truth from them. They will think that you have been sent by the white man, and give you no information of any value. As for the chiefs, if you ask one about his district or about his chieftainship, he will be afraid to give you the true facts of the case, lest you go and tell the European, who will depose him and give the office to whom it rightly belongs. Moreover, some of the old men still believe that the white man will soon be going,[1] so why should they tell him about these things, in order that he may take them away from them, or forbid them their use? Others think, when you ask them something and they see you write it down, that you are making a report to give to a govern-ment official, who will increase their tax.

Especially is this so in the case of one whom they know to be in government service; they will never give him a true answer, unless he force it from them, for fear that he may tell the white man. They put him off with lies, and if one of them tries to tell him the truth, the others pull faces and wink at him, till he desists and falls back on misleading statements, so that the inquirer goes away with a mass of false information. Far better results would be obtained if a European conducted a systematic inquiry himself, and pinned them down to facts. But in the case of a missionary, or a follower of the Mission, they say, 'A missionary is not a white man of any consequence: he neither tries cases, nor collects tax, nor inflicts punish-ment; all he does is to pray. We can tell him frankly about our affairs, and he will do no harm'.

As for myself, I am known by a large number of the tribe, and they understand me. There is no Tiv chief to-day who does not know me well. I am favoured, too, by Providence in my relations with them, in that they never fear to tell me what I ask them; while I, on the other hand, am careful not to put questions to them in such a way that they will not answer. But I take no credit to myself for this.

[1] This is a common belief amongst the people of Northern Nigeria.

❡ The rest of his introduction is chiefly concerned with the work which we have done together, and the slight help I have been able to give towards arranging the material and getting it published. He concludes:

I PRAISE God who inspired me with the desire to write this book, and has not left me with it still unfinished. For who am I, with the knowledge that I have, to write a work of any value?

This book fulfils a father's duty to all Tiv who have a care for that which concerns their own tribe. You, then, my Tiv brothers of the new generation that can read, read it and tell others, who cannot, of the things of our ancestors; so that, whether we have learnt to read or not, we all may still know something of our fathers who have gone before us. And do you, however great your knowledge may be, remember that you are a Tiv, remain a Tiv, and know the things of Tiv; for therein lies your pride. Let us take heart. The old mushroom rots, another springs up, but the mushroom tribe lives on.

❡ Akiga sees himself as the spokesman of a passing age, and indeed he is one of the very few who are fitted to play such a role. In a sense he belongs to the old order, rather than to the young generation which has been growing up in the changed environment of the European occupation. In spite of his Christian training, he has spent a large part of his life amongst his unenlightened kinsfolk, and a broad and tolerant mind has enabled him to understand and represent their point of view with sympathy and, as far as is humanly possible, without bias, while still holding to his personal convictions. He does not therefore record the practices and traditions of his people from the standpoint of a detached observer, but as part of his own mental experience. While one half of him is bound up with the loyalties due to his calling, the other half is identified with the inner life of his own tribe. It is because he has been able to keep the balance between these two sides of his spiritual make-up, and has not allowed either one unduly to influence or prejudice the other, that he is so well able to interpret both the old thought to those whose minds are trained in the new way, and the New Knowledge to those who have grown up in the old. The latter task he helped to accomplish in the translation of the Bible, and performs every day of his life as an evangelist; the former is the object which he sets out to achieve in this book.

Much of the credit for producing a man capable of such an achievement is due to his teachers. From the beginning, the aim of the Mission has been to train its pupils for the work which they are to do, without taking them out of their environment. It has sheltered them from the harmful externals of Western culture, and encouraged them to develop along their own lines, as far as was consistent with their main objective as Christian missionaries. The genuine, and essentially African, tone of Akiga's writings proves the success of this policy. Indeed the value of the book to us lies in the fact that the author has been so little affected by European ways of thought. He has learnt a little English, but not enough, fortunately, to have read any literature or be influenced by foreign models; for the Mission at first wisely concentrated on developing the vernacular as an educational medium. His work is, therefore, in every sense an original effort, as, of course, he had no precedent to follow in his own language. He writes as freely as he would talk, in his own natural style, untrammelled by any literary conventions or inhibitions which might have been induced by studying the work of others.

Other books have been written by Africans about the life of their own people, though not yet in Northern Nigeria. Others will be written, but they will be written by more sophisticated authors who have the advantage, or disadvantage, of a modern education, whose outlook is no longer primitive and whose knowledge is no longer subjective. The old men have that knowledge, but they are inarticulate, or rather have no channel of communication with us. Only a man such as Akiga can act as the mouthpiece of the elders and of the old order. True, he has spent many years in contact with the white man, and has learnt something of our ways and our ideals, but if this were not so he could not have done the work at all. His book represents, as it were, a last struggle of the old Africa to express itself before it dies, and to make its voice carry across the abyss which divides us from the mind of primitive man.

The author's greatest asset is perhaps his ability to see the humour and the pathos of his own people's reaction to contact

with more advanced civilizations: the childish eagerness to copy
their masters: the desire of the sturdy thick-set Tiv to dress himself up in absurd European clothes, or in the even more incon-
gruous draperies of the lean northern peoples: the ease with
which he is gulled and robbed by more astute traders or spell-
mongers. There is hope for a people who can laugh at themselves
like this. Here is none of the snobbish bitterness that one sometimes sees in the newly emancipated products of our schools, whose
essays breathe a pharisaical contempt of the 'bush man', the
'witch doctor', and the 'superstitions' of their ignorant kinsfolk.
Akiga has a deep affection for the old people and customs, and
nothing but scorn for the young imitators of foreign fashions.

Akiga set out to write a History of the Tiv. He has not succeeded in this, because the Tiv, like most African tribes,
have no history in our sense of the word. But he has given an
account, from the native point of view, of the events of recent
years, and particularly of the effects of contact with European
culture. He has also achieved his main object in recording the
dying traditions of his people for the benefit of posterity. The
book must not be judged as an anthropological treatise, but as a
contribution to the newly born African literature. Anthropology has already grown up, and is preparing to enter the age-
grade of the exact sciences. A modern observer who wishes to be
taken seriously may no longer, like the old explorers, write pic-
turesquely about anything that takes his fancy, but is expected to
give detailed information on definite subjects, and to answer a
large number of set questions, systematically arranged under
headings and sub-headings. His first duty, like that of the com-
piler of a government report, is not to interest his readers, or to
advance theories of his own, but to furnish accurate evidence on
each point, which will add to the common store of knowledge, and
perhaps form the basis of a general survey written by some one
else.

Let it be said at once that this book makes no pretence to fill any
of these requirements. Many essential questions which would
form the subject of an objective inquiry are left unanswered, or
only partially dealt with. Parts of the book have no scientific
value as a record of facts, but have been included in this edition
for their human interest and for the light which they throw on the
African's mentality and his attitude to current problems. The

author has chosen his own subjects and discarded those which have no interest for him. A few suggestions have been made to him which he has followed, but rather with the object of completing the picture for the Tiv readers for whom he is writing. Even the most ambitious monograph can be no more than the briefest of summaries, for a full description of the life of a tribe, or even one side of it, is not to be contained in a single book. It is only the apparent simplicity of the life of more primitive peoples, and the lack of literature on the subject, that has led writers even to attempt such a task. So that although the number of pertinent facts which have not even been mentioned in this book greatly exceeds those which have, room has still been found for things which would never be included in a better proportioned study by a trained anthropologist.

The extracts which have been translated and reproduced in this book form only about a half of the original manuscript. They have been chosen not so much for their intrinsic merit as for their general interest to Europeans. The parts which have not been included deal chiefly with the detailed history of each clan, a record of local events attending the British occupation, of which only those having a direct bearing on present-day problems are here given, and an intimate description of the activities and character of each European officer. Indeed the whole book is concerned with persons rather than with things. This is to be expected, for no normal African could, or would wish to, write an impersonal review of contemporary events such as might be demanded from a European historian. But for obvious reasons it has been necessary to keep personalities out of the English version, and names of government officers have therefore been omitted, or replaced by the titles of their appointment. It will be understood, naturally, that this substitution is contrary to the character of the original; for an office, as apart from the man who holds it, means little to a Tiv. There are also sections dealing with the work of various departments, Agriculture, Education, Medical, Missionary, and the British Cotton Growing Association. These, unfortunately, have also had to be omitted owing to lack of space, and because they are mostly records of purely local interest. They will be included in the Tiv edition of the book which it is hoped eventually to publish.

It must be admitted that the necessity for cutting out much of the local material has somewhat upset the proportions of the book. It is now still less a 'history' than it was in its original form, and we are both conscious of its lack of arrangement and ordered sequence. As Akiga said, when this was pointed out to him, it is as if one set out to go to a neighbouring village, and, instead of keeping to the path, turned aside continually to visit friends along the route, chat with them about their crops and household affairs, paused to look at the trees and birds by the side of the road, or to meditate on God and the Universe. . . . The historical framework of the book is consequently somewhat obscured by the digressions. Nevertheless, except for a few minor transpositions and re-wording of headings, it has been thought best to keep the manuscript, that is as much of it as has been translated, in its original form, and not try to make it look like an ordered scientific work, which it is not. It should be added that, as regards logical arrangement of data and sustained continuity of thought, the manuscript as a whole is far in advance of any African effort which has hitherto come to the notice of the Northern Provinces Literature Bureau.

Akiga has been criticized for attributing to the Tiv tribe as a whole characteristics and practices which apply strictly only to the Shitire clan to which he belongs. It is inevitable that his outlook should be coloured to a certain extent by his own immediate knowledge and experience, in the same way that, on a larger scale, the writer who speaks of 'the African' or 'the European' is sometimes inclined to generalize from the peoples with whom he has personal acquaintance. But I believe he has made a conscientious attempt to treat his subject without clan bias, and has on the whole succeeded. He has travelled in every part of Tiv country, and spent much time studying the local lore and history. Especially in the section where he deals with the history of each individual clan has he been careful not to give preference to any one section of the tribe over the rest. In any case, the life and practices of the various clans differ only in points of detail.

As to the parts of the book, printed in smaller type and marked with a ⅏, which were not written by Akiga, I offer an apology. It is feared that these connecting passages and explanatory notes interrupt rather than carry forward the train of thought. They are necessitated by the inability of the translator to reproduce, through the medium of a European language, the full meaning of the passages and all the ideas which lie behind. The book is self-explanatory to those for whom it was originally intended. It is unnecessary for the author to describe an environment, or explain allusions, which are familiar to everybody. The object of these additional paragraphs is not to add information which he has omitted to supply, but to sketch in, as it were, the background which he takes for granted, and to explain or underline passages whose significance might otherwise only be appreciated by his own countrymen.

The difficulty is to separate, for purposes of inspection, the threads of a pattern which in Akiga's description forms a natural whole. 'The world of the primitive African is characterized by its unity and completeness. No sharply defined aspect exists by itself. . . . It is therefore difficult to study one single feature of African life in isolation. Because it is cohesive one inevitably passes from one region into the other without noticing it; and a correct understanding can only be obtained by surveying the life as a whole.'[1] Magic and witchcraft, farming and medicine, marriage and social organization, cannot be separated into water-tight compartments, for they are all interrelated and interdependent. This is especially true of the many allusions to the supernatural factors at work in the Tiv's everyday life, and the attempt to give cross-references or explain these as they occur has inevitably given a patched appearance to the book which it does not have in the original.

My second object has been to explain from the European standpoint, but not to explain away, certain incidents and matters of policy which are recorded by Akiga as seen through the eyes of the people whom they affected. Some of these, taken out of the context of Akiga's real appreciation of the aims of the present administration, cannot but appear in the light of a serious criticism. Mistakes have certainly been made and many have been recognized, but it is only fair to the Government which has approved and made possible the publication of these passages, and to the individuals concerned in formulating the policy, that certain factors and causes should be noted which lie on the side of the picture which is hidden from the Tiv author, and that mention should be made of the steps which have been taken to rectify errors, or reconsider experiments which have proved unsatisfactory.

[1] Professor Diedrich Westermann, *The African To-day*, pp. 178–179.

For the rest, a translation of this kind can reproduce the substance, but hardly the spirit, of the original. A book written in a European language can be read in another without very much loss, because the two peoples look out on much the same world. But a book by an African cannot really be 'translated' into a European language at all, because whatever words are used they must always mean something different to members of the two races. Linguistically, we lack points of contact for expressing even the most familiar objects, let alone more intimate or abstract ideas. Words like 'house', 'farm', 'brother', 'family', not only represent different concepts in themselves, but the associations which form their setting, especially the mystical associations, are many leagues apart. You can call a spade a spade, but the African may not see it as such. Moreover, two races that live in such dissimilar environments naturally differ widely in the range of vocabulary in common use. The result of this is that many African objects and ideas can only be described in a European language, if at all, by a technical word. But this book is not about technical subjects. It deals with the things of everyday life, and is written in everyday language. A Tiv does not need a training in anthropology to understand it, and an English version filled with specialized terms gives a very false impression of the nature of Akiga's work.

Similarly, the terms used in the descriptions of magic ceremonies are not exotic or departmental, but amongst the commonest words in the language. For this reason it has seemed best, as far as possible, to render them in the basic meaning which they have in Tiv, and to avoid technical or semi-technical terms, particularly those associated with other cultures or religious systems. By this means the underlying idea will not be made more obscure than it is in the original language, and it will still be possible to draw comparisons, without the prejudice of question-begging terms. For example, it has been the custom to speak of the 'propitiation' ceremonies carried out by the Tiv; but the word he uses himself means no more than to 'mend' or 'put right', and has accordingly been so translated here. None of our own terms for dealing with the supernatural will serve the purpose, because they imply personal intervention. Whether or not such a conception forms a part of the Tiv beliefs at the present time is matter of doubt; in any case it would be unjustifiable to assume it implicitly in translation of the primitive idea. Similarly, 'sacrifice' is merely 'killing', 'offering' is no more than 'pouring out beer', 'initiation'— though this word could not always be avoided—the 'seizing' (of control over supernatural forces).

So it is in every department of life. There is no technical vocabulary, because there are no professional classes, and little specialization beyond that which is the result of sex or age. Every aspect of tribal life is everybody's business. Consequently, with the exception of those terms which are used chiefly by the women, and the words which belong to the inner circle of elders, practically the whole of a huge vocabulary is in common daily use.

I wish to join with Akiga in thanking the large number of his countrymen who have supplied material for this book, and to express my personal indebtedness to the members of the Administrative staff, especially Captain R. M. Downes and Mr. K. Dewar, who contributed many ideas to the discussion of social and political problems, and to Professor Westermann and Mr. E. S. Pembleton for reading the manuscript. We also acknowledge the kindness of the Mission in allowing Akiga to work with me on the book, and the generosity of the International Institute, the Nigerian Government, and the Tiv Native Administration, in defraying the cost of its production.

I.

THE ORIGIN OF THE TIV TRIBE, AND OF SOME OF THE TRIBAL CUSTOMS

⁋ The setting of the story, into which the author plunges without preliminaries, is as follows: In the pleasant savanna country to the south of the River Benue, and in a narrow strip along its north bank, lives a tribe of 530,000 people. They are a stockily built, virile race of farmers, whose two great aims in life are to fill their yam stores and granaries with food, and their homes with children; an independent people, who have little respect for princes, and have never felt the need for cohesion, or obedience to a central authority, or unifying code. Cheerful, and on the whole contented, they are not afraid of tangible foes or misfortunes, though always on their guard against the great unseen army of evil forces and the occult machinations of their fellow men. They have a quick-tempered and somewhat unstable nature, and are always ready to go after strange gods, or to copy and adopt anything which takes their fancy, whether it be a hat, a new word, or a social movement; but they soon tire of it and throw it on one side. In this, as in almost everything else, they are the antithesis of the northern Muhammadan peoples. Everywhere you go in the northern states you will hear social and administrative workers complain of the difficulty of making any progress owing to the stubborn reactionary temper of the people. Amongst the Tiv you will hear the same complaint of the lack of any consolidated advance, and exactly the opposite reason given for it.

This contrast in temperaments is only one of the results of a fundamental difference in origin, culture, and environment. Indeed it would hardly occur to any one even to compare such obviously disparate races, were it not for the fact that, owing to a more or less fortuitous circumstance, the British approach to the Tiv has been, both culturally and linguistically, through the Hausa-speaking peoples of the Muhammadan states. That is to say, when the whole of the territory which is now known as Nigeria came under British control at the beginning of the present century, and was divided into two sections, each of which had, for practical purposes, its own staff of Administrative, Police, and (later) Education officers, the Tiv tribe (with the exception of about one-fifth which remained in the southern section until 1914) was included in the Northern Provinces. As a result of this, the great majority of European government officers who have been posted to Tiv have first served an apprenticeship amongst Muhammadans and learnt the Hausa language. This, in the past, has inevitably had an unconscious effect in determining our psychological approach to the tribe, and, as will be seen later, in shaping the administrative policy.

In recent years a change has been taking place, and the Administration has made more direct contact with this people by encouraging European officers to learn their language, and to study them first-hand, instead of through the medium of Hausa interpreters. The adoption by us of their own name 'Tiv', in place of 'Munshi', the term by which the Hausa calls them, is significant of this changed attitude.

It is appropriate, therefore, for any one who studies the local problems at the present time to compare the two types of people, and note how great is the difference in their mental equipment and outlook. There are, of course, many pagan tribes in the Northern Provinces to which the same distinction would apply, but the Tiv tribe is far the largest and most homogeneous; moreover, since it was never conquered or even seriously penetrated by the Fulani or other Muhammadan people, it has been affected less than most by northern culture. Nowhere is the contrast between the characters of the two races more clearly marked than in their personal relationships with the European, and their reactions to contact with Western civilization. The Muhammadan citizen of the northern emirates may privately despise the white man, with his undignified clothes, frivolous behaviour, and indifference to religion; he may regard his tiresome restrictions and regulations as an affliction; yet outwardly he pays him the greatest respect. He flatters him with such titles as 'The Great Reformer' and 'My Father and Mother', but he will not willingly give up one iota of his own creed, or any part of the culture which is based on it, in favour of Western customs and ideals. The Tiv, on the other hand, tells the white man quite openly that everything was better before he came, and that it is he who has 'spoilt the land'; but inwardly he has a strong affection and respect for the individuals he knows, and recognizes many good points in the new régime. One of our chief difficulties is to prevent him from slavishly copying the worst manifestations of Western culture and ruthlessly discarding what is good in his own.

You will see no walled towns in Tivland, and scarcely any large villages. There are no big areas that have been under intensive cultivation for generations, as in the north, nor, on the other hand, any wide stretches of uninhabited country. Everywhere dotted about are small homesteads, well built, clean, and in good repair, each belonging to one man with his family and relations, and surrounded by his farms. They will remain there till the land is exhausted, or until the father dies, when in course of time the site will be abandoned and each son will go out to find a place near by in which to build his own home. In this way the population is distributed fairly evenly over the whole area, which, except in the crowded southern districts, is big enough to allow the people to practise their system of shifting cultivation without serious land shortage, yet not so large as to prevent every man being within easy reach of his neighbour. We once took a party of Tiv on a visit to Hausa country, where they saw relatively big towns and people living under urban conditions; but what impressed them most was not the crowds or comparative wealth concentrated in a small space, but the large areas of bush that were not occupied at all; not the dust and noise of the towns, but the great silences in between. Tiv country is a friendly place, and generally speaking it is impossible to walk along a path for more than half a mile without meeting one of your fellow men, or coming to a little settlement where the householder is glad to welcome you into his guest-house to smoke a pipe and chat with you, whether your skin be black or white. Almost wherever you may be you can hear the voices of people passing along the bush paths or working on the farms, and, when evening comes, the sound of singing and piping in the hamlets round about.

The Tiv language belongs to a group which has usually been called 'Semi-Bantu', or, more recently, 'Classifying Sudanic'. The tribe certainly has Bantu affinities, both ethnological and linguistic, and the view held by Malherbe[1] and others is that in the remote past they once formed a part of the main body of Bantu people, far to the east and south-east of their present

[1] *Tiv-English Dictionary*; introduction.

territory. Their own tradition, which is given in the following
pages, is that they came down from the hilly country to the
south-east, and there seems no reason to doubt that this statement
is accurate in so far as it refers to comparatively recent migrations.
Even to-day, although they live in the plains of the Benue valley,
they still refer to the south and south-east as 'up' (*sha*) and to
the opposite direction as 'down' (*shin*). As to their movements
before this, the theory put forward by Captain Downes is that they
came to the Sonkwala hills from the Ekoi country to the south-
west,[1] but I have here accepted the tradition given by Akiga of
an entrance from further to the east, for reasons hereafter shown.

At all events the people who now live in the hills to the east of
Takum (Undir, Ukwese, Ugbe, &c.), whom the Tiv now include,
together with the tribes on the southern border, under the con-
temptuous name of *atɔatiev*, 'rustics', are so like to themselves
in appearance, customs, and language, that one can hardly doubt
that at one time they all belonged to the same branch of a race
which had been driven up into the less hospitable country by
some unknown pressure in the past. Eventually a small sub-
division of this tribe, or collection of tribes, whose members now
call themselves Tiv, being more adventurous than the rest, pushed
down from the hills and rocky country into the more attractive
farming lands where they now live. Here, through contact with
such peoples as the Jukun, Chamba, and Hausa, aided by their
natural ability for copying and adapting the ideas of others, and
by the more favourable environment in which they now found
themselves, they developed a relatively advanced culture. This
development, which is traced by Akiga in the second chapter,
seems to have happened very rapidly, and has been brought about
mainly by culture contact: for instance, by the introduction of
weaving from the Hausa; various cereals, and possibly black-
smithing, from the Chamba; the cultivated yam and certain
domestic animals, such as the duck and the sheep, from the south
(Dam); some political institutions from the Jukun, and so forth.
But the change has also been to some extent evolutionary, and due
to their own inventive genius; as, for example, in the case of their
house construction, which, of its type, is now unsurpassed in
workmanship and design by any people in Nigeria.

Meanwhile, their brothers whom they have left behind in the

---

[1] R. M. Downes, *The Tiv Tribe*, p. 2 and map.

hills have mostly advanced little beyond the stage of development that the Tiv attribute to their forefathers. Beans, millet (*agase*), and the koko yam, which the Tiv say were the first foodstuffs known to them, are still cultivated by the more backward of these tribes as their chief crops. It is true that they now wear cotton clothes (though bark cloth is still made) and use iron tools, but they buy these from the Jukun peoples or the Bafum, and do not seem to have learnt the craft of blacksmithing or weaving themselves.

Once having settled in the plains which they now occupy, the Tiv increased and multiplied in a very short space of time, and this is no doubt the reason why there is little disparity between their different sections, either in appearance, language, or customs. They regard themselves almost literally as one huge family—a family, however, between whose members there have been constant feuds and much jealousy. Every one of this family of half a million members can trace his descent to the common ancestor, and so can in theory tell his relationship to any other member. This is made possible by the fact that every kinship group, from the smallest unit up to the main divisions of the tribe, is called after its common parent. As the tribe now traces descent patrilineally, the parent in the majority of cases is the father, but a few maternal ancestors appear further back in the family tree. The significance of this fact is discussed in a later chapter. A complete genealogical table, giving the position of every family in the tribe in relation to the common ancestor, was prepared by Akiga in his original manuscript. The data contained in this, being generally well known to every one in the respective groups, are an accurate representation of the social organization of the tribe as it exists to-day, though from an historical point of view the founders of the larger and older sections of the tribe must doubtless be regarded as mythical.

But whether these remote ancestors actually lived under the names after which their children now call themselves is to a Tiv not a matter of dispute, because to him they still live in the persons of their descendants. This personification of the groups, reminiscent of the references to the tribes of Israel in the Old Testament poets, is no mere figure of speech, but a reality, which must be appreciated for a clear understanding of some of the following passages. It is, in fact, an extension of the concept, familiar in

c

Africa, and developed later in this book, of the close association
between the group and each individual member of it. As the
individual is spiritually identified with the group to which he
belongs, so is the group regarded as an individual, personified
in the name of its founder. The idea is contained in Akiga's opening sentence: 'Tiv has only two children.' To the Tiv these two,
Icɔŋgo and Ipusu, are not mythical figures óf antiquity, but still
very much present, as any one may seę, in the persons of their
hundreds of thousands of living representatives. This viewpoint
is shown even more clearly in the concluding sentences of the
first chapter.

Every man refers to himself by the name of his group. When
questioned, he replies, 'My name is So-and-so; I am Mbakor'
(or whatever his group and clan may be). Similarly, the land is
identified in Tiv nomenclature with the people who live on it.
Every hamlet is called by the name of the householder, and every
part of the country is known by the name of the group which
occupies it at the time. Excepting the names of hills and rivers,
there are no other place names.

The Tiv, then, are divided into two main sections, Mbaicɔŋgo
and Mbaipusu. The terms mean the Circumcised and the Uncircumcised, and though nowadays, and as far back as the people
can remember, circumcision is practised by everybody, the names
obviously suggest a stage in which this was not the case. Yet so
strong is the kinship-group idea amongst the Tiv that they will not
accept this inference, but have invented a legend on the analogy
of the other patronymics (for one can hardly accept it as fact)
that the sections are called after their two first ancestors, Icɔŋgo
and Ipusu, the coincidence of whose names is explained in the
following account. The Tiv tradition, on the other hand, admits
that the practice of circumcision had a foreign origin, and there
is a certain amount of internal evidence to support this view. In
the first place, it belongs to that class of operations for which the
right to practise can be 'bought': these are commonly acknowledged to be comparatively recent introductions, as opposed to the
older Tiv practices which cannot be performed without ceremonial initiation.[1] Secondly, the fact that the use of an iron
razor of foreign pattern is expressly enjoined gives very strong
support to the Tiv belief that it was first done by a foreigner

[1] P. 210.

using this instrument; because, as is well known, in the practice of medicine (which is closely allied with magic), and especially in a critical operation like circumcision, evil effects may result from the slightest deviation from traditional procedure. If circumcision were an indigenous custom it is more probable, on the analogy of practices in other parts of Africa, that the use of iron would be expressly forbidden.

With these introductory remarks I leave Akiga to tell his story.

TIV AND HIS CHILDREN: THE ORIGIN OF CIRCUMCISION

TIV has only two children, Ipusu and Icɔŋgo. Ipusu was the first-born, and at that time his father was uncircumcised. He was born on the farm. Now a certain foreigner[1] who was out hunting elephant chanced to come that way and, seeing Tiv with his child Ipusu, asked him how it was that he had begotten a child without having been circumcised. Tiv replied that he did not know what circumcision was, but would like to be shown. The foreigner showed him, and it pleased him, so that he asked if he might also be circumcised. The other agreed, but added, 'Circumcision is a very big thing, and can only be done on certain conditions. You must give me something before I can circumcise you'. Tiv said, 'Yes indeed, that is quite right. Tell me what I must give'. The foreigner told him to give a chicken. Tiv asked, 'A hen or a cock?' The foreigner said, 'Neither is taboo, but there must be two of them'.

So Tiv got up, chased and caught two chickens, gave them to the foreigner, and he circumcised him. When he had done, Tiv said that he would now like to buy the practice of circumcision, in order that he might in his turn circumcise his race for ever, from generation to generation. 'Very well', said the other. 'If you ask me to teach you, I will certainly do so; but not for nothing.

---

[1] The word *uke* translated here, and throughout the book, as 'foreigner' was apparently the name given by the Tiv to the first people they met from the northern districts of Nigeria, such as individual elephant hunters and the like. It was afterwards extended to include all races who wore clothes and appeared to have a relatively advanced culture, such as the Chamba, the Jukun, and the Hausa. Finally, it was also applied to the European. The more primitive tribes who live to the south and east are not called *uke* but *atɔatiev*, the word which is here translated 'bush tribes'.

You must buy. If you perform the operation without
having bought the right to do so, it will go wrong.'[1] Tiv
said that he readily agreed; what must he give? The
foreigner told him to give two chickens and a 'ten-twenty',
which meant a young chicken. For at that time a hen or a
cock was a 'twenty', but a young pullet or cockerel would
be a 'ten-twenty'.[2] This fee, which the foreigner prescribed, was for showing Tiv the medicine which he
should apply to stop the bleeding, if there was much loss
of blood after the operation.

Tiv did not dispute this. He got up, caught two
chickens and a young pullet for the showing of the
medicine, and gave them to the foreigner, who thereupon
taught him how to perform the act of circumcision. It was
with his own type of razor that the foreigner circumcised
Tiv, and afterwards he drew out a razor of the kind which
he had used and gave it to him. He told him never to use
any other kind of razor, save only the foreign razor
which he had given him, and to make no mistake about it.
That is why the Tiv from that time have always used a
foreign razor for circumcising. They have nothing of
their own with which to do it, since originally Tiv had no
knowledge of circumcision whatever, until he was shown
by the foreigner. It was the foreigner who taught him
how to circumcise and also gave him the razor to use for
the purpose.

When Tiv had recovered from the operation, his wife
again became pregnant and in due course gave birth to
another son. So Tiv gave him the name Icɔŋgo, because
he was born after he had been circumcised. That is why
he called this child his 'Circumcision', and the first son his
'Uncircumcision'.[3]

When Tiv died his children were called after him. For
a time they were known as 'Tiv's Children',[4] but this
term was afterwards dropped, as it did not sound well, and
the whole tribe came to be included under the name 'Tiv'.

¹ P. 208, 9.
² For an explanation of these terms, and the significance of fees in general,
see p. 210.
³ Icɔŋgo, Circumcision; Ipusu, Uncircumcised (from ipusugh, foreskin).
⁴ An analogy drawn from present custom, see p. 107.

THE MIGRATION

The Tiv married women from the neighbouring Bush Tribes, and had children by them, both sons and daughters. When their sons grew to manhood and their daughters reached puberty, the Bush People cast their eyes upon them, and demanded that the Tiv should now give them their daughters to marry in return. When they refused to do this, the Bush Men were angry. 'What!' they cried. 'Why are these Tiv becoming so assertive? We used to give them our daughters to marry, thinking of our children who were yet unborn; why will they not give their daughters to our sons? Is it we who have been the fools, then?' This was the beginning of the quarrel.[1]

Faced with the hostility of the Bush Tribes, the Tiv abandoned their site and began to move down. They left the east on the one hand, the south on the other, and came down between, until they met with the people called Fulani. The Fulani shepherded them and escorted them down. They never troubled them, or oppressed them in any way, but came down in company with the Tiv, quite peacefully. Thus the Tiv formed a close friendship with them. Whenever they came up against any other tribe that wanted to fight with them, the Fulani would attack their enemies and drive them off. When the Tiv saw the strength of the Fulani, they gave them the name of 'Pul', which in the Tiv language means 'to be stronger'. For the Fulani were stronger than all others at that time; whatever tribe they attacked they were sure to overcome it.

The Fulani fought with staves, little white spears, and swords, but they never agreed to give the Tiv any of these weapons of war, for they did not want to teach them all they knew. Some, judging only by outward appearances, say that the Tiv are slaves of the Fulani. This was never so; but in so far that they greatly helped the Tiv in delivering them from the hands of the Bush Tribes, so the Tiv repaid them by giving the help of their labour. For

---

[1] Up to the present day it is almost unknown for a Tiv woman to marry outside the tribe, though the men, especially in the border clans, will take non-Tiv wives. This, since they now are patriarchal, has doubtless contributed to their expansion at the expense of the surrounding tribes.

the Tiv were a people who understood how to cultivate the soil, whereas the Fulani were a tribe of herdsmen, and knew nothing about farming. So when they went out with the cattle to graze, the Tiv would do their farm work for them. The two races differed in appearance because the Fulani wore clothes, but the Tiv were unkempt; and for this reason the Fulani children used to jeer at the Tiv children, whenever there was a quarrel, saying, 'Your fathers are slaves who work for our fathers'. But their fathers never took any notice of this, nor did the Tiv.

The Fulani and the Tiv, however, were not together very long before they parted company. The two peoples were so intimately connected that they did not refrain from intermarriage. But the Tiv did not like the Fulani marrying their daughters. When the elders saw that this was their intention, they were not at all pleased. 'For', they said, 'this is just the thing which we have already refused to allow, and here it is again! We do not let the Bush Tribes marry our daughters, so why should the Fulani be scheming to take them? They are not of our race, and it is best that we should separate. We will go our way, and they shall go theirs. But let us not part with ill feeling; let us part good friends.' So the Tiv elders, having first talked the matter over amongst themselves, called all the chief men of the Fulani, and they sat down and discussed it together. . . . The Fulani elders agreed to the Tiv proposal, but they said, 'Since our parting is without rancour, it seems to us that each of us should leave some memorial of the event. What do you think? It may be that some day hence our children and your children will not know of the good fellowship which exists between us to-day. Let us then appoint a token'. The Tiv said, 'That is not necessary. Even though we have no token, the resemblance between us is the main thing. For our daughters have borne children to you, and your daughters have married our sons and borne children to us, so that we have indeed intermingled our blood; this is a fact which will never be forgotten'. The Fulani said, 'Nevertheless, let us make it an occasion for giving small presents. We will set aside a month in which you may catch us and take a little money from us, or a cloth which has been burnt in the fire'. 'Very well, then', said the Tiv; but it did not seem to them to matter very much. They agreed in order that the Fulani should leave them to go their own way. And that is why, even down to the present day, the Tiv do not trouble to catch the Fulani, and receive their cloths.

So they separated. The Fulani turned back towards the rising sun, and the Tiv passed on down alone.

It is possible to find some slight evidence to show that the Tiv were once connected with the Fulani. They are alike in outward appearance,[1] and one or two of their words are the same. For example, if the Fulani wish to say to one of their brothers, 'Come, let us go', they say '*Shin ja*', exactly like a Tiv, and their name for a tree-felling axe is *ijembe*, as in Tiv.[2] These facts may possibly show that there is some truth in the story of a connexion between the Tiv and the Fulani. And another thing: The Europeans, who know about the country, say that in the days before the white man came the Fulani in these parts grew more powerful than all other peoples, and eventually it was they who became the rulers of the great Hausa states, such as Sokoto. Is this evidence perhaps sufficient to let us believe that the Fulani were at one time in contact with the Tiv? Otherwise, how is it that of all the other different tribes none are mentioned, save only the Fulani, who were certainly the most powerful at that time?

[1] This refers chiefly to colour. A number of Tiv have light skins, but this is not peculiar to the tribe; it is commonly found in individuals of many races in the Southern Provinces. The Fulani of to-day would certainly not recognize this as evidence of kinship. They are an exceedingly race- and colour-conscious people, and look upon all other tribes of West Africa as 'black men', although they themselves are often indistinguishable in colour from their despised neighbours. A light-skinned slave will not even be called 'white' or 'red', which are honourable terms, but 'yellow' (*saiwajo*); and the black-skinned slaves are said to have been preferred. Apart from the occasional resemblance in colour it would be difficult to find two African peoples more dissimilar than the stocky Tiv farmer and the slim, small-boned, sharp-featured Fulani herdsman.

[2] *Shin ja = sei en njah*. *Ijembe* (axe) appears in western Fulani as *jambere*, and is a common Bantu root. There are a large number of Bantu roots both in Tiv and Fulani, but this, of course, is not necessarily proof of direct contact.

¶.The tradition, here recorded, of a former connexion between the Tiv and the Fulani seems at first sight improbable, if one accepts the theory that the Tiv came into their present position from a south-westerly direction. If, however, one believes the account given here of a migration over the mountains from the south-east, there is every likelihood of their having come into contact, during their wanderings, with the southern fringe of the Fulani penetration. According to Lemoigne,[1] the main advance of the Fulani into Adamawa from the north took place in the eighteenth century, at which time also were founded Tibati, Ngaundere, Banyo, Tingere, and other Fulani towns, which are not far off the Tiv hypothetical line of march. But before this time wandering bands of Fulani herdsmen, known to later immigrants as 'Kitije', had already penetrated into Adamawa, and it is probably these to whom the Tiv tradition refers. The Fulani are said to have first reached Bornu and Bauchi in the fifteenth century, and Bagarmi 150 years later, so that it is unlikely that they had penetrated sufficiently far south to come into contact with the Tiv before the end of the seventeenth century, which, if the Tiv tradition is correct, fixes the earliest date for the Tiv migration. There is nothing improbable in the account of the arrangement between the Tiv and the Fulani by which the former did farm work in return for protection. To the present day the true Fulani seldom farms himself; this work, in the latter days of their ascendancy, was always done by slaves. Before the Jihad (early nineteenth century) the Fulani were not in a position to requisition labour for this purpose, but were themselves subject to the indigenous inhabitants of the country.

The attempted derivation of the Tiv name for the Fulani is clearly a false one. The Tiv are fond of finding plausible meanings for the obscure terms in their own language, if necessary inventing a story to explain their origin. Akiga's efforts in this direction must not be taken too seriously. *Pul* is the true root of the name by which the Fulani call themselves, and of which the term 'Fulani' is a Hausa corruption. But this error is in itself evidence in favour of the authenticity of the tradition. For if the Tiv were once in such close contact with the Fulani as they claim, it is evidently thus that they came to learn their real name. Later generations, having been cut off from direct contact with the Fulani, and being

[1] *Renseignements Coloniaux*, 1918.

more closely associated with the Hausa, have learnt from the latter the name 'Fulani'. So, not recognizing this as the same as their own term 'Upul', they have invented the derivation given in the text.

The month referred to as having been set aside by the Fulani for the giving of presents is Muharram, and the original Fulani custom on which the story is based concerns the relationship between cousins. On the eve of the tenth day of Muharram (Ashura), and for the remaining days of the month, a Fulani may go up to his cousin and throw him some small present of money, cloth, &c., saying the words '*Mi haɓɓi ma*' ('I have bound you'). In some parts, he at the same time lays a piece of string across his cousin's wrist, this being apparently a relic of former times when he actually tied him up. Thereupon the man thus addressed is bound to give a return present of at least twice the value of the original gift; the object therefore is to get one's present in first. The custom of giving presents during Muharram has come to be extended by the Fulani to other tribes whom they regard as their 'cousins', that is to say, those with whom they have at one time been in close relationship, as, for instance (in the case of the Adamawa clans who came down from Bornu), the Kanuri. This is what is meant by saying that a Tiv who meets a Fulani during this month may 'catch' him and demand a present. The fact that this custom still survives between the Tiv and the few isolated Fulani with whom they occasionally come into contact is another strong proof of an earlier connexion. For the Fulani to-day look upon all the pagan tribes of the Benue valley as slave peoples, and would not normally be at all disposed to give them the status of 'cousins'.

THE ORIGIN OF THE RAISED SCARS ON THE FACE
AND OTHER TRIBAL MARKINGS AND PRACTICES

AT the time when the Tiv were with the Fulani their faces were unmarked; nor did they make any mark on their bodies. It was when they came to separate from the Fulani that they decided that they had too much trouble with other people, and would adopt some symbol which should be peculiar to the Tiv tribe.[1] So they learnt the

---

[1] I.e. they would henceforth cut themselves off from extra-tribal relationships.

art of raising scars on the face, and began to practise it.
(Where can they have seen these markings? We do not
know.[1]) They always wanted to be different from other
tribes, and as they came down they kept strictly to themselves. It was in fact owing to this exclusiveness that they
took to cicatrizing the face. Nor was this enough for them.
Later on they added other marks on their bodies, and
began to make marks on the bodies of the women, of
many different types and names, till the practice became
for them not merely a symbol, but a mode of adornment,
so that now those who do not know say that it is natural to
them.[2]

They laid down that these practices should be carried
out in due order: piercing the ears; cutting the teeth;
circumcision; raising scars on the faces; marking the
women on the belly; and other different kinds, both for
men and women.

❧Much of what follows is written in the past tense, because the
author has still his historical purpose in mind. But, unless otherwise stated, these descriptions may be taken to apply equally
well to the present day.

PIERCING THE EARS

IN the old days a boy had his ears pierced as soon as he
started to go about with arrows in his hand.[3] The
custom was for a child,. who wanted to have his ears
pierced, first to go and tell his mother or father, or
whichever of the elders was acting as his guardian, that
he was going to pierce his ears, and they would then give
their consent. But sometimes they said, 'No, you are
still too young. You have not yet reached the age for the
piercing. If you pierce your ears now you will take no
care, and your ears will break off or form a lump'. So the

---

[1] They are also practised by some of the tribes through which the Tiv are
said to have passed, e.g. Iyɔn and Utaŋge.

[2] Cf. C. K. Meek, *The Northern Tribes of Nigeria*, vol. i, p. 45: '. . . as tribal
marks are now—and were even in pre-European days—commonly regarded as
adornments, their original significance as tribal badges has been to a great
extent blurred, if not entirely lost.'

[3] Nowadays about nine or ten years old; formerly said to have been later,
see p. 306–7.

boy had to give up the idea for the time being. But another, although forbidden by his people, would go and pierce his ears in secret, and they would only find out afterwards. They might scold him, but the deed had already been done.

As to the actual piercing, the boy would go to a man who knew how to pierce ears, and say, 'Will you please pierce my ears for me?'[1] The man who was to do the piercing would then say, 'Very well. Go and sharpen two implements, and massage your ears, then come back and I will pierce them for you'. At this the boy would go home, pleased as anything, and, having first split off two dry splinters of *gbaaye*[2] wood, he would pare them down till they were smooth, slender, and sharpened to a fine point. Then he would warm his hands at the fire, and massage his ears. When they were quite soft he would get up and go off to the ear-piercer, and give him the two wooden needles. The man pierced his ears, and then he went back home. He left the needles in for about three days, after which the ears would begin to fester. It was then time to bathe them. The boy would seek out a man of good blood[3] to come and bathe the wounds. When he had finished bathing them, he extracted the wooden needles, inserted a feather in the hole in the ear, and drew it through. Having thus cleaned it, he broke off a piece of smoke-covered sword-grass[4] and thrust it in (the soot on the grass acting as a medicine), and continued this treatment until the sores on the ears had completely healed.

When his ears were quite well again, the boy started to go round taunting the other members of his age-grade. If he saw a boy of his own age, he said, 'Here's a little mouse!' Whereupon those who were there would take up the cry, jeering loudly at the boy who had not had his

---

[1] No fee is charged for ear piercing, and the art does not have to be 'bought', as in the case of circumcision (see below).

[2] *Prosopis oblonga :* a very hard red wood.

[3] To have 'good blood' is considered a natural, not acquired, characteristic, and a man whose own wounds heal up quickly is expected to be the most successful when dressing the wounds of others.

[4] I.e. he pulled out a piece of the thatch (sword-grass being used by the Tiv for this purpose) from the inside of the hut, where it would be coated with soot.

ears pierced, and who had been called a mouse. And if there were a number of boys there who had their ears pierced, one of them would start the taunting Ear-song: '*Aŋgyeto!*'[1] and the rest joined in: 'Your ears will quickly go lumpy!' Whereupon all the boys who had not had their ears pierced were overcome with shame, and some would actually cry. After that they would go and have it done without fail, so as not to have ears like a mouse, with no holes in them. Nevertheless, the reason why they had their ears pierced was not because it was a fundamental custom of the tribe, but because of the taunts which were hurled at them by the other members of their own age-grade.

CUTTING THE TEETH[2]

A few days after having had his ears pierced, a boy would start thinking about having his teeth cut. When the time came for this, he went to a man who cut teeth, and said to him, 'I should like you to cut my teeth, if you can'. The other would say, 'Bring along something, then, and I will cut them'. (Cutting the teeth was not done for nothing; a fee was paid. In the old days it was a strand of tobacco, for there were no arrows then; it was later, when these came into use, that an arrow was sometimes given.)

For example: Abo has come to Jape to have his teeth cut. He gives him a strand of tobacco. Jape agrees to do it, goes and fetches his instruments, and places them on the ground. What are the instruments? They consist of a chisel and a small round stone. Having seated himself, Jape takes Abo's head and lays it on his bosom, Abo lying on his back. Jape then opens Abo's mouth and cuts a piece of corn-stalk to place across inside, so that the mouth may be kept open and there will be room for him to cut properly. He then takes the chisel and rests its edge against the front teeth of the upper jaw. Having placed it in position, he takes the stone and taps the base

---

[1] Meaning not now known. Probably the name of some one who had swollen ear lobes.

[2] Note that the common term 'filing the teeth' is due to a misconception, when applied to the Tiv. See below.

of the chisel. He starts chipping the two front teeth of the upper jaw, first this one, then that, and when he has finished there is a gap left between the two. If no more than this was done, it was said that Jape had only 'opened out' Abo's teeth, but not sharpened them all to a point. One boy would stop at the 'opening-out' stage, finding it too painful; but another would go on and sharpen the teeth on either side. This type of cutting is called *kɔgh* or *iase*.

Abo, then, gets up and bakes a yam with which to make a fomentation. But in the old days, before yams were known, he would have filled his mouth with hot water, so that there should be no swelling. After this he goes off to taunt the others in his age-grade about their teeth.

Let us suppose that Adi, one of Abo's age-grade, is smoking a pipe, and Abo has asked him to give him a smoke:

ADI: Wait a minute, I'll just have a pull, and then I'll give it you. I have only just lit it.

ABO: I forbid you that pipe by virtue of my teeth. If you disobey and start smoking, when you have your teeth cut they will swell up.[1]

ADI: Here you are then.

ABO: And don't try being funny with me, because you're only a kid. You with your teeth all round and even like a monkey's! 'Handsome little sharp-teeth' is what the girls call me.

ADI: Dash it! I'm going straight away to get Jape to cut my teeth too.

So Adi has his teeth cut by Jape, after which he goes about happy.

CIRCUMCISION

A boy having had his ears pierced, and also his teeth cut, next set his heart on being circumcised. In the old days the Tiv did not circumcise early. Some boys would be sixteen, and others would reach eighteen years, before they were circumcised.[2] Formerly they were afraid that if a boy were circumcised too young he would become

---

[1] P. 41.   [2] Nowadays the normal time is at the age of puberty.

sickly. Moreover, when the time came for a man to circumcise his son, he greatly dreaded the operation, lest
the *mbatsav*[1] should bewitch the boy, and he should bleed
to death. Sometimes a father would take his son to be
circumcised in his mother's group. Only a brave man
would circumcise his son amongst his paternal relatives.

When the time for circumcision had arrived, the father
of the boy who was to be circumcised, or one of his relatives, would take him to the senior elder of his group, who
had power over the *Igbe*, *Megh*, and *Ahumbe*. The elder
would thoroughly purge the boy with the aid of a chicken,
before he returned home. The washing away of the
akombo was done as follows: While the master of the
akombo was carrying out the purging with a chicken, or
sometimes merely with an egg-shell, he pronounced this
incantation, 'If you have looked into the *Ahumbe* bin, I
purge you this day. A woman looks not upon an *akombo*
that is behind her. Flow away Evil, come Good. Or if
you have looked upon the fire of the *Igbe*, or have taken
something on which a magic guard has been placed, I
purge you this day. The Moon is a maiden, and the Sun
a man-child. If the guardian emblem of *Megh* has been
laid upon something which you have taken without
knowing, it is death, a quick death from bleeding. But
to-day I purge you of all these things. Flow away Evil,
come Good. The Moon is a maiden, and the Sun a man-
child'.

While he uttered this incantation he swung the chicken
rapidly round the boy's head. Having done this, he took
some mud and smeared it on the big toe of the boy's right
foot. This was the cleansing from the *akombo*.

So the boy would go off home. Sometimes this rite was
performed in the village, sometimes by the stream. To
the man to whom you took your child to be cleansed you
would give a strand of tobacco, but the chicken with
which the rite was performed would be set free. A boy
who returned home in the evening after being purged
would sometimes be circumcised the same day; if not, he
would be done early the next morning.

[1] Witches. But see p. 236 et seq.

¶, A detailed description of the practices connected with the *akombo* is given in Chapter IV, but a short explanation is necessary at this point to understand the meaning of the foregoing passage.

The *akombo* are supernatural agencies. If a man is continually unlucky, or is attacked by illness which does not yield to normal treatment, he assumes that he has committed an offence against one of them. He accordingly discovers by divination which it is, and then goes to a man who has control over that particular *akombo* (the singular *kombo* is not in general use), who performs a magical act, or, as the Tiv say, 'puts it right' for him. But at the critical periods of life, as when a boy is being circumcised, or a woman is giving birth, it is thought wise to forestall disaster by giving the person a general ceremonial purging (the Tiv word simply means 'to wash'), in order to guard against the possible evil intervention of an *akombo*, against which he or she may have unwittingly transgressed, and which is waiting for a chance to do harm. These precautionary measures can only be carried out by a man who has acquired control over the *akombo* in question, and the best man to do it is obviously the senior elder of the group, who has the strongest magic power (*tsav*), and is probably master of the largest number of *akombo*.

To take the incantation phrase by phrase: The '*Ahumbe* bin' is the mud container, built like a corn store, in which are kept the arcana of this particular *akombo*. It is an offence for any uninitiated person to look on these. *Ahumbe* means 'wind'; it attacks people by breaking down their crops or tearing the roofs off their houses, and also causes bleeding after circumcision. When one of this class of rites is being performed the women and uninitiated keep inside their houses, lest they should see what they must not. But a woman is not guilty if she is looking the other way. This plea is here urged in extenuation of any occasion on which the boy may, through ignorance, have placed himself under the evil influence of an *akombo*. In the *Igbe* ceremonies torches are·lighted in the central meeting house (*ate*), and are also carried round the neighbouring villages. All unauthorized persons remain indoors, and bury their faces in their hands, so that they may not see even the reflection of the *Igbe* fire. If they see it they will be 'caught' by the *Igbe*, and die of dysentery.[1] The power of the *akombo* can also be directed by a man against evil-intentioned persons, by placing its

[1] Cf. note on p. 270.

emblems on the thing which he wishes to guard. The boy is therefore also purged of any offence that he may have committed by
touching an object protected in this way. 'The Moon is a maiden',
&c., is a form of words used in most incantations, but the meaning
has been lost; it may be a relic of an older belief which is now forgotten. The smearing of the mud is the concluding act of every
akombo rite; sometimes it is also done on the wrist and stomach.
The exact significance of this is not now known by the Tiv, who,
when asked, reply that the mud is to give health (*kpe iyol*). It is
probably derived from the idea of virtue present in the soil, and
seems especially appropriate in connexion with the *akombo* of the
crops.

The object of performing the rite by the stream is that
Evil may 'flow away' with the water. If it is done in the village a
little water is placed in a vessel, and poured out on the ground
when the ceremony is over. The significance in both cases is the
same. In this rite, and in others of the same kind practised by the
Tiv, the chicken acts as a scapegoat. When the bird is swung
round the boy's head, the Bad is drawn out of his body and enters
into that of the chicken, which must afterwards be set free in order
that it may carry the evil away with it. But here there is a confusion
of two ideas, for in the words of the incantation Evil is adjured to
flow away on the water. In Downes's account of a similar rite the
cock is actually thrown into the stream;[1] here there is no doubt at
all as to its function. In other cases the bird is taken out into the
bush and left to roam about loose in a marsh or by the side of some
water. The two ideas are therefore closely connected, but the
matter must not be pressed to a logical conclusion. Usually the
chicken is wounded, either by breaking a limb or plucking a
feather violently from its throat so as to draw blood, but it is
important that, in its capacity of a scapegoat, it should not be
killed, at any rate at that time. This point is clearly shown in a
parallel formula for the removal of a spell. In this case the bird is
swung round the bewitched person's head until it becomes unconscious, and is then laid on the ground. If it comes to life, all is
well, for the spell has been transferred to the chicken; if it dies,
the spell is still potent, and indeed is shown to be of an especially
virulent kind, so that its victim is said to have 'death on him'.
Steps must then immediately be taken to detect the witch by

[1] Op. cit., p. 64.

divination, and to take action against him before it is too late. Finally it may be noted that the egg-shell, which is said to be sometimes used, has no virtue in itself, but acts in the place of a chicken, being well qualified to do so by the laws of contagious magic. On the same principle, if you are undergoing a rite which demands the slaughter of a he-goat, and are not able to provide one, a hair from the animal's body will do as well. This fact is so well known that it has passed into a saying: 'Here is the goat; there is no need to look for a hair' (used when referring some one to the person whom the matter under discussion primarily concerns).

HERE is an example of the actual operation:
The boy's name is Ker, and Atso is his father. The man who does the circumcising is Adagba. The elder in whose ate[1] Atso will put Ker, so that he may look after him, is called Agwabi. This Agwabi is an elder kinsman of Atso, and a man of strong spiritual power.[2] So, as Atso has given Ker into his hands, there is nothing to fear, and the *mbatsav* will not dare to do him harm. Adagba has begun the operation. He has taken a large stone, about the size of a hearth-stone, and set it in place. Ker comes and sits down. Adum, a young man, comes and props him up from behind, in order that he shall not move and cause the circumcision to be done badly.[3]

ADAGBA: Hold tight, Adum. He has a frightened look, as if he is going to struggle. Close his eyes.

ADUM: I am holding him very tight.

ADAGBA: It's all up with you to-day. I'll have your foreskin off!

With these words, Adagba takes out a small foreign knife,[4] and starts to sharpen it in front of Ker. Ker trembles all over. Adagba takes hold of the foreskin, pulls it and lets go again, cuts a blade of sword-grass, measures it against one of his finger-joints, spits on it, and

---

[1] The big common hut in the centre of the village, used as a guest-house.—See p. 61.

[2] This corresponds roughly to the common conception of 'mana', and is treated fully in Chapter V. From now on the Tiv term *tsav* will be used.

[3] I.e. Adum sits on the floor behind the patient, who leans against him, and is held tight by the arms.

[4] P. 20.

D

then measures with it the exact place on the foreskin which he wishes to cut.[1] Having done this, he takes his small foreign knife, while Atso, or some one else, digs a small hole in which to bury the foreskin.[2] Then he gets up and runs backwards and forwards, saying, 'Many are the deeds I've done! I have taken women, both dark and fair! I have cut off the red leopard's tail, and I shall cut a man to-day!'

Adagba comes back and squats on his haunches, takes hold of the foreskin, and makes a swift cut. Ker bursts out crying.

ATSO: Ker! You are not like your father. Look at me; have I ever cried about anything like that? Goodness me, you're just like a girl.

KER: Leave me alone, Atso! It hurts like anything. (At this point some boys do the hyena's trick.[3])

ADAGBA: Be brave, Ker. Here, Adum, why are you not holding your hands over his eyes? Is it not because you are letting him look at it that it is hurting him so much? There is still the inner membrane to do. The blood is making my hands terribly slippery.

KER: Atso, my father! They are killing me! They are killing me!

ATSO: Quiet, my son.

ADAGBA: Be a man. It's all over now except for the part under the cord—— There, now I have done that too. Hand me that water, to pour over it. Let him get up, Adum.

ATSO: Adagba, take that cock of yours I gave you just now.[4]

ADAGBA: Right! I am going now. If there is any bleeding, send a boy down at once to call me.

ATSO: Where are you going?

ADAGBA: Down to Mbaadam.

---

[1] I.e. he cuts off a length of grass equal to his finger-joint, and lays it length-ways on the end of the foreskin. The spittle which he applies sticks to the skin, and can be seen when the grass is taken away.

[2] The prepuce is buried, according to the custom in most tribes, lest it should fall into the possession of some evil-minded person who might do harm to the owner by sympathetic magic. In the case of the Tiv the man who has your foreskin can prevent you from having children.

[3] The hyena is said to defecate on the smallest provocation, when alarmed.

[4] I.e. a 'twenty', the fee prescribed by custom.

ATSO: Good-bye, then. Agwabi, I give Ker into your hands. I have eaten human flesh with no man. If a man comes with spells to bewitch my son, ask him if I am in his debt,[1] and he will tell you. I am going.

AGWABI: Ker, get up, and go into the *ate*. You, take a chair in for him. I shall tie an *Igbe* to the chair, and also an *Ambi-a-iwagh*, and if any one comes to give you the evil eye,[2] his bowels will gush out, and he will die; or a thunder-bolt will fall on him. Atso has hung Death around my neck,[3] and I will not trifle with the matter.

(Agwabi accordingly ties on all the *akombo*. But when he has sat down and started to smoke his pipe, a boy comes running to tell him that Ker is bleeding badly from the circumcision.)

AGWABI: Aba, run quickly and tell Atso to come!

(Atso comes back.)

ATSO: What is it, Agwabi?

AGWABI: Ker is not doing well, so I thought you had better come and help me look at him.

ATSO: Aba, run and call Adagba from Mbaadam.

(Adagba comes.)

ADAGBA: What is the matter, Atso?

ATSO: The boy is bleeding terribly; see, he is showing all the whites of his eyes.

ADAGBA: Is there any *alufu*[4] growing round here?

Alu, wife of Ajaga, says that there is some growing under the eaves of her house. Adagba goes and picks some blades of *alufu* grass, rubs them well between his hands, and squeezes them on to the wound, saying, 'The blades of *alufu* are the remedy for wounds. Since I have squeezed it on like this, the bleeding will certainly stop. Save only if it be the work of the People of Darkness, is there no hope'. (Here, in some cases, the bleeding would stop; in others, however, it would go on, till finally the boy died; then it was said that the son of So-and-so had bled to death.)

So when he has squeezed all the juice from the grass the

---

[1] I.e. flesh debt, see p. 255.   [2] *Ishe i bo:* a literal translation.
[3] I.e. he will demand the blood of his son at my hands.
[4] *Alufu* (*Pennisetum pedicellatum*) is a coarse grass, common in West Africa, and well known to Northern Nigerian herbalists for the styptic property of its juice.

bleeding stops. The people disperse to their homes, saying,
'Adagba has a medicine for stopping bleeding!' Others reply,
'As to that, he *bought* it, did he not?' (It would merely
be foolish for any one to apply the treatment if he had
not bought the right to do so, for it would do no good.)[1]

❡ The supernatural character of the dangers inherent in a
ticklish operation like circumcision are here strongly emphasized.
The reason for tying the two *akombo* to the boy's chair is not to
avert the consequences of the 'evil eye', as will become clear
later, but to discourage any evil-intentioned person from giving it,
for fear of the results which might react on himself. Hence the
advantage of choosing a man like Agwabi, the potency of whose
tsav is well-known, to act as protector of the boy during the
critical period. The *Igbe* has already been mentioned; any one
offending against it is liable to be seized with a violent attack of
dysentery. The *Ambi-a-iwagh* is the slag of the furnace, and, like
other things connected with the blacksmith's craft, has the power
to cause an offender to be struck down by lightning. The real
danger is from the People of Darkness, that is, the *mbatsav*, who
are always the older members of the victim's group, and who may
wish to 'kill' their kinsman (by witchcraft) in payment of a flesh
debt, or for other reasons which will appear later. This is why
Atso protests that he has eaten human flesh with no man. It also
explains what is meant by saying that only a brave man would
circumcise his son amongst his paternal relatives.

The Bathing After Circumcision. In former times,
when a boy had been circumcised, he would never eat
good sauce, but only sorrel. The sorrel was crushed on
the grindstone, and eaten with *ruam*.[2] It was said that if
he ate good sauce the wound would fester badly.[3]

---

[1] P. 209, bottom.

[2] The solid part of the meal, made either of pounded yam or flour boiled in
water to a compact mass.

[3] The Fulani and Hausa practice, on the other hand, is to give especially
good food to the boys who have been circumcised, and Fulani boys are allowed
an especial licence, during the period of their convalescence, to criticize the
food brought to them, if it is not quite to their liking. The Tiv belief is that
if a man has a wound and eats the richer kinds of sauce, the oil with which they
are made comes out of the wound in the form of blood. For this reason the
sorrel diet is prescribed in all cases of illness which are the result of injury, and
for any man who is undergoing the magico-pathological rites of *atakpa* and *idyo*.

After about five days, it was time to bathe the wound. The bathing was more painful than the circumcision. When the time came, a man with good blood was sought to come and bathe the sores. A man with 'good blood' means one who soon recovers from any misfortune or wound.[1] This man poured some water into a potsherd, took a piece of kapok, broke off from three to six stalks of grass, pulled out the kapok and twisted it round the stalks, then stuck the ends into the ground.[2] Thereupon he scooped up some water in his hand and poured it over the boy's wound until it became soft. When it was soft, he carefully removed the blood which had adhered to it. This did not hurt the boy much. But when he took the kapok on the stalks and wiped away the pus, the boy would be sure to cry out and beat his hands against his hips, for it was very painful. Having finished bathing the wound, he took a leaf of the meni oil tree[3] and baked it over the fire. When it became soft he took it and split it to exactly the same width as the wound, and covered up the place with it. Then the boy got up.

This treatment was continued until the circumcision healed up. When it was all finished, the boy powdered up some charcoal and blackened the scar with it,[4] and his father gave him strings of beads to put on in honour of his circumcision. So he began to go about in full view of every one, and if he happened to come across any of his own age-grade who had not been circumcised, he would start bragging in front of them. When he came up to one of them, he would sniff, and say, 'What a smell of billy-goat!'[5] And if the other happened to be eating something, the boy who had been circumcised would forbid him by virtue of his circumcision, and he had to stop. Then every one jeered and laughed at the uncircumcised one, who was covered with shame. And, feeling very heart-sore,

---

[1] Note on p. 27.
[2] I.e. to be ready to his hand when required.
[3] *Lophira alata*, a tree much used in Tiv magic, possibly owing to the fact (or belief) that it is especially liable to be struck by lightning, the same reason for which Sir James Frazer believes that the oak was venerated by the Aryans of ancient Europe.
[4] Being ashamed of the light colour.
[5] I.e. because a goat is also uncircumcised.

he went and worried his father, demanding that he should be circumcised.

The Taking of a Toll from the Mother's Group.[1] Some days later the boy who had been circumcised went off to his mother's home, where he killed a chicken and brought it back to eat. The owner of the bird would not take it away from him. If he did so, the boy would go home quietly and tell his mother.

For example: Ker, having been circumcised, goes and kills a chicken at the village of Afo in his mother's group. Afo is a near paternal kinsman of Iju, who has the same mother as Adei, the mother of Ker. Adei hears that Ker has been to kill a chicken, and that Afo has taken it away from him; she is angry, and goes to tell Iju. When Iju hears this, he snaps his fingers[2] and says, 'Never mind, Adei. Go home now. If ever a child of one of Afo's daughters kills something, I'll take it from him, and then we shall be quits. I'm not going to let this matter rest here. I am very angry about it, and shall certainly retaliate. No one shall do Ker a wrong in my group, the Mbaigu, and get off free. I shall get it back again, so that's that!'[3]

From that time onwards Ker turns his mind seriously to the question of women.

CICATRIZATION

A boy being circumcised, and having started to go after women, would next want to have the raised face-marks.[4] So he went to a man who knew how to make them.

For example: Apav is the man who makes the cicatrices,

---

[1] *Igba yan:* lit. 'eating the *igba*'. The terms *ityɔ* and *igba* mean, respectively, the paternal and maternal groups, or any individual member of them. They are here translated 'father's (or mother's) kinsman', 'home', 'group', &c., as the context requires.

[2] A gesture expressing the intention to get even with some one.

[3] This is a special instance of the hospitality which any man may demand from the group to which his mother belongs. Under the present conditions of security and increased intercourse, this privilege has been much abused by the young men, and has had to be checked. Moreover, the size of the *igba* on which the demand may be made is elastic, and depends on factors which are explained later (p. 130 et seq.).

[4] *Abaji*, the keloids made in the shape of a crescent on each temple.

and Asɔm has come to him to have them done. (The young people call them 'Cics'.[1])

Asɔm: I have come to ask if you will cut me some 'cics', please.

Apav: All right, sit down then.

Asɔm: There! I'm ready.

Apav: Daughter of Akeri, pour some water in a vessel and bring it out to me.

Apav gets up, goes and grinds up some charcoal, pours water over it, gets a stalk of grass and dips it into the charcoal, then makes some marks with it on Asɔm's face in the places where he wishes to raise the scars. Having finished this, he takes the 'hook', catches up the skin with it, and makes an incision with a razor. This he does in five places. (Sometimes they made five marks, sometimes only three. Some also had 'Mosquitoes'[2] done on the forehead.)

Apav next cuts some blades of *alufu* grass, and squeezes the juice on to the wounds. Although it stings, Asɔm must bear it. When Apav has squeezed out the *alufu* juice, and the bleeding has stopped, he takes the charcoal which he has previously ground up and rubs it on. It is by hard rubbing that it gets right in, and causes the cicatrices to swell up and form big lumps. When Apav has finished, Asɔm gets up and goes off.

The Bathing of the Cicatrices. When the time comes for Asɔm to bathe the scars, he looks for a man of good blood to come and bathe them for him. Ayɔɔ is the 'Man of good blood'.

Asɔm: Ayɔɔ, come and bathe my 'cics'.

Ayɔɔ: Is there any palm oil?

Asɔm gets some, and when Ayɔɔ has bathed all Asɔm's scars, he takes up some oil on a feather and paints them with it. He continues to dress the scars in this manner, until they have quite healed. When they have healed up, and are itching, Asɔm takes some powdered camwood and rubs it on. And if the cicatrices show no sign of coming up, he takes some shoots of the indigo plant, crushes them in his hands and rubs them on. The scars then swell

---

[1] *Aba.*   [2] A small circle of keloids over each eye.

into big cones. The girls call Asɔm 'The boy with the
handsome cics', and he begins to go round throwing
taunts at the other members of his age-grade. Going up
to Ugor, and seeing that his face is quite smooth, he chases
him off. 'Out of my way,' he says, 'you with your silly face
like a foreigner's!' Whereupon all present hoot with
laughter at Ugor. Ugor is humiliated, and hangs his head
in gloom. After this he will move heaven and earth to
have the marks done on his face, for Asɔm's taunts about
'cics' have stung him to the quick.

AGE-GRADES

¶ The age-grade system, like many other Tiv institutions, has
the appearance of having lost some of its original functions and
meaning. Nevertheless, the word *kwagh* still has a strong theoretical significance in so far as it represents the accepted African
idea of a society built up in a series of strata dependent on age,
each group having its special place in the life of the community.
Progress up the social scale is (or was) marked by a series of mile-
stones, the earliest of which are the outward and visible signs of
ear-piercing, teeth-cutting, and such-like, described above. But
though the mounting of these steps is roughly, it is not rigidly,
determined on an age basis; the members of each grade do not
necessarily move up together, and there are no formal transition
rites to mark the progress of the class as a whole from one stage to
the next. Moreover, although the idea contained in *kwagh* is
fundamentally concerned with age, and includes all those who
were born within about a year of each other, it is apt to be modi-
fied in individual cases, because a young man of superior strength
or personality will often force his way into a higher grade than
that to which he properly belongs on the age qualification.

Circumcision is naturally one of the most important of the
early steps; but though boys of the same age-grade are usually
circumcised at the same time, the rite has not the communal
significance which it has in some other tribes, nor are any initiation ceremonies practised in connexion with it. As already said, it
is probably not indigenous. It is not correct even to say that contemporary circumcision is an essential qualification for membership of an age-grade, though it often happens that boys who have
been circumcised at the same time regard each other as age-mates.

As Abraham says, 'the age at which this operation is carried out varies with the health and physical development of the boy',[1] and, it might be added, with the disposition of the omens, and the courage of the father in risking the maleficent intervention of the *mbatsav*. The description given above is of an individual operation, and it is significant that, when it is over, the boy is said to go round and taunt the other members of his age-grade who have not yet been circumcised.

After circumcision the next big event in a man's life is marriage, and in comparatively recent times the most important type from the point of view of the present question was marriage by 'capture', because of the prestige which this gave to a young man amongst the fellow members of his age-grade.[2] The later stages of the Tiv's social progress consist in acquiring the authority to practise the numerous *akombo* rites, culminating in initiation to the *Biamegh* and the *Poor*,[3] which is the peak of social and spiritual eminence.

The idea contained in the word *sɔgh*, here very inadequately rendered in English by 'taunt', may be noted, because it is largely the fear of this which, in the absence of any formal institution, keeps the members of an age-grade at the same level as they move up the social ladder. With this word you not only boast of having something which the other person has not, but can forbid him to do whatever he is doing by virtue of your possession. For instance, the boy who has just had his teeth cut stops his friend smoking his pipe, under penalty of getting tooth-ache if he disobeys. The boy who has been circumcised forbids the other to eat his food; otherwise when he himself is circumcised he will bleed to death. A man who has acquired a wife or a horse will go up to one of his age-mates, who is less fortunate, and give him some order which he is afraid to disobey, lest he should never be able to get a wife (or horse) himself. If some women trespass on your fishing, you can prevent them from having the use of the fish by using the name of one of the men's *akombo* in the same way.[4] This practice is carried on in every stratum of society, and acts—so great is the power of ridicule—as a strong incentive for every one to emulate the most fortunate or ambitious members of

<hr>

[1] R. C. Abraham, *The Tiv People*, p. 211.   [2] P. 154.   [3] P. 196 et seq.
[4] The formula is '*m sɔgh u ityu (msɔrom mara, ishu la), m sɔgh u anyi (kwase, Swaŋge)*'. The second part of the sentence shows the authority by which he is able to put his threat into force, i.e. his superior teeth (wife, *akombo*).   Lit.: 'I forbid you that pipe (&c.), I forbid you (by the power of my) teeth'.

his grade. But, as Akiga says, the old landmarks are disappearing, and when values alter, and the fear of public mockery is no longer effective, tribal markings and practices, which used to be thought so essential, lose their attraction.

The most important practical aspect of the age-grades is that they run at right-angles to the family organization, and so serve as a protection to each of their members from the elders of his own paternal group. The need of such protection, as it appears to the Tiv, will become evident later, when the question of the fleshdebt is considered. The measures which were taken by the young men to protect or avenge their age-mates, and which have been resorted to in quite recent years, are also described in a later chapter.[1] Formerly it was the custom in all clans for the young men to meet together to pledge their mutual help in age-grades from fifteen years upwards. They were summoned together by one of their number, who brewed beer and prepared a feast for them. But nowadays this custom seems to be dying out, except amongst the Kparev clans, in which the age-grade system has still a certain functional significance.

THE MARKS ON WOMEN

CICATRIZATION and teeth-cutting are practices which apply also to women, not only to men. A woman whose marks suited her used to be called by the young men 'So-and-so's daughter with the pretty cics', and similarly in the case of cutting the teeth. Women also used to have marks made on the stomach, but not as many as they have now. The man who did the marking examined the woman's stomach, ground up some charcoal and placed it ready, then dipped a blade of sword-grass in the charcoal and drew lines with it round the navel.

For example: Agabi is the artist, Ahɔbee a young girl who wishes to have the marks made on her. Ayawer is Ahɔbee's mother.

AYAWER: Agabi, I am bringing my daughter to-morrow to have the body-markings done. Although she has quite reached puberty, her stomach is unmarked.

AGABI: All right, come along to-morrow and I'll do her.

*　　*　　*　　*　　*

[1] P. 329.

AYAWER: Come out, Agabi. I've brought my little girl that I came to see you about yesterday.

AGABI: Come, come, Ayawer. Won't you sit down and just let me fill a pipe for you? Then when you have had a smoke, we'll get down to the marking.

AYAWER: No, no. Better do it while it is early, before the blood begins to circulate.[1]

AGABI: Very well. Ahɔbee, go and lie down in the chair,[2] and loosen your cloth.

Agabi goes and sits down on the ground, takes a razor and makes the incisions. He cuts three circles round the navel, and a vertical line to the chest which is continued right on up to the neck. Formerly, that was all; marks were not made all over the stomach. But afterwards, with the introduction of new fashions, other lines were made branching out to either side of the woman's body and downwards, in addition to those drawn round the navel. And later on there were added still further decorations.

When Agabi has finished making the incisions, he pours some water over them and washes away all the blood. Then he takes the charcoal, which he has previously ground up, and rubs it on. Ahɔbee gets up and goes off. She leaves it for about two days, and then, when the cuts have festered, Ayawer looks for a man of good blood to come and bathe them. Having washed them thoroughly, he paints them lightly with palm oil, and continues to dress them in this manner until the sores have healed. In subsequent washings Ahɔbee puts on some powdered camwood. When all is quite finished, the young man who is courting her kills a chicken for her, and Ahɔbee can go and make fun of the girls who have not been marked. Other marks on women were done in the small of the back, and on the calf. The treatment was the same in each case.

The Tiv used to say that if a woman did not have the decorations made on her stomach the skin would not be

---

[1] The blood is thought to be thicker in the cool of the morning, on the analogy of oil. When the sun gets up the blood loses its viscosity, and flows more freely through the body. It is therefore safer to operate in the early morning, to avoid bleeding.

[2] A Tiv chair is made in two pieces, and the back slopes at an angle of 45 degrees or more, so that the patient can 'lie' in it.

drawn tight, but become flabby like that of the foreign women, and this was ugly. That was the reason why they made these marks. But nowadays they do not consider the stomach markings so important, and many women have no decoration on their stomachs at all. In Kunav the majority of women are unmarked. On the other hand, in some other clans, such as Nɔŋgov, stomach marking is on the increase, and new forms of ornamentation are being added.

THE NEW MARKINGS

The 'Nail' is a type of marking that has recently been brought in by the younger Tiv, who have seen it in foreign parts, amongst the Jukun. The people who actually introduced it were the young men who had entered the service of foreigners. It was they who started the Nail fashion, which has subsequently spread all over Tiv country, and become such a big thing amongst the young men and women.

Now the way that this type of mark came to be called the 'Nail' was as follows: The lad who originated it had been a carrier, travelling in foreign parts with a white man's loads. Thus he saw how the foreigners made their tribal marks. One day, when he was out of work, and in doubt where to turn for his next meal, he picked up a large nail on the ground. Taking it into a blacksmith's shop, he beat out the pointed end to a flat edge and ground it down till it was as sharp as a razor. Then he called a very small child, whom he knew to be without fear, telling him to come and be marked with the nail. The child came, and he cut a small mark on his cheek, close to the eyes, of the kind that he had seen on the foreigners. After a few days, the cuts which had been made by the nail healed up, and scars appeared, black, and nice to look at.[1] Seeing this, some boys and girls came to the lad who had the nail, asking him to make cuts on them too, like the ones he had done on the other child. Whereupon he demanded a small fee, saying that

[1] The result was produced by rubbing in charcoal, as in the case of the other marks already described.

he would not do it for nothing. And since the children wanted it badly, they each gave him something—one two tenths of a penny, another three—and he marked them. When the young people saw this, they rose up in a body and crowded round him, demanding to have the Nail cuts, and he marked them with various patterns. After this other boys began to forge nails and to cut the marks on each other, and in this way all these marks came to be called the 'Nail'. A young man on whom the markings have come out well is called a 'Nail Boy' by the girls.

Those who had already reached the age of puberty before the Nail had appeared have the raised cicatrices, but all those who are now growing up are having the Nail done instead. Moreover, the women will have nothing to do with those who have the raised scars, saying that they belong to a past generation, and are not young at all; they do not like men with raised marks, because they carry the symbols of the past. So the young men, knowing this, make the Nail mark on every part of their body. They mark not only their faces, but also their necks, their forearms, and their stomachs, while some are marked all over. In these days, if you come to Tiv country, or if, without necessarily coming here, you see a young Tiv who has recently left it, he will certainly bear the mark of the Nail on his face.

This affair of the Nail is now doing a great deal of harm in Tiv country, owing to the fact that the women will have nothing to do with those who have the old markings. For in as much as marriage by exchange has been replaced by the bride-price system,[1] and a woman can no longer be given away in marriage forcibly, but only if she consents of her own free will, it goes badly nowadays with those who have the raised scars on their faces. A woman may have been married for a long time to a husband with raised markings, but leaves him on the ground that the white man has said that women must do as they wish, and she, for her part, does not wish to have a husband with a lumpy face. So the men who have raised scars do not

[1] Chap. III.

know where to turn, and sometimes, in despair, a man
who already has the lumps on his face will take a nail and
make cuts on the top of them, thinking thereby to please
the women; but this does not hit the mark either. So
there is loud lamentation in Tivland. The younger Tiv
are split into two factions, and there is bitter feeling
between them. Those with the lumps make up mocking
songs about the Nail Men, and the Nail Men about the
Lumpy-faced. Those with the lumps are backed up by
the old men, because the old men have these markings
themselves, but the Nail Men have the women behind
them, and for this reason they are getting the best of it.
A man who has the raised marks can do little against a
man who has the Nail, for amongst the Tiv the women
have more influence than the elders. You may do something of which the elders do not approve, but if the women
approve there is no more to be said. If, on the other hand,
you do something which is praised by the elders, but
meets with disapproval from the women, you are not
satisfied.

The Nail Men have lately introduced another type of
mark which they call 'Ukari', after the town of Wukari,
where they first saw it. This mark is not usually made
high up, but is cut close under the eyes in a downward
direction, as though a man were weeping, and a tear-drop
were running down his face. It is quite short, made with
a deep cut, and when it heals leaves a big black scar. This
is a sure woman-killer. Women who see it never stop
admiring it, declaring that the boy looked nice with his
Nail markings, and now that he has had the Ukari done as
well, it really suits him wonderfully! If the Lumpy-faced
Men hear this, they start to quarrel with the women. Thus
has the Nail shaken the country of Tiv. The men with
the lumps on their faces shrink into their shells like the
tortoise, but the Nail Men shoot forth their necks.

This question of the Nail is one of the reasons why the
older men are always asking to have exchange marriage
back again, and recounting its various advantages.
Because if there were marriage by exchange the women
would not dare to refuse them, that is, the men with the

lumps; and they would not mind if the owners[1] of the women took them by force and gave them to the Lumpy-faced Men, for then the world would be a good place. But the old men are ashamed to state the matter in its true light, so instead of this they sing the praises of the old exchange system. And what they say is quite true; but the Nail is also at the bottom of it. Nevertheless, the elders do not mention the matter of the Nail Men, fearing that, if they did so, the Nail Men would say that they were stronger than the elders, and that was why they were making complaints against them. So the old men of the lumps, being more wily than the young men of the Nail mark, go round by devious paths in order to get the Nail Men on to their side. They point out the many advantages of exchange marriage, which even the Nail Men cannot deny. But in spite of all this, since the system has not been changed, the Nail Men are getting the better of the Lumpy-faced.[2]

In these days, also, Tiv boys no longer set much store by the ear-piercing custom. For they say that originally a boy used to pierce his ears in order to insert an *iŋga*. (The *iŋga* was an old type of ear ornament, made out of the root of the indigo plant, pared down carefully till it was about the length of a man's finger, and bound closely round with the hair of the hippopotamus's mane, or (later) horse-hair. On to this was threaded a bead, for example, the red bead known as *matse*.) The *iŋga* used to be admired by the women, but nowadays it is not worn. And the practice of cutting the teeth, too, which used to be such a big thing in former times, is not now held in much account by the young Tiv, because the women of to-day will like you just as well without it. The days are past when a woman would refuse you for not having your teeth cut, and rail at you for having flat teeth like a monkey

---

[1] This is not a very satisfactory rendering of the Tiv word *tien*, but it conveys the idea better than 'guardian', which is generally used. The 'ownership' means the right to use the woman (i.e. daughter, sister, &c.) to make an exchange marriage, or (at the present time) obtain a bride-price. There was never, of course, absolute ownership of women, except slaves, but, as will be seen, the *tien* has, in a sense, greater and more permanent rights than the husband.

[2] To remove any suspicion of personal bias, it is only fair to mention that Akiga himself is practically unmarked.

or a foreigner; for nowadays even the foreigners themselves marry Tiv women.[1] So that the young men who have had their teeth cut in the past are now sorry, saying that if they had known they would not have spoilt their teeth by cutting them. And some take hold of them and break off the points, in order to have teeth like the foreigner, and thus be able to speak Hausa or English well (for they imagine that it is the teeth which cause difficulty in speaking other languages). It is the modern Tiv women who have caused all these troubles, and many others like them, to come upon the land of Tiv.

Nor are the Tiv so proud of their circumcision as they used to be. A boy who is ten years old, or in some cases even less, will be circumcised by his father, in order that he can go after women. The only reason why they delay circumcising a boy nowadays is on account of the tax. The white man has said that every boy who is circumcised is old enough to be taxed, and for this reason they hesitate. Were it not for this, the Tiv would circumcise a boy even before he reached the age of ten.

The girls, too, have departed from the old custom of having the marks made after reaching puberty. Nowadays, when a girl is only about eight years old she cuts the Nail mark, and not the marks of her forefathers. If her people compel her she will have the old marks done, but she will certainly also have the Nail marks put on as well before she is satisfied. After this she starts singing songs in praise of the Nail Boys. Moreover, if it were not that the white men who look after the country have said that a girl must not go to a man before she reaches puberty, they would go to the Nail Men even before they reached the age of ten. The Tiv say that the Boys of the Nail have ruined the country, and subverted the traditions of the ancestors. This is how the symbolic idea of body marks has become changed into what it is now.

¶ To sum up: The body marks were originally intended as a symbol of tribal indentity (p. 25). Afterwards their significance was forgotten, and they came to be used merely for purposes of

---

[1] This has happened in very few cases.

adornment. Finally, owing to the adoption of the foreign 'Nail'
marking by the younger set, the tribal marks have again taken on
their old function as distinguishing 'badges', but this time as
symbols not of racial difference, but of the split within the tribe
between the Old and the Young. Behind all this can be seen the
influence of the women, who, freed from the compulsion of the
exchange marriage system, are defying the authority of their
parents and marrying the young men of their choice.

FURTHER RELATIONS WITH THE BUSH TRIBES

ALL these markings on the body were originated by
the Tiv when they separated from the Fulani. It
was at this time that they came and settled on the hill of
Yavwua, in the midst of the Bush Tribes. The names of
these tribes were Undir, Ukwese, Ugbe, Iyɔnov, and
Utaŋge. After they left Yavwua they came down and
lived by a certain river called Muanawuha, which has a
very strong current. Even to-day cattle brought by the
foreigners from Cepe are carried away by the stream. It
is about thirteen miles south-east of Kashimbila. I went
there with Mr. Malherbe and Mr. Orffer in July, 1934.

But they did not stay there very long. Their nearest
neighbours were the Ugbe and Iyɔnov, and when these
also began to give them trouble over the question of
women, they moved again and came on down to Muan.
Muan and Muanawuha are not far from each other; the
distance between them is about nine miles. If you start
from Kashimbila, and set out in a south-easterly direction,
you come to Muan about four miles from Kashimbila.
It was there that the Tiv first came into contact with the
Chamba, though the Chamba say that they were there
before them.[1] When the Tiv arrived they lived together
quite peacefully; but the Tiv did not want to be amongst
them permanently, so moved on again from there. However they did not come straight on down, but changed
their direction towards the west, that is to say amongst
the tribes which I have mentioned above—the Undir,

---

[1] The main body of the Chamba did not come till about 1830, having been
driven out from the district round Tibati by Fulani pressure; but groups of
Chamba had settled in the neighbourhood of Kashimbila long before this.

E

Ukwese, Utaŋge, Ugbe, and Iyɔnov, until they came and
settled at Mkɔmon.

By the time that the Tiv had come to live at Mkɔmon
they had begun to grow quite accustomed to the Bush
Tribes, and to understand their ways. They watched
what they did, and tried to learn from them. They even
came to call them their brothers, and were not so afraid to
intermarry with them. In short, it was here that they first
came into close touch with them. They took to cutting
the mark down the bridge of the nose,[1] as they do, and
the Bush People, also, learnt some of the Tiv customs.
In fact, the Tiv very nearly remained permanently
amongst them, for they were happy there; and they used
to go back again to visit the Ugbe and Iyɔnov, too.

After the Tiv left Mkɔmon, they did not settle on the
plains, but went up on to the hill of Ibenda. Ibenda Hill
is in the present district of Turan; if you stand in Jato
Aka's village, you can see it to the south-east. At Ibenda
they chose sites according to their clans. The children of
Ipusu settled on the greater Ibenda, which was called
Ibenda Shitire, and the children of Icɔŋgo on the lesser
Ibenda, which was called Ibenda Iharev.

THE CHILDREN OF IPUSU AND ICƆŊGO

The Children of Ipusu are Shitire, Kpar, and Kum.[2]
Kum was a girl, Ipusu's daughter. Her real name was
Ikumura, and the reason why she was so called was that
she was a girl with a broken leg which she used to drag
along the ground. When the rain fell, it poured down
upon her. Ipusu called her his 'Ikumura'.[3] She inclined
more towards Shitire, and did not go with Kpar, because
he was very troublesome to her.

The Children of Icɔŋgo are more numerous. They are:
Ihar, Gondo, Nɔŋgo, Ikura, Ikɔrakpe, Mase, and a
daughter, Toŋgo. With regard to Toŋgo, some say that
her mother was captured by Icɔŋgo in the bush. This

---

[1] *Ikuŋgwa*. This mark is sometimes seen on the old men, but is now no
longer made by the Tiv, though they sometimes cut a small vertical mark down
the centre of the forehead (*icul i paven*).

[2] Kpar is the ancestor of the Kparev clans, Kum of Ukum, &c., cf. p. 108.

[3] = 'Drenched with rain.'

opinion is held by most. And there is another thing which shows that she is not a true daughter, that is, although Toŋgo has come in between Ukum and Shitire, yet they cut off the heads of the Toŋgo men. How, then, can she be their sister?

⁋, The last few sentences show clearly how the clans are identified with their original ancestors. The tendencies of their members are attributed eponymously to their founders. That is to say, there is a closer connexion to-day, in dialect and customs, between Ukum and Shitire, than between Ukum and Kparev, and this fact is personified by the Tiv in the traditional preference shown by Kum, the lame daughter, for her brother Shitire rather than for Kpar. The final passage runs literally: 'although she has come in between Ukum and Shitire, yet they are [in the habit of] cutting off her head. So how is she a sister?' Toŋgo, the clan, is, in fact, still regarded as the illegitimate daughter.

It was the custom to cut off the head of an enemy killed in battle, but not if he belonged to the same tribe as yourself. The practice of head-hunting seems to have been learnt from the Bush Tribes, amongst whom it was fairly common. The skull was kept, and produced at the dance known as *girnya* (also an importation from the south), in which only those who had killed a man could participate. This does not, however, appear to be connected with any cannibalistic practices. On the contrary, the Tiv say that the eating of the enemy was strictly forbidden, on the grounds that this would give the enemy power over them. The body was therefore cut up into small pieces and burnt, to prevent any one eating it, and if any Tiv was discovered eating the body of a slain adversary he was handed over to the enemy to be killed by them.

II

THE HOMESTEAD, THE FARM, AND THE BUSH

IBENDA was the Gateway to Tivland. When the Tiv
had settled on Ibenda Hill, and looked all round without
seeing any other tribe near enough to worry them, their
minds were set at rest. At that time the people living in
Tiv country were the Dam and the foreign tribes of the
North.[1]

THE *AKWAGI* SHELTER

So they began to build their homes and live in contentment. At first they made shelters. They made a large type
of shelter, wide but not very high, called *Akwagi*[2] after one
of the Mbaipusu, who knew best how to make it. . . . If a
man wanted to make an *akwagi* shelter, he decided where
he was going to put it, and prepared the site by taking out
all the stumps. Then he went into the bush, cut down
some young trees, slender and whippy, brought them in
and put them down close to the place he had already
prepared. Next he drew a circle having the same circumference as the *akwagi* which he proposed to make. Then
he sharpened a stick, called the 'digging stick', and with
this dug holes all round the circle, leaving a space where
the door was to be. He took the withies, buried the ends,
and rammed the earth down hard. Then he went into the
forest and pulled down some *ikaver* or 'dog-gut' creepers,
and another thing called *mkamande*, which is like the
'dog-gut' but is not so thick, and is more common in the
thickets. Having brought this, he stood in the centre of
the *akwagi*, took hold of the withies, bent them over, and
tied them tightly to the creepers. When he had finished
the framework he put on the thatch.

After a time they began to make other shelters of

---

[1] *Uke*; see note on p. 19.
[2] This type of shelter, which is similar to that used by Fulani herdsmen,
is still made by the Tiv, but is used only for storing yams. If temporary shelter
is needed for sleeping in, e.g. on the farm, it is made by planting a ring of posts
and placing a small conical roof on them.

different types and called by different names, but the method of construction was the same in all. One they made in an elongated shape, which they called the 'Hippo' shelter. Finally, they began to build houses in which to sleep, and others to sit in, shaded from the sun.

THE SLEEPING HUT

The Building. A man who wished to build a house first prepared the ground on the site which he had chosen. He collected some earth, made a mound like a yam-heap, and then marked out the plan of the hut in a circle with the earth in the centre. He dug a trench following exactly the circumference of the hut, about one inch in depth only. . . . He told his wife to draw water for him, mixed the mud, and left it till the moisture had drained away. Then he started to build. He told a boy to shape the mud into balls for him, and another boy to collect them and hand them to him.[1] He built the wall wide at the base, in the trench which had been made round the house, and this was known as the 'pressed-down course'.[2] People said, 'So-and-so has laid the foundations'. When he had built a low wall, about one foot in height, it was high enough for the base,[3] so he put on a thick layer of mud and smoothed it over. Others drew their fingers over it, and made patterns, but their work was very rough. It was then said, 'So-and-so has finished the base of the house'. Then he began to build up on this. After he had laid about two courses above the base, he left a place for the door,[4] and did not build all the way round. When he had laid about another sixteen courses he put the lintel in place, after

---

[1] The wet mud is handed in a ball to the builder, who rolls it out into a sausage shape before laying it. (N.B.—The past tense is used, but *vide* note on p. 26).

[2] I.e. the first layer of mud is merely pressed down into the trench to form a foundation.

[3] In modern Tiv houses the plastered base of the wall (*imagh*) is usually about 3 or 4 ft. high. Above this the courses are laid on wet as described above, and are not plastered over on the outside, as this part is protected by the thatch. This gives the house a decorative appearance.

[4] I.e. the bottom of the entrance was, as in modern sleeping huts, some distance from the ground. Nowadays it is usually about three feet up, and the threshold consists of a smooth log of wood, either built into the wall or resting on two forked posts placed up against it on the outside, over which the inmates slide as they climb in and out.

which he added a further two courses, and then left it. He
had finished the wall.

The men of former times did not build houses as high
as those built to-day. Sometimes they collected stones and
built with these. They laid them on without mortar and
plastered them over with mud. Building with mud only
was more highly esteemed, but for strength the stonework
lasted longer. A stone wall, when the rain had washed
away all the mud, would subside till the stones rested on
each other, and so it would remain indefinitely. I climbed
the Hill of Ibenda Shitire with Mr. Botha in September,
1916, and so saw some of the work done by the people of
former days.

The Roofing. The house-builder next set to work to
make the roof-frame. He first went and cut long straight
poles for the rafters, and put them aside to dry. When they
were dry he cut some *icen* grass and dried it in the sun, or
scorched it over the fire till it was withered up and tough
as raffia-fibre, then twisted it and plaited it carefully into
rope. Having finished making the rope, he collected the
other materials; he cut *agegha* shoots and *ikaver* creepers
for the roof-tie rings, brought them in, and set them down.
Then he started to make the framework. This he did
not do alone, but called one of his relations or friends to
come and help him. First they bent the *ikaver* into a ring
large enough for about three of the rafter-poles to pass
through.[1] Next they dug a hole, or used that which had
already been dug for the mixing of the earth, and put the
ends of the rafters in it. They took hold of these and
pulled them apart,[2] and then started binding on the
horizontal rings. There would be about three of them
working: the first man laid on the *agegha*, the second
followed behind tying it on, and the third handed them
the materials one after the other; he would give more rope
to the man who was doing the binding when his was
finished, or *agegha* to the man who was laying it on in

[1] This ring is put over the three main rafters at the end which will eventually
be the top of the roof. The framework, however, is made *up-side down*, so that
it is this end which is put in the hole in the ground.

[2] I.e. the top ends are pulled outwards, but the bottom ends are held by the
ring and the sides of the hole, forming an inverted cone.

front, if he had not enough. People said, 'So-and-so has begun the framework of his roof to-day, and is tying on the cross-rings'. Having tied on the rings, more sticks were inserted, in addition to the three original rafters.

When the framework was complete, it was time to put it on the house. For this purpose a number of people were called in to come and hold it; one man had a pole with which he levered up the base of the roof, another tied on a rope to the inside and pulled on it, so that it should not fall back again. The rest took hold all round and lifted it on. Thereupon a general hubbub arose, all shouting instructions. Some said, 'Push it forward!' and some cried, 'No! Pull it back!' Some said, 'It's all right as it is', and some said, 'It just wants to be tilted a bit in the direction of the stream. . . . There! That's fine! All finished, all finished! Why, So-and-so, you *can* make a roof!'

The Thatching. The men of former days did not use sword-grass for thatching. When a man was ready to thatch his house, he went down to the marsh and pulled up some *dur* grass. He took about five bundles of this, and joined the pieces of grass together. This was called 'plaiting the *dur*'. When he had plaited all this, he went back again and pulled up only another ten bundles or so, for they did not build big houses in those days. This second lot of grass he left unplaited. Then he started on the thatching. First he took one roll of plaited *dur* grass, and began to thatch from the bottom of the roof with the lower ends of the grass pointing downwards. Having gone once round, he took another roll and laid it on, this time pointing the tips of the grass towards the ground. When he came round again he left off using the plaited grass, and started to thatch with the loose bundles. But if he did not himself know how to thatch, he called some one else to come and do it for him.[1]

The Beating of the Floor. When the thatch was finished, the wife for whom the husband had built the house set about beating the floor. She dug up some red soil and brought it in. Then, having first levelled out the

[1] Naturally a meal was provided, but no other payment was expected for mutual help of this kind, nor is it to-day, if both men are of the same group.

heap of earth which her husband had collected when he was preparing to build the house, she took the red soil, scattered it all over the floor, then drew some water and sprinkled it on. This done, she looked about for a smooth stone, which she called a 'mallet', and started to beat the floor with it. After the first beating it was not very smooth, and she was said to have done the rough preparation. Then she went to look for a 'mushroom' ant-hill, which she broke up and powdered over the floor, sprinkling some more water on the top. When the earth from the ant-hill had quite dissolved, she took the mallet and beat the floor again till it was nice and smooth. The ant-hill earth prevented the floor from cracking. People would then express their admiration, saying that the woman certainly knew how to beat floors!

THE THINGS IN THE HOUSE

The Hearthstones. When the woman had finished beating the floor, she set up the hearthstones and cooked a meal. For the hearthstones she went to find three round stones as big as a man's head. Then she scraped out three holes in the centre of the hut. In these she set the stones, filled in the earth, sprinkled on some water, and beat it well down. Sometimes she would add another small stone close to the others, for cooking the sauce. The three large ones were for cooking the *ruam*. A woman who was skilful would make a very fine-looking fire-place. Sometimes she would put on a mud coating over the out-side of the stones.

The Stand for the Water-pots. When the woman had finished the hearth, she built a stand for the water. If she were lazy, she would not take the trouble to make this carefully; she merely put three stones on the ground like hearthstones and rested the pot on them. But if the stand belonged to a woman of importance, she would draw some water, a boy would mix mud for her, and she would build it properly. Sometimes a man would help her. She built it high, oblong in shape, and scooped out hollows to hold the water-pots. She also fixed a small stake by the side of the stand on which to hang the dipper.

The String Holder. When a house had been built for a woman, and she had made the fire-place for cooking the food, and a stand for the water, she would then hang up a string holder in which to keep her cooking utensils. First she pulled up some *icen* grass—for they made rope with this before they learnt the use of raffia—and separated it out well. If she were a strong-minded woman, she would plait some flat-sided cord[1] herself, but another would look for a man, and give it to him to plait properly for her.

In those days a woman did not take much pains over making the holder. Having been given the cord, she cut it into four lengths. One piece she made into a loop, then took the other three pieces and tied them on at points round the circle. Finally she bound the ends together, and hung it from the rafters on the right-hand side as you entered the house, this being also the side where the water was kept. These were the things which the woman made in the house.

The Wooden Platform. When the woman had made all the women's articles in the house that her husband had built for her, the man set to work on the things to be done by him. First, he cut down four forked posts, and stripped off the bark. Then he cut two more straight poles which he called the girders of the platform, the forked posts being intended for the upright supports. In addition to these he cut about twenty sticks to form the flooring of the platform. He dug four holes in the centre of the hut in which he set the uprights, packed in earth, and rammed it down hard. Next he took the two beams, lay one across from this post to that, and the other in the same way. Finally, he laid the cross-timbers.

The Drying-Mat. Having completed the platform, he was now ready to make the drying-mat. The men of those times did not understand the uses of the raffia palm, so that for everything which they would have made with raffia they used some other material. They cut some slender rods about 2 ft. long, and some *icen* grass to make string, which they plaited between the rods in three

---

[1] *Ipekor.* In this type of rope the blades of grass (or palm-fronds) are plaited flat, so that it has the appearance of a narrow band.

places, one at each end, and one in the middle. When it was finished, they tied it up underneath the centre of the platform, and used it for drying purposes.[1]

The Door. Although a man had done all this, the work of making the things in the hut was not yet finished; there was still the door to be made. Originally the type which was made of slender sticks was called an 'Honour-door',[2] because when it was put over the entrance the house looked important. That was the origin of the name. The word is still used for a door in Kparev.

When a man was ready to make the door, he first went into the forest and cut some thin sticks, or else it might be *agegha* shoots. He brought them back, and made some string from *icen* grass. When the sticks were dry he arranged them carefully on the ground. He measured the height and width of the door, and spread out the sticks so as to be the same width as the measure. Then he carefully cut a piece of wood to the same length as the width of the door, placed it across the sticks which he had already spread out, and bound them to the cross-piece with the string made of *icen* grass. This he did in three places, exactly in the same manner as for the drying-mat.[3] Finally, he took the thing with which he had measured the height of the doorway and cut off the door to the same length.

Ever since the time that they lived on Ibenda the Tiv have never tied the door to the right-hand side, but always to the left. The stand for the water is on the right side, and the string holder is tied up on the same side as the stand. When the door was to be tied in position, a straight post of dry wood was cut, and set up at the side of the doorway close up against the wall. The door was tied to this in two places, at the top, and at the bottom. For the 'lock' another post was set up behind the door. When it was required to shut up the house, the door was pushed

---

[1] Nowadays the mat is made of lengths cut from the narrow end of the stem of the raffia palm, tied together with string made from the leaf.

[2] *Civir-hunda*.

[3] But, of course, the door was rigid, whereas the drying-mat was not. According to this account the rails were placed horizontally, as in European doors, but nowadays the framework usually consists of three vertical stiles, and the cornstalks are tied across horizontally.

to, so as to close the entrance, and the locking-stick was placed with its forked end against the post behind, and the other end resting firmly against the door, so that no one coming from outside could open it.

The Bed. In the old days before the Tiv knew how to make beds as they do now, they used to build an oblong mud platform inside the house, like the stand for water-pots made by women of importance, and sleep upon that. Later on they took to cutting blocks of wood to sleep on, and so eventually they evolved the bed. They cut four forked sticks about 2 ft. high, and fixed them in the ground on the side of the hut nearest the door. They placed them so that the bed would be just long enough to take a man's body, and broad enough for two people to sleep on it. The posts having been set in position, some more poles were cut, about the thickness of a man's forearm, long and slender, and stripped clean of bark. Another two were quite short, equal to the width of the bed; these they placed crosswise on the forked sticks which had been already stuck in the ground, one at the head and one at the foot. Then they took the long poles, laid them on lengthwise, and bound them with rope. That was the bed of the people of those days. The head was towards the door, and the foot towards the wall.[1]

The Manner of Sleeping. The Tiv do not sleep anyhow. The man sleeps by the side of the fire, and the woman next to the wall.[2] If their child is suckling, he sleeps between them, but when he grows up he sleeps next to the wall. The guest[3] sleeps on the side where the water is kept. So it has been from earliest times down to the present day. The man, his wife, his children, his

---

[1] Two kinds of beds are now made by the Tiv. The one (*gambe*) has developed out of the type described here, and is constructed in much the same way, except that the 'planks' are made of raffia palm, and it is no longer fixed to the floor. The other kind (*kpande*) has been developed out of the original 'blocks of wood'. These are common in parts of Kunav, where raffia palm is scarce. They are carved in one piece with considerable skill, and some have been in use for several generations.

[2] The point, of course, is not that the man should be near the fire, but that he should be between his wife and the door, in order to protect her in case of danger, and to keep her safe from interference. This is the rule in most tribes.

[3] I.e. a friend of the household. A casual visitor would normally sleep in the *ate*.

relations and guests all sleep in one house. And his mother-in-law, too, if she comes to visit her son-in-law, sleeps in the same house, and so also his brother-in-law. If he were to put his mother-in-law in another house she would be angry.[1]

DIVISION OF LABOUR

¶. The sleeping house, when it is complete, is the property of the woman, and she therefore contributes as much to its construction and furnishing as her physical capabilities allow, on the same principle that, as the production and preparation of food are the woman's province, so the farm belongs to her, and she does as much of the work on it as she can. The heavy work in each case, on the one hand the building and carpentry, on the other the initial clearing and hoeing, is done by the man. The woman draws the water, because this is associated with the preparation of food. The man mixes the mud and builds the house, but the woman 'builds' the hearth-stones, the pots and other utensils, which are her especial care. Some of the work, such as the building of the stand for the water-pots, falls between the two categories, and can be done by either sex.

In some of the Kparev clans the women do more work on the construction of their own house. They mix the mud for the building, cut the corn-stalks, and help the men bring in the roof-poles and thatching grass. It is said that the women prefer to do this, because it gives them a stronger claim to call the house their own, and to refuse admittance to whom they will. In Shitire and Ukum, on the other hand, if a woman were told to mix mud, she would go to her father's home and complain that she had been treated as a slave, and this might be enough cause to dissolve the marriage. But apart from the restrictions imposed by local usage, and the fear of ridicule, there do not appear to be any immutable laws governing the work which may be done by each sex, and a man will quite often lend his wife a hand even in the most essentially female tasks, such as the sowing of the seed.[2]

Of the houses which are next described the *ate*, the *dwer*, and the smithy belong to the men, and the women accordingly take

---

[1] It is not usual for a woman to visit her son-in-law until after the first child has been born. When she does so, she must be treated with especial respect.
[2] Cf. L. H. Dudley Buxton, *Primitive Labour*, p. 21 et seq.

no part in their construction, with the exception of beating the floor, which is woman's work in most Nigerian tribes. The food stores, however, and the *tsum*, of which the corn store in the centre forms an essential feature, belong to the women.

COMMON MEETING HUTS AND FOOD STORES.

The 'Ate'. In the time when the Tiv were few, the *ate* was their common meeting-place. Every man who settled down with his family would build one in the middle of his village, and there all would come and sit together, men, women, and children. (The name *ate* is an abbreviation, and meant originally 'central house'.) In those days they did not make the *ate* as big as they do now. They cut down the forked posts, and set them up in a circle, according to the size of *ate* that they wished to make. Then they cut the curved cross-poles, and placed them in the form of a circle on the top of the uprights. After this they roofed it and thatched it, and the women made a good floor of beaten mud. But they did not sleep there, for fear of wild beasts; for in those days, when the population of Tivland was smaller than it is now, the country was full of beasts of prey, and any one sleeping in the *ate* was liable to be seized by one of them.

But when they became more numerous and started to live in big villages, and as their knowledge increased and the number of wild animals diminished, an advance was made in the development of the *ate*. Nowadays, in a big village, a man of importance will build a *tsum* for each wife in front of her house, in which to store the food or sit with her friends. And before the house of his chief wife he will build an *ate*, which he can use himself. In construction, moreover, the *ate* is no longer the small and badly made shack of the past. It is a spacious building, which can be made in several different styles. The posts are selected and handsomely carved, and the framework of the roof is a work of art; more care is spent on it than on any of the other houses. In the centre is a broad ceiling,[1] and the outside is covered with a good thatch. The

[1] Made of a series of concentric rings of grass or straw, bound closely round with rope.

floor is beaten down hard by the women, and a wall is built round it under the eaves, but not so high as to shut out the breeze. It is in this house that the head of the family is accustomed to sit with his chief wife and his guests, and when he makes beer it is here that the people sit round and drink. The young men hold their dances and keep their drums there. In the centre he sets up a drying platform, and fills it with millet. His fame goes round, and every one says, 'So-and-so has built a great *ate*, and his millet is piled up to the roof!'

Such is the modern *ate*. It has come to be a mark of the old and respected, and of the younger men of substance.

The Smithy. The smithy is another kind of *ate*. It dates from the time when the Tiv first started black-smithing, and has not altered in the smallest detail from the earliest times down to the present day. Little care is taken over its construction, and when you see a smithy to-day you see the *ate* of the ancestors, a small and un-sightly hut. The framework of the roof consists merely of long sticks.

The smithy is not usually set up in the middle of the village, but on the outside, owing to the danger of fire. Inside it the blacksmith keeps his tools—the bellows, the tongs, the heavy iron hammer and the small hammer with the wooden handle, the rake, the iron and stone anvils, the clay nozzle for the furnace, the water-trough, and the magic pot hanging from the rafters. Beside his tools, he also used to keep in the smithy any hoes, axes, or such-like, which had been brought to him to mend. No one who saw them there would dare to steal them by night, for if he did so Aɔndo would surely strike him with a thunderbolt. But nowadays, if the blacksmith is entrusted with some implements and puts them in the smithy, some one who has been looking comes in the night and steals them, and in the morning the smith cries 'Thief!' in vain. In the end he has to pay the owner for what he has lost. So now, when a man comes to him with something to be done, he no longer keeps it in the smithy, but puts it carefully away in his house.

In the old days children on the slightest pretext were

made to take the Oath on the Forge. If a child was suspected of having taken something, but denied it when
questioned, you told him, if he were speaking the truth,
to swear by the Smithy. Whereupon, if he really had not
stolen anything, he said, 'So-and-so's Forge is very evil'.
But if he were guilty he would be afraid to swear, and
would remain silent, so that you could tell at once that he
was the thief. But afterwards children got used to hearing
their elders say that Aɔndo did not kill people by the
Powers of the Day, but only through the People of the
Night, so that the oath soon came to mean little to them.
Children nowadays, even though guilty, are not afraid to
swear falsely by the Forge.[1]

The 'Tsum'. The *tsum* is very much like the *ate*, but not
the same. The difference is this: in the case of the *tsum* a
platform is made first, the horizontals of which consist of
sticks or raffia poles. This is plastered over with mud, and
a corn store, provided with an opening, is built on top of
it. This store is covered with a roof which comes right
down to the ground, and is supported by one circle of
short posts under the eaves. The *ate*, on the other hand,
always has two circles of posts, one in the centre, and one
round the edge.

When the thatch is completed, the woman for whom
the *tsum* has been built tells one of the boys to make a
heap of earth for her. This she fetches in, spreads over
the floor, and beats down hard. Her husband builds a
low wall round it, as in the case of the *ate*, and people
come and sit there, and sometimes sleep there, too. But a
tsum is never so roomy as an *ate*, because it is only so
called when it has a corn store built up on the top of the
central staging, whereas an *ate* has simply a wooden
platform, and sometimes not even that. The millet is put
on the platform in the *ate*, but the guinea-corn is kept in

[1] For the identification of Aɔndo with the sky see p. 230, and Abraham p. 43
et seq. According to Akiga the tendency has been to ascribe more and more
power to the *mbatsav* (i.e. human agency), so that the supernatural forces
(*akombo*) are now considered to have little effect without their intervention.
Even Aɔndo, the Sky God, is subject to their control, and cannot kill (by his
thunderbolt) unless the victim has already been 'doomed' by them to die that
particular death (p. 250). For the connexion between blacksmithing and the
lightning see p. 207.

the mud corn-bin, inside the *tsum*. This is how the *tsum* has always been made, right from the beginning.

The Grass Yam Store. When our ancestors began to build houses, they left off sleeping in grass shelters on account of snakes, and the same type of shelter in which they used to sleep came to be used as a place to store yam seed. Sometimes they made one store for the yams and another for the seed. The seed store could either be on the farm or at the edge of the village, but the yam store was always put in the space between the sleeping huts, otherwise, if it were away on the farm, the yams would be stolen. But the Tiv never used to steal yam seed; for they said that if you planted stolen seed, not only would the yams not grow, but the rest of the crop, which you had already planted, would also be ruined. That is why they did not dare to steal yam seed. But nowadays people steal seed without any fear at all.

The 'Dwer'. The *dwer* is a house in which men can sit together. It has not been known long by the Tiv, but was introduced at the time when the Tiv started to go amongst the foreigners,[1] and to receive the chieftainship from them. They brought the idea of the *dwer* back with them, and built one in their own home. But it is foreign, not Tiv. It was first introduced by Ukum and Shitire, and afterwards copied by other clans. The Hausa name for it is *zaure*. Originally it was not every one who had a *dwer*, but only the chief. A commoner who built one built his own pyre,[2] for he would surely die;[3] so men did not dare.

If a chief wished to have a *dwer*, he chose an expert to build it for him. It was set in the middle of the village, and had four entrances, or, in the case of a *pua-dwer*, only two. The roof was also made by a skilled craftsman, and the rope-work ceiling extended from the apex to more than a man's height.[4] There the chief set his throne, and beds and chairs on which people might sit; and if he bought a horse he would tie it up inside, too. The chief's

---

[1] I.e. the Jukun.   [2] P. 333.   [3] By witchcraft.
[4] I.e. when the roof was inverted on the ground, before being placed in position.

drums were also hung up in the *dwer*, and when the day was over his drummers would take them down and start drumming. And this pleased the chief, who sat on his throne, smoking his long pipe in contentment. But if any one else were to build a *dwer*, he was furious, because the man was setting himself up as a rival. The young men slept in the chief's *dwer* to guard his horse, lest the *mbatsav* should cast a spell on it, and any strangers who came to the village would also spend the night there.

Such was the *dwer* of former days. It was the prerogative of the chiefs; all others, whatever their position, built only an *ate*. But as time went by things changed, and many of the more important men, beside the chiefs, built themselves a *dwer*.

FARMING AND FOOD

Tools. The Tiv used not to have as many tools to work with as they have now. They had the digging stick, the wooden hoe for farming, and machetes for felling trees. The machetes they got from the Umbu, a section of the Dam people. They used to be called *agondo*, or 'Utur axes'. (The Utur[1] are said by the Tiv to be a sub-division that has split off from the Umbu.) The adze was not used in the past.

The wooden hoe was made as follows: The farmer cut down part of a *gbaaye* tree at a point where it branched, and stripped off all the bark. Then he split off a piece of wood from another *gbaaye*, or any hard-wood tree, and worked it into a flat blade. He fixed this on to the forked branch which he had previously stripped, . . . cut down some *uwer* vine, and with it bound the wooden blade tightly to the handle. It was thus like a hoe, and he could use it for digging the farm. At first it was not at all easy for them to make a farm with this tool, but they went on trying until they got used to it. Even to the present day it is still used by a small division of Ikurav South, called Ityuav.

---

[1] A small tribe of fishermen living by the river near Katsina Ala, known to the Hausa as the Turu.

F

FOOD CROPS

The 'Alev' Bean.[1] In the beginning the Tiv did not
have the great variety of foodstuffs which they have
to-day. Their crops were *alev* beans, koko yams, pearl
millet and *anumbe* yams. Those were all the foodstuffs
they had at the outset. Originally they farmed *alev* beans
only, and the farm was called the 'bean patch', because no
other crop was grown on it.

When the time came to hoe the ground for the beans,
the farmer would first choose a piece of bushland where
the soil was nice and black, and there were plenty of
trees.[2] During the rains he rooted up the grass, and killed
all the trees by fire. A few days later he burnt off the
grass which he had pulled up, and the place was then
clear. Then he took his wooden hoe and went off to the
farm to start hoeing, making the heaps round but not
high, of the type known as 'elephant's feet'. When he had
finished hoeing he did not plant the farm at once, but
waited until there had been many days' rain on it.

The planting was done by the woman.[3] Having first
shelled the beans, she took the seed and went out to plant
it. She made a deep hole with her heel in the 'elephant's
foot', dropped in two seeds, pushed up some soil with her
hand, and covered them over. She went on doing this
until she had planted all the heaps. After some days the
beans sprouted. . . .

The young leaves are picked by the women, and used to
make sauce for eating with *ruam*.[4] Sauce made of bean
leaves is called *mhiandem*, but if the leaves are first boiled
and then dried before cooking, it is called *akafi*. . . . But
it was the fruit which was really called the bean in the
first instance, and indeed still is. In a rainy season in
which a great many men are drowned, the Tiv say that
that year there will be a wonderful bean harvest; but what

[1] The *alev* class includes roughly all the varieties known as cow-peas.
[2] As an indication of the fertility of the soil.
[3] I.e. the wife for whom the farm had been dug. This applies to all crops.
The man digs a separate plot for each wife, and once the initial clearing and
hoeing has been finished, she takes over the farm, and does the rest of the work.
[4] The same tense is used throughout in Tiv, and may refer to past or present.
Here, and in similar passages, the author has obviously forgotten his historical
purpose, so the past tense has been dropped in translation.

they really mean is that the beans will bear a better crop for the kinsmen of those who were drowned.[1]

Beans are eaten at two seasons. First, while they are still green, the women pick them and cook them in their pods. They are eaten like this by the women and children. The other way of eating them is to leave them till they have quite ripened, and dried up. Then the women go out to harvest them. If not many are gathered they are carried home in a calabash, laid out on the drying-platform until they are quite dry, then collected and put into the small store in the space between the houses, known as the bean store. But to give the bean the deference due to it, it should be carried home in a basket, and in the old days even if a woman had only gathered a few she would put them in a basket before bringing them home. So a saying has arisen amongst the Tiv: When a man talks big words, though he is really nobody at all, they say, 'Look at the bean trying to get into the basket! You are not that man's match, but you think you must needs compete against him'.

As soon as the beans are dry, they are ready for eating. The woman shells them and pours them into the pot, adds water, and cooks them. When they are quite cooked she fries some beniseed, grinds it up, pours it in, and stirs. Then she serves it out to her husband and children to eat. Some do not like the beans to be stirred into a mash, but eat them whole. If beans do not agree with you, they will give you a swollen stomach and a sleepless night.

Alev beans are of many different varieties, but the manner of planting, of growth, and of preparation for food is the same for all. The chief difference is in the seed. The beans of the ancestors were the *tende*, and the 'beniseed bean'.[2]

[1] In the Tiv language the word for 'to bear fruit' as applied to the bean is *gbà*, which also means 'to fall'. Therefore the connexion between casualties from drowning and the bean harvest is probably due to the association between the two meanings of the word. That is to say, the fact that many people have fallen into the water and been drowned may be expected to have a sympathetic effect on the 'falling' of the bean crop.

[2] With regard to the plants mentioned in this section, many of the varieties recognized by the Tiv are not distinct species, and have no corresponding English, or botanical, names. Some of the terms apply to the colour or appearance of the individual fruit, seed, or tuber. But the Tiv understands perfectly well the difference between a distinct variety which will grow true to type, and an individual peculiarity due to local conditions (see p. 77).

The 'Ahuma' Bean.[1] The *ahuma* is another species of bean. Usually it is planted early, but some women plant it at the same time as the *alev*. It does not mature so quickly, however. It forms tubers under the ground, like cassava, and the women of former times used to dig them up and cook them for their children. These tubers were called '*ahuma* stones', and were very good to eat. But when they were eaten roasted they gave a man a bad headache, or else he would have pains in the stomach and be very sick. But *ahuma* stones were mostly eaten by the children. Like the *alev*, the beans of the *ahuma* can be eaten either green or dry.

In former times the *ahuma* bean was the great food of the elders. It was gathered and bound into bundles, and in times of famine one bundle was worth a 'twenty'. An important woman would become famous for her cooking through giving a feast of pounded *ahuma* beans. She shelled all the beans, started to cook them from the hour at which people sit together in the evening, and kept on making up the fire throughout the night. At first cock-crow they were done. Then she got up, roasted some beniseed, ground it, and brought it into the house.[2] She took a mortar and started pounding at cock-crow, added the beniseed, and poured in palm oil. At the break of dawn she served it out into a large calabash and gave it to her husband, who would call the people together. Indeed some of them would come of their own accord when they heard the pounding. They came and ate, and were loud in their praises. 'The daughter of So-and-so', they said, 'has become a great lady in the house of So-and-so; she has cooked a meal which men have eaten and left over!' That was how women of importance formerly used to cook the biggest meals of pounded *ahuma* bean.[3]

---

[1] *Vigna ornata.*   [2] The grinding is usually done outside the house, under the eaves.
[3] The food was (and is) in the hands of the woman, and since she had done practically all the work since the time of the planting, she rightly got the credit for her hospitality, and not her husband, as would be the case, say, in Muhammadan society. It was she (subject, of course, to a certain amount of control by her husband) who decided when to invite the neighbours to the Bean Feast. Bulrush millet is an exception to the above rule (see p. 77), because it is the grain from which beer is made (this being the man's department), and is also nowadays the chief economic crop sold in local markets. In Kunav the yams are also in the husband's control.

The Koko Yam. The koko yam was of great importance to the men of former days. When the time comes to
prepare the ground for it, the farmer roots up the grass in
some marshland and burns it. Then he makes the heaps,
divides the tubers and plants them. When it comes up it
spreads out its leaves in a thick canopy; for there is no
plant which has such a broad leaf as the koko yam. The
women cut off its young shoots, and make from them the
sauce known as *ishɔŋgo*. When the koko yam is ripe, its
leaves turn yellow and fall off. The woman goes out and
digs it up, pounds it into *ruam*, and the people eat it. At
other times it is baked.

Pearl Millet.[1] Pearl millet, even in the old days, was
broadcast, and a separate field was not dug for it. It was
sown on the piece of land from which koko yams had been
harvested in the previous dry season. When the rains
came, the millet seed, after having been pounded,[2] was
sown on the old koko yam field, and the surface of the
soil was scratched up with the wooden hoe.[3] After some
days the corn came up, and when it was above the knees
it was cleared of grass, and the weaker plants were weeded
out. The corn did not bear till the following dry season.
The farmer then reaped it, tied it into bundles, brought
it home and put it on the drying-platform.[4] When it was
dry, the women made it into *ruam*. But the millet was
best for gruel, and still is so. In fact there is no other corn
which makes such good gruel as pearl millet.

'Anumbe'.[5] In the old days, if a man wanted to grow
anumbe, he first rooted up the grass on new bushland
during the rains, made low heaps, then took the tubers,
divided them between the fingers, and planted them. The
plant grew up, putting out broad leaves, until it was
ready to be harvested at the beginning of the dry season.
The woman then boiled and ate it with her husband; or
sometimes she baked it. The tuber was yellowish in

[1] *Pennisetum spicatum.*
[2] The stalks are pounded in a mortar and the seed comes off.
[3] The seed is first broadcast, and the surface hoed up afterwards.
[4] Actually the boys cut down the standing corn (*gber*), the women cut off the
heads (*sunda*), and the men bind it into bundles, cf. p. 76.
[5] A small and inferior type of yam, said by the Tiv to be the original kind
grown by their forefathers.

appearance, and had an unpleasant taste, being slightly bitter.   If the woman who dug it up threw it down heavily, it formed hard parts which would remain un-cooked even after they had been boiled.

These were all the foodstuffs that the Tiv had at first. Later they discovered other valuable kinds of food, which they still have to-day, such as guinea-corn, bulrush millet, maize, and yams.   Also luxury crops[1] such as sweet potatoes, white cassava, ground-nuts, Bambarra ground-nuts, 'king of the rains',[2] kaffir potato, pumpkin, and marrow.   The soupstuffs[3] are: *bushi*, red sorrel, okra, *afialegh*, and *igar*.   Chilli, beniseed, pumpkin seed, and black pepper are also put in the sauce.

Guinea-corn.   It was from the Chamba that the Tiv first learnt the use of guinea-corn,[4] which they have re-tained down to the present day.   Guinea-corn ranks first amongst the food-crops of the Tiv.[5]   They grow it on different kinds of land.   A man who has no other place in which to grow it makes his guinea-corn farm on new land, and that is the way in which men first used to grow guinea-corn, before yams had been discovered.   But ever since they started to grow yams, and the land on which last year's yam crop was grown has been available, they have grown guinea-corn on this, too.   Some grow a crop on

---

[1] *Abeer a uyia :* lit. 'fooling' crops, i.e. not serious farming, but the sort of things you plant in your spare time. A Tiv who has not had a meal made out of one of his staple foods will say that he has eaten nothing.

[2] See below.

[3] I.e. the main constituents of the sauce, as opposed to the seasonings men-tioned in the next sentence. These plants are cultivated by the Tiv. In Hausa-land they are not cultivated (except okra), but are sometimes picked in the wild state and used as sauce ingredients. In the case of *igar* (*stylochiton dalzielii, aroideae*) and *bushi* (?) it is the leaves which are eaten; in the case of *afialegh* (*grewia mollis, tiliaceae*) the juice expressed from the bark.

[4] The Tiv have only been in contact with the Chamba for about 200 years, and their knowledge of guinea-corn is probably much older than this. But they certainly obtained some species from the Chamba (see below).

[5] The crop which now supplies the major part of the tribe's food, and is the most popular, especially amongst the younger people, is undoubtedly the yam. But guinea-corn is given the place of honour by the elders, because it was one of the old crops, can be kept and eaten throughout the year and used for a variety of purposes, but more especially because it is made into beer. Beer (the Tiv word is *msɔrom*, the drink which 'sets right') has a very strong social and ritual significance amongst the Tiv. Thus the use of guinea-corn for this purpose, coupled with the fact that it was one of the foods of the ancestors, gives it a prestige which the yam can never attain.

new land as well, in order to get a big harvest,[1] but a farmer who is not prepared to work very hard is content with the ground left by the old yam farm. In the case of new land, he roots up the grass and throws it on the ground, cuts down all the small trees, and burns them after a few days, when they are dry. Having done this, he broadcasts the guinea-corn seed, and hoes up the ground. Others grow guinea-corn on the beniseed patch, and others merely use any old land.

When the corn first appears the bush-fowl start to pull up the seed from under the ground. And there is another thing which grows in the bush called striga.[2] The farmer does not see this while he is actually making the farm, but no sooner has he made it, and left off working, than it starts to come up. When it begins to grow, the corn is rapidly scorched up as though it had been burnt by fire, and never comes to maturity. And where it is present in large quantities, not one head of corn will the farmer reap in that field, for the crop will be completely spoilt.

When the corn is high enough to cover a man's knees, it is time for the weeding. During the weeding those maize-cobs which did not mature at the right time are gleaned and eaten on the spot.[3] And if you are weeding, and another man has come out to help you, you share them between you. But if on another day, when he had not been working with you, he felt hungry and came to glean the maize, you who were weeding your farm would say, 'No. Leave my maize-cobs alone'. So the Tiv have a saying: 'If you refuse to weed a man's guinea-corn, leave him the gleanings of his maize crop.'

By the time the weeding has been finished it is the height of the rainy season, and nodes begin to appear on the corn-stalks. At this time the rain is accompanied by many loud crashes of thunder, and the Tiv say, 'The

---

[1] Not because the crop grown on the new land will give a better yield, but in order that the total produce may be greater.

[2] A parasitic weed which grows round the roots of the corn.

[3] The maize is planted at the beginning of the rains (March–April) and reaped in June and July, after which the guinea-corn is sown on the same land, and harvested in November–December. The maize-cobs which are not fully developed at the time of the harvest are left to ripen amongst the young guinea-corn.

guinea-corn is jumping into nodes'.[1] When the nodes
have formed, and the corn is high, the head begins to
appear, and after this the seed starts to form. When it
begins to turn red, a bird with a long beak, called the
grey-headed hornbill, breaks off a head and goes and
throws it into the water, in order that the big fish may
see it, and know that the dry season is at hand. Whereupon they swim away to a deep pool in the stream, and
hide themselves there, so that the women shall not
catch them.[2] The hornbill, too, starts to sing his song at
that time, and people say, 'There's the hornbill! The
dry season is here'.[3] So they set to work on the dry
season's tasks.

When the corn is in ear, and has started to turn red,
there is said to be great activity amongst the *mbatsav*,
who want to kill some one and dry his flesh to eat with
the guinea-corn. During this time no one goes out after
dark.

The guinea-corn is ripe at about the time when the
crackling of burning grass is first heard. From the time
when the seed starts to form it is subject to a great many
pests. The birds collect together and spoil it. If a roan
gets into a man's field of guinea-corn, it is the end of it.
He will not reap a single head; the roan will eat the lot.
This animal comes out at night. The big red monkey, too,
breaks down the corn, and so also the small grey monkey;
these do a great deal of damage to the guinea-corn. And
beside these there is also the baboon. If a pack of baboons
gets into a man's farm, they will break off all his corn,
leaving not one head untouched. That man will certainly
go hungry.

So, when the harmattan begins to blow, the men cut
posts and set up the drying-platform. The farmer goes
out and does the *icegh* rite[4] in the evening, and on the

---

[1] I.e. the corn, being startled by the clap of thunder, jumps out of its stalk,
and so forms another node!

[2] Fish cut off in the shallow pools are caught by communal drives.

[3] The hornbill does not appear to migrate during the rainy season, but is
silent. The Tiv say that the hen, having laid its eggs, loses all its feathers, sits
on the eggs in a hollow tree trunk, and is not seen again till the young are ready
to fly.

[4] See below.

following morning the boys go to the farm, and tread down the corn-stalks. In the old days the corn was always trodden in such a way that it bent over and fell with the heads pointing towards Tiv country, for it was said that if it were trodden down in the direction of the land of the foreigner the corn would actually go there, and the supply would run short. But nowadays they do not care.

On the day after the boys have come home from the farm the women go out to reap. They cut off the heads, and collect them into heaps. Then the men go to the farm and separate out the corn, dividing the 'full heads' from the 'leavings'. The full heads are the good ones, and the leavings those which are poor. For in former times, when there was an abundance of food,[1] they used not to carry the bad corn, but left it in the fields, and that is how the bad corn which was left came to be called the leavings.

When it has all been separated out, it is bound into bundles, carried home, and laid out on the drying-platform. But it is not just put down anyhow; the stalks are arranged neatly in rows one above the other, and make a fine show. The men of former days did not eat the guinea-corn so soon as people do now, but left it on the platform till it had had many days' rain upon it, before they finally collected it and stored it in the bins. The reason, they said, why they let the corn first be soaked by the rain was that there was a poison in it, which would be washed away by letting the rain fall on the corn, and a man could then eat it without getting pains in the stomach.

Guinea-corn is used for food; but it cannot be eaten as it is. Some make it into gruel and drink it. Some women stir it into *ruam* for their people to eat, and it is also roasted to make *mumu*.[2] When it is first harvested, one of the elders calls his wife and says to her quietly, 'Daughter

---

[1] The older men say that food was more plentiful in their youth, and after making due allowance for the usual disparagement of modern times by an older generation, there is no doubt that in many districts the soil is getting used up, and owing to the rapidly increasing population it is not so easy as it was to keep on finding new land. Accordingly the yield is not so good. Moreover, with their improved standard of living and increased needs the Tiv are selling more of their foodstuffs, and giving more attention to economic crops, than formerly.

[2] Grain roasted first and ground afterwards, used as provisions for a journey.

of So-and-so, make some gruel, so that my group may come again and see my place'. That means that she is to make beer. So the woman pounds the corn, and brews some beer. On the day that it is ready the guests come for the beer-drinking, and the host serves it out to them in pots. They drink it, and become drunk. If the beer is sweet, the men say it is not good; it is the beer of women and children, and not a fit drink for men of their position. But if it is bitter: 'Aha! How does that taste? That's good beer!' The people strike up a song, and the revels begin; they shout the praises of their host, and finally return to their homes late at night. That is what the Tiv have used the guinea-corn for in the past, and still do to-day.

The names of the different kinds of guinea-corn are: Chamba corn, 'wait-by-the-road', 'sheep-will-snatch', *jinawa*, and 'trouble-corn'. Chamba corn is white, not much to look at, and has a hard grain. 'Wait-by-the-road' is pure white, and its grains are large. 'Sheep-will-snatch' is white, and has the biggest head of all the white guinea-corns; it has a black sheath, and looks very handsome. But *jinawa* has the biggest grain of all; it is bright red in colour, and nice to look at.

Bulrush Millet.[1] The Tiv had bulrush millet in the early days, but they never cared for it. They nearly gave it up altogether, because its cultivation was too much trouble. However, they tried to grow a little, and the Chamba used to buy it to mix with their guinea-corn and make *tashi*, that is Chamba beer, or to make into *ruam*, or grind into *aso* cakes[2] for drinking in water when they went a journey into the bush. The reason why the Tiv thought of giving up millet was the care required to grow it, that is, the continuous protection from the birds. They very nearly tired of it on this account, and the only reason why they did not give it up was that it was a wet-season crop.[3] It ripened just at the time when they were suffering from food shortage, and so saved them from famine.

---

[1] *Pennisetum typhoideum.*
[2] The Chamba equivalent of *mumu*. The grain is first boiled, then ground and made into balls.
[3] It is harvested about July, in the middle of the rains.

Moreover, in the days before they had begun to evaporate salt, it was this crop that they exchanged for salt with the foreigners. It was owing to these considerations that the Tiv continued to grow millet, though only in small quantities. They also used to make *ruam* and gruel from it. There are several distinct varieties of bulrush millet, which are quite different in appearance. They are all sown at the same time, but some kinds ripen more quickly than others. The names of the different varieties are: 'Tiv millet', 'monkey's tail', 'big baboon', 'headache', and *tsafa*. 'Monkey's tail' is a variety of Tiv millet, and is so called because it is long and slender like the tail of the grey monkey. 'Big baboon' is also fairly long in the head, and slightly thicker than 'monkey's tail'. 'Headache' has the same sort of leaf sheath, but is red. These are all varieties of Tiv millet. *Tsafa* is the millet of the Chamba. It is sown at the same time as Tiv millet, but when Tiv millet has formed its seed, ripened, and already been harvested, *tsafa* is still putting out its bright-green leaves. When it starts to bear, it forms a huge head, far larger than the Tiv varieties; but it always takes a long time to ripen, and for this reason does not find much favour with the Tiv.

The Tiv grow bulrush millet on the land from which they have harvested the yams. In former days they sowed it on the old *anumbe* farm. When the first rain falls the women go out and pull up the grass, collect it into heaps, together with the foliage left by the yams, and burn it as soon as it is dry. The ground is then quite cleared. When there has been a good fall of rain, they say, 'This is a sowing rain', and the head of the family makes a proclamation that on the following day, after the rain, the women will sow the millet. So the women start to pound the millet at day-break, and when this is done they go out to sow. They make a hole with their heel in the old yam heap, pick up some grains of millet between two fingers and let them fall. Then they push up some soil with their toes, and cover them over. In each heap they sow seed in four places round the side, and one on the top.

Millet is not long in the ground before it comes up. As

soon as it appears, the bush-fowl and guinea-fowl start to scratch up the ground and pull out the seeds, and the boys go out to drive them off. When millet is about the height of a man's finger, it is called 'the crown-bird's crest'. After this, it is time for the women and children to go and weed out the plants. This is called 'dividing the millet'. The woman pulls up the weaker plants and those which are red, and leaves only those with strong stems. These she makes to lean away from each other, in this direction and in that, taking up a handful of soil and placing it in the space between the stems. After it has been thinned out the millet is more healthy, and begins to shoot up and form nodes. Having formed its nodes and reached a good height, it starts to bear. At this stage it is said that the millet is putting out rats' tails. After this comes the flower. When the rain falls it washes away the pollen, and the millet turns quite white. Then the boys go out to keep watch.

Bulrush millet has a great many enemies. As soon as it appears above the ground the bush-fowl do damage to it. If it survives this, and reaches the stage when it turns white, it is attacked by the *mkurum*[1] and the stem borer. At other times it suffers from gumming. This may happen to guinea-corn as well as to millet. If it gets over the time of these little pests, the millet ripens and its leaves turn red. At this stage the Tiv say, 'The millet has put on its red tassels. It is ripe, and ready for harvest'. The owner of the millet field goes out in the evening, and performs the *icegh* rite. Having done this he roots up a little of the crop, and people say, 'So-and-so has initiated the millet harvest to-day; it will be reaped to-morrow'.

The next morning the boys go off to the farm, pull up the corn by the roots and lay it on the ground, and the women go out and cut off the heads. They call these by three different names, according to their grade: the 'full', the 'undeveloped', and the 'birds' beaks'. The 'full' is the fine healthy corn with good grain, the 'undeveloped' is the poor corn with little seed on it, and the 'birds' beaks' are the good heads which have been eaten by the birds, so

---

[1] A little black beetle.

that the grain is left only at one end, or on one side. The 'birds' beaks' are collected and taken away by the women harvesters, who make them into *ruam*, and eat them. The 'undeveloped' heads are taken by the woman to whom the millet belongs. She collects them in a basket and puts them in her house, takes a little at a time to put on the drying-mat, and makes it into *ruam*, as soon as it is dry. As to the 'full' corn, the young men, having cut some raffia fronds, tie it up into bundles and take it home. Formerly they used to give it to the head of their family to put on the platform in the *ate*, and if the woman needed it he would take some and give it to her. Bulrush millet was not a woman's crop, but was in the hands of the man. But nowadays, since there is plenty, the crop is divided. The woman's share is put on the platform in the sleeping house for making *ruam*, and the man's share is put in the *ate* for the brewing of beer.[1]

Maize. Maize grows well in certain places, but not every kind of soil suits it. It does best when sown on the old yam farm, or at the edge of the village, or in marshy land by the river banks. In former times, before men realized how good the marshland was, they used to make clearings in the woods, killing the trees by fire, and the maize did very well there, too. But light, sandy soils do not suit it.

There are several different kinds of maize, such as *iusu*, *santa*, 'blood maize', the Nɔŋgov and Kparev varieties, 'bad teeth', and 'monkey's belly'. *Iusu* is the first to ripen. It has a white sheath and big grains. The grains are also white, and not very hard. *Santa* ripens rather slowly; it does not reach a great height, and forms slender cobs covered with a large number of hard, bright red grains. Nɔŋgov maize has large grains and thick cobs; it is very satisfying, and you cannot eat more than three cobs or so by yourself. Kparev corn is a quick ripening, dwarf variety. 'Blood maize' is not a distinct variety, but may appear in any type of maize crop, and is so called from its blood-red colour. So also 'bad teeth', which is the name given to any plant with variegated black and

[1] Note on p. 68.

white grains, like a man who has a number of discoloured teeth amongst the white ones. 'Monkey's belly' can also appear in any type of maize crop, and is the name given to a cob which has grains on one side, and on the other only the white sheath, like the red monkey with his white stomach.

As soon as the maize appears above the ground the bush-fowl start to scratch up the seed, and the boys must go out and keep a continuous watch, if the crop is to mature. But as it grows the seed gets used up, and when it has reached a certain height people say, 'The maize has now survived the bush-fowl'. Guinea-corn is then sown amongst it, but some wait until the grain forms. Guinea-corn sown through maize grows slowly and poorly, owing to the harmful effect of the maize pollen. Some time after the maize has flowered the cobs start to grow. These put out tassels, and in due course reach their full size. The small grains form in the cob, and the elders drive out the boys to go and scare away the red monkeys. Monkeys give the boys a great deal of trouble, for there is no crop which they like better than maize.

When the sheath of the cob begins to dry up, the maize is ripe. The children who are keeping watch in the fields are strictly forbidden by their elders to eat the cobs. But it never does any good; they know too well how to steal the corn. A boy will take a sharp knife with a pointed end, and when he has looked out a cob which takes his fancy will cut off the stem of the plant under the ground. Lifting it clear, he carries it into the bush, breaks off the cob, and throws the stalks away. Then he goes back to the spot where he cut it, carefully fills up the hole, treads it down, and covers it over with worm-cast.. Then off he goes to bake and eat his corn-cob, throwing the remains well away into the bush. And they have other ways of stealing the corn, too.

When the corn is ripe, the head of the family goes out and cuts one cob to place on the *akombo*.

When the maize is dry, the boys go and reap it, and the women break off the cobs and knot them together. The men go out and bind them into bundles, which are carried home and placed on the drying-platform. Here the best are picked out and tied up in bunches over the hearth, to be used for seed.

Like other foodstuffs, maize can be made into *ruam*, but it is not very good for this purpose. When it is green, women pick off the grains and make them into *akpekpa*,[1] and some prefer this to *akpekpa* made with ground-nuts. But the Tiv do not have so many different ways of preparing it as the foreigners.

The Yam. The yam was first discovered by an orphan child. A long time ago there was a great famine, so terrible that a man would take his daughter and sell her to buy food, saving only his son to inherit his home. This happened at the time when the *ijev* dance was in fashion.[2] The famine brought with it many evils. The Dam used to kill a Tiv and hang his corpse in a tree by the road-side, so that the others might see and fear to pester them with demands for food. But they did not succeed in stopping them from begging. With things in this state, little attention was paid to orphans; they were left to die of hunger. They wandered about in the woods, eating roots. Some ate what was poisonous and died.

One day a young orphan saw, growing in the forest, a yam. He dug it up, and said, 'I will try it. For what is death? And since I am dying, what have I to fear?' So he baked it, and when it was ready he peeled it and ate it. And having eaten it, he found it was good, and, moreover, that he did not die. After that he went on digging up yams, baking and eating them always. Eventually one of the elders noticed him, and asked, 'How is it that though children who have both fathers and mothers are starved, and some have died of hunger, you on the contrary are growing fat, as though the famine has not touched you?' So the orphan told him all. When he had finished, the old man asked him to come and show him, and they went together into the wood. He showed him the yam, and dug it up and gave it to him. The old man looked at it for a

---

[1] A kind of cold food, taken when travelling.
[2] This fact is only mentioned to date it.

long time, and then said, 'It is like the *anumbe*, which we had in former days, and which also bore fruit under the ground. When the famine came upon us it was all finished, though even now there are some here and there who still jealously hoard the few stumps which remain'. Thereupon he took the yam which the orphan had dug up to show him, and cooked it in the same way as they used to cook the *anumbe* in the past. When he ate it, he found that it tasted even better than the *anumbe*. And perceiving that this was indeed a means of deliverance from the famine, he told his household, 'Let this be openly proclaimed, that others also may be saved, for it is certainly not a matter to be kept secret'. So his young men went round the homesteads, crying, 'Come out, come out, there is food in the forest!' And the people rose up in a body, and poured into the forest, where they found the old man and his wife, who told them everything, saying, 'Dig! You may eat this, and not die. This is not death but life!' Then the people set about digging up the yams in mad haste as though they would trample each other to death.

Although the orphan discovered the yam, and taught the Tiv to eat it, they did not know how to grow it themselves, but merely gathered it in the forest. Now at that time the Dam were not far from the Tiv, and one day one of the Dam people came with his wife to visit a Tiv, who was his friend. His host cooked a yam for him, and when he had eaten it he asked his friend where he had got it. The Tiv told him all about it. When he had heard the story, he said that they had yams too, but that they kept them to themselves and did not give them to any other tribe. His friend asked him whether they too dug them out of the forest, and he said Yes, they had done so in the first place, but afterwards they had learnt to cultivate them. When the Tiv asked him how they did this, he replied, 'Were you not my friend, I would not tell you this for nothing, but for our friendship's sake I will teach you'. Then he asked the Tiv whether he had a field prepared for guinea-corn after the Tiv fashion, and the other replied that he had indeed a large field. So they rose up, taking with them a wooden hoe, and went out to the farm. The Dam took the wooden hoe—for at that time there were no iron hoes—first broke up the soil, and then made a heap. When he had finished, he gave the hoe to the Tiv and told him to make a heap, for him to see. The other took the hoe and quickly finished making his heap, but without first breaking up the earth as the Dam had shown him. The Dam said, 'As you have not first broken the soil your heap will not yield such a big yam as mine'.

The next day they went out to plant, taking their wives with them. The men made the heaps, and the Dam's wife taught the Tiv woman how to plant. The Dam told his friend all about yam farming; how, when he had made all the heaps, he must kill the trees by fire, so that the leaves might fall and serve as manure, to make the yams grow; and how, when the yams began to grow, he must cut stakes and plant them in the space between the heaps, so that the plants might climb over them, and not cover up the heap with their thick foliage; for too much shade is not good for yams. So after the Dam had gone, his Tiv friend did exactly as he had told him. When about two months later the yams started to come up, he cut sticks to plant in between the rows of heaps, and trained the vines on to them. And after a few days they began to climb and form a thick canopy some distance from the ground. When seven months had gone by, the yams had made big cracks in the soil, and when he opened up a heap he found that the tuber had formed inside. So he took one out secretly, that no one might see, and baked it and ate it with his wife and children. And a few days later his wife went and dug one out, and eventually they began to eat them openly, in full view of every one. So when the people saw it, they all took up yam farming; for the cultivated yam yielded a better crop than the wild yam which grew in the forest. 'This is a stroke of luck!' they said; and this is how the word for 'good luck' (*ikɔr*) came to be applied to the yam seed.

The Tiv first baked the yam whole, and did not know how to make it into *ruam*, except by cutting it up small,

G

drying it, and then grinding it into flour. Later on the same man of the Dam people came and showed them how to make pounded yam. But even then they had no mortars; they stamped it to pulp on a hollow grindstone.

This, then, was the origin of the yam. And this is why some people say that the Tiv got it from the Dam. But this is not so; it was an orphan who discovered the yam in the forest, and the Dam showed the Tiv how to use it.

❦ This story, like others in this book, is an attempt to account for the bare fact that the cultivated yam is believed to have been introduced from Dam country. The details are obviously supplied from current custom, rather than historical knowledge. For instance, when it is recounted that the Tiv did not make the heaps as taught by his Dam friend, this reflects the fact that there are still two ways of making yam heaps, one according to Dam custom and one not, and that Akiga, or his informant, prefers the former. Similarly, it is a common practice for the women and children to start eating the new yams before the rites have been performed and the crop is officially declared ready for public consumption (see below).

Next follows a list of names for the different kinds of yams, with a short description of each. The author divides yams into three main classes: *Nuaŋge* (hard yams), which he calls 'male yams'; *agbo* (water yams), the 'slow-ripening' variety; and *anumbe*, 'the yams of the men of former days'. The first division has thirty-nine varieties (Malherbe states that the Tiv distinguish fifty or more[1]), the second twenty. The male members of the tribe, whose interest in the yam is confined mainly to the initial preparation of the farm, and to the harvested and cooked article, naturally do not know the names of all the different varieties, for which an inquirer is usually referred to the women. But the length of the list, and the technical vocabulary connected with it, indicate how large a place the yam now occupies in the life of the tribe, although according to Akiga it is a comparatively recent innovation, and even now has not the same honour amongst foodstuffs as is accorded to the guinea-corn.

[1] Op. cit., p. 131.

ROTATION OF CROPS

WHEN the Tiv acquired all the different foodstuffs which they now have, in the manner which we have described, and as you may see for yourself if you come to Tivland, they started to grow them in rotation. The minor crops, however, are usually sown by the women on a farm which has already been prepared for one of the main crops, but they are occasionally grown on a plot by themselves.

All Tiv clear new land for the yam farm, and the time of the clearing is during the rains. The best month is October, though some do not start till November. When the time comes to clear the bush, all the older men in the village go out early in the morning to choose a site for the new farm. In former times they did not each have their own separate farms as they do nowadays, for they were afraid lest, if they did so, any one of them might be cut off by enemies before he could obtain help. When they have selected the site, each of the elders pulls up a handful of grass to mark the place where they will start clearing. Then they go home and tell their sons to cut treading-poles, and plait the rope for them.[1] The next day one of the elders shows the lad who is to tread down the grass the place they marked on the previous day, and he treads out a lane the width of one pole from the bottom end of the farm up to the top. The other workers pull up the grass, but he takes no part in this. Then they go home, and do no more that day. And since the *akombo* came to be practised, it has been the custom for the head of the family, to whom the farm belongs, to go out after the young men have all gone home and place an *akombo* at the edge of the field, in order that the *mbatsav* may not damage his farm by witchcraft; for if the *mbatsav* cast a spell on it, the crop will fail. Down to the present day, if you pass by a farm belonging to one of the older men anywhere in Tivland, you are sure to see an *akombo*, which has been set there from fear lest the *mbatsav* should spoil the crop.

---

[1] The rope is tied to each end of the pole, to form a loop which is held in the hands. The pole hangs horizontally, and is pressed down against the tall grass with the foot.

So all set about rooting up the grass. In the old days, while this work was in progress, the boys used to look out for the *dzumbe*. This is a kind of locust, which is most common at the time of the clearing of the bush, and which the Tiv are very fond of eating. These locusts, when disturbed by the grass being pulled up, fly off in front of the workers, and the children used to catch them and spit them on a piece of stick. It was in the catching of the *dzumbe* that a child showed whether he had any sense or not. There is a poisonous locust called *hurukuku* which looks exactly like the *dzumbe*, except that its wings lie closer against its body. So when a boy who had no sense caught a *dzumbe*, a sharp child would hoodwink him, saying, 'That's not a *dzumbe* you've caught, it's a *hurukuku*; give it to me, I'll throw it away for you'. But when the silly child handed it to him, he did not throw it away at all, but put it on his skewer and went off with it. And for a long time afterwards, whenever any argument came up between them, the wily boy would say to the stupid one, 'What do you know about it anyhow? You, who let me have your *dzumbe*, because I told you it was a *hurukuku*!' And this has become a well-known saying, used by the Tiv to the present day; if some one calls you stupid you say, 'I may be a fool, but you're not taking my *dzumbe* off me', meaning, you won't trick me into giving anything away.

From the earliest times women have gone out with the men to the first clearing of the bush, and have taken part in the pulling of the grass, but they break off early to go and dig up the yams and prepare the meal. Some are afraid of the grass-pulling, and when the time comes for the clearing a woman will sometimes sham sickness, though she is perfectly all right again as soon as the others have gone out to the farm. Another, who has a child, will pretend that he is sick and therefore she cannot go. But nowadays women do not go out much to the clearing, except those with bad husbands who force their wives to go and work.

On their return from work on the new farm all the men and women bathe, and eat their *ruam*. And when the day is over they rub camwood on their bodies, and the men walk about looking for women. For the Tiv say that people look their best at the time of the bush-clearing. But nowadays they do not use camwood so much as they did.

After the clearing of the bush comes the making of the heaps. The head of the family first gets up very early in the morning before any one is astir, goes to the farm, and makes the first heap with an *iyiase* pod, before starting work on the farm with a hoe. The reason for this is that the *iyiase* pod is one of the emblems of the *Twel*, which is an *akombo* of the crops. But only a man who has been initiated into the *Twel* may inaugurate his farming with an *iyiase* pod. He must do this in complete silence. If he meets any one on the road he must not open his lips; if he does so, it means that he gives the other man his crop. Moreover, he must only make one heap that day. On the following day his young men go to the farm and start hoeing.

The Kparev clans make their yam farms according to a definite plan. First they hoe what they call the *dece*, which is one line of huge heaps exactly down the middle of the field. Then they make a row of heaps on each side, which they call the *dece's* children, and continue in this manner, hoeing up the farm in a series of rows. The rest of the Tiv know nothing of the *dece*, but start hoeing in the ordinary way, first making a row down one side, which they call *gwer*. The actual method of hoeing is also different; the Kparev build up the heaps with clods,[1] but the others have no special system. The Kparev laugh at the other clans, saying that their farms are all higgledy-piggledy; and this is quite true, for none of the Tiv make such good heaps as the Kparev. But the yams are just the same.

The hoeing of the yam heaps is, amongst the Tiv, the greatest of all the tasks. The Tiv say that if a man comes and works for you on your farm, even though you may cook for him human flesh, he will not be in your debt

---

[1] Slabs of earth are taken up by the hoe in one piece and thrown flat against the side of the heap.

(and if you read the chapter on the *mbatsav* you will realize how much this means). The women make food and bring it to the workers when the sun begins to show his strength. If, when the Tiv are out on the fields, you were to stand on a path leading from the village at the time when the women come out with the morning meal, and shoot an arrow towards the farm, you would be certain to hit some one on the forehead or in the eye, for all heads are turned in the direction of the road along which the food will come.

When the farm is made early it is called the 'standing corn' hoeing, because it is done before the guinea-corn is reaped, or else the 'dry season' hoeing, as it takes place in December or January. Others call it the 'thatched-heap' farm.[1] If you do not make your wife a thatched-heap farm, she will not love you. Women say that this is the only proper kind of farm, and gives more and bigger seed. It will produce plenty of seed, even if the yams themselves are eaten by the beetle.[2]

When all the heaps have been made, the women go to the farm and prepare the seed for planting. This consists of cutting up the tubers to a suitable size. The seed should be planted about one hand's depth; if it is planted too deep the yam will grow thicker, but not so long. When the planting is finished, and the ground is hard, the people return to do what work there is in the village; they also reap the guinea-corn. Later on a little rain falls; this is known as the 'black-stalk' rain, because it comes at the time when all the grass stalks are charred. The people go out and hoe up the old cornfield, for sowing beniseed. After a time there is some more rain, and this is heavy. Then there is much work to be done, and every one sets about doing what he feels to be necessary. Some still have building to do. The women go out to sow the millet and maize, or to get the farm ready

---

[1] The heaps are covered with grass to protect the seed yams from the heat of the sun through the dry season.

[2] That is to say, it is considered best to finish making the heaps before the ground gets too hard. If the farmer leaves it too late he must wait till the beginning of the rains to finish the work, by which time the seed ought to have been planted for some months, and be starting to germinate.

for the beniseed. Others make a yam farm, which is known as the 'new-rain' farm; it does not yield such big yams, but they are good ones, and the best for storing. At this time, also, the women sow the herbs for the sauce, already mentioned, on the farm made in the dry season.

When the leaves of the wild plants begin to appear on the yam farm, the women go out to weed. At the same time they take away the grass with which they covered the yams at the time of the planting, and open up the heap to see if the seed has rotted. If so, they take it out and put in a fresh one. By the time that the farm is ready for the second weeding the yams have already formed. The women go out to weed, and dig some up secretly to give to their children. This is called 'new yam stealing'. Some time after this the yams harden, and begin to be eaten in public. But before this the head of the family, who is an initiate of the *akombo*, first tells his wife to dig up a yam for him to perform the necessary rite before he starts eating. The *akombo* which are set right before the new yams are eaten are *Wayo*, *Agashi* (*Akombo-a-dam*), *Ribi*, and *Gwarmou*.[1]

When a little of the crop has been eaten, the head of the family tells the women to display the yams for every one to see. So the women go to the farm early, dig up a number of large yams, bring them home, and lay them out in the middle of the village, or on the drying-platform, so that people may see that the yams are ready. And if he is a man of standing, he kills a beast and broaches a pot of palm oil, which he divides amongst the women to cook, that men may come together and eat. The people are loud in their praises, saying, 'So-and-so's wives have laid out the yams to-day; we have had a great feast, and food still remains over!' From then onwards every one eats yams till the time for clearing the bush comes round again.

When the dry season is well advanced, about the month

---

[1] These cults, or at least some of them, have been copied from the same southern tribes from which the Tiv say that they got the yam, and this fact supports their theory of its origin.

of January, it is time to dig up the seed yams.[1] The women dig up the yams, put the seed on one side, and the yams for eating on the other, and store them away. The seed is either kept in a hole in the ground, or in grass shelters; but the whole yams are stored in a small hut, and ashes are sprinkled over them to keep them from rotting.

When all the seed yams have been taken out, the yam farm is called *akuur*. The women clean it up nicely, ready for the millet. Formerly they used always to broadcast the seed, and then scatter the heaps over it, and this method gives a better yield. But if a man has too much work on hand to do this, he merely presses in the seed with his heel. The sowing time for maize is the same as for bulrush millet. After these have been harvested, the land is sown with guinea-corn, and when this crop has also ripened and been reaped, the field is called *tsa*. It is then laid down to beniseed. After the women and children have taken out the stubble, and the first rain has fallen, the people go and sow the wet season beniseed. When this has been harvested, the field is called *tsa kurkur*, which means old land. Formerly no other crop of importance was grown on land which had reached this stage, only sweet potatoes.

White cassava, like the red kind, used to be planted by the women on heaps, by cutting pieces of the stem and sticking them in the ground. But it was not a very useful crop, and so not much store was set by it. It is still grown in small quantities.

Bambarra ground-nuts came from the Chamba. They used to be grown in a field by themselves, but nowadays women sow them in amongst the yam heaps. They are harvested at the same time as the seed yams.[2]

The ordinary ground-nuts also came from the Chamba, but are sown on the *tsa*. If you plant them on a high heap,

---

[1] The yams which are harvested during the last months of the rains are cut off near the top, and the remaining end to which the vine is attached is replaced in the ground, where it goes on growing. It is then dug up again about January and used for seed.

[2] December and January: see above.

they will not give any yield, and they must not be weeded like other crops. If they are weeded the leaves will not spread.[1] They are very nice, but if you eat too many they will give you a headache, or stomach trouble. They are also made into oil, which is very good for cooking and is also used by the Tiv when rubbing camwood on their bodies. The clan which grows most ground-nuts, and knows best how to farm them, is Masev, and in particular the section of Masev known as Ingyenev.

The 'king of the rains' was introduced into Tivland quite recently. It is a species of ground-nut, but has bigger kernels than the ordinary ground-nut, and often contains three or four to each pod. It is so called because it is a wet-season crop, and will do well at whatever time you sow it during the rains. This name, however, is not generally known in Kparev, where it is called *igar*.

The Kaffir potato[2] used formerly to be grown on its own piece of ground, and was of great importance to our ancestors. But when the Tiv got plenty of other crops they lost interest in it, and nowadays the women merely sow it amongst the yam heaps. This was also first seen in foreign parts, and is not really a Tiv crop.

Agbadu[3] and *furum*[3] are plants which creep over the ground, and are sown amongst refuse. The *agbadu* is about the size of a calabash, and is not good in the rains, unless eaten as soon as it reaches full size. Otherwise it must be picked and the moisture allowed to drain off. It may not be ready to eat till the beginning of the next dry season. It is cooked with beniseed, or eaten whole, and its leaves are good for sauce. The *furum* is eaten in the same way as the *agbadu*, but if you leave it too long before picking it becomes uneatable. The fruit is also shredded and dried, and used to make sauce.

Bushi, *ashwe*, and *igar* are called by the Tiv 'strong' vegetables, that is to say, ingredients which are not stirred

---

[1] This apparently refers to the bunching effect on the leaves caused by Rosette disease. The soundness of the Tiv theory is supported by recent experiments on the Gambia, which show that the presence of weeds tends to inhibit this disease; cf. R. T. Hayes, 'Groundnut Rosette Disease in the Gambia', *Tropical Agriculture*, vol. ix, p. 211.

[2] A species of *plectranthus*: Hausa, *rizga*.   [3] Pumpkins.

into the sauce. But okra and *afialegh* must be stirred while the sauce is being cooked. These are all sown by the women on the yam farm during the wet season.

Of the things used for seasoning, pepper is sown on the yam farm in the shade of a tree. Beniseed, besides being a seasoning, is nowadays also an economic crop. The *icegher*[1] is of two kinds, the white and the red, both of which are sown on the yam farm. The red variety is sown first, about the beginning of the rains. It is only used in sauce; if you eat it raw you will become deaf. The white kind, however, is eaten raw by men; it is not very good for sauce, having no oil. The Tiv got the *icegher* from the Dam.

❡ The following is a summary and brief explanation of the magic rites connected with farming which are mentioned in this section: First, before any work is started on the new farm the householder must go out alone and scrape the soil (for this 'heap' means little more) with a pod of the *iyiase* tree. It is said that the reason for using this is that it is an emblem of the chief *akombo* of the crops (*Twel*), but it seems more probable that the rite is a relic of the days when farming was done with more primitive tools than the Tiv have now, and is a precaution against the misfortune which may accrue from departing entirely from the methods laid down by the ancestors who first cultivated the soil. If a 'day's work' is done in the old way the demands of tradition are satisfied. In this case the *iyiase* pod doubtless became an emblem of the farm cult because it was used as a primitive hoe, and not vice versa. The pods of this tree (*Afzelia Africana*) measure about 6 in. by 3, and, being very hard and thick, might perhaps once have been used by early Tiv agriculturists to scratch the surface of the soil. But it is not necessary to presuppose this. The prescribed ritual is in the nature of a prohibition rather than a positive rule, namely a taboo against the use of iron. This is shown by the fact that in some parts the wooden handle of a hoe, without the blade, is used for the purpose. The immediate predecessor of the present farming tool was the wooden hoe, but it would be difficult in most places to find one of these with which to perform the ceremony. The circumstances surrounding this rite

---

[1] A kind of small pumpkin.

are therefore the converse of those which gave rise to the procedure in circumcision, where the use of iron is laid down as essential. Lastly, the whole thing must be done in complete silence, and if on the way back to his village the farmer is asked for something and gives it, or even answers a greeting, he thereby gives away all the benefit which he hoped to get by performing the rite. The use of the *iyiase* pod, however, is not common nowadays, and the whole custom seems to be dying out.

Next the farmer sets up the familiar cult objects at the edge of the farm. These have no positive function in relation to the fertility of the crop, but are put there, as in the case of those tied to the chair of the boy who was undergoing circumcision, in order to warn off potential evil-doers. These may be of two kinds, and the precautions taken for each are slightly different. First, and most dangerous, are the *mbatsav*, those who out of spite or jealousy wish to damage the crop by black magic. To guard against these the householder sets up the emblems of any *akombo* over which he has obtained control by initiation; the most commonly seen are the *Agashi* which produces (and is) syphilis, and the *Igbe* which attacks the enemy with dysentery. Secondly, it may be necessary to guard the farm against thieves; there is no urgency for this, and the emblems are often not placed in position till the crop is nearly ripe. The difference in method employed when taking these precautions is this: If you want to ensure against people taking some of the produce, it is not very much use setting up the emblems of the common *akombo* of which almost every householder is an initiate, because if the thief has control of the *akombo* himself it cannot harm him. It is therefore better to ask some one from another district to set up an *akombo* which is not well known locally; in this case, of course, the farmer himself cannot touch his crop until the owner of the *akombo* has been summoned to remove it. For anti-witchcraft, on the other hand, any powerful *akombo* of which the farmer is an initiate will serve, because the practice of witchcraft is taboo to any one who holds an *akombo* and automatically breaks his control over it.

The *icegh*, which is mentioned in connexion with the millet and guinea-corn, but may be done for any grain crop, is not an *akombo*, but a rite which is performed by any one who has been initiated to one of the fertility cults. It is carried out as follows: A leaf of the wild apple tree (*hul*), or an *iyiase* pod, is laid on the ground, and a little of the soil from the farm is mixed with water and put on it. Then a few stalks of corn are pulled up and laid by its side. In some cases the wet mud is sprinkled over the growing crop. This has every appearance of being a rain charm, and in former times is said to have been so used at the public rites of the *Ilyum* and *Iwoyaŋgegh*,[1] when rain-making was more common than it is now. Nowadays the meaning of this rite seems to have been forgotten, and it is merely preparatory to the harvesting of the crop. The *icegh* rite is also carried out with appropriate modifications in connexion with the *idyugh* ceremony (q.v.) performed at conception. This suggests that it is applied, by analogy, to the fertility of human beings. The magic fertilizing principle in each is supplied by the wet soil on the leaf.

The word for initiating the harvest (*kɔr*) is the same as that used for making the first heap, and the idea in each case is that the householder, who is an initiate of the fertility cult, should go through the form of digging the farm, or harvesting the crop, alone, before his family start work. If he is not an initiate this formality is not observed.

Finally, before he eats any of the crop, he must lay a head of corn, or maize-cob, or whatever it may be, on the cult emblems outside his house. (In the case of the yam crop a more elaborate rite is required.) The obvious inference is that the *akombo* is given the first-fruits in recognition of its help, but the Tiv, having always in mind the negative rather than the positive attributes of the supernatural, invariably say that both this and the *icegh* rite are carried out because otherwise the farmer, even though he had harvested the crop, would derive little benefit from it: the food would go bad, or come to an end long before it should.

MEAT

IN the past, game was very difficult indeed to get, and young people did not have meat to eat as they do now. If an older man felt a strong desire to eat flesh he told one of his children, or one of his wives, to go and dig out a cricket. When it was brought in, his wife took it and fried it for him; but she did not season it with salt, for there was none at that time, only potash. It might be that when

---

[1] P. 194.

the boy had gone to catch his cricket, he met a grown man who, seeing him with it, asked him to give it to him. If he refused, there would be ill feeling between them, and henceforth they would never be seen sitting together enjoying the warmth of the morning sun. The older man would always have his knife into the boy, and whenever some cause brought them together, however long after it might be, he would remember the incident of the cricket and hold it up against him. The matter would not be allowed to drop until the boy had made amends.

When the elders gathered round for the meal, the cricket was shared by many. The owner ate the head himself, gave one of the hind legs to a guest, and the other to some one else. He took the thorax and divided it between two, saying, 'Eat this. It is not a very big piece, but one of your teeth is sure to bite on it!' Finally he cut off the insect's abdomen, and shared it out amongst three or so. The one cricket would have to serve for the whole calabash of *ruam*, however large it might be. A child would not dare even to dip into the gravy; if he did, one of the older people would take a handful of *ruam*, dip it in pepper sauce, and throw it in his eyes. The child would have to go on being content with his poor soup, unless he could catch a cricket and eat it in secret. It was through the cricket that the Tiv first learnt the habit of sharing with their fellows.[1]

Another way of getting meat was by means of dogs, of which the Tiv always kept a large number for hunting. They set out in a body, and went down into the wood with their dogs and sharpened staves. They beat the bush, while the dogs cast round to pick up the trail of a bandicoot. If they put one up, all the hunters and the dogs rushed to the spot, chased it and killed it. After the kill the carcass was given to the owner of the dog which drew first blood. The man who speared the rat with his

---

[1] This clearly does not apply to children at meal-times, and the reason is said to be that if a child forms the habit of joining in the meal with his elders he may one day, in a strange house, unwittingly eat human flesh, with the terrible result of contracting a flesh debt. See p. 255. Cf. also Dr. A. I. Richards, *Hunger and Work in a Savage Tribe*, pp. 71, 74.

wooden lance, after the dogs had seized it, received the tail, and the man to whom it was handed over to carry home was given the entrails as reward. 'The strong boy eats the bandicoot's tail.'

A third method of catching game was the net. This was not known to the Tiv originally; they got it from the Chamba. Amongst the Tiv it was not every one who could own a net, but only a big man, who bought it from the foreigners. In course of time, however, they learnt the art of net-making from them, and made nets for themselves.

WEAPONS

What weapons were used by the Tiv for hunting in the old days? They had the net, the pointed stick, and the palm lance. But they had no arrows, broad-bladed spears, barbed lances, or any of the other weapons which we see nowadays.

When a man wished to make a net, according to the method which had been learnt from the foreign tribes, he first of all cut down some raffia palm, stripped off the outer covering, and laid it out to dry. When it began to dry up, he took it and twisted it into cord, or else he plaited the kind of rope used for roofing. The type of net which was made with twisted cord would be used for rabbit snares, and that made with plaited rope for bigger game. Having finished making the rope, he wound it up into balls about the size of an *amaku* fruit, and, when he had prepared enough, started on the net, which he made with a square mesh. (The mesh is the space between the strings of the net. When the chameleon said, 'Agashi, the world is like a network', what he meant was that nothing in the whole of creation exists without cause. All things are arranged in due order and with set purpose, and are complementary to each other, like squares in the mesh of a net.)

The 'pointed stick' consisted of a straight pole cut from the bush, about the thickness of a man's big toe, and in length equal to a man's height. Its head was sharpened to a fine point, and hardened in the fire. 'The Stick is an *ɪŋɔl* that is shared by many. It passes from hand to hand.'[1]

The 'palm lance' was a weapon of great importance to our ancestors, and corresponded to our broad-bladed spear. A man who was preparing to do deeds of valour broke off a number of branches of the oil palm. He pared them down to a sharp point, and put them in the fire till they were so hard that if you speared a beast in the flank with them they would break its ribs into small pieces. The old Kparev warriors, who inspired such terror in the Dam that they would not live in the same country with them, fought with the palm lance. Agaku Akpacum of Mbakaaŋge in Kunav, a famous fighter in the days when the people were few in number, and Dzerasuwa of Usar in Mbadzaka of the Mbaitiav, the greatest warrior of all, were armed only with this weapon.

The shield, which was carried in war, was made like a round winnowing tray, woven with grass, and covered with cowrie shells, to ward off arrows. Both this and the palm lance played a part in the rites which they performed to bring success in battle, when they went to war with the Bush Tribes. Before going out to fight, they carried out the *Mku* rites[2] in the name of the warriors of old, then gave the palm lance to a slave, who, holding it in his hand, went in front of the people as they marched to battle.

These were all the weapons which the Tiv had in the beginning. In course of time they came to use arrows, broad-bladed spears, barbed lances, and swords. To-day some have guns, which they use for hunting.

NETTING GAME

This was done as follows: A man who was experienced in bush-craft went out after rain. If he saw tracks, he walked round in a circle till he came back to the same spot, and if the animal had not come out of this circle, he went to tell the news in the village. Thereupon a large crowd

---

[1] *Iŋɔl* is an 'exchange sister'. The meaning of this saying is that for the purpose of making exchange marriages the available women must be shared by the whole group, and not all taken by the senior member to obtain wives for himself. See p. 109.

[2] P. 213.

would set out, old and young, carrying nets which they borrowed from those who had them, pointed staves, palm lances, and shafts for propping up the net. Having arrived at the spot, they first trod down a path through the grass, making a circle round the patch of bush into which the quarry had entered. Next they set up the shafts on the path which they had trodden out, along the side where the animal's track was seen to enter, and fixed the net on to them. The net was placed here, because game always breaks back and comes out at the same point at which it went in. Then the whole crowd of hunters, with their staves, palm lances, or branches which they had broken off the trees, went round and came in from the far side, beating and shouting, and moving in the direction of the net. The quarry, even if it had been asleep, started up on hearing the noise, and came running back along the track by which it had entered. When it reached the edge of the circle the hunters closed in on it, and as it rushed past to break out it fell into the net, and was beaten to death.

There is an old saying, 'My net is wide', which means that a man has the power to obtain whatever his heart desires. His opportunities are wide as a net, and nothing can stand in his way.

HUNTING LAWS

If when the quarry was put up it made for the net, and some one speared it with his pointed stick or palm lance, but the wounded beast went on and was afterwards caught in the net and killed, it was not given to the man who speared it, but to the owner of the net; because even if it had not been already wounded, it would have fallen into the net in any case. But if it fell into the net without being speared, but tore through it and broke away, and some one speared it afterwards, it then belonged to the man who first wounded it, and if it was killed it was handed over to him, and was not counted as 'netted game'. This rule holds good to the present day.

When the quarry came into the net and was killed, the man who first speared it was given the right shoulder;

that was his portion as first 'sharer'.[1] The man who made the second thrust took the neck, and the man who followed after him got four ribs. So they set about cutting up the carcass. When they brought the meat into the village, the actual owner of the net was given the head, a hind-leg, and the skin. The man who had taken out the net to kill the game received a hind-leg and a shoulder, and the hunter who had originally drawn the circle round the quarry got the tail.

The general law of Tiv hunting is that the beast belongs to the man who first hit it. It may only have been wounded, and may eventually fall to some one else's weapon, but if the man who first touched it can show a spot of blood, or a hair, on his weapon it is given to him, and the two hunters who subsequently hit it are only counted, respectively, as the first and second 'sharers'. If a man sees a python and points it out to some one else, who kills it, it is given to the man who saw it, and the man who killed it gets only a share. His share in this case is the *tswam*, that is, the part of the body which adjoins the neck. So also for every animal which lives in a hole in the ground: when it has been dug out it belongs to the man who first noticed the smooth entrance to the hole, and only a certain part of the meat goes to the diggers.

DOMESTIC ANIMALS

The only domestic animals which the Tiv had at the beginning were the dog, the cow, and the chicken. Later they got the sheep from the Gee.[2] Sheep were much prized by them, and were only owned by important people. Even to-day the Tiv say that the sheep is not a thing for children. The goat they got from the Chamba, whom at that time they called Ilyufu. These were the people who came down and settled close to Akwana, and afterwards came to be known as Alufu. They possessed many goats.

How did the Tiv get the pig? We do not know. You

---

[1] I.e. the 'owner' of the kill is not reckoned as one of the 'sharers'. Each of the first three 'sharers' has a special name in Tiv.
[2] One of the tribes to the south of Tiv country.

H

may ask any Tiv about the pig, but he will not be able to tell you anything for certain. Many of them believe that it was caught first in the wild state; others hold that it came from the Dam. However this may be, the Tiv certainly prefer eating pig to all other kinds of meat, and if you want to give a Tiv a meal which he will really appreciate, give him pork. Amongst some of the Tiv, pig's meat is taboo to women.[1]

[1] See also p. 310.

III

MARRIAGE AND TRIBAL ORGANIZATION

❦ At the time when the Tiv first became known to Europeans the affairs of the tribe were in a state of considerable confusion, owing to the number of different forms of marriage which were in use. It must, indeed, be unusual to find amongst any one people examples of so many types of marriage in existence at the same time. The forms described in this chapter are marriage by exchange, with and without payment of 'gifts', marriage by payment of a bride-price or by labour, consanguineous marriage, patrilocal and matrilocal marriage, marriage by capture, both real and formal (mutual agreement between groups to sanction elopement), and marriage by true purchase. In 1927 the Administration decided to recognize marriage by payment of a bride-price only, and all other forms were declared illegal. Much of the following, therefore, must be taken to refer to conditions previous to that date. But the social organization and internal relationships of the tribe cannot be understood without an appreciation of the Tiv attitude towards these different forms of marriage, particularly that of exchange, and it would not be an exaggeration to say that these now obsolete systems have a direct bearing on almost every social or political problem with which the Administration is faced in its present dealings with the tribe.

Marriage by exchange, that is, the method of obtaining a wife by giving your sister (in the classificatory sense) to the girl's brother, or more exactly, the system by which one group exchanges one of its women for a woman of another group, is common amongst the pagan tribes of Nigeria, and, in Dr. Meek's view, was probably practised by many others who have now abandoned it for the purchase system.[1] It is also found elsewhere in West Africa, and in other parts of the world, usually as a subsidiary or alternative form to obtaining a wife by capture or purchase. It has not, however, on the whole been given a very prominent place in general works on marriage, and is dismissed as a 'much less dignified' type of marriage by consideration,[2] or as being often

[1] Meek, op. cit., vol. i, p. 204; and *Tribal Studies in Northern Nigeria*, i, 538.
[2] Hobhouse, *Morals in Evolution*, p. 156.

'an economic measure intended to save the bride-price'.[1] But with the Tiv the exchange system cannot be considered merely as a better or worse way of getting a wife. It is, or has been, an institution of paramount importance, and lies at the base of the whole present tribal organization. Moreover, it is bound up with the strongest of supernatural sanctions; for although the spiritual life of the tribe has been severely shaken by events of recent years, the orthodox belief, still held by the old men, is that the fertility of the crops and of the women—in fact, the very existence of the tribe—is dependent on exchange marriage and the rites which are associated with it. The view set forth by Akiga, and held by the tribe as a whole, is that this was the original form of marriage, all others being later accretions, introduced from foreign sources. Whether this is the most probable theory, or not, will be considered later. It is, at any rate, undoubtedly older than marriage by 'capture' or payment of a bride-price, in the form in which they have been practised in recent years.

In this account Akiga first discusses the 'theory' of exchange, and shows how the present tribal organization has been evolved out of it. He then describes the actual procedure in making an exchange, as it was carried out before this form of marriage was abolished, and finally alludes to its magico-religious significance. The first part is hardly intelligible without an understanding of the peculiar Tiv point of view with regard to exchange, which is taken by the author for granted. The 'theory' is summarized in the first paragraph:

IN the past the Tiv did not have the many different forms of marriage which they have practised in recent years: the only kind of marriage was by exchange. For they would not allow the name of their child to be lost to their house for any cause except death. If a man had children he wanted all of them to remain his. So if, for instance, he had two sons and three daughters, he divided the daughters amongst the sons, to give in exchange for wives, who should bear children in the place of his own daughters who were with their husbands, that his house might expand and go forward.

[1] Westermarck, *The History of Human Marriage*, ii, 358.

¶. Clearly, in any patrilocal society the loss of the daughters is compensated by the wives who are brought into the family by the sons, and vice versa where the principle is matrilocal. But the Tiv conception of exchange implies much more than mere compensation. The essence of the idea is that the wife who is introduced into the group takes the place, in a very real sense, of the daughter of the family. She not only acts as her deputy, but, for the purpose of bearing children, actually becomes the woman for whom she has been exchanged. Therefore, although under the patrilocal system the father cannot keep his daughter in the family as well as his sons, by means of this theory of exchange she can still bear children to his family *by proxy*. She is, in fact, regarded as the real mother of the children born to the wife for whom she has been exchanged. Their descendants are even spoken of as having 'come out of her womb'.[1] There is, as it were, a transposition of personalities. Only the outward and visible forms of the women are exchanged, the inner procreative principle remains with the group. By this means the Tiv contrive to combine the patrilineal and matrilineal principles. Although the group is built on a patrilineal system, the members trace their descent also through the female side. That is to say, in any group the grandchildren are descended from their grandfather through their father, but also, by means of the Tiv view of exchange, through their mother. This is, then, what is meant by saying that the Tiv wanted both their sons and their daughters to remain theirs, and 'would not allow the name of their child to be lost'.

If the matter be considered from our purely physiological standpoint, it is clear that descent cannot be traced to the same grandparent through both mother and father, except in the case of a brother-and-sister marriage. Similarly, it will be anticipated that the only way in which the Tiv principle could be realized in its true sense was when the person given in exchange for a wife was a full sister. Only in this case would the wife become the daughter, by substitution, of both the father and the mother of her husband, and thus be able to carry on the line through both sides of the family to the next generation. The true sister exchange marriage had, in fact, a very special significance. For although a man could obtain a wife in exchange for any

[1] Cf. p. 107.

of the women in his group whom he was entitled to use for this purpose, and the marriage would be perfectly valid, the other wives had inferior status, and it was only in the case of true sister exchange marriage that the complete fertility rites were performed.

There is, however, another case, mentioned more than once in the following account, where a marriage counts as a true maternal exchange,[1] even though not effected through a true sister. If there were a number of male children in the family, the elder sons took the daughters first to make exchange marriages, and a younger son would have to wait until a daughter was born in the next generation. His niece was then given to him for the purpose of obtaining an exchange wife, and this was counted a true maternal exchange marriage, because this niece 'was of the same "stem" (*ityɔ*) as his mother'. In other words, she was the daughter (by proxy) of his true sister. This is illustrated by examples in the following pages.

It is now almost a truism to say that to the African the main purpose of marriage is the propagation of children. But from the point of view of the group it would not be an over-statement to say that it is the only purpose considered. The normal individual certainly desires children above everything, and has a stronger incentive to build up a large family than the modern European, but the desire to possess a wife, apart from the question of children, with all the added comfort and prestige which this implies, is at least as strong an incentive to marriage in Africa as in other parts of the world. The group, as such, on the other hand, is primarily concerned, not with the comfort of the individual, but with its own continued existence, and any theory of marriage held by the community must be evolved with a view to the children rather than to the wife. This is particularly true of the Tiv exchange theory. The exchange was not complete until children had been born. Until then the marriage was in the nature of a trial, and the wives were regarded somewhat as being 'on loan' from their fathers' groups. If one of the women bore children and the other proved barren, the group into which the latter had married could annul the contract and demand the return of their own daughter,

---

[1] The vernacular term is *kwase u yamen u sha ŋgɔ*, 'an exchange wife through the mother'. The ordinary term 'full-sister exchange' is inadequate in the present context.

together with her children, or, alternatively, another woman to take the place of the one previously provided. Or, if one of the women bore more children than the other, the group which had the less fruitful mother could demand an equalization. This question is treated more fully by Akiga. It will also be shown that under the elopement form of marriage, which was introduced in later times as a preliminary to ultimate exchange, the girl's group made no demand for compensation until she had her first child, or, in some cases, until she had borne a number of children. If she had borne two daughters before an exchange was given for her, her group would demand one of the daughters in addition, so that each party should have the same number of women. This law of equalization is the logical corollary of the theory that each of the exchanged women bears children on behalf of the other. If one fails to produce as large a family as the other, the group to which she is attached feels that she is not fulfilling her function as a deputy for their daughter. It should be added, however, that in practice the principle of equalization was not rigidly enforced, provided that both the women bore a reasonable number of children to their respective groups.

The most probable explanation of the Tiv theory of exchange marriage is that it represents an unconscious attempt to reconcile the patrilineal and matrilineal principles. In the foregoing brief description, it will have been noticed that the Tiv exchange marriage system bears very strong traces of mother-right, and without committing oneself to the theory that mother-right represents an earlier stage in human development than father-right, it is difficult to escape the conviction in the present case that marriage by exchange developed out of an older form of matri-potestal and matrilocal marriage. For if the custom at one time was that the daughter should remain with her mother's brother to bear children to his group, and the practice of allowing her to be taken away by another group, on condition that a substitute was provided, grew up later as a result of conditions postulated below, then the Tiv conception of exchange becomes far more logical and intelligible.

The tendency for mother-right to give way to father-right has been frequently noted, and is no doubt due to a natural desire on the part of the father to have control of his own children.[1]

---

[1] Cf. Westermann, op. cit., pp. 124, 134.

But this desire could only be achieved by members of exceptionally powerful groups, who were able to take the women of the weaker groups by force. At the same time they did not relinquish their own women, so that in the next generation their numbers would tend to increase at the expense of their neighbours. They were also reinforced by young men from the weaker groups, whose only chance of obtaining wives was to attach themselves to the groups which had all the women, and would probably be expected in return to contribute labour on the farm and assistance in time of war. Marriage in these powerful groups would, in fact, be patrilocal as regards their male members, and matrilocal as regards their females. The males, moreover, would naturally favour their own natural children, and give them superior status. This can be seen in the present tribal organization, the sections of the clans which are traditionally descended from a female ancestor having inferior status to those which are descended from a parallel male line. For all these reasons the groups which were strong enough to enforce the right of their sons to bring up their own families would increase at the expense of the matrilocal groups, and the tribe would tend to become more and more patripotestal and patrilineal.

During this process of elimination of the weaker groups by absorption into the stronger, a stage may be pictured at which a number of powerful groups have come into being, no one of which is sufficiently stronger than the rest to seize their women, against the matrilocal law, which still theoretically holds good. Each wants to acquire wives for its sons, yet not part with its daughters. It is a case of father-right for us, but mother-right for you. After (we may imagine) some attempts by the rival groups to find a solution by force of arms, society looks for compromise, and exchange presents itself as means of reconciling the two mutually exclusive principles. The old men come together (as they did in later years to make the *iye* pact, when forcible marriage by capture was splitting the tribe with interclan warfare). Each group insists on the right to bring up its own families through its sons, but agrees to lend its daughters, subject to many conditions, and provided that a satisfactory substitute be given who will be in no wise inferior to their own in the matter of bearing children. Yet they cannot entirely give up the deeply seated idea of descent through the female line, so still regard their own daughter, who under the matrilocal system would have borne children to the group, as the real mother, although she has been, in a physical sense, replaced by a stranger. The essential principle, which will carry on the family in direct matrilineal succession from the grandmother to her grandchildren, still remains, and for this purpose the foreign female element which has been introduced in the middle generation has no significant existence.

It must be admitted that this hypothesis is contrary to the view held by the Tiv themselves, who say, first, that exchange was the original form of marriage, and, secondly, that their descent is to be traced to the first ancestor through the male line in the vast majority of groups. There is, however, some reason to suppose that the people are mistaken in this matter, and that mother-right did, at one time, form the basis of their organization. As these notes are only intended to offer an explanation, and not to state a theory, it is not proposed to produce any detailed evidence to support this view, beyond noting that some of the groups, especially in the older clans, do show traces of matrilineal succession in the past. Most of the recognized female ancestors occur about five or six generations back in the family tree, that is to say, about the time when the transition from mother-right to father-right was most probably taking place. Since then normal succession has undoubtedly been patrilineal in fact, and before that time the sex of the ancestors may well have become obscured in the mists of antiquity, so that many who are described as male were in reality female. Failing a definite tradition to the contrary, it is natural that all groups should claim descent from a male ancestor where possible, as this nowadays carries a superior status. It is also noteworthy that wherever a female ancestor appears in the genealogy, there is almost always a difference of opinion as to how she came to be there, and what was her relationship to the other members of the family. Her descendants do not, in fact, like to admit the once honourable, but now distasteful, fact that her children were born in her brother's group, and their father was a more or less casual visitor of unknown origin.[1]

[1] See also an article by Dr. C. K. Meek in *Africa*, vol. ix, p. 64. His description of exchange marriage customs amongst the Mambila and Kona (who are said to have been matrilineal until recently) is of special interest in the light of the Tiv theory, and suggests that the view of its origin expounded here may be found to apply also to exchange marriage in other Nigerian tribes.

THE ORGANIZATION OF THE TRIBE, BASED ON EXCHANGE
MARRIAGE

IF a man had five sons and two daughters, the sons had
the use of the *aŋgɔl*[1] in order of seniority. The elder
sons took them first, and the younger sons had to await
their turn. When the elder sons begat daughters they took
some and gave to their brothers who came next after
them. But the youngest would still be left. He might be
well on in years before his turn came to take an *iŋgɔl*, and
all this time he would be still a bachelor.[2] This was the
reason why men who lived in former times did not marry
early. But when daughters were eventually born to the
other brothers they went on giving them to him, one after
the other, so that in the end he had a host of *aŋgɔl*. From
this the saying has arisen, 'The youngest gets the most
aŋgɔl'. When the youngest son had obtained wives by
exchange, and they had borne children, he took one of his
daughters and gave her to his brother who had previously
given him the *iŋgɔl*, because she was of the same stem as
his mother,[3] and his brother exchanged her for a wife.
Thus it has come about that all the sons of one man who
share the *aŋgɔl* between them constitute an '*iŋgɔl* group'.
All the members of this group also take part in the *akombo*
rites together.[4] When they become numerous, and begin
to occupy a number of different villages, the name of their
father is given to the whole group, and it is called 'So-and-
so' after him. But when they become more numerous
still they are called 'The people of So-and-so'.[5]

It happens in this way; I will take the instance of one
man, Jato Aka, and use him as an example. 'The people
of So-and-so', then, shall be the children of Jato Aka.
Jato Aka has now only two sons, Cia and Adam. But if he

---

[1] *iŋgɔl*, pl. *aŋgɔl* : a woman available for the purpose of making an exchange
marriage, or (nowadays) obtaining a bride-price.

[2] I.e. the two eldest sons only were given exchanges by their father. The
next two got the daughters of their elder brothers, and the youngest had to
wait for the third generation.

[3] P. 102, and note on p. 107.

[4] The constitution of these groups is explained on pp. 109 and 110. The
expressions used are 'eat (i.e. use) the same *aŋgɔl*', and 'eat the same *akombo*'.
In the latter case the word 'eat' has a more literal meaning, because the initiates
in the group have a share in the meat which must be provided every time a
rite is performed.

[5] I.e. they take the prefix *Mba–*.

had daughters he would divide these between them as their *aŋɔl*. Cia and Adam have different mothers. So when they have obtained wives by exchange, and begotten a large number of children, their sons would share the *aŋɔl* derived from the original *iŋɔl* which Jato Aka gave to Cia, or Adam, as the case might be.[1] Nevertheless, as long as Jato Aka were alive, they would be called 'Jato Aka', however many of them there might be, and they would live in the same village. Any one who was going there would say, 'I am going to Jato Aka'. And if one of the family split off and lived in his own hamlet, it would still belong to Jato Aka, and to no one else. Even after Jato Aka's death, as long as his sons remained in his village, any one who was going there would say, 'I am going to Jato Aka's old home'; till finally they moved from there, and Cia and Adam went to build their own homes, and live there with their children. They would then be spoken of as 'The children of Jato Aka'. But when their numbers increased, and their descendants split up again into separate homesteads, they would begin to be known as 'Mba-jato-aka' or 'Mba-aka'. The children of Cia would call the children of Adam their half-brothers,[2] being all of Jato Aka's stock. The children of Cia would say of each other that they were of the same 'stem'.[3] The meaning of this is that they have all come out of the womb of one woman, namely the *iŋɔl* which Jato Aka originally gave Cia to exchange for the woman who bore them. That is the reason why it is called a 'stem'. So if a descendant of Cia or of Adam went on a journey, and some one asked him, 'What is your clan?'[4] he would say, 'I am Mbaaka, and my stem is Mbacia', or 'Mbaadam', as the case might be. Eventually the homes of the descendants of Cia and Adam might grow to a very large number, and

---

[1] I.e. the daughters of the woman who was exchanged for the sister of Cia or of Adam, according to which branch of the family their descendants belonged.

[2] *Anterev* : lit. 'father's children', i.e. related on the father's side only, not full brothers (*anmgbianev* : 'mother's children'). Here it means that they were descended from a common male ancestor, but from his two different wives.

[3] *Ityɔ*. This is now the ordinary word used for the paternal group (see note on p. 38), but Akiga's explanation clearly indicates a matrilineal origin, although he does not himself believe in the matrilineal theory.

[4] *U ŋgu unɔ?* lit. 'Whose are you?'

when an initiation to an *akombo* were held, the Mbacia
would eat alone, and not invite the Mbaadam. (By this
time Cia and Adam would be dead.) Nevertheless, they
would keep their clan name,[1] Mbaaka, for all time. This
is how the Tiv tribe has grown; it has been entirely
through exchange marriage.

Since the *aŋgɔl* were limited in number, marriage was
not haphazard, but the son relied on his father. And it is
because a man who had children used to give the *aŋgɔl* to
his elder sons first that the majority of Tiv clans have two
divisions, which are half-brothers by same father,[2] like
Cia and Adam. You will find this in Tiv again and again:
'The So-and-sos and the So-and-sos', two sections of a
clan descended from different maternal ancestors. So that
if to-day you wish to know about some section of the
tribe, say, for example, Ipav, and ask, 'How many divisions are there in the clan descended from your father?'
you will get the answer, 'Two: Kpegh and Igɔr'. The
first division is called Mbakpegh, and the second, now
that its members are many, Igɔrov.[3] You do not find
three or four divisions, except very occasionally, but
mostly two, as in the case of Mbacia and Mbaadam.

❡. The prevalence of clans having only two sub-divisions is, then,
attributed to the custom of allowing only the two eldest sons to
make exchanges with the first generation of *aŋgɔl*, that is, their
own sisters. A point, however, which needs explanation (though
not, of course, to a Tiv) is that the children of the younger sons
are regarded as being descended from the elder brother who provided the *iŋgɔl* that was exchanged for their mother. For example,
a family consists of three boys A, B, and C, and two girls, D and
E, all by the same mother. A and B take D and E, and exchange
them for wives. C has to wait. A eventually has a daughter
whom he gives to C for the purpose of making an exchange,
because 'she is of the same stem as his mother', and thus provides
a true maternal exchange. C's children, however, do not form a

---

[1] Lit., 'big name'.
[2] In recording relationships the groups are treated as individuals: cf. p. 18.
[3] The names of these groups are formed from the name of the founder in
different ways, and represent different plural forms of the personal class. There
is no rule, except that of euphony, to determine which form they shall take.

separate sub-division, but are counted amongst the descendants of A, because *their mother was exchanged for A's daughter*, and is therefore identified with her. This clearly shows the matrilineal bias in the Tiv theory of succession, and how it has been adapted to the idea of father-right. C is treated as though he had no place on the family tree, exactly, in fact, as if he were a matrilocal husband from a strange group, allowed to have intercourse with his wife, only in order that she may bear children to her group and not his. She is the person who counts in the succession, in her capacity as deputy for A's daughter, for whom she has been exchanged. From our point of view she has no blood-relationship with the group at all, yet in her role of substitute for a female member of the family she is reckoned in preference to her husband who is a true member, for purposes of succession. This curious reversal of ideas is difficult to explain without presupposing an older matrilocal stage of society, out of which the exchange system was evolved.

It is easy to understand why, even in a family where girls predominated, the younger sons would not necessarily be given the *aŋgɔl* in the first generation. The father's duty to his sons ceased after he had provided the first two with wives. After this he was entitled, if he wished, to use his daughters to obtain more wives for himself. And there were other closely related members of the group who had to be considered. A younger brother, for instance, might be waiting his turn for a niece, as in the case of C in the example given above; or another brother, who had obtained a wife in the first generation, might have produced only male children, and these nephews would need *aŋgɔl* to obtain wives. For this reason there had to be a certain amount of give-and-take amongst the members of the extended family, and these members, who shared the *aŋgɔl* between them (*mba ve ye aŋgɔl imɔŋgo*), formed a definite tribal unit, which has been called above the '*iŋgɔl* group'.

The actual size of this group, like all other Tiv tribal units, has theoretically no defined limits, and naturally depends on the distribution of males and females within the family. But for practical purposes it may be taken as a unit comprising one man, his children and grandchildren, together with any full younger brothers who are dependent on him for *aŋgɔl*, with their sons and grandchildren. This group would normally live in one village, or in several hamlets very close to one another. In arranging marriages within this group, preference would always be given to a true sister exchange, whenever possible.

It is said in the passage quoted above that all these take part in the same *akombo* rites (*mba ye kombo mɔm*). But those who share the ritual feast do not necessarily all share the same *aŋgɔl*. These, in fact, whom it is proposed to call the '*akombo* group', form a larger unit which may include a number of *iŋgɔl* groups. This unit consists of all those who partake of the food or presents, which must be given by any member who undergoes an *akombo* rite to all those of his group who have been through it before. Like the *iŋgɔl* group, the size of the *akombo* group varies within wide limits, but at the present time it may be taken as comprising usually about 600 to 2,000 persons. The nature and functions of this group are treated more fully later under the heading of exogamy.[1]

At this point it may also be noted that there exists a larger functioning unit, composed of several related *akombo* groups. This unit is controlled by a council consisting of the chief elders of its component groups. It takes an important part in the present administrative machinery, and is now termed the 'kindred group'. The component groups never lose their identity, but act in concert for dealing with administrative and magico-religious questions which concern the community as a whole. It is therefore an essential factor in the constitution of the kindred group that it should have at least one elder of sufficient standing to possess the equipment and authority to 'set right the land', that is, to carry out the rites which affect the whole group, as opposed to the individual. The political leadership of one such elder is also usually recognized by the whole kindred, but he would have no power of direct action in any *akombo* group other than his own.

Finally, there are the larger divisions of the tribe, which we call clans or sub-clans. There are now 52 of these (34 before the recent re-organization). The place which they hold in the present tribal organization is described in the final chapter. Here it is only necessary to say that these bigger units have no rigid constitution, and little to unite their component groups beyond a common name and a general sense of kinship. A 'clan' is merely

---

[1] In local official nomenclature this group is called the 'family group'. I have not adopted this term as, although very convenient for administrative purposes, it is even less definite than the vernacular term, and could be equally well, or better, applied to the '*iŋgɔl* group'.

a 'kindred' at a later stage of development. The terminology which distinguishes the constitution of the 'tribe', 'clan', 'kindred', 'district', and so forth, is our own. In Tiv the largest unit which has a definite name, limiting its function, is the *akombo* group.

THE PRACTICE OF EXCHANGE MARRIAGE

HERE is a description of an exchange marriage according to ancient custom: Suppose that some one had a daughter, or an *iŋɔl*, whom you saw had reached puberty, and who pleased you. You went to her father and asked him to give her to you, and said that you would give him an exchange. Thereupon he referred you to the senior men of his group, and told you, if you were in earnest, to speak to them first; afterwards, when you had heard what they had to say, he would tell you what was in his mind. So you, the girl's suitor, laid the matter before them, and if they agreed, you came back and told the owner[1] of the *iŋɔl*. Then, if he wished to make a marriage compact with you, he said, 'I cannot judge of your sincerity by only one visit. If you really mean it, you must go away and come back again'. Thereupon you went home and told your kinsmen that you had been to the So-and-sos, and had seen this man's daughter, who pleased you; to which they replied, 'If you have an *iŋɔl*, go and make an exchange by all means!' So you started to go round making preparations.[2] When you were ready you went to the man and told him to come and see your *iŋɔl*. 'All right,' he agreed. 'You go on, I am coming.' A few days after you had left he asked some friend of his to accompany him, and set out to come and see your *iŋɔl*. When they arrived you called your *iŋɔl* and told her to bring water for the guests. She went and fetched it, and he saw her. After she had gone out you said to him, 'That is my little arrow with which I am risking an encounter'. He replied, 'She seems all right to look at, but of course one cannot tell what her character may be. Anyhow, one doesn't refuse a man's invitation without

---

[1] Footnote on p. 47.
[2] I.e. collecting presents to take to the girl's relations. In later times this meant a cloth for her mother, and a pig.

going into his house. If he asks you to a meal you go in and try it; if you find you don't like the sauce you can always refuse to eat it. Very well, then,' he says, 'I have no objection. You can come and spend the night at the bride's home.'[1]

In the old days the Tiv did not refuse any woman, however ugly she might be. As long as she was capable of bearing children, and had a good character, that was all that was required; they said she would bear them a son to carry on their line. In fact, it was the ugly women and the cripples through which in the past families were founded. It was only later that men began to pick and choose. Nowadays a man will give anything to marry a pretty woman, even though she may not be able to bear children at all, so that every one may say what a handsome wife he has got. The old idea is not considered so important as it used to be; in these days it is good looks which count.

Some days later, then, you who first went to see the other man's *iŋɔl* would catch a chicken and set off towards the place where he lived. But first you went to one of your *igba*[2] who lived in the same district, and told him all about it. He was the man on whom you depended in making the marriage contract. In the evening you would go with him to the home of the man with whom you were arranging the marriage, and the latter told the head of his group that the suitor had come to spend the night at the bride's home. This meant sleeping in the house of the woman whom you were seeking to marry. In former times a man who was making an exchange marriage would sometimes sleep with the woman, and actually have connexion with her, and the next morning she would bring him water to wash his face.[3] But sometimes he and

---

[1] *Tsa kwase:* a technical term (see below).

[2] See footnote on p. 38. The relationship works both ways. Here it does not mean one of your mother's relations (since you are not necessarily marrying into your mother's group), but the son of a man who married into your group, that is to say, some one who looks upon you as his *igba*. You are his *igba*, and he is also yours.

[3] Cf. H. A. Stayt, *The Bavenda*: 'The father asks the young man to stay the night. . . . The following morning the girl . . . creeps into the hut in which the man is sleeping, with water for him to wash. This is the first menial duty she performs for her future husband.' Here not only does he not sleep with the girl, but may not even see her except for a consideration.

the woman would sleep apart, though in the same house. However hard he might try to sleep with her during the night, she would not consent. To spend the night in the bride's home, and actually sleep with her, showed that she was a bad woman. In the old days, if a man had connexion with the woman at whose home he was staying, he would sometimes refuse to marry her. He said that she had a weak character, and if he married her she would behave in the same way when she was his wife. But the woman who could not be seduced by the man who was staying with her, however hard he might try—yes, that was a woman with a strong will! This was how men used to test women before they married them.

You went back, then, and told your kinsmen when you proposed to hand over the woman. When the day came you set out with your *iŋgɔl*, the mother-in-law[1] (who need not necessarily be the mother of the *iŋgɔl*), one of your kinsmen, and a singer; and if any other members of your group wished to go as well, they could do so. Having arrived there, you all went and sat down in the home of your *igba* whom you called on to support you before, when you went to spend the night at the bride's home. You would arrive there some time in the evening, and as soon as it was dusk your *igba* set out and led you to the man to whom you were taking the woman. Having arrived there, the singer would keep up a continuous song. People heard, and said, 'So-and-so of such-and-such a group is bringing in So-and-so's bride'. The bride would remain standing, and the bridegroom had to give some little present before she would sit down. This gift was therefore known as the 'Standing-up'. The bride-groom then brought a chicken, which was killed, and *ruam* was prepared; but when the meal was ready the bride would not eat, and the bridegroom had to give another present before she would take any food. This gift was called the 'Refusal of *ruam*'.[2]

When the meal was finished, they slept. But the bridegroom did not sleep with the girl, for she had not

---

[1] I.e. the 'mother-in-law' of the other bridegroom.
[2] Cf. Meek, art. cit. in *Africa*, vol. ix, p. 70.

I

yet become his wife. The mother-in-law slept with her daughter. The next morning, a kinsman of the man to whom the bride had been brought on the previous day sent a message to summon all the elders who shared in the same *akombo* rites and who sat together in council.[1] When all had assembled and were seated on the ground, the chief elder in the group of the man to whom the woman had been brought stood up, and, calling the senior member of the party which had come with the bride, asked him, 'Why is it that I see you here?' The other would reply, 'I have seen a cup in So-and-so's house which I like, and have come to take it away that I may drink water from it'. 'What you say,' said the first elder, 'is not good. You would commit such an act of violence with no provocation? You say you have seen a cup which you like, and have come to get it for nothing?' 'No, no,' replied the other. 'I have not come empty-handed. I have brought a strand of tobacco to give you in return for your cup.' The first man then turned to the other elders of his group and asked them, 'Do you hear what he says?' 'We hear,' they answered. 'Tell him to bring out his strand of tobacco for us to see.' So the first elder asked the other to send to the mother-in-law who was in the house, and tell her to bring out the girl. The man to whom the girl had been brought also told them to bring out his *iŋɔl*. Each girl, however, remained by her mother's side. The head of the visiting party told his *iŋɔl* to stand up. Turning to the head of the local group, he said, 'This is the strand of tobacco which I was telling you that I had brought to exchange for your cup'. The other agreed, saying that he saw her and liked her; he told him also to ask her whether she liked him. The mother-in-law then asked the girl. She would be too shy to speak, but her mother in any case would say, 'The girl agrees'. The leader of the visitors would then say to the local elder, 'The girl accepts you. Now ask your *iŋɔl*. If she does not like me I shall not bear you any ill will'. So the old man told her mother to ask the girl, and though the girl did not open her mouth, her mother would say that she accepted her

[1] Cf. p. 132.

husband. Should the girl refuse, her people would scold
her, and sometimes even beat her.[1]

The women having both given their consent, the head
of the local group stood up, called the head of the visiting
party, and said to him, 'Ask your *iŋgɔl* to say whether she
has ever had relations with a young man, or whether she is
still a virgin. If she has had intercourse with a man, but
does not say so now, and the matter comes out later, the
young man will have to pay a fine[2] of one full-grown cow
without fail'. So the question was put to her. Sometimes
a girl would deny that she had ever known a man since the
day of her birth, but another would admit having had
such relations. If she confessed it at the time it was no
great matter, but if she insistently denied it, and it was
discovered after the contract had been concluded, the
man who had deflowered her would certainly have to pay
a fine of a cow, otherwise it would give rise to a quarrel,
which might end in the annulment of the marriage contract.

The elders, having questioned their respective *aŋgɔl*,
then said, 'Let the women embrace the husbands'. The
heads of the two groups then stood up, one on this side
and one on that, and their wives which they had exchanged
rose up and embraced them.

The Concluding Words. After the women had embraced the husbands, the elders spoke the final solemn
words. The head of the home group said to the
other, 'I have this to say to you: Although the marriage
contract has thus been concluded between us, you may
do as you please with the body, but take care of the head.[3]
Should some need compel you, take your own property
and use it, but give me mine alive'.[4] The other agreed,
and said that he also demanded the same.

[1] The argument between the elders, and the asking of the brides' consent was,
of course, a pure formality, since all arrangements had been made before.

[2] The word used is *megh*, and is actually the name of an *akombo* which has to
be put right if the girl has previously been seduced; otherwise it will seize the
husband, who will break a limb. The fine is theoretically the cost of the fee for
setting right this *akombo*, but the customary chicken is replaced by a cow in
view of the gravity of the offence.

[3] Lit.: '. . . one plays with the waist but looks after the head' (=life).

[4] I.e. if the need arises for you to take a human life in connexion with the
rites which require this, or to pay off a flesh debt, then kill your own child, and
not mine.

When the elders had finished speaking, the man to whom the bride had been brought got up and killed a chicken for the people to eat. This chicken was called the 'End of the compact'.[1] When the meal was finished, he gave presents to the people who had brought him the wife, to one a bag of salt, to another a piece of tobacco. But the 'Standing-up' and 'Refusal of *ruam*' he gave to be taken to the mother of the bride. When all was over, the people dispersed to their homes. The bridegroom stayed the night, and the next day, if he wished, could take his wife home; but if not, he told his brother-in-law to bring her to him a few days later.

LATER INNOVATIONS

This is all that was done by the men of former times when they made an exchange marriage. But later on, when wealth increased, and men began to vie with each other on account of it, money came to play a part in the negotiations. One man might see some one's daughter who had reached puberty, and who pleased him, but when he came to ask whether he might make an exchange, another who was rich would go and spoil his wooing by spending a lot of money, in order to get the girl himself as an exchange. When it came to speaking to the relations, he did not approach them without gifts, but distributed money here and there amongst the elders. Thus they all became favourably disposed towards him, and told the owner of the *iŋgɔl* that he was the man with whom the exchange should be made. But as for the suitor who came without anything, they paid no attention to him.

Moreover, when the exchange was concluded, the 'End of the compact', which used to mean only a chicken, now came to mean the killing of a pig; and whereas in the old days there was only one singer, it now became the fashion for a large number of young men to go with them, and when these arrived they each found a friend amongst the local youths, and spent the night singing, so that no one had any sleep. The next morning, when the sun was well

---

[1] The phrase literally means the 'postponement of the contract'; I have not been able to discover the reason for its use in this context.

up, and the time came to hold the marriage ceremony, they all came and sat round, to listen to the elders concluding the contract. The marriage presents were not limited to packets of salt, but also included chickens, brass rods, and bars of iron. And when the guests had gone, whereas formerly it was the practice for the owner afterwards to go alone with his *iŋgɔl* and give her to his brother-in-law, this was now no longer done. He set out with a large company, and they went to hold another marriage ceremony in the other man's village. He gave marriage presents just as the other had done, and tried all he could to win people's approval by outdoing his brother-in-law. This is how exchange marriage became expensive, and gave rise to mutual rivalry.

THE *AKOMBO* OF EXCHANGE MARRIAGE

Formerly, when a man made an exchange marriage, he set up the *akombo* at the door of his wife's house. This was not done, however, for every exchange wife, but only for a wife received in exchange for an *iŋgɔl* who had the same mother as himself. Or, in the case of an *iŋgɔl* by his mother, who was exchanged for a wife by one of his father's sons: if the wife thus procured gave birth to a daughter, who was in turn given back to him when he used this girl to make an exchange marriage, he would say that the wife he obtained was of his mother's stem; so in this case also he would set up an *akombo* at the door of her house.[1] All the other exchange wives were left as they were, and he set up no *akombo* outside their houses. At the inauguration of the farm,[2] he turned the first sod on the plot of his maternal exchange wife, and hoed her farm first before making farms for the other wives. Even though she might be quite a small girl, it was the maternal exchange wife who took precedence over all the others. She might also be quite witless, but according to ancient Tiv custom, she was the chief wife. Moreover, when they took to marrying wives in all sorts of other ways, the *akombo* was never set up before the house of any except that of the maternal exchange wife, and a woman married

[1] P. 102.   [2] P. 90.

by any other way could only attain the position of an honoured wife, however wise she might be; she was never called the 'great' wife.

The *akombo* set up at the door of the exchange wife's house are the paternal and maternal *Ihambe-icigh*, and the *Twel* with its enclosure.[1] These are all that were set up according to ancient Tiv custom. You will find a description of them in the chapter on *akombo*. The actual place where they stand is on the left-hand side of the entrance, as you go in. You may travel all over Tivland, but you will never see the exchange marriage *akombo* placed on the right of the doorway. If you see an *akombo* on the right-hand side, it is some foreign hunting *akombo*. The reason that all exchange marriage *akombo* are placed on the left is because this is the side on which the Tiv fix the door, and on which the owner of the house sleeps.[2] They are put on this side, in order that the wife who sleeps there may have good health and happiness, through the mother of the man who has made the exchange marriage. This is to show that the man holds his mother in high regard, for even though she is dead he is doing these things that her name may not be forgotten. Also by doing this he will not be visited by bad dreams about his mother.[3]

THE CHILDREN BY EXCHANGE MARRIAGE. EQUALIZATION

The children born by exchange marriage were the rightful heirs, and were free to do as they pleased in their father's family and in his group, without hindrance. It was the son by an exchange marriage who built the *Poor*, and performed the rites of the *Biamegh* and other big *akombo*. It was he also who must have the use of the *iŋgɔl*, lest trouble should ensue.[4] And when the idea of chieftainship arose, it was a son of an exchange marriage who was made chief.[5] Even when the Tiv began to adopt

[1] The emblems can still be seen in any village founded previous to the abolition of exchange marriage.

[2] P. 58, 9.

[3] The mother bears a close mystical relationship to the wife, because it was she who bore the *iŋgɔl* who is identified with the wife for whom this *iŋgɔl* was exchanged. This question is treated more fully on p. 191 et seq.

[4] The trouble is that he would bewitch, or cause to be bewitched, any other man who took her; see p. 327, etc.

[5] Cf. Meek, art. cit., p. 70.

other forms of marriage, and have children by them, a son by exchange was still of the utmost importance. It is only lately that they have ceased to trouble about this to such an amazing extent.

When a man made an exchange marriage with some one, and his *iŋgɔl* bore more children to her husband than the other man's *iŋgɔl* bore to him, the first man took one of the daughters which had been born to his *iŋgɔl*, to use himself. Here is an example:

Owners	*Angɔl*
Igba	Ayamar
Atɔm	Iwuhe

Igba takes Ayamar and uses her to make a contract with Atɔm; Atɔm gives him his *iŋgɔl*, Iwuhe, in exchange. Ayamar, Igba's *iŋgɔl*, bears Atɔm five daughters and two sons. Iwuhe, Atɔm's *iŋgɔl*, bears Igba three sons and one daughter. So Igba goes to Atɔm, and says, 'My *iŋgɔl* has borne more children to you, so give me one of her daughters to exchange for a wife, that I also may build'.[1] Atɔm will reply, 'Brother-in-law, you have well spoken. Go back now; I will speak to the elders of my group, and then send you a message to come'.

So after Igba has departed Atɔm starts off quietly in the evening to go and see Agbaibu, his kinsman, and tells him what Igba has said. Agbaibu, having heard everything, asks Atɔm what he thinks about Igba's request.

ATƆM: What I think! In a case like this I would not venture to make a hasty answer without coming to consult you first, as long as you are alive.

AGBAIBU: Well then, give him a daughter. By settling a matter in a friendly way you can reap the benefits from it without further argument.

So Atɔm sends a message to Igba, his brother-in-law, and when he comes calls one of his daughters and shows her to him, saying, 'Igba, this is my child that I am giving to you. Since my house has grown big through your

---

[1] I.e. 'found a family', but the word has a literal significance in as much as a new hut is built for each wife (and her children).

iŋɔl, I will not let yours fall in ruins. Take her and marry a wife, that you also may build'.

IGBA: Ah. That is a very friendly way to get something from a man. Bring water, that we may wash away all feelings of resentment,[1] and call my *iŋɔl*, too, that she may sit with us and do the same.

So when water has been brought, and each has purged his heart of all malice, they lie down to sleep. The next morning Igba takes the daughter of his *iŋɔl*, and his hosts courteously escort them along the road. When Atɔm is about to turn back to the village he says to Igba, 'Igba, I have given you my daughter; do not keep her away from me. If anything happens which must be set right, do not stay and do it alone, but bring her to me that I may set it right and then send her back to you'.

IGBA: Atɔm, I will not refuse to do anything you may ask of me.

Atɔm then returns home with his wife, Igba's *iŋɔl*, and Igba passes on with the girl, who has now become his *iŋɔl*. When they arrive home they sleep, and the next morning early he takes her to show Akɔso, the head of his group. When he has told him everything, Akɔso says, 'Igba, Atɔm has done well indeed. Let no harm come to this girl. Exchange her for a wife, and beget children to carry on your line'. So Igba returns home with the girl, and exchanges her for a wife. This is how the Tiv used to take away[2] an *iŋɔl* with the best of goodwill. This type of friendly arrangement continued unaltered until the time when the Tiv finally gave up exchange marriage.

KEM

The word '*kem*' means to give a number of small things till they grow to a big total. The word is used in Tiv for many things: If you want to buy a cow or a horse, you start saving up for it, setting aside a penny here, a shilling there, and when any one comes and asks you for something you say, 'I can't give it you, because I am trying to *kem* enough money to buy a cow'. So also in the case of

---

[1] *Hamber ifan;* see note on p. 298.
[2] For purposes of equalization. The word *dugh* (deduct) is used in this technical sense.

exchange marriage, formerly when a man started to make overtures he gave the girl's mother a small hoe and an iron spike for the *ruam*, and her father a cloth to tie round his waist. He also approached the elder members of the owner's group with presents on the question of making an exchange. (This is the origin of the terms *ŋɔkem* and *terkem*.[1]) But if the marriage arrangements fell through, the suitor demanded the return of all the presents he had given, since they were not making an exchange with him, and this was accordingly done. If everything was not paid back, and he afterwards caught a member of that section of the clan, he would sell him, saying that they had appropriated his presents but refused to give him the woman.

❡. The institution described below corresponds roughly to what has been termed marriage by 'purchase' or 'payment of a bride-price'. Marriage by true purchase certainly existed amongst the Tiv, but the term conveys a very misleading idea of the type of marriage dealt with here, at least in the form in which it was originally practised. No apology, therefore, is offered for using the vernacular word in place of the better-known terms mentioned above. Except in the case of slave marriage, a husband cannot, in any society, 'buy' his wife by paying a bride-price, but only certain rights sanctioned by custom,[2] and in the case of the Tiv these rights were very few indeed, originally, in fact, limited practically to right of intercourse only. It must be admitted that here, as elsewhere, with the development of the idea of property, the introduction of money, and of the Western habit of valuing all things in terms of cash, marriage has come to assume more and more the nature of a commercial transaction. In fact European civilization, by its influence on the institution, has itself done much to justify the name which it has given to it.

The origin and nature of marriage by payment of a bride-price amongst the Tiv is of especial interest, because it is this system

[1] The words are translated in this book as mother-in-law and father-in-law, but note that the terms differ from ours in that
(*a*) they can be used in a wider classificatory sense (cf. p. 113);
(*b*) they are applied before marriage as well as after (as is clear from the derivation). The terms are used for exchange marriage relationships as well as for marriage by payment of gifts only, and, on the theory given here, date back to the time before the latter custom came into use.

[2] Westermarck, *A Short History of Marriage*, p. 162. The word for 'buy' or 'pay' is never used in this connexion: the presents are always 'given'.

which has now been recognized by the Administration as the only legal form of marriage.[1] The basic meaning of *kem*, as Akiga explains, is the collecting of small amounts, either as gifts for the parents of a prospective bride, or with a view to buying a cow, or any other purpose. The only difference is that in the case of a wife you hand everything over to her parents as soon as you get it, whereas in the case of a cow you do not *kem* any particular beast, and therefore must bank the money yourself until it is sufficient to buy one. Now his opinion of the origin of this custom, which there seems no reason to doubt, is that it was not a form of marriage in itself, but merely a preliminary to obtaining a wife by exchange. The presents were not, at first, reciprocal (though the custom of giving big exchange presents and feasts is said to have grown up later), but were given, as might be expected, by the man who made the initial move in the negotiations. He had, in fact, to pay for the privilege of choice. The second man would have to accept whatever wife the first was able to provide in exchange for his sister. It was natural, therefore, that his group should have the advantage in receiving the gifts. These gifts originally 'bought' nothing at all, except the goodwill of the girl's relatives. In later times, owing to foreign influence (according to Akiga), they were considered to give the suitor the right of cohabitation, but no rights of marriage in the true sense, which, from the Tiv point of view, means the possession of the children. This is the crux of the Tiv marriage question to-day.

The idea of *kem* is also closely associated in this account with consanguineous and matrilocal marriage. According to Akiga's view, these practices grew up in later times alongside the exchange marriage system, but were always considered as a temporary arrangement, to be broken off as soon as opportunity occurred to make a proper marriage by exchange. Consanguineous and matrilocal marriage, he implies, are different forms of the same thing. That is to say, the custom of obtaining a partner by gifts alone was only practised inside the group. Sometimes the 'husband' went to live in the girl's village, and sometimes he carried her away to his own home (Kparev). In either case, he had to pay

---

[1] Strictly speaking, before the present régime, this means of obtaining a wife was not regarded as marriage at all, in the same sense as marriage by exchange, and the same attitude is still maintained by the more conservative elements of the tribe. For convenience, however, the terms 'marriage', 'husband', &c. are here applied to the relationships described in this and the following sections.

a certain consideration to her parents, which gave him the right of cohabitation but nothing further. The term *kem* is used for the giving of this consideration, as in the case of the presents given as a preliminary to making an exchange. So in this case, also, *kem* does not signify a form of marriage in itself, but a custom practised in connexion with other forms.

The practice of taking a temporary wife within the group may very well have grown up as a consequence of the difficulties of making an exchange marriage, especially for the younger sons. It is said that in former times a man was often quite old before his turn came to use an *iŋɔl*. In these circumstances it was natural that irregular unions should have been common. It also seems intelligible that, as long as they were considered irregular, they should only be permitted between members of the same clan. Shortage of women is one of the commonest causes of incest, and these appear to have been incestuous connexions, tolerated, but not encouraged, by society to mitigate the hardship of remaining single, which arose from the difficulty of finding wives for the young men, and husbands for the girls, when these had to be procured from outside the group. Apart from the question of finding sufficient *aŋɔl*, it must have been very difficult to arrange exchange marriages with other clans, when the tribe grew and covered a large area of country, especially in the unsettled times before the British occupation. There were constant journeyings backwards and forwards with presents for the bride's relations; there were long delays while the elders of each group met together to discuss the proposed alliance, and sent word to, or visited, the other party. Finally, when the agreement had been reached, and the bridegroom went to fetch away the girl, there was always a chance of her being seized while passing through the territory of another clan on the way home.

But whether these irregular unions within the exogamous group are, in themselves, of recent origin or not, there is reason to suppose that the matrilocal type of incestuous marriage, or 'companionship', as it is euphemistically termed by the Tiv, is founded on a much older custom. In the following description of this custom, as practised in Masev, the husband who first marries the girl and goes to live in her village is pictured as holding a very honourable position. The marriage is, indeed, only temporary, and the girl eventually makes an exchange marriage with a man from another group, when such is forthcoming, but when the girl becomes pregnant the second (exchange) husband has to bring her back to her own group, in order to observe certain rites intended to ensure a successful delivery. On this occasion the two husbands engage in a kind of dressing-up and dancing competition. The first (matrilocal) husband takes a prominent part in the ceremonies, and the second (exchange) husband on the whole takes a back seat. In this instance the two men doubtless represent their respective groups and the rivalry which is always present between the relatives of the husband and of the wife, but they may also be regarded as representatives of the two fundamental principles of father-right and mother-right. It is significant that the custom is performed at the first sign of potential descendants. The whole ceremony is suggestive of the matrilocal idea in conflict with the patrilocal, of mother-right making a last symbolic gesture to assert its claim to the children.

A similar form of marriage is found in other clans, but it is chiefly practised by Masev and Iharev, and this fact is important, because these were amongst the last to leave the hills and come into their present position. On their way they had to pass through the strong Kparev clans, who seized a large number of their women. Kparev was thus able to enforce the patrilocal system in favour of its male members, in accordance with the natural tendencies already indicated. Matrilocal marriage persisted longer in Iharev and Masev, by force of circumstances, and assumed its present consanguineous form from the same cause. The men of Kparev, having recently asserted their right to bring up their own families, and having, moreover, acquired more than their fair share of women at the expense of the unfortunate Iharev and Masev clans, would not be disposed to submit to the somewhat undignified and unsatisfactory role of matrilocal husbands in the families of their weaker neighbours. So, in default of men from outside, the Iharev and Masev groups would be compelled to admit husbands for their daughters from amongst their nearer kinsmen. The men, on the other hand, might well choose to remain in the relatively honourable position of a matrilocal husband in a group where this was the normal form of marriage, in preference to suffering the added indignity of attaching themselves to a group in which it had already fallen into disrepute, and implied a very inferior status to that held by the coexistent patrilocal households.

ALTHOUGH at the beginning the Tiv had only the exchange form of marriage, after a time they saw the *kem* system practised by foreigners (Chamba), and began to adopt it. In this form of marriage, if a man saw a girl who took his fancy, he started to *kem* her, whether she had reached puberty or not, and even though she might be only about ten years old. First of all he bought a small open-work cloth for the girl to bind round her waist. This he called 'tying on the medicine'. Others were then afraid to pay court to her, saying that this man had 'tied medicine' on the girl with the intent to *kem* her. Then he set about making the payments in earnest. If he killed some small creature he took it to the girl's mother, or if he got some farm produce he would give this. When the farming season came round, he went to hoe a farm for his future mother-in-law. At that time, when there was not much property, these were the only kinds of payment that were made. Finally he picked a mushroom and gave it to the mother. This concluded the affair, and he was given the girl to take away with him.

But when in due course of time people began to possess more property, they developed the idea of *kem*, and added to it other practices. They also invented new terms, such as 'Entering into companionship with a woman', and 'Daughter of the family' or 'Sister'[1] [marriage]. The meaning of 'Entering into companionship' was that when a man started to *kem* a woman, he went and cohabited with her, and called her his 'companion'. It was called 'Daughter of the family', because the woman was one of your own group, and of the same section, within which you would not intermarry;[2] in some cases she might even be of the same family.[3] The name 'Sister' indicated quite plainly that she was a close relation.

With the increase of property and development of the -*kem* idea, the father was no longer satisfied with all these small presents from the suitor. When the girl reached

[1] In the classificatory sense. Actually the closest relationships permitted are said to have been between third cousins.

[2] Lit., 'accept each other', i.e. under the exchange system, which was the only genuine form of marriage.

[3] *Ya.*

puberty, her father or owner told him the price[1] which he had still to pay; this might be four or six 'twenties', or in some cases as much as a cow. The price depended on the girl. If she were an exceptional woman an exceptionally high price would be demanded from her suitor; but if she were just an ordinary woman, only a little would be given for her. When the suitor had paid off the whole of the bride-price, he had to give a bed and a she-goat. The goat was slaughtered by the owner of the girl, and the meat divided up amongst his kinsmen. Some days later the mother of the girl asked her co-wives to go with her and take the bride to her husband. They set out with the girl at night, about the time when people have finished the evening meal, and went to give the man his bride. The bridegroom killed a chicken for the women, and after this they returned home, leaving him to settle down with his wife.

The above is a description of the *kem* as it is practised in Shitire, Ukum, and other clans. Kparev and Masev have the same customs with some slight variations. In Kparev payment is made largely in brass rods. When a man sees a girl he likes, he starts by paying attentions to her mother. If he gets a little scrap of something he gives it to the mother, and the girl's father, too, he treats in the same way. In Kparev, if you make these small presents to the father and mother of a girl you like, you can go and sleep with her. And if while you are staying there some one else also comes prowling round as a rival, you try to get the better of him. The way in which you do this is to go and get two or three bundles of twenty brass rods and give them to the father. This means that you have 'bought the house'. If, after this, some one else comes, the mother herself will drive him away, saying, 'Stop making trouble. My son So-and-so has already bought this house'. Then you also bring a bed as a present, after which you can say that you have made a 'Sister' marriage, bought the house, and actually set up[2] a bed. Sometimes

---

[1] The Tiv is *inyaregh*, a word now used for 'money'. The words do not in themselves mean 'pay', 'price', &c.; this meaning is suggested by the context.
[2] Because the uprights were originally planted in the floor, see p. 59.

a man will stay with the girl in the house of her mother, until she conceives and gives birth there. Another, on the contrary, will elope with her and take her to his own home, even before she is with child. In this case, the mother sets off in pursuit, and goes to demand her daughter's return. The man gives her one bundle of brass rods, or possibly two, which he calls 'tying a cloth round the mother-in-law's waist'. The mother goes home again, and some time later the father of the girl sets out and goes to tell the man to *kem* his daughter, naming the price which he must pay. This may be, for example, five bundles of twenty rods; but he need not necessarily pay it all at once. Sometimes he is unable to find the money, and in this case the owner comes and takes his *iŋɔl* away, to exchange for a wife for himself. 'Sister' marriage is the name used in Kparev.

COMPANIONSHIP MARRIAGE IN MASEV

To the people of Masev the companionship marriage is of great importance. Originally they entered into 'companionship' with a woman in the same way as other clans, but afterwards their customs diverged. In Masev, if a girl reaches puberty and does not first have a male companion at her home, she is laughed at as being not much of a woman. They say that when she grew up she was so unattractive that no man came near her. In all other clans not much importance is attached to these local love-affairs; the elders in former times did not by any means approve of their children entering into such a relationship, but it was beyond their power to prevent it. In Masev, however, it is a big thing. If a woman who has formed an alliance in her home afterwards breaks it off and gets married,[1] but does not become pregnant, the matter ends there; but if she conceives a child by her second husband, the occasion on which he brings her to her home for the purpose of performing the 'Purging of the *akombo*' ceremony is a great day of rivalry between the two men—the one who had been her husband at her home, and the man whom she has since married and by whom

[1] I.e. by exchange.

she is with child. When the woman conceives, and her
husband is about to bring her to be purged, her owner
brews beer, and on the day that it is ready all the elders
assemble at his village and spend the day drinking, while
the young men and girls spend the time making themselves ready to come to the Purging in the evening.

On the day of the Purging the man who was formerly
the woman's local husband buys a calabash bowl, which
he carves with careful workmanship, and a necklace or
bead girdle. He also buys a woman's loin-cloth of the
type known as *ashila*, on to which he sews an ornamental
pattern of cowrie shells and ties a row of rattles round the
edge. Then he collects all these things together, puts
them into the decorated calabash bowl, and goes early
in the morning to give them to the girl. He calls her his
'companion'. When the sun is overhead, the people
arrive for the dance. The relations of the new husband
vie with the relations of the girl's former lover in dancing,
and the husband of the girl vies with her companion in
smartness of appearance; each of the two husbands ties a
'rubbed' cloth round his waist (a 'rubbed' cloth is a piece
of black cloth rubbed with a snail-shell till it shines). The
man who is acclaimed by all as the winner is he who has
the shiniest cloth, and the one who is acknowledged to
belong to the superior group is he whose relatives prove
themselves the best dancers.

When evening comes, all the people sit down on the
ground. The girl's companion gets up and stands by her
side in the middle of the open space, and the two join
hands,[1] while the husband who has brought her remains
in the background. The senior man stands up and
performs the purging rite, purging her from the various
akombo. The object of this rite is to purge the woman of
the *akombo* against which she may have trangressed in the
past whether wittingly or unwittingly;[2] in either case
they are set right for her. So it is said that they are

[1] Amongst other peoples the joining of hands is usually the symbolic act
associated with the conclusion of the marriage ceremony. So here also it
emphasizes the strength of the relationship between the woman and her own
group, as represented by her local 'husband'.
[2] Cf. p. 31.

purging her free of the *akombo*, that she may have a safe delivery. When all have been set right, a he-goat is taken out to the back of the village, by the *Ilyum*,[1] and slaughtered. After the killing of the goat the husband departs with his wife.

This is companionship marriage, as it is practised in Masev. All these customs are observed by the Tiv to the present day. But with regard to the *kem* system as practised within the home, though a man may do this he does not say that he is married,[2] but calls himself a bachelor, and others look upon him in the same way. He says that it is his 'sister' with whom he is living.

THE CHILDREN BORN OF COMPANIONSHIP MARRIAGES

From the oldest times down to the present day, if you *kem* a girl at home, any children which you may have by her do not belong to you, but are called the children of the woman's father; although, if you beget a number of children, your father-in-law may take one of them and give to you for the gate of the cattle pen.[3] If the children you have by the woman are sons, they may perhaps later not like living with their mother's family, and so come to join their natural father, but they would not get an *iŋgɔl* in their father's family. They would be given this by their mother's family, if they went and begged them for it. Nevertheless, if at their father's home the other sons or brothers of their father were weak, these children by marriage within the group would compel them,[4] and so

[1] The *Ilyum* was one of the old fertility cults (see p. 195), but its rites are not now generally practised, so this presumably refers to the past. In this connexion the rites were carried out in view of the coming birth, and also to cement the relationships between the two groups, the emblems being placed on the boundary which divided them.

[2] Yet Akiga himself uses the same term (*er kwase*) in this connexion above, and also calls the 'companion' a husband. The fact is, since the abolition of exchange the Tiv ideas about marriage have become somewhat inconsistent, and the old terminology is no longer appropriate.

[3] An expression used, in the first place, in connexion with the practice of farming out livestock. The custom amongst the Tiv, and other Nigerian tribes, is to give the man who looks after your cattle, &c., one or more of the offspring in return for his trouble, or, figuratively speaking, in payment for the gate used to shut them up at night. Cf. also footnote on p. 156, but the child referred to here is a daughter, as the Tiv have not much interest in claiming the sons; see p. 157.

[4] E.g. by witchcraft. 'Weak' implies weak in *tsav*.

K

get full use of the *aŋɔl*. Nothing would happen, and no one would dare to oppose them; they could even be made chiefs, and become powerful members of their father's family. Hom, the present chief of Mbagen, is the son of a consanguineous *kem* marriage. Any one who is born in this way is called by the Tiv a 'woman's child'.[1]

EXOGAMY

❡ It seems advisable at this point to try to determine the size of the group within which true marriage was not recognized, that is to say, marriage by exchange, as opposed to the temporary relationships described here. Theoretically, there has been no true marriage in the old sense since exchange was abolished, and the following deductions cannot apply to the present system; but in practice, there seems good reason to believe that the considerations on which the Tiv attitude to exogamy is based are fundamental and permanent, and that when the present transitional period is over there will be no great change in the feeling of the people on this question, whatever form of marriage may be finally accepted by them.

It must be said at once that the exogamic unit has never had any very well defined limits; moreover, owing to the speed at which the tribe has grown, these limits have been continually shifting. There is no tribal code forbidding marriage within definite degrees of kinship. At any one point in the history of the tribe each member knows the extent of the group within which he may marry. But in the next generation, though the identity of the groups remains, their size may have been much increased, and the necessity for exogamy is less apparent. In this way new exogamous sections come into existence within the groups. The extent to which this may happen is dependent largely on the closely allied organization of the *akombo* groups, which are also continually undergoing sub-division and rearrangement. These groups, as already shown, are composed of a number of *iŋɔl* groups, which are bound together by a close bond of kinship, and recognize the leadership of a common elder. If there are several

---

[1] *Wankwase* is a child descended from the female side of the family. Any one is reckoned a 'woman's child' in his mother's group, whether he is living there permanently or not, and the same term is applied to his children. But the children of a matrilocal marriage are always 'woman's children', wherever they are, as they have no legitimate standing in their father's group.

senior elders within the group, they will usually split up out of mutual jealousy, with the result that the older clans, owing to the length of their history, often have smaller groups. In the younger clans, like Ukan, the growth has been so rapid that sometimes a thousand people or more are descended from a man whose children are still alive. It seems absurd to split up when many of the group can remember their common ancestor, and so they are held together by sentiment. The reverse process of amalgamation also sometimes occurs, as, for instance, when a group cannot remain as an independent unit, owing to lack of elders of sufficient standing. It should be added, however, that from the spiritual point of view it is not absolutely necessary that an *akombo* group should have within its ranks an elder of sufficient authority to perform all the important rites, because for this purpose the group will often call in a more senior elder from another group inside the kindred.

The *akombo* group, however, is not only a magico-religious, but a kinship, unit, and the senior elder is regarded as the living representative of the ancestor from whom the group is descended, whose name it bears, and with whom it is identified. As such he is representative of the group, present and past, and also 'father' of its living members. This 'family' is normally coextensive with the social and administrative unit. In its social aspect it is referred to as those who 'have one drum-stick', or 'use the same big drum', (*mba ve koho geŋga mɔm*) that is to say, those who meet together for any occasion of festivity. In its administrative capacity it has been termed the 'council group' (*mba ve dze ijir imɔŋgo*), and is the largest unit of which all the members habitually meet to settle disputes or discuss matters affecting the common good. The essential characteristic of this unit, from whichever point of view it be considered, whether that of the rites, the dancing, or the council, is that it should be of such a size that frequent meetings of the whole group are practicable.

All the main functions of this *akombo*-kinship group have an important bearing on the question of exogamy, and tended to make it, in practice, the smallest unit within which exchange marriage did not take place. From the point of view of the family, marriage within this group would confuse the essential attributes and functions of the father's and the mother's kindred, two conceptions which, to the Tiv, are totally different and mutually exclusive. This idea of the two opposite kinship groups is very closely bound up with the whole Tiv theory of exchange marriage, and finds its mystical expression in the erection of the paternal and maternal *Ihambe-icigh*.[1] A man whose father had married inside the group would be in an impossible position. His father's and mother's group would coincide, his paternal and maternal kinsmen, both living and dead, would be the same people, and there would be no difference between the rites appropriate to the two sides of his family, which in each case would have to be conducted by the same elder, as representative of a single group.

Socially, the *akombo* group was the smallest unit which contained the necessary elements for celebration of the marriage dance, a very important, and indeed indispensable, part of the ceremony, without which a true marriage could not take place. For administrative purposes the group had the necessary constitution to arrange the marriage, that is to say, an elder of sufficient influence to back the preliminary negotiations and carry out the ceremony (see p. 114), and was large enough to take corporate action in any subsequent disputes arising out of the marriage, as for example, a question of equalization of the children, or return of an unsatisfactory wife. These functions of the group are described in the account given by Akiga. Those who came together to ratify the marriage agreement were 'all the elders who shared in the same *akombo* rites and sat together in council', and it is the same elders of the group who were consulted when the question of equalization arose (p. 119).

Although the minimum exogamic unit for the purposes of exchange corresponded more or less to the *akombo* group, an exchange between members of two groups inside the same clan was not considered so satisfactory as a more distant marriage. The ideal, as amongst the Australians, was always to marry as far away as possible.[2] An exchange marriage with another clan was preferred, wherever it could be arranged, and was celebrated with feasting and dancing on a large scale. The origin of this idea may appear, at first sight, to lie in the indefinite and variable nature of the exogamic unit, and the feeling of near kinship between all members of the clan, which is due to the rapid growth of the tribe. But it is doubtful whether the Tiv see any physiological or eugenic

---

[1] P. 188.   [2] Howitt, *Native Tribes of South-east Australia*, p. 262.

virtue in exogamy, except within very close degrees of kinship. Nor can their desire to avoid marriage between comparatively near relations be due to any natural repugnance, or fear of breaking taboos against incest. If this were so, it is unlikely that the consanguineous unions, already described, even though admittedly only of a temporary nature, would be tolerated with such complacency. It is perhaps worth noting in this connexion that the *iye* inter-clan pact to exchange wives was sealed by a mingling of the blood of the contracting parties.[1] If blood relationship were in itself considered an insuperable bar to marriage, this symbolic act would have exactly the opposite effect from that which was intended, by making subsequent intermarriage impossible.

The suggestion is here advanced that the whole of the Tiv conception of exogamy is based on the sense of unity which exists between the individual and the group with which he associates, and in a sense identifies, himself. This group he calls his *ityɔ*, a term which may be applied to the group as a corporate body, or to any individual member of it. The fact that the same word is used for the two meanings is no semantic accident, but reflects a manner of thought that conceives two ideas, which to us are quite distinct, as essentially one. The individual acts as the group, the group as the individual. A marriage between members of two groups is an alliance between the groups themselves. This idea is very clearly shown in Akiga's description of the exchange marriage proceedings. At every stage of the negotiations the elders are consulted. Each group takes action as a whole on behalf of its members, and speaks for them through the mouth of its representative, the senior elder. The marriage ceremony is conducted. as though the two old men themselves were marrying the girls, instead of the bridegrooms whose group they represent. The one stands up and says, 'Why is it that I see you here?' and the other replies, 'I have seen a cup in So-and-so's house . . .' and so on. When the two brides are brought, one of the elders asks the other whether the girl accepts him as a husband, that is to say, whether she accepts the group which he is representing, and which in turn includes, and is identified with, the man whom she is actually marrying. The other replies on behalf of the girl (and her group). The marriage compact between the groups is symbolized by the two brides embracing their 'husbands', who, again, are not the

[1] P. 142.

actual members of the group whose wives they will be, but its representatives.[1]

The conception of the group as husband finds its fullest public expression in the marriage dance. The group feasts and dances, not as guests of the husband, but as co-hosts. It is the marriage dance of the group, and it is the group that 'stays the night'. 'Staying the night' is an integral part of the marriage ceremony. The Tiv term for it (*tsa-utu*) has a specific implication and is not used in any other connexion. The circumstances of this custom, and the amatory nature of the dances which accompany it, cannot fail to suggest that it represents, for the group, the consummation of the marriage. The especial significance of this in the present connexion is that, although guests from other groups are not excluded from the initial festivities which take part in the day time, the only people who are entitled to 'stay the night' are members of the group with which the bridegroom is identified for the purpose of this marriage.

The girl addresses all the other men of the group as 'my husbands', the married women as 'my co-wives', and the unmarried women as 'my children'; and they call her, respectively, 'our wife', 'co-wife', and 'mother'.

If the group is identified with the husband, true marriage within the group is obviously impossible. Therefore, the minimum exogamic unit is that which habitually acts 'as one man', and is indivisible for magico-religious, social, and administrative purposes. This unit is the *akombo* group. Now if a man married into a neighbouring group, he had with him, as co-partners to the marriage, only the members of his own *akombo* group, and it was only these who could take part in the marriage dance, and 'stay the night'. The group which acted as 'husband' naturally could not include any of the group which was the 'wife', or of any larger unit of which the bride's group formed a part. But if he married into another clan, the whole of his own clan were theoretically

[1] It is hardly necessary to add that no suggestion is here made of 'group marriage' in the literal sense, or anything of the kind. The husband had an exclusive right to the woman he married, and the children, although they belonged to, and were part of, the group, acknowledged him as their own father as fully as in any civilized society. It is true that a son might inherit his father's wives (apart from his mother), and occasionally had access to them during his father's lifetime, but this practice may originate from quite other causes. The theory which insists on the essential unity of the group with its component parts does not, in practice, necessarily imply community of women or even of property belonging to its members.

partners to the marriage, and could take part in the marriage festivities in the role of collective husband. The importance of the occasion was emphasized by the number of guests entitled to take part in the celebrations. Apart from the added prestige which this gave to the husband, he had the satisfaction of knowing that the whole of his clan was taking part in his marriage and interested in its success; moreover, that he had behind him, not only the authority of its most influential elders to support him in case of trouble, but also the great weight of all its members, living and dead, and the greatly increased power of the supernatural sanctions which this implied.

From the point of view of the clan, it was also considered more satisfactory for its members to marry outside, if possible. But here there was no intention of cementing a friendship between two communities.[1] On the contrary, the complexity of the rules which had grown up around the Tiv exchange marriage system seems to have given rise more often to bad feeling than amicable relationship between the contracting parties. As disputes were almost certain to arise, it was better for the sake of internal harmony that they should not occur between members of the same clan. These disputes were not concerned merely with the 'legal' aspects of the exchange, the ownership of the children, and so forth, but were bound up with the Tiv beliefs in relation to witchcraft. If one of the exchanged wives died, the two groups were unavoidably involved in an argument as to which was responsible for her death, and this might well lead to war. Any two clans which were in the habit of exchanging women were always liable to come to blows (see p. 143).

It was, however, in the next generation that the advantages of an exchange with a distant group became most apparent, because the more remote the marriage of the parents, the larger the size of the child's *ityɔ* (father's group). Theoretically, *ityɔ* is explained by Akiga as including all those who 'have come out of the womb of one woman', that is to say, all who trace their descent to (the woman who was exchanged for) a common maternal ancestor. But *ityɔ* is one of the vaguest of all the Tiv tribal units. When Akiga's explanation is considered it will be realized that this must be so. According to tradition the whole tribe traces its descent

---

[1] The need for forming a bond between families has been advanced by Prof. Hobhouse as a possible explanation of the exogamic impulse, op. cit., p. 51.

to a common ancestor, who had two sons, Icɔŋgo and Ipusu. The mothers of these (or, according to the Tiv view, the women who were given in exchange for their mothers) each founded an *ityɔ*, to which, in theory, every one of their descendants belongs. From the individual's point of view, the word *ityɔ* may be, and is in actual practice, applied to any kinship group to which he belongs, varying from the smallest exogamic unit to the whole clan. But the practical implication of the term is *the group with which his father identified himself when marrying his mother*. If the two groups are closely related to each other, both will be small, for they are mutually exclusive; but if the marriage was a more distant one, the child will enjoy membership of larger and stronger paternal and maternal groups. A man whose parents belong to two different clans holds a privileged position as regards protection and hospitality throughout both these clans, whereas the child of a marriage between two related *akombo* groups would be treated like any other stranger outside these groups. These practical considerations are all that concern the ordinary man; but at the back of the tribal consciousness there lies a deeper mystical reason, which probably once formed an essential part of the whole theory of exogamy, but is not now very clearly conceived by the tribe as a whole, namely, that since the group consists of its dead as well as its living members, the larger a man's paternal and maternal groups the more powerful are the supernatural sanctions behind the marriage of his parents.

To sum up: The ideal exchange marriage was between two clans. Marriage between smaller groups was recognized, but less satisfactory. True marriage within the *akombo* group was impossible, because the group was identified with its members. Nevertheless, it was customary for young people to form temporary relationships within the group, the man paying for the privilege of intercourse by presents to the girl's parents. This was not recognized as true marriage, and any children that were born belonged to the girl's 'owner'. The Tiv tradition is that these practices, including matrilocal marriage, are of recent origin; that their tribal organization is patrilineal, and is based on a system of exchange marriage which dates back to their first ancestor. But it is more probable that the existing traces of matrilocal marriage are relics of a much older system based on mother-right, out of which exchange marriage has itself developed.

MARRIAGE BY CAPTURE

MARRIAGE by capture originated amongt the Tiv as a hostile act. It first took the form of retaliation on that section of the Dam tribe known as Mbaiyɔŋgo, who seized their women by force at the time when they were passing down through the Bush Tribes, and as a result of this experience the Tiv in later years took to seizing the women of their own tribesmen. When they turned their faces down towards the plains, and came out amongst the Mbaiyɔŋgo, they suffered so much at their hands by having their women taken from them, that if they had not had recourse to cunning they would not have arrived at Ibenda with a single one. The Mbaiyɔŋgo lay in wait for them on the road by which they would pass with their womenfolk, and when the Tiv approached they fell upon them and seized the women. But if a woman was a cripple they left her alone, for in former times none of the Dam people would marry a woman with any physical infirmity, even though it were no more than a missing toe. They carried this so far that they would not go near a woman who had a sore on her body. When the Tiv discovered this they resorted to guile. Every man crushed some of the bark of the *ikpine*[1] tree and laid it on the skin of his wife or daughter. He covered this over with bark-cloth or netting which he made for the purpose, and tied it in position. The *ikpine* juice trickled down the woman's shin as though it were the pus from a wound. When the Mbaiyɔŋgo saw this they thought that she had a bad chronic sore, and would not touch her. For this reason they conceived an aversion for the Tiv women, and the Tiv were able to pass peacefully through the midst of them with their wives and daughters.

One or two of the Tiv who had bold and vindictive natures cherished the memory of these things in their hearts, and this eventually led them to start feuds which afterwards became common throughout the tribe, and increased rather than abated as time went on. These feuds originated in this way: A man of the Ukan clan would set out with his wife to go to Tɔmbo. When he

[1] The juice expressed from the bark of this tree is a dark red colour.

arrived in Ipav, meaning to pass through on his way,
some Ipav scoundrel, having inquired and made quite
certain that he was not of his own clan but of Ukan,
would seize the woman by force and drive her husband
away, or pin him into the stocks[1] and afterwards sell him
to buy a cow for the marriage feast.

For example: Gande is a man of Ukan. He is on his
way to visit his mother's home, Abɔgor in Yandev, and is
accompanied by his wife. When he arrives in Ipav, a
member of the Ipav clan called Ugbadi, who has neither
an *iŋgɔl* nor money to pay a bride-price, meets him on the
road outside his village. (At that time each section of the
Tiv consisted of only one village.)

UGBADI: You there, what's your clan?

GANDE: Ukan.

UGBADI: Where are you going?

GANDE: I am going to Yandev, to visit Abɔgor, my
mother's home.

UGBADI: And who is that nice-looking girl you've got
with you?

GANDE: She's my wife.

UGBADI: How is that you ugly men always marry·
women much better looking than yourselves?

GANDE: Come now, no one is unworthy of his own
property.

UGBADI: You fool! What do you mean by contradicting
me? No one is unworthy of his own property indeed!

GANDE: Why are you trying to pick a quarrel with me?

UGBADI: Well, if I choose to pick a quarrel with you,
what do you propose to do to me?

GANDE: What have I said to cause you offence?

UGBADI: Oh, you'd answer me back, would you? Right!
In that case I'll take that wife of yours by force.

GANDE: No! I'd rather die than that!

Now Ugbadi has three young men with him, Ihɔ, Ada,
and Iyoŋgo, making with himself four persons in all,
whereas Gande and his wife are only two.

---

[1] The *igbe* was a heavy log of wood with a hole bored through it transversely.
The prisoner's leg was thrust through this, and fixed tight by a peg hammered
perpendicularly through the larger hole, and at right angles to it.

UGBADI: Go and catch that woman for me, I want to take her away.

The young men go and seize her, while her husband runs off yelling. Ugbadi takes the woman into his village and puts her in a house. People say, 'Ugbadi has captured a wife off a man of Ukan to-day'.

At first, if the man who had his wife taken from him fled back to his own country, he told one of the elders of the district who was well known for his tact in handling such matters. The latter sent for one of the *igba*.[1] He gave him some *iyandegh*[2] leaves, and told him, 'Take these, go to the head of such-and-such a group, and say that it is not fit that he and I should quarrel. Why does he jest? Let him hand over my wife to be brought back to me.'[3] When the *igba* brought the *iyandegh* leaves, and gave the elder's message, peace would be made. The elder who had received the branch would send for the man who had captured the woman, and say to him, 'So-and-so of such-and-such a group has sent me the *iyandegh*, and asked me to send that woman back to him. So give her up to me that I may deliver her to our *igba* here, to take away with him, for it is not good that we should quarrel with them'. The woman's captor would not venture to refuse, for in olden times no one dared to disobey the word of the elders. He brought the woman to the old man, who handed her over to the *igba* to take away, and the dispute came to an end. But in later years conditions changed, and a man who captured the wife of another refused to let her go, even though the elder should send an *igba* with the *iyandegh*. He beat the drums, and shouted his defiance.[4]

For example: Ugbadi has carried off Gande's wife. That evening the young men drag a log-drum into the village and place the band instruments ready. When night comes on, and the evening meal is over, the time is

---

[1] In this case, a man whose mother came from the clan to whom he wished to send the message; see note on p. 112.

[2] The sign that the errand was peaceful.

[3] Cf. p. 133 (elder representing the group, including the individual).

[4] *Ger*: a word applied to a type of declamation, shouted or sung, in defiance and derision of rivals.

ready to celebrate the capture of the woman with shouts
of defiance. All the people come together in the centre of
the village, men, women, and children. When all have
assembled, two young men climb up on to the fence[1] round
the village, or into a fig-tree, and declaim in song. After
this they call to the man whose wife has been captured:
'Gande o-o! Wanaga bids me tell you she has cooked the
meal, and eaten hers. She has put some by for you in a
corner of the hut, take it and eat it, wash out the scourings
and drink them; as for her, she has gone off with a real
man, Ugbadi, o-o!' A yell of defiance goes up from the
crowd below; drums are beaten, horns blown, and shrill
cries of triumph add to the deafening noise and general
uproar. They repeat this six times, and then start the
marriage drumming. This was the critical moment, the
time when they used to go out to fight.

Perhaps when the young men climb up and hurl insults
at the man whose wife has been taken, the other, stung to
the quick, creeps up close, and during the general hubbub
takes an arrow and shoots one of the youths in the tree.
As he falls to the ground the people scatter, and a cry goes
up, while every one calls out, 'Save my child!' The man
who shot the arrow slips away under cover of the night,
and goes to tell his clansmen that he has killed a man.
Both parties make ready for war that very night. At the
first light of dawn the battle-cry is raised, and the two
forces meet at the border. The fight waxes hot, and dead
bodies strew the ground. The *atakpa*[2] man passes swiftly
round behind, and when any of his clansmen is hit
quickly picks him up and carries him out of the fight
down into the water-grove, to tend his wounds. Some
may yield to his treatment, but others die, and are num-
bered amongst those who have fallen in battle.

At first, the elders of the Tiv strictly forbade this, and
condemned the forcible capture of other men's wives as an
evil thing, but the lawless spirits took no notice, and the

---

[1] *Kon-gar*. These have mostly been given up long ago, and Tiv villages are
open.
[2] An antidote for poisoned-arrow wounds or snake bites, consisting of a
decoction from the stem of the red sorrel and other herbs, allowed to go
thoroughly putrid, and given to the patient to drink.

capture of women became more and more frequent as time went on.

HONOURABLE MARRIAGE BY CAPTURE: THE *IYE*

A cause which led to increased intercourse between the Tiv was the *iye* agreement, by which men could go and seek[1] wives in neighbouring clans, though not outside the tribe. When the elders found that they were unable to prevent the good-for-nothings from stirring up trouble by forcibly carrying off their brothers' wives, and also perceived that it was a means by which the younger men could obtain wives early, they left off trying to stop it. For before they started to take each other's wives, and could only obtain them by exchange according to immemorial custom, it sometimes happened that a man grew up and had reached his fortieth year before his turn came to take an *iŋgɔl*, and he would still be a bachelor. Whereas under the system of marriage by capture a man of twenty could seize some one's wife and have a child by her. This was quite agreeable to his father that, is to say the local elder, and this was the reason that the opposition of the elders to these disputes was never very whole-hearted.

So the old men all assembled together and decided to change the nature of marriage by capture, so that, instead of being an act of aggression, it should become both right and honourable. They would go about amongst each other in large numbers like the black ants,[2] which used to be called *iye*, hence the name for this method of wife-seeking. So the neighbouring clans came together, and each made an *iye* agreement with the clan whose territory adjoined its own,[3] that they should go into each other's country to seek for wives, Shitire with Ukum, Ukum with Ugondo, Ugondo with Ikurav, and so on. But an *iye* could not be started merely on the consent of both parties. Before it could be put into force, the elders of the two clans first met together to discuss the matter, and

---

[1] *Sɔɔr*, also here translated 'court'. The word is only used for the direct wooing of a girl by a man, without the intervention of parents in the initial stages, and only when the two belong to different groups.

[2] *Iyiye.*

[3] Chiefly to avoid the danger of passing through a third clan, with whom they had no treaty.

concluded a pact. A true *iye* pact required a human life.
When the Kpav section of Shitire were making an *iye* pact
with the Mbagen division of Kparev, and were looking
for a victim to be slaughtered for the sealing of the
treaty, Avaan, father of Hom, the present chief of
Mbagen, laid himself down on the ground and told Cire[1]
to cut his throat, that a pact might be made with Shitire,
and the land become good. Cire acceded to his request,
and slaughtered him. The pact was made, and Shitire
obtained wives by it, many as the waters of the river in
flood; and Kparev likewise. Ukum also concluded an *iye*
pact with Shitire, but for this a dog was hanged.[2] This
was in the time of Chief Dajo, son of Mshanjo, of the
Isherev section of Ukum, and, on the Shitire side, Chief
Kon of Mbavughur and Chief Akaanya of Mbajir.
Ukum took an enormous number of wives from Shitire
under this treaty.

 Another way of sealing the pact was this: The old men
came together, and a large grindstone was set on the
ground. A member of one of the two clans stood up, and
laid his hand upon it. This was then cut with a razor so
that the blood flowed out on to the stone. After this one
man from the other clan came and placed his hand there,
and this was also cut so that the blood flowed on to the
stone. Then some locust-bean seasoning was powdered
over the blood, together with a little salt and red palm
oil, and these were mixed together. The men of both
clans stood up, and each took up a little of the mixture and
ate it. When it was finished the elders said, 'This day we
have made a bond between us. Let there never be bloodshed between our two clans, that the land be good, the
people go about in safety, and there be no war'. In olden
times, if they sealed a pact with their blood, they feared
even to shave each others' heads lest they should break the
skin. And if they did so, and the razor should accidentally
make some tiny wound, however slight, the man who
had been cut must take the razor and with it make a cut

---

[1] Father of Cia, drum-chief of Mbagen, both famous leaders in the past.
[2] The dog is probably used as a substitute for a human victim, being of all
animals the closest associate of man. Cf. also p. 206: a dead dog is taboo to
women, like a human corpse.

on the other, but not with any ill feeling. Treaties, in the old days, were very strictly observed, and not regarded lightly.

These were all the things which had to be done before they could go to seek wives under the *iye* agreement[1] without causing friction. Nevertheless, as the Tiv have never had a single thing which they have not thrown away, over this, too, disputes again arose from time to time; war broke out between the very people who had made a treaty with each other not to let any act of folly spoil their friendship, and numbers of men were killed before peace was restored and they started to go about amongst each other again.

THE COURTING

When an *iye* pact for mutual wife-seeking had been made, a large body of young men would start out from their homes, and go off in a long line to the clan with whom they had the agreement. They did not go without due preparation. Camwood was ground up, and clothes were well covered with it. Heads were dressed in the smartest styles, some in patterns, and some shaved clean to be coloured red with powdered camwood. The young men's dress of former times consisted in a striped loin-cloth and a loosely woven covering.[2] When they arrived in the country of the other clan they did not just go any-where, but stayed with a man whose mother was of their own clan, that is, one of their *igba*. If they were a very large number they did not all stay with the same man, but split up amongst all their relatives.[3] If they had friends in the district, these would give them secret information. They were called 'go-betweens'. It was these go-betweens who told them about all the girls in their district who were of a marriageable age. 'So-and-so's daughter has quite reached the age of puberty,' they would say, 'and when

---

[1] The term is simply *dzende iye*, 'go on an *iye*'.

[2] The loin-cloth (*gere*) is woven in one piece on an upright frame, and the pattern generally consists of indigo and white stripes of different widths. The 'covering' (*andzagher-ikondo* or *ijɔmon*) is woven in strips on a narrow loom, and parts are left unwoven with only the warp to hold it together. Both are still seen, but their use is dying out owing to the introduction of European stuffs.

[3] *Ɔnov vev*: lit., 'their children', i.e. 'children' of their group on the female side.

you see her she is sure to take your fancy', and they would mention the girl's name, and that of her father. The young wife-seeker would ask where the water-hole was, and his go-between would furnish him with a full description, before they went to sleep.

The next morning at cock-crow the young man got up and rubbed camwood over himself, powdered his head till it was a bright-red colour, and went and sat by the side of the water-hole. When the girls started to come down in the morning to draw water, he called the one about whom he had been asking on the previous day by her nickname,[1] and asked her to give him some water to wash his face.[2] When the girl drew water and brought it to him to wash his face and his feet, the courtship had begun. That day the girl had a hard time. When she had drawn the water and set the pot upon her head, the youth followed behind. He might be alone, but more usually he had a companion with him. When she had set down the water, and taken up her things to go to the farm, the young man went with her. All the time he kept up a continuous stream of talk, which consisted chiefly of remarks intended to make a favourable impression on her. He paid her the highest compliments. 'Daughter of So-and-so,' he said, 'if you will marry me I shall think myself the luckiest man on earth! I shall leave all other women alone.' He also spoke highly of himself, telling her what a big man his father was, and what a lot of property he had. 'If I get you,' he said, 'as soon as I arrive home my father will knock down[3] a cow, and he won't have to look about for one either! Are you going to stay about at home? Don't you want to become famous?' The man who was helping him also told any number of lies, saying that amongst the So-and-sos there was no one in the whole countryside to be compared with his friend.

When they arrived at the farm, the girl took a leaf and put it on a yam heap for her swain to sit on, while his

---

[1] *Iti i kwagh*, i.e. the name by which she was known to her own age-mates.
[2] Cf. note on p. 112.
[3] The usual word is *sɔŋgo*, which means to cut its throat. Here *gber* is used to increase the impression of a care-free father who had so many cattle that he did not trouble to have them properly slaughtered!

friend walked round with her,[1] telling her the things which women like to hear. As for her, even though she were pleased by the flattery, she would not say anything at first. She would finish her work and set off home. When she had collected some firewood the young man and his friend would also carry a small stick on their shoulders[2] and follow her back to the village. They would stay with her while she ground the corn, and the man who was courting her must sit on the palm stem on which she knelt while she was grinding. If he were a piper, he would pipe to her while she ground to the rhythm of his piping. Or if he were not a piper, but his friend was, his friend would pipe for him, till the girl had finished and swept up the corn. Having done this, she went out to collect corn-stalks,[3] and they went with her. Then she came and cooked the meal, but she would not eat it, for she would be ashamed to do so. When the time came to sleep they went back to the place where they were staying and had some food, and the girl would then also get a chance to eat her meal, for since they had risen in the morning this was the only time that any of them would get anything to eat. The next day was the same, and for five days they all went hungry, while both the girl and her suitors grew thin. After they had gone the man who was acting as a go-between spoke privately to the girl on their behalf.

When they came the next time, they arrived in full force. The young men made up a song in praise of the girl, and sang all night before her door till the break of dawn. Sometimes they accompanied their singing with the calabash rattle, and sometimes with the small conical drum.[4] Kparev mostly sang to the beating of gongs,[5] and in later times they used two drums, a male and a female, and the dancers moved to the rhythm of the singing and drumming. And sometimes the young men took a large number of drums, and spent the night in

[1] I.e. while she went on with her farm work.
[2] This gesture was the limit to which they could go, without making themselves ridiculous by carrying a woman's load.
[3] To use as a torch.
[4] *Wangbande.*
[5] *Kwen.* These are made in the shape of a large flat-sided bell, without a clapper, and struck with a piece of wood or metal.

L

revelry, so that no one had any sleep. Yet in spite of all this it sometimes happened that the man failed completely to get the girl. Some one else took her, and hurled scorn and defiance at the name of his rival. But if the girl were going to marry him, she gave him a pledge at the time when he was doing all he could to woo her. In the days before the Tiv had any property this pledge took the form of finger rings. Later on the girl gave him, beside the rings, some strings of beads and a woman's loin-cloth.[1] These she put into a small calabash bowl of the kind used for holding camwood, and gave them to the go-between to take to her suitor. But this was done in secret, because if her people got to know about it they would keep a watch on her. At the same time that she gave him the pledge she would name the day on which he should come and fetch her away, and tell him the place at which he was to wait for her to join him.

If you pleased the girl whom you were courting, when you entered the house she would set a seat for you on the far side of the room, and sit down beside you and talk to you. But if she did not like you she put the seat down in the *ishenbar*,[2] that is, by the entrance, on the side where the water is kept. Then she went outside, saying that she found it very hot in the house, and when you spoke to her she answered in a loud voice, and became restless and irritable. In this case, if you were a man of perception, you quietly left her alone, and went off to pay your attentions to some other girl. Only a fool would fail to take the hint, and go on wasting his time there till some one else came and took her.

THE CAPTURE[3]

When the girl had named the day to her plighted lover, he came and waited at the trysting-place till she came out to join him, and then they went off together. Sometimes

---

[1] *Wanashisha.*

[2] This word means lit. 'begging for salt', and is so called because a female visitor stands there when she wishes to show the woman of the house that she would like a present. It is on the side of the entrance opposite the door, and so the unpopular suitor would be in full view of passers-by.

[3] It will be seen that this was only a nominal 'capture', but the same word is used throughout, as it is recognized as a survival from ruder times. The Tiv word '*ŋgohol*', which is used in both cases, does not necessarily imply the use of force.

a girl would come, and then be seized by misgivings, so that the man had to drag her away by force. The time mostly chosen by women for elopement was either at dusk or in the morning when the sun began to get hot.[1]

When the capture had been effected, the man took the girl to the home of one of his near relatives, or else one of his age-mates.[2] As he came near to the village he gave vent to shrill cries of triumph and announced his approach in song. When he had finished his song he uttered the cries again, and proclaimed the news with the words 'Zaki-o-o! Tidings! Tidings spread quickly, rest not by the way!'[3] Then he took up his song once more. When the people heard this they knew at once that a wife had been captured, and recognizing his voice, too, they rushed out; those who were asleep awoke, and with all the women and children in the village ran to meet him on the road. They sang, and shouted the news. The women set the captured bride in the midst of them, covered her head with a cloth, and brought her slowly in. She was taken into the house of the bridegroom's kinsman. All the young men of the neighbourhood came in, and sang and danced to the beating of the cone-shaped drums. That night was not one to be spent in sleep.

When the bride had been brought into the kinsman's house, he gave a 'dew chicken'[4] to be killed, and *ruam* was prepared. The 'dew chicken', however, was not eaten by everybody, but only by the bridegroom and those who had previously captured wives,[5] and, of the women, only

[1] These are two times of the day when the people, especially the women, are most busy, fetching water, preparing and eating the meal, &c., so the elopement would have the best chance of being unnoticed.

[2] N.B.—Not necessarily his parents, as the marriage had not been officially sanctioned and arranged by them.

[3] In Kparev the form is *aŋgwe ye nyamnyam*, 'Tidings eat meat', apparently referring to the feast to be prepared for the bride, but the words have little meaning nowadays.

[4] To recompense the travellers for their trouble, or, figuratively speaking, the dew through which they had to walk. Cf. p. 258.

[5] Cf. initiation to the *akombo*. The capture of a wife gives the man a status to be compared with that given by becoming master of an *akombo*. The punishment for breaking the taboo is similar. This seems to be an example of a taboo definitely invented to preserve the prerogative of a class, and is not very different from the taboos which are well known in our public schools, and probably arose from the same motives, viz. the preservation of exclusive privileges. But see Marett, *The Threshold of Religion*, p. 81 et seq.

the captured bride. If you had never captured a wife and ate of the 'dew chicken' because you wanted some meat, you would have bad luck. In some sections of the tribe, such as Mbamar of Ishaŋgev, the woman for whom the chicken is killed does not eat of it, but only her husband and the others. But this custom is not common to all the Tiv.

The next morning the news is given out in all the hamlets which belong to the same drum-circle[1] (that is to say, the people who have the same grandfather, and come together to drum in the same place when one of their members captures a wife), and that night they all collect at the village into which the bride has been brought, and celebrate the marriage with songs of defiance. For, just as in former times, when they captured other men's wives by force, they used to shout defiance at the husband, so when they afterwards came to capture unmarried girls instead, they used to ask the bride the names of the suitors whom she had refused before she eloped with her present lover. If she had been courted before she would tell them about one of her suitors whom she particularly disliked, and they would then call out his name six times with shouts of defiance and abuse. But if there were any men of whom she had been fond, she kept quiet about them. After this they moved into the centre of the village to start the marriage drumming in real earnest, and this was continued through the night till the break of dawn. The next morning the captor of the girl gave a feast, and slaughtered beasts to divide amongst those who had stayed through the night,[2] according to their families. After this the people dispersed to their homes.

While the bridegroom was in his kinsman's house each of his age-mates who had previously captured a wife came and received a present from him. This might be an arrow or a packet of salt, and was called the 'icegh'. From the day on which the bride was taken into the house, she did not appear again during the day-time. She only came

---

[1] *Ikoho-geŋga*, also called *shav-geŋga*, 'drum-stick' = (roughly) the *akombo* group; see p. 131.
[2] *Tsa-utu*. See p. 134.

out at night, secretly, and then went back again. In the house in which she was, a screen was placed across the side where she slept, and no one went in there except the bridegroom and young girls and the woman to whom the house belonged.[1] When the woman of the house prepared food and took it to the bride, she would not eat. Her hostess might make *ruam*, and even kill a chicken, but she would only take a little when entreated to do so. So also the bridegroom; if he felt that he must eat something, he went out to have a meal privately somewhere else, and then came back again. They both grew thin. The bride remained inside the house in this manner sometimes for as long as two months before she gradually started to come outside after dark.

THE ESCORTING OF THE BRIDEGROOM TO HIS HOME

After a wife had been captured and taken to the home of the bridegroom's kinsman, and all these delays were at an end, the kinsman announced that he was now going to brew beer and escort his brother to his home. On the day that the beer was ready the people came in to celebrate the escorting of the bridegroom, and when the sun had passed over towards the western sky the host, having proclaimed that all should be seated, brought out sheep and goats to kill for his guests. Sometimes he gave as many as four or five beasts, in addition to the she-goat whose blood was to be poured on the threshold.[2] He also brought out a cloth and bound it round the bride for all to see. When night fell he rose up with his brother and the captured wife, and they went to the home of the bridegroom's father. The father killed a chicken for him, and then he returned to his own home. There he boasted to the other men of his age of having escorted his brother, and threw it in their teeth.[3]

The next morning the father of the bridegroom caught and killed a large boar to feast the bride. After this she

---

[1] Normally there is little privacy in the Tiv's life. Any one (except a complete stranger) can go in and out of the sleeping huts as he pleases.

[2] The Tiv do not recognize any meaning in this act, beyond a gesture of triumph (*ihagh*) by the bridegroom.

[3] *Sɔgh*. See p. 41. By giving the feast, &c., he had made a definite step forward in the tribal society.

gradually began to come out during the daytime. She would get up early and go to fetch water for her husband to wash his face, then take her calabash bowl[1] and go out to the farm.

The adornment of the bride did not take place before the time when she first began to appear in public. In former days, before young people had any property, it was the bridegroom's father who provided the ornaments for his son's wife. He put brass rings[2] on her legs and hung fine strings of beads of different kinds upon her. He put a hair ornament[3] in her ears and a *luwa* or *agɔm* girdle around her waist. All these things did not necessarily belong to him; some he would ask others to give him.

THE MARRIAGE DANCE

After some days the father announced that he was going to give a marriage feast for his son. He proclaimed that a dance would be held, and told a minstrel to compose a song in his honour, and in honour of his son and his bride, and a song in praise of the chief men in his group, and a song for the bride's family. Songs of this kind, if they were very good, were passed down from one generation to the next, to be sung always at the celebrations for the marriage of any one in the group. Every night, when the evening meal was finished, the people met together at the village of the bridegroom's father to learn the song. The news went round that So-and-so had proclaimed a marriage dance for his son. 'Listen!' said every one. 'They are practising the song!' This became a most important and honourable custom. All the young men who had captured wives at that time, but had not yet been given a marriage feast, were also included, and the song touched rapidly on this one and that: 'So-and-so rose up and captured the daughter of such-and-such a clan, and the tree-drum's voice was heard!'

[1] *Kwese:* a big calabash divided vertically, used for carrying herbs, farm produce, &c.
[2] *Bashi:* the 'brass rods' used as currency, welded into a continuous length, and bent loosely round the lower leg into a spiral, sometimes reaching from the ankle up to just below the knee; also on the forearm, see plate, p. 43.
[3] *Iŋga*, see p. 47.

The song would be practised perhaps for several
months, and then, when the time was ready, the father
of the bridegroom brewed beer, and all his kinsmen did
the same. He went to tell the father or owner of the
woman, and he in turn informed his group. When the
beer was ready to drink the people came in according to
their clans, bringing with them many different kinds of
dances. They adorned their bodies, and let off their
guns. The great dance of olden times, which the Tiv
had from the beginning, was the *aŋge*. It was by dancing
the *aŋge* that the old men made a name for themselves,
and the young men by the *agbaga* and leaping dances. In
the very early days these were the only three kinds of
dances that they had.

The chief would be at the dance, too, dressed in a
locally woven gown and indigo waist-cloth. Or he would
tie a blue Hausa cloth round his waist, and wear a cap of
the same material; and if he were very rich he would
sometimes put on a white Hausa gown made of the
material called 'Vault of heaven', 'Egg-shell',[1] or *Mgena*.
The most important of his wives would wear a cloth of
red flannel, and a string of beads of the kind belonging
to chiefs called *tukure*, which was much admired by
every one. The chief remained standing and would not
sit down until the man who was giving the dance had
paid something for a throne to be set for him to sit on,[2]
together with his wife.

The drumming for the dance went on without pause
till the sun grew red. Then it was announced that all
should sit down according to their families, and when
all were seated on the ground in silence, the father who
was giving the dance for his son dressed up the bride and
bridegroom. A bed was set in the middle of the village,
and the bride was led out, bedecked, into the open.[3]
She had a red-flannel cloth about her loins, and a leopard
skin over her shoulder. She wore a girdle of fine beads

---

[1] Calico. Both names refer to its whiteness (in comparison with native
cloth).

[2] Cf. p. 370.

[3] The dressing up of the bride and bridegroom was done in the bush at the
edge of the village.

around her waist, a tall red fez upon her head, and in her hand she carried a horse-tail whisk. The other women went before her, dancing to the beat of the big drum; but she did not dance herself. When they arrived in the middle of the open space where the bed had been set for her, her kinswomen, who had already married husbands of that district, stood before the bed on which their daughter was to mount, and would not give permission for her to stand upon it until they had been given some present. Then the procession went back to drum in the bridegroom. He was dressed in a shiny or patchwork cloth, and as he came he danced with all his might, while the drums beat for his dancing. Then the father gave his young men the cow which he was providing for the feast, and told them to bring it for all the people to see, while the bridegroom and his bride looked on. The minstrel stood up and sang his song, and the kinsmen of the bridegroom answered in chorus. Every one who was mentioned in the song gave some present to the singer. Time was passed in this manner till night came on, and at dusk the bridegroom took chickens and prepared food for the bride's relations, slaughtered beasts for his own group, and one for the chief. The night was spent in drinking beer and singing. Some of the guests departed during the night, but others stayed till the morning.

On the day after the dance the host called all his clansmen, who were members of the same drum-circle and belonged to the same *akombo* and *iŋgɔl* group, to come in the early morning and slaughter the cow which he had brought out to show them the day before. The elders divided up the meat, and the host took the right foreleg, some salt, and a 'twenty', to send to the father or owner of the bride. Those who went with the leg of the marriage cow would be the brothers of the bridegroom, unless the capture had given rise to ill feeling and they were afraid to go, in which case one of their *igba* would be sent instead. These *igba* relations were of the utmost importance in the old days. When a man went on a journey it was with them that he could safely lodge, and it was often they who made peace when quarrels arose.

THE COMPENSATION

After a man had captured a wife, her family did not immediately come to see him. It was time for them to come when a child was born.[1] Then the owner of the girl (who might be her father or uncle, or whoever had the use of the *iŋgɔl*) came to his brother-in-law, who had captured his kinswoman and had children by her, and asked him to do what he could to help him, that he too might stop going down to drink at the well drumming on an empty gourd.[2] So the other spoke to his father, who sat and discussed the whole matter with his brothers. Then they took an *iŋgɔl*, a sister of the husband, and gave her to the owner of the woman. But if two daughters had been borne to you by your wife, her owner would take one of them, in addition to the woman who was given to him, saying that he wished to have two doors to enter, as well as you.[3] The owner of the girl did not do all this by himself. He obtained the support of one of his *igba* in that district. It was this man who conducted all the business, and afterwards handed the wife over to him; and if anything went wrong it was he who put matters right again. The owner of the *iŋgɔl* that had been captured had children by the wife who was given to him in exchange for her, and took the daughter of his *iŋgɔl* to exchange for a second wife for himself.

Whether a wife was obtained by payment, or was captured for nothing, the result was the same. In either case you had [eventually] to provide an *iŋgɔl* in compensation. But when the question was being discussed amongst friends of the same age, the man who had got a wife for nothing would say that he was the better of the

[1] Or children; see below. The significance of this is that until children had been born there was no case for an exchange; see p. 102.

[2] 'Drumming on the gourd' is expressive of the idle diversion of a bachelor who must go and fetch his own drinking water. Women do not draw water in a gourd, but in a pot.

[3] A separate house being built for each wife and her children. The daughters are potential wives by exchange, so, to make things even, each man takes one and thereby has the chance of acquiring two wives, the original wife and the one which he will get by exchanging the daughter. There was no definite age at which the child would be taken away, so long as she were old enough to leave her mother. Sometimes, if her owner was in no hurry to make an exchange, she would be left till after she had reached puberty.

two. He was, in fact, so handsome that he could get
women by dint of his good looks alone, whereas the other,
having no personal attractions, had to collect money and
pay for the woman to be caught, beaten, and handed over
to him. The man who had paid a bride-price, on the
other hand, would say that he was so rich that he did not
have to keep going backwards and forwards for the same
thing. He merely paid out the money and was rid of the
matter, so that he could turn his attention to something
else; whereas the other fellow had nothing better to do
than spend all his time on the road, till eventually the
girl gave in from sheer exhaustion. It was not a question
of good looks, but of dogged persistence. 'Nonsense,'
said the other. 'You people with the ugliest faces always
have the glibbest tongues. How can you have had more
to do than I have? I have captured a wife, So-and-so of
such-and-such a group, and the night was spent in
celebrations. I brewed beer for the marriage feast, and
slaughtered a cow. I have had children by her, and have
given a wife to her owner in compensation.' His opponent
replied that he had also obtained a wife, paid out money,
and done all the things that the other had. But people
said that the one who had got his wife for nothing was the
better man. The other, though he said he had married
a wife, had paid a price as though he were buying a slave.[1]

If his wife heard this she would say that rather than be
called a slave she would leave him to go and marry some
one for nothing, and be a free woman. For a cause such
as this alone a woman would certainly leave her husband
and return to her home, even though she might have borne
him many children. She would not go back to him,
however often he went to persuade her, but would marry
some one else without the payment of a bride-price. If
her owner had had children by her husband's *iŋgɔl*, they
would then transfer the exchange agreement to the
children.[2] The man who had got the woman for nothing,
having heard that this had been done, then gave her owner
another woman in exchange for her.[3] Thus the owner was

---

[1] Cf. p. 174.   [2] *Ve mase yamen sha uɔn.*
[3] In order, of course, to establish his claim to any children he might have by her.

able to build one house for this wife given as compensation, and could also obtain another wife by exchanging the daughter of the woman who had been given to him in exchange for his *iŋɔl* when she had gone to her original husband, so that he became possessed of many houses.[1]

If the woman remained with her second husband till she died, the matter ended; but if she lived on, it sometimes happened that after she had been with him many years, and even though she had borne several children to him and was growing old, she would suddenly go off to join the children that she had had by her first husband, whom she had formerly rejected, and left in order to marry the other. Her owner would say, 'Why are you causing me so much trouble, my *iŋɔl*? I gave you a husband and you rejected him, saying that you did not care for him. I had already had children by his *iŋɔl* which he gave me in exchange for you, and was very fond of her; yet when you insisted I gave her up in order that you should leave him, and we transferred the exchange agreement to the children, he keeping your children, and I those who had been borne to me by his *iŋɔl*. One of them I have exchanged for a wife. Moreover, the husband whom you married of your own free choice gave me a wife in exchange for you, and I have built her a house. And now you are going to change back again! Do you want to break up my home? I did what you wished, thinking to please you, but you do not like it, so what am I to do?' The woman answered, 'The female gives her life for her young. I will go back to my children, to die and be buried by them'.

THE *ISHEIKɔ* CONDITION

Formerly, if you captured a wife and did not give a woman in exchange for her, however much money you paid, her connexion with you was unrecognized.[2] If she bore you children they were said to be *isheikɔ*, that is to say, no exchange had been given for them. The owner of the *iŋɔl* could come and take them away, together with their mother, whenever he pleased. This held good long before the Tiv thought of marriage by capture, in the days when exchange

---

[1] = Wives.   [2] *Gbilin.*

was the only form of marriage they had. Here is an example:

Owners	_Aŋɔl_
Agaku	Adei
Abam	Dzendaun

Agaku takes his _iŋɔl_, Adei, and marries her to Abam, who gives him his _iŋɔl_, Dzendaun, in exchange. Before either of the two women have borne children Adei dies. Abam accuses Agaku of killing his _iŋɔl_.

Agaku denies that he is responsible for her death, so they resort to trial by ordeal. The draught is administered to chickens; Abam's chicken vomits the poison, Agaku's dies. Agaku, having thus lost his case, tells Abam to go home for the time being; meanwhile he will discuss the matter with his kinsmen, and let him know. He says that he is very fond of his wife and does not wish to lose her; he promises to give Abam another woman in exchange. But after Abam has left, Agaku pays no further attention to the matter, and goes on having children by his wife, Abam's _iŋɔl_, as though nothing had happened. So eventually Abam gets up and goes to him, and demands that he should be given those belonging to him, who are _isheikɔ_, since Agaku has given nothing for them. That is to say, he gave him a wife, but afterwards killed her. Every one would agree that Abam was right, and tell Agaku to stop making trouble. Thus both the mother and the children are _isheikɔ_. If the children are all female Abam will take every one, but if some are males he will take one of the daughters and give her to her brothers, because she is of the stem of their mother, and in order that they shall not at some future time fall victims to the sasswood at another woman's door. Their mother he will also leave, but nevertheless they are all said to be _isheikɔ_. If anything should happen to them, Abam's group would not forgive the group of Agaku.[1]

---

[1] Cf. Meek, art. cit. (referring to the procedure amongst the Kona on dissolution of marriage owing to an unsatisfactory exchange): 'As an act of grace one son might be left with the father. The other sons became the wards of their maternal uncle, who made himself responsible for their upbringing and for providing them with wives, _using when possible the lads' sisters as exchanges for this purpose._' The words italicized (by me) are very significant in the light of the Tiv 'true sister exchange' theory.

❡ *Ishe-i-kɔ* means literally 'unripe (i.e. unfulfilled) contract', and was applied, as shown above, to a woman who was in the anomalous position of having been taken as a wife by 'capture', or other means, but for whom no exchange had been given, or to the children of such a union. Until the exchange had been given, the marriage was not valid, and the 'husband' had no claim either to the woman or to the children. In the example given, the exchange contract had been completed, but one of the women had died. This, from the Tiv point of view, came to the same thing, because the owner and his group would be held responsible for her death unless they could prove their innocence. Although they had originally carried out their share of the contract by giving an *iŋgɔl*, they had subsequently withdrawn from it by 'taking her back again' (p. 253), that is to say, they had killed her (by magical means) for their own purposes. What these purposes were is described in the section on *tsav*. The owner of the other *iŋgɔl* was therefore quite justified in claiming back his unredeemed property, but in practice he might, as in the example, allow his *iŋgɔl* to stay with her unlawful husband, probably because at this stage he would in any case have little control over her. He might also renounce his claim to one of the daughters, in order that the sons should not be left without any means of obtaining a wife by exchange, and so 'fall victims to the sasswood at another woman's door'.

The meaning of this allusive phrase is as follows: The sons would probably choose to stay with their mother and natural father, where they would have a fair chance of establishing a position for themselves, although they were not recognized members of the group.[1] The owner of their mother was only concerned with the daughters, whom he needed for the purpose of exchange, and could not in any case compel the sons to go with him after they had reached a certain age. These sons, however, would be *isheikɔ*, and have no rights to the *aŋgɔl* belonging to the group in which they were living. Finding, therefore, that they had no chance of obtaining a wife by fair means, they might be tempted to bewitch the sons of another wife of their father (this is the meaning of 'another woman's door'), or other members of the same *iŋgɔl* group, in the hope of intimidating them into giving them one of their *aŋgɔl*. When one of the group fell ill,

[1] P. 129.

suspicion would accordingly fall on them; if the spell were not removed, and the sick man died, they would be forced to submit to trial by ordeal, and, being guilty, succumb. Although they had chosen to live with their natural parents, they were still technically members of their mother's group, who would hold their adopted group responsible for any harm that might come to them; so in any case it was better for all concerned that their mother's owner should act generously and allow them an *iŋɔl*, to avoid future trouble.

MARRIAGE BY PURCHASE

THIS was the form of marriage which built big villages. A wife by purchase was one that a man bought as a slave and then married. Women of this kind were mostly purchased from the Utyusha,[1] from the Dam, and from the more distant clans. Marriage by purchase did not take place within the group. The children by these marriages used often to have more power in their father's family than the children by exchange marriage, but when it was a question of standing it was the son by an exchange marriage who was considered the rightful heir. He was a true member of the group, and even though he might fall on evil times the home was still said to be his.

On the other hand, the child of a marriage by capture, for whose mother no exchange had been given, would always be considered as a sojourner, even though he might be more powerful than any one. If he were persecuted by his father's group, he might go away to live with his mother's owner, and become powerful there too. But his owner's[2] group would always treat him with contempt. 'He is only a woman's child,' they would say, 'and why does he come here putting on airs? Whose son is he here?' And when they started to have chiefs, the son of a marriage by capture was not appointed. His group said he was just a visitor, and they were not going to give the chieftainship to a man who might abscond with it and

---

[1] The name given to some of the southern Tiv clans.
[2] I.e. the man who owned the rights over his mother and any children she might have.

go to live amongst his mother's children;[1] the chief
should be a son by exchange marriage.

A son of an [unredeemed] marriage by capture would
not dare to look into an *akombo* bin, as, for example, the
Poor; but the son of a marriage by purchase could
become strong enough to put his hands on all these
things. He could be made chief, and could build an
akombo bin, because since his mother had been bought
for a price he had no place to which he could take away
the things of their land.

❡ The term 'marriage by purchase', as used here, roughly
translates the Tiv *kwase u sha uika* (woman in exchange for property), but has not the same meaning as the now somewhat
discredited anthropological term for the marriage of a free woman
in consideration of a bride-price, which corresponds rather to the
Tiv *kem* system. Although the form described is a true purchase,
it has not here been called slave marriage, as this is not the vernacular term. Moreover, a woman married in this way was, in
practice, no more a slave than the other wives, and her children
were in a better position than those of a free wife for whom no
exchange had been given. The advantages of this type of marriage
are clear. When a man had bought and paid for his wife there
could be no further argument, and he could 'build a big village',
that is, become the father of a large family, without fear of complications. Under the exchange system, the husband's hold on
his wife was not at all secure. He had her, as it were, on loan
from her group, to whom he was in a measure responsible. He
could 'play with the body, but not the head'. His children could
always appeal to their mother's group against their father's group,
and many of the rites could only be carried out by elders from
their mother's home. Moreover, if the woman he had given in
exchange misbehaved herself, proved barren, or died, he was
liable, in default of finding a substitute, to lose not only his wife,
but his children as well. But a woman bought as slave (from a
conveniently remote district) belonged to him unconditionally,

---

[1] Chieftainship is conceived not merely as an abstract idea, but as being
inseparable from the insignia which always go with it. So if he carried off the
symbols and magic apparatus, he would take the chieftainship itself. There
are many tales founded on this theme in Africa, e.g. *Stories of Old Adamawa*,
p. 77.

and if anything went wrong he was not responsible for her to any one. The children, having no *igba*, felt themselves the more completely members of, and dependent on, their father's group. They could safely be trusted with the 'things of the land', that is, the arcana of the *akombo* rites, chieftainship, and so forth, without fear of their transferring their allegiance to their mother's clan, as in the case of the children of a *kem* marriage or an unredeemed marriage by capture.

Summing up, the real difference between the Tiv marriage systems is this: The *kem* form gave the husband only the right to cohabit with the woman, and no claim whatever to the children. This also applied to marriage by capture until it was redeemed by an exchange. Exchange marriage carried with it also a right to the children, provided that an equivalent number was borne by the *iŋgɔl*, but no rights over the woman's life, which still belonged to the original owner. (For this reason, if she fell ill, she had to be sent back to her own group to be 'set right'. If the husband failed to do this, he was accounted responsible for her death.) In marriage by purchase the ownership of the woman was transferred unconditionally to the husband, body and soul, with all rights to any children she might afterwards bear.

CHANGES

IN later years the Tiv ceased to regard their traditions, and looked only for a man of ability, who would take good care of their land,[1] and be generous with his hospitality. So whether he were the son of exchange marriage, or of a marriage by purchase or capture, if he became strong enough, it was all the same to them. He lived his life as he pleased, and people would say amongst themselves, 'So-and-so rides the high horse in his group, because there is no one else'. But if it were the son of [an unredeemed] marriage by capture who attained to such a state of affluence in his own group, those who had the rights over him[2] would always say, 'He may be strong, but he has not redeemed himself. However powerful he may be, no man is invulnerable, and we will arrange with some one to kill him'. So he would be afraid,

---

[1] Magically speaking.   [2] *Mba nan lu ishe ve.*

and take one of his *aŋɔl* to redeem himself. After this he could live his life amongst his kinsmen with an easy conscience.

THE ABOLITION OF EXCHANGE MARRIAGE

As the Tiv added to the number of different forms of marriage, so their troubles increased. Administrative officers, chiefs and judges were continually harassed by marriage suits. Every case was connected with a woman. Even to-day, if you were to take all the cases that are tried in Tivland, you would find that three out of four were disputes about women, and that in the remaining one, if you looked into it carefully, a woman was also involved. In the days before the coming of the Europeans women were at the bottom of most of the wars which were fought amongst the Tiv, and even at the time when the white man appeared they were giving rise to much troublesome litigation. One man would say, 'I made an exchange marriage with So-and-so. His *iŋɔl* died, and when I consulted the divining chain he was shown to be guilty. But when I asked him to give me another woman he refused. I have therefore brought my complaint to the chief, and demand that he be arrested and made to hand over the *iŋɔl* which I gave him when the exchange was made'. Another would complain, 'I gave So-and-so some money for a wife. He has spent the money, but has not handed over the woman'. The white man or the native court sent policemen to arrest the defendant. When he was brought in he might say that the other had not paid what he stated, and give a different account of the matter. Witnesses had therefore to be found, but these often did not tell the truth, because each would give evidence in favour of his friend, and a settlement was reached only after the greatest difficulty.

Another, again, would bring the following case: 'So-and-so of such-and-such a group owes me a debt of long standing, but when I go and ask for payment he merely threatens to beat me.' When the reason for the debt was investigated it was found to have its origin in a marriage question. Sometimes a man would bring a

M

complaint about an old contract which was made by his father years and years ago, before he was born. Cases were unending. Another kind was: 'So-and-so took my *iŋɔl* for nothing, and gave no woman in exchange. When she had borne children to him, I asked him, even if he could not fulfil the contract, to give me one of my *iŋɔl's* daughters to exchange for a wife, but he refused and adopted a threatening attitude. Being unable to do any more, I have come to court to claim the return of my *iŋɔl* and all the children.' Murders were also committed over the question of women, and many other complications arose as a result of the Tiv marriage systems. For this reason the white men living amongst the Tiv resolved to allow them to have one form of mariage only, and abolish all others.

In the year 1927, therefore, the European officers in charge of Tiv country met together at Abinsi and called in the District Heads and their courts, together with all the chief men from every clan. After welcoming them, they told them that the reason why they had come together was that they wished all the Tiv to agree with them to adopt one form of marriage only, and do away with the rest. When the Tiv heard this their hearts sank, for it seemed to them a great disaster. 'Now I have told you,' said the white man, 'so think it over well and then let me know.' It was at this time that Chief Ugba had just been deported to Kaduna,[1] and for this reason the chiefs were particularly frightened of the white man, because they thought that if they did not do as he wished he would take them away to Kaduna as well. And to add to their fears, Captain ——, the very man who had seized Ugba and sent him to Kaduna, was on the council!

So the Tiv were in a state of great agitation. For many days after the white man had asked them to declare which form of marriage they wished to choose, they were unable to find an answer. The white man, however, had set his heart on having only the *kem* marriage by payment of money, and abolishing all other kinds. When the Tiv learnt this they said that they could not abandon marriage

[1] P. 397.

by exchange, because this was the immemorial custom of the tribe, and because it was at the door of the exchange wife that they set up the *akombo*, in order that the crops should be good, the women give birth, and the land prosper. If they were to give up exchange marriage the land would be spoilt, the women would cease to bear children, and the crops would fail. The white man told them to explain to him all their different forms of marriage, and they did so. He heard them all, but inclined most to the *kem* form.

Now about this time the young men had lately returned from the work of making the railway, and having plenty of money in their hands were also much in favour of the *kem* marriage, so that the only dissentients were a few of the chiefs. Thus the opinion of the people was divided, some demanding marriage by exchange, and others the *kem* form. The matter reached a deadlock, and the discussion went on for about seven days. Mue Ityɔka- tyever, the Chief of Ukan, told me that the proposals which were being discussed were so distasteful to him that he was at a loss to know how to act. So he shammed illness. When they got up from the council he affected to stagger right in front of the white man, as though he were about to fall on his face, in order that the white man should think he was unwell and refrain from plaguing him with questions. The next day, at the time when the council was due to sit, he sent a message to say that he had not slept a wink. He had pains in the back and stomach, and had spent the night vomiting. He was therefore unable to attend the conference. The white man believed this story, as he had seen that Mue was not well the evening before when he left the council. By this means he avoided attendance at the meeting that day. What annoyed him most, he said, was that he realized the white man was seeking the truth, and wanted to tell him, but knew quite well that if he explained the facts in their true light there were fools present who would get up and contradict everything he said, and give an entirely different account; whereupon the white man, seeing that they were many and spoke with one voice, whereas he was alone with a handful of supporters, would give more credence to the opinion of the others.

With so many chiefs divided in counsel a solution seemed difficult, when an incident occurred to hasten their decision. While the conference was in progress a number of motor lorries came in from Makurdi and stopped near by. As to why they were brought, who knows? Thereupon the officials in the white man's employ told the Tiv that these lorries had been sent for them. If they did not finish their argument and come to an agreement, they would all be put inside and taken to Kaduna, where they would have to stay, together with Ugba, and never come back to Tivland again. Directly they heard the name Kaduna, the few chiefs who till then had held out against the *kem* marriage gave in, and all agreed unanimously to have the *kem* and no other kind. The white man then recorded the consent of the Tiv, and told them how they were to arrange the marriages. Nevertheless, all the laws which he laid down were those which had been observed by the Tiv in connexion with the *kem* for a long time before.

When the chiefs dispersed and returned to their districts they found themselves in trouble with their clansmen, who said, 'The chiefs have been down to meet the white man at riverside, and completely spoilt the land! Ever since the white man came he has never done anything so disastrous to our country as this'. There was general indignation against the chiefs. People said that they were paid by the white man, and because they had the money they supported the *kem* marriage. The chiefs denied this, declaring that it was the white man who had forbidden exchange marriage and ordered the *kem*; they themselves had no say in the matter.

So there has been lamentation amongst the Tiv to the present day. Wherever you go in Tivland you hear the same thing, 'The white man has spoilt the land! If he wishes that our land shall prosper he must permit two forms of marriage'. The forms which they wish, in order that the land may be good, are marriage by exchange and marriage by capture. They point out that in marriage by capture, though the man gets his wife for nothing, her owner is always given a woman in exchange when he comes to ask for one, so that each gets a wife in the end. If you say, 'Very well, then, take your *iŋɔl* and get a bride-price for her, then take the money and *kem* a wife with it. Won't you both have wives then?' they reply, 'No. It will not do. Suppose you take your *iŋɔl* and give her to some one to *kem*. He gives you a cow, and you turn it out to graze. While you are looking for a wife the cow may die, and you are left with nothing. The other man has your *iŋɔl* and gets children by her, while you dare not take away even one child.[1] If you were to do so in these days, the white man would not spare you. So you must remain destitute. Or, again, the man to whom you give your *iŋɔl* may pay the bride-price in cash, and you set this aside while you go in search for a wife. But meanwhile your child may fall ill, and on consulting the diviner you learn that an *akombo* is the cause of his sickness. You go home and put your hand into the money, take a little to buy a chicken, or a larger beast if the nature of the *akombo* demands it, in order that it may be set right and your child cured of his illness. Once some of the money has been spent it is no longer sufficient to pay a bride-price, and is soon wasted to no purpose. The other man has your *iŋɔl*, and you have nothing'. This is the reason, they say, why there have been so many deaths in recent years. A man gives his *iŋɔl* away in marriage in return for a cow or for cash. The money disappears, his brother-in-law has children by his *iŋɔl*, and he is left without anything. Thereupon in the bitterness of his heart he proceeds to kill his *iŋɔl*, or her children, by witchcraft, saying that if he must be desolate his brother-in-law shall be desolate also.

They always say, too, that they have given up trial by ordeal because the white man has forbidden it, but this question of exchange marriage they will never drop. At first some tried to evade the law, but circumstances were too strong for them. Some refused to give away their daughters for a bride-price, though they were already

[1] Cf. p. 155.

marriageable, saying that they would keep them until the law against exchange marriage was repealed, and then obtain wives with them. They waited and waited till they could hold out no longer, and then in despair gave them away for a price, with a sob in their throat.

For the old men the most galling aspect of the matter is that when exchange marriage was forbidden the young girls would have nothing to do with them. Under the old system an elder who had an *iŋɔl* could always marry a young girl, however senile he might be, even though he were a leper with no hands or feet; no girl would dare to refuse him. If another man were attracted by his *iŋɔl* he would take his own and give her to the old man by force, in order to make an exchange. The girl had to go with the old man, sorrowfully carrying his goat-skin bag. If she ran back to her home her owner caught her and beat her, then bound her and brought her back to the elder. The old man was pleased, and grinned till he showed his blackened molars. 'Wherever you go,' he told her, 'you will be brought back here to me; so stop worrying, and settle down as my wife.' The girl fretted, till she wished the earth might swallow her. Some women even stabbed themselves to death when they were given to an old man against their will; but, in spite of all, the Tiv did not care.

So when the white man made it illegal to give a woman in marriage without her consent, and laid down that marriage payments should only be made by a man if the girl herself accepted him, there was great rejoicing amongst the women and young men. Nowadays, if one of the older men ventures to speak to a young girl, she snaps her fingers at him and tells him to stop talking nonsense, for the women are no longer slaves as they used to be. In the old days, she says, their owners could give them away by force, but now the white man has put a stop to slavery, and has said they can do just as they please. If they like a man they can marry him, if not they can refuse; the days of compulsion are over. So the old men are loud in their lamentations, complaining that the white man has spoilt the land, and that the women are insolent. The girls reply, 'The dance is merriest when the dancers are of the same age. Let the old men run after the old women, and leave us to find husbands amongst the companions of our youth'. The women say that this is the best thing the white man has done since he came. Instead of being slaves, they are now free women. The young men are also glad that there is no more exchange marriage. In the past, they say, the old men had got above themselves!

So the women and youths, and all those who have grown up since the coming of the European, are of one mind about this. But there is one more thing that they would like, and that is that there should be not only the *kem* marriage by payment of money, but also marriage by capture, without payment, under the *iye* system. As to exchange marriage, they say, when the present generation of old men has died off, it will be forgotten. When the old men hear this they say, 'The white man has spoilt the land!' Whenever they come together for a big tribal council, the elders are fully expecting to hear that the white man has decided to repeal the law against exchange marriage, while the young men are all agog for the news that he is going to allow them to go out on the *iye* and get wives for nothing. But the white man has never opened his mouth to speak of any of these matters on which they have set their hearts.

❡ The adjustment of the Tiv marriage systems is probably the biggest problem with which the Administration has been faced in its relations with the tribe, and that which has had the most far-reaching results. It arose, like most other problems in modern Africa, directly and indirectly from the clash of two different cultures and moral standards. Akiga has accurately described the reactions on the two opposite sections of tribal society. I propose briefly to consider the facts from the European side. The proposal to change the Tiv marriage customs was first made by the Dutch Reformed Church Mission on the grounds that these were not in accordance with Christian principles. From the practical point of view, the existing laws bore hardly on the Christian community; the youths were unable to get wives, and the women had no power to marry according to their natural inclinations or religious convictions. On general grounds it was urged that there was no certified permanency; that young men were unable to obtain wives at a desirable age, which led to much immorality and abduction; and that a woman might have several successive husbands, thus bringing the destruction of home life and suffering to the children.

The news that a change was in the air quickly spread to every part of Tiv country, and deputations of men and women who were dissatisfied with the old system waited on the District Officer to demand its abolition. It was thought by some that unless action were taken, serious disturbances might follow. Added to this there was a strong practical consideration: the amount of litigation resulting from so many different and complicated systems had become so enormous that the courts had time to deal with little else. From the European point of view, then, there were good grounds for abolishing exchange marriage, and when this move appeared to have the support of a large section of the people there seemed little to stand in the way of a much needed reform. The decision was generally welcomed in European circles as a most important social advance.

But the opinion generally held to-day by those who have had an opportunity of observing the effects of the change is that the step taken was too big. 'A gradual adjustment and the elimination of unsatisfactory features, after full inquiry, would have been far better for the tribe than the sudden abolition of exchange marriage.'[1] 'The basic foundation of the Tiv social system was abolished.'[2] It implied that in future, according to ancient custom, no marriage would be ratified, and no man would have a moral

[1] Captain R. M. Downes, Annual Report, 1934.
[2] Mr. E. S. Pembleton, 1933. The following are some more opinions extracted from reports or comments on the subject by administrative officers: 'The demand for the abolition of exchange marriages comes largely, I imagine, from individuals who do not want to carry out their part of the bargain; and is backed by district chiefs who are tired of excessive court work arising principally in connexion with claims for the custody of children' (Dr. C. K. Meek, 1927). 'The question was never considered in relation to the social organization of the Tiv generally. . . . The practical question which arises now is how are we to expect the *tors* and their elders to enforce an exotic system they don't approve of?' (Captain J. J. Emberton, 1932; endorsed by Mr. Pembleton). 'The remedy was too drastic. A simplification of the many different variations of marriage, and not the abolition of the fundamental one, would perhaps have been a wiser step for the District Heads to have advocated' (Mr. A. B. Matthews, 1934; endorsed by Mr. Pembleton).

right to his children. It also shook the spiritual life of the tribe, because with the end of exchange marriage the greatest of the family cults, which were closely bound up with it, lost their true purpose and significance. It will be seen, however, that the harm done in this respect is probably not so great as the elders imagine (p. 193, 4).

But the most profound effects of the change have been indirect. It drove the first wedge into the crack which had just begun to make its appearance between the old generation and the new, and which was itself due to causes brought about by our arrival, such as the beginnings of education and facilities for travel, and the newly found economic independence of the young men, who had been working for the European and were disposed to regard their wages as personal rather than family property. The abolition of exchange brought about two interacting results: On the one hand, it was a heavy blow to the prestige of the elders, who had lost the case to their renegade children. The practice which they had upheld as an integral part of the tribal life was declared a criminal offence. At first, having no property except the women of their family, they could not get wives, while some of those whom they had, being released from the constraint of the exchange system, ran away from them. They had only one weapon with which to enforce their authority, but it was a powerful one, namely the fear of witchcraft, and they proceeded to use it to the greatest possible effect against those who were the cause of their troubles. The younger generation, on the other hand, had gained a great victory, which led them to believe that the white man was the champion of youth against traditional authority, and gave them confidence to defy the elders. These two factors working together were largely responsible, two years later, for the rising of the young against the power of the old which is described below (p. 275 et seq.).

There is doubtless some truth in Akiga's cynical remark that the white man had already made up his mind when he asked the people to choose. A solution had to be found, and the only arguments that the elders could bring against the change—that the women would cease to bear children, &c.—did not carry much weight against more practical considerations. It may be that the Tiv themselves did not see the full implications at the time; it is certain, not only that their opinion was asked, but that there was a strong movement in favour of the bride-price system, led by the younger generation, but also backed by some of the chiefs and salaried officials, who doubtless, as their critics alleged, saw that it would work to their personal advantage. It certainly never had the support of those whom we now recognize as the true leaders of the tribe. Probably, as Akiga says, it was started by young men of the type that had been working on the new railway. Here they had seen the bride-price system practised by other tribes, and came back to their own country with money enough to get a wife, but no means of using it. Many of these, and others who had left home to seek work under the European, had spoilt their chances of being given a wife in the normal way by deliberately cutting themselves off from their own groups. For the same reason it was they who were the most articulate, and in the best position to make their opinions heard. But whichever section of tribal society played the greatest part in bringing about the downfall of the old system, it is certain that now the blame is invariably laid on the shoulders of the white man.

The difference in moral standards which led to our interference in the Tiv marriage customs is due ultimately to the conflict of two ideals, the communal and the individualistic. To us it is intolerable that a woman should be forced to marry a man for whom she feels no affection, and inhuman that a man should be content to accept almost any wife as an exchange, 'so long as she was capable of bearing children and had a good character'. We could not sanction a custom which permitted children to be taken away from their mothers, or wives from their husbands, to satisfy a theory of inter-group justice. Yet, although with the Tiv individual preferences must be subordinate to the interests of the community, it would be wrong to suppose that under the exchange system a woman was a mere chattel. Her status was far higher than, for instance, in Muhammadan tribes, which use the bride-price. She had complete control of the food supply, and her authority in domestic affairs was hardly questioned. She held an honourable position as the true representative of her husband's sister, to bear children and carry on the direct line from his mother. At the same time his group was responsible for her safety and well-being to the group to whom they had given one of their own members. If things went wrong (which to the Tiv implied supernatural interference, usually directed by human agency) they were bound to send her back to the protection of her own group, who in turn were liable to lose their own wife if the cause of the trouble were not removed.

It is possible also that we have overstressed the evils inherent in equalization of children. The practice only applied to the daughters, who would have to leave home in any case as soon as they reached puberty. In theory, at least, there was no reason why they should be taken away before this, so long as their owner's group had asserted its claim to use them for making an exchange marriage, and in practice they were often allowed to grow up with their parents. It is true that girls were sometimes sent to the group of their future husbands before they had reached a marriageable age, but this practice is equally liable to happen under any system of marriage by consideration.

Besides its disregard of personal feelings, the Tiv exchange marriage system was unsatisfactory because it compelled the younger members of the family to remain bachelors till comparatively late in life, and thus led to irregular unions and forcible wife-capture. In point of fact, this had already been recognized by the Tiv themselves before we came, and a partial remedy had been found. The invention of the *iye* agreement was perhaps the most brilliant piece of inter-clan collaboration and collective legislation which the tribe has yet achieved, and shows that they are, by themselves, capable of adapting old forms to new conditions, when the necessity arises. Up to a point, and so long as the rules were observed, the *iye* was almost an ideal form of marriage. It gave an equal chance to every one to procure a wife for himself. It allowed real freedom of choice for both individuals, and provided the romance necessary to veil the more sordid aspects of the contract, yet at the same time was carried out with the approval of society, and, almost always, the connivance of the girl's parents. By the proviso of an eventual exchange, it took into account the interests of all sections of the community. The rule that the presents should be given afterwards eliminated the mercenary element in most African marriage; and, finally, it made a virtue of necessity by regularizing the practice of woman-stealing which it had become impossible to control. Unfortunately, it could not be preserved, because it was ultimately dependent on the exchange system. Sooner or later an exchange had to be given, and this second match was of necessity a *mariage de convenance*. Only half the women of the tribe could marry the men they chose.

By stating these few points in extenuation of the old forms, there is no intention to suggest that reform was not needed, or even that the old system was capable of more than temporary modification. Eventually exchange marriage had to go: it could never have survived the changing conditions, the increasing claims of the individual to recognition, and the growing independence of the younger generation. The break-down of the system was in reality the result of factors which had no apparent connexion with it. One of these was our appointment of chiefs and clan courts with executive powers. Before our arrival there were no legal means of divorce, but a woman who was unhappy with her husband would run back to her own group. She would, of course, be returned, because otherwise the exchange would break down; but if she were sufficiently persistent she must get her own way in the end, as in Akiga's illuminating example of the woman whose unreasonable attitude caused so much trouble to her unfortunate owner (p. 155). If the evil were serious enough it provided its own remedy. But with the introduction of clan authorities and a Native Administration police force the unhappy wife had no chance; she would be compelled to return, however often she escaped.

Formerly, the number of wives which a man could have was limited by the women whom his group had available for exchange and by the demands of the other male members in it, so that distribution was comparatively even. The selfish practice of collecting large numbers of wives at the expense of the rest of the group was started by the chiefs, and would have been impossible without the authority given to them by us. The establishment of district and provincial courts encouraged hundreds of litigants to make claims which in the old days they would never have thought of pressing, or would have settled amicably between themselves.[1] It was this that brought about the downfall of the *iye* system. As soon as a lad had eloped with his bride, her parents followed on his heels with a complaint to the authorities, demanding immediate compensation or return. A payment had to be made at once, and an exchange given later. If not, the girl was forcibly sent back. Thus the critics had good grounds for complaining of impermanency and immorality. But this could never have happened without our intervention. Formerly the claim was made after a

[1] See Akiga's example on p. 119, which is a model of good sense and courtesy.

decent interval, when children had been born, and even then could never have been enforced against another clan, except by friendly agreement. One may be certain that the husband's group would make every effort to find an exchange, as otherwise they would eventually lose the children. As for exchange itself, the charge against it should not be of impermanency, but of over-rigidity.

It is idle now to speculate whether the Tiv would have found a way to meet these changed circumstances if left to themselves. Possibly the initiative would have to have come from without. The question now is what they will make of the system we have suggested to them. A few notes on this system and its immediate results are here set down for the sake of completeness.[1] On July 15th, 1927, marriage by payment of a bride-price became the only recognized form of marriage, and all other forms were declared illegal. At first the maximum price was fixed at £5 for a virgin and £4 for other categories, but at present there is no such limit. Existing exchange marriages were not interfered with, but in the case of an incomplete contract the affair was regularized by payment, so much for the wife, and so much for the children. Women were not to be given in marriage against their will, or before they reached the age of puberty.

These regulations had the effect of eliminating some of the abuses of the previous systems, but unfortunately had the immediate result of introducing certain fresh evils. Some of these have already been remedied by legislation, others will need time and education to eradicate. They are chiefly due to the fact that the people still interpret the new form of marriage in terms of the old. Thus the first tendency was to make marriage less stable. Whereas in exchange it had been too difficult for a woman to obtain release from an unhappy marriage, under the bride-price system she was inclined to leave her husband on the slenderest grounds; for in the past this type of marriage had always been of a temporary and provisional nature. She was no longer sent back by her group, because it was to their material advantage that she should have as many suitors as possible, and if she had borne a child they felt that the group to whom she had been married already had the

[1] For much of the information that follows, I am indebted to members of the present administrative staff, who have studied the results of the change at first hand.

advantage. From the husband's point of view, an unsatisfactory aspect was that he had to pay the full and final price for a woman whose potentialities as a child-bearer were unknown. This was obviated in the *iye* by not giving the exchange till she had proved herself fertile, and even a regular exchange was not ratified until children had been born on both sides. As to the women, for whose sake the change was largely made, they have undoubtedly benefited in that they have gained their independence, and are, in theory at least, free to choose their own husbands; but it should not be forgotten that, as long as the old ideas persist, they cannot rise to the same honourable position in their husband's group as a true sister exchange wife, nor claim the group's spiritual protection.[1]

Another regrettable result of the change, which seems inevitable in everything we touch, is that the Tiv marriage contract has now become much commercialized. Amongst many peoples whose custom it is to pay a bride-price the transaction is by no means equivalent to a sale of property, and the sordid aspect of it is usually discreetly veiled, but amongst the Tiv it will be remembered that formerly the only lasting form of marriage by purchase was slave marriage, and this idea is not yet dead. The attitude of the 'owner' towards his *iŋgɔl* has not changed. He still regards her as an asset: formerly she was a potential exchange wife for himself or his sons; now he is inclined to value her, not more honourably, in terms of cash. The people themselves are fully aware of this weakness in their character, and at the last tribal council there was an almost unanimous demand to mitigate the mercenary aspect of the marriage contract by limiting the bride-price to a maximum of £2.

[1] In this connexion, K. Dewar writes: 'It is here that the real secret of the failure of bride-price marriage lies. Even supposing ideal conditions, namely the wife being fond of the husband and her guardian giving full support to the match, such marriages are apt to break down from this cause. Everything goes well until some disaster, possibly quite a minor one, befalls the wife or her child. Not being a member of the husband's group, she cannot go to the group elders for treatment or satisfactory diagnosis—or if she does go she goes without that *sine qua non* of "magical" cure, faith—and eventually goes home for treatment. She probably returns a little later satisfied, but before long suffers a recurrence of the illness or some other minor disaster. When this has happened two or three times it gets on her mind; she is always seeing evil omens and feeling imaginary pains and comes to the conclusion that, unprotected as she is, she is living in a group containing unknown ominous and hostile forces. Thus the idea that she must get out of that group before long becomes dominant in her mind to the exclusion of other considerations, such as the attachment which she may still feel towards her husband.'

Nevertheless, should it appear that the unfortunate aspects of the change have been unduly stressed, it must be pointed out that in their present state of development marriage by payment of a bride-price was practically the only alternative. During the short time that it has been in force the people have already begun to find solutions to the problems which confront them. The younger men and women are mostly satisfied with the new conditions, and even some of the older people are becoming reconciled. The direct effect on the ordinary life of the tribe has not been as great as might be expected from the drastic nature of the step taken, and the fact that such a revolutionary measure could be carried through without active opposition is an indication of the confidence of the tribe in its present Administration. Hope of the ultimate development of a satisfactory form of marriage lies in the spread of Christianity, bringing with it a higher view of the status of women, and the growth of Christian ideals to replace the old sanctions.

IV.

AKOMBO

⊏, This section, dealing with Tiv magico-religious practices, does not profess, even in the original, to give a complete account of all the cults, of which there are a large number in common use. Akiga mentions fifty-three in his manuscript, and this does not nearly exhaust the list. Here only a few typical examples have been chosen, including the more important, and a few notes are added to supplement Akiga's account, with the object of explaining the nature of the Tiv beliefs from within, rather than of discussing the general magic principles involved, which can be done more ably by others in a different type of work.

It is not easy to give a clear account of the subject, because the attitude of the Tiv themselves towards it is very indefinite, both in theory and in practice, and the manner of conducting the rites and the reasons given vary greatly, not only between clans, but even between individual elders. Therefore Akiga's descriptions, the details of which have been collected with considerable trouble and cross-checking from all parts of Tiv country, should not be condemned as untrustworthy if some are contradicted by other informants. The Tiv have been called reticent or deliberately misleading, but more often it seems that even the older men, who should know, are uncertain not only of the meaning of the rites, as is to be expected, but also of their form and purpose. There is nothing secret about the cults themselves, and so long as an informant is satisfied that his inquirer has no ulterior motive he is willing to discuss them as readily as farming, or hunting, or any other aspect of his everyday life, of which indeed they form an inseparable part. Even the 'mysteries' are precluded only from the sight and touch of the uninitiated, not from their knowledge.

To the vast majority of the tribe the practices are nothing but an empty formula, of which the true meaning has been forgotten. European investigators, arguing from internal evidence, such as the relics, emblems and forms used, and from knowledge of cognate races, have justly assumed that the Tiv magico-religious system is based on a cult of ancestors. But, to be honest, the people themselves, with very few exceptions, know nothing of this.

PLATE I

a. A Tiv village (see p. 15)

b. Building corn stores (see p. 53)

PLATE II

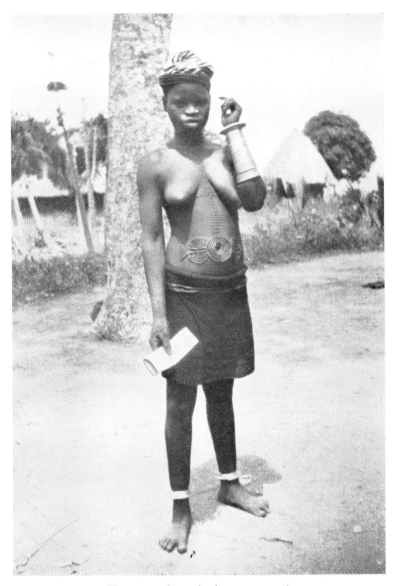

The stomach marks (see pp. 42–44)

PLATE III

Millet stacked in the *ate* (see pp. 61–62)

PLATE IV

a. Pounding corn (see Chapter II)

b. At the water-hole (see p. 144)

PLATE V

a. Dance of the young men (see Chapter III)

b. The marriage dance (see Chapter III)

PLATE VI

The *itumbyu* rite (see pp. 303–5)

PLATE VII

b. The *ihambe-icigh* (see pp. 189–94)

a. One of the last guardians of the old knowledge
(see pp. 176–80)

PLATE VIII

b. Childhood (see pp. 305–8)

a. The *twel* (see pp. 188–94)

PLATE IX

a. Market day (see p. 222)

b. The band (see pp. 150–2)

PLATE X

Flint and steel (see p. 358)

PLATE XI

a. Poor skulls and *imborivuŋgu* pipes (see p. 278)

b. A trial (see pp. 373–9)

PLATE XII

a. 'The White Man's Chief' (see pp. 383–403)

b. The tribal council (see p. 410)

To them an *akombo*, that is the actual object over which the rites are performed, is a force in itself. The sprinkling of the blood and the beer is now no more than a purely magical act which influences the *akombo* in such a way that the cause of the trouble is removed: 'Health is in the blood of the chicken.' Only a few, chiefly the very old men—the generation which will in a few years be gone—understand that the true meaning of the rite is a gift of food to the 'fathers who are under the soil', and even this is little more to them than a form of words. It is doubtful even whether any seriously believe that the dead have a continued individual existence, except in the sense already explained that they are represented collectively by the group which is descended from them.

Even the old men seem to feel a sense of unreality in the ancestral rites. One confessed that it was like calling down a road after a man who had passed out of sight: you could not say where he was, or if he could hear you; all you knew for certain about him was the direction in which he had gone. The same applies to dreams. The fact that a special rite is prescribed in cases where a man is troubled by dreams of a departed parent, and this also takes the form of a libation, is clear evidence of a former belief in the possible return of the spirits of the dead and their effective interference in human affairs. There are practices connected with burial which point to the same thing (p. 332). But none of these customs can be taken as proof that the people have a well-defined belief in survival or return of the dead now, and in the face of their own generally expressed testimony to the contrary, they can, I think, only be regarded as survivals. Nowadays the attitude of the normal Tiv towards these practices and experiences is purely formal. To dream of the dead is attributed to memory of the past, and the influence of the revenant is only considered effective in that it reminds the dreamer of the wishes and injunctions of his father while he was still alive. The lack of terms is at least a negative indication of the absence of clear thinking on this subject. There is no word for spirit except *jijiŋgi* (shadow), and this could not be used for a dream phantom. It is occasionally used of the soul which passes from a dead man into the womb of his son's wife, or the wife of his grandson, to be reborn in one of his descendants; but this trace of the Bantu reincarnation beliefs remains now as little more than a figure of

N

speech, and the familiar conception of a country of the dead, usually pictured as being under the earth, lives only in folk-lore.

Some of the rites are in their origin undoubtedly directed to procuring the goodwill of the ancestors, and their favourable co-operation in the affairs of the living. The most conspicuous of the public cults of this kind is the *Poor*, whose ritual centred round an ancestor's skull kept as a sacred relic, and of the family cults, the *Twel* and *Ihambe-icigh* group, which will be shown to have had special reference to the spirit of the mother. But not all the *akombo* can be explained in this way. Many of the so-called 'birth *akombo*' appear to be nothing more than the personification, or rather representation (for they are regarded merely as undefined 'forces'), of various evils which may afflict the human race. Some are diseases, such as *Igbe* (dysentery), *Akombo-a-dam* (syphilis), *Ikuŋgu* (epilepsy);[1] others are physical phenomena, like *Ahumbe* (the stormwind) and *Wanaɔndo* (the thunderbolt). There seems to be a confusion between two types of beliefs or rites, the one essentially religious and the other more magical in character, which must once have been, at least in function, quite distinct. The word *akombo* is now used as a general term for all the cults and objects, and the prevailing idea contained in it is always of an evil which is liable to attack a man's person or property and must be brought under control by magical means.

This is true of the ancestral as well as of the purely 'defensive' cults. For example, the *Ihambe-icigh*, whose ritual bears unmistakable signs of having been directed towards the immediate forerunners of the group, is associated with a skin-disease called *icigh*, and other ailments and misfortunes of which it is said to be the cause. The *Poor* (*Biamegh*) mentioned above, which is connected primarily with hunting, may attack the hunter and cause him to lose his way in the bush. So also with the rest of them. Their influence is almost entirely negative; all would be well if it were not for their intervention. A man's normal condition is one

---

[1] The ailments attributed to the maleficence of each *akombo* do not, however, necessarily coincide with the symptoms of any one disease according to a European diagnosis. For instance, of the *Agashi* Akiga writes: 'This is the cause of the sunken nose and all sorts of other deformities. It dries up a man's throat, so that he suffers from a permanent cough in the chest and makes him weaker and weaker, till finally it kills him.' The *Atseŋge* 'attacks children and prevents them becoming strong. They always remain weak and sickly, and grow soft, straight hair on their heads'. The *Ikòmbo* 'causes a red skin, soft hair and a furrow in the skull'.

of good health, the nature of woman is to bear children and of the soil to produce good crops. The *akombo* are liable to interfere with the course of nature, and if any disease or misfortune occurs, or even if the optimum is not being attained, as, for instance, in the case of child-birth or harvest, the offending *akombo* must be isolated by divination and 'set right' (*sɔr*). If the victim wishes to be saved from any further visitation of this particular *akombo*, he may, if he has the means to do so, bring it under his control (*kɔr*). These two fundamental ideas underlying Tiv magic are fully illustrated in what follows. The point that it is wished to emphasize here is that, whatever may have been the significance of the rites in the past, their main object now is not to obtain the support of the ancestors or of any other supernatural power in acquiring prosperity or success, but to neutralize or take precautions against potential evils. Although the positive aspect of the greater cults may appear to survive in the often-repeated formula, 'That the land may be good, the women bear children, &c.', in the context the words always imply that previously the Universe had got somewhat out of man's control. This aspect of Tiv magic is stressed in this book wherever *akombo* are mentioned, but is shown with especial clearness in the descriptions of the purging of circumcision candidates, and of women at the time of conception.

It may also be noticed that in the descriptions of some of the practices there are faint traces of a third type of cult, connected with the sun and moon. But except for the words used in incantations, 'The Moon is a maiden, the Sun a boy', which are now meaningless, and the custom of throwing a little of the ceremonial food to the east and west, these beliefs, if ever they existed, are now forgotten.

It would seem, then, that at one time the cult of ancestors had a more vital and independent existence, and that it has become confused with, and subordinated to, a type of maleficent animatism,[1] which now pervades the whole of Tiv magico-religious thought. These two forms of belief are common to most West African peoples, and may perhaps in origin be different aspects of the same idea, a 'vital animating principle which permeates men, animals and matter'.[2] In support of this theory, it should be

---

[1] 'Animatism' (a word coined by Dr. R. R. Marett) 'is the attribution of life and personality to things, but not of a separate or apparitional soul': *Notes and Queries on Anthropology.*

[2] J. H. Driberg, *At Home with the Savage*, p. 182.

noted that the essential ritual, namely the offering of blood and
beer, is the same for all, and is religious in form, though magic
in purpose. That is to say, no distinction is made in treatment
between the spirits of things and the spirits of men.[1] The traces
of a cult of the sun and moon may also perhaps be ascribed to the
same origin. But the view of primitive religion as an all-inclusive
ancestor-nature cult does not very well represent the Tiv outlook
on the world as it exists to-day. Apart from the traces of ancestor
worship alluded to, the cults in practice are all magical rather than
religious in their nature and purpose. Only certain things of a
destructive or harmful nature are credited with an individuality
and inherent force, which is subject to control by man. Their
potency is strictly specialized in its effect, and should not be confused with the power concept called *tsav*, which is, as will been
seen in the next section, a personal thing, restricted to living
members of the human race. Moreover, the cults are directed
only towards things of an abstract or intangible nature. They
provide an explanation and a concrete representation of forces
which otherwise would be difficult to control. The effects of the
disease are apparent; the disease itself has no material existence.
But when the master of the *akombo* fashions the emblem, he makes
the disease itself, and thereby has a tangible object on which he
can work. This is pure magic. To us, in theory, the magico-
religious practices of the Tiv may appear to be based on an
attribution of life to inanimate things, but to him, on the contrary,
they mean the giving of a material form to invisible animate forces.

Akiga divides the cults into two main classes, the 'birth *akombo*'
and the 'hunting *akombo*'. This is a useful classification and accurate for most purposes, though there are a number of sub-divisions
and a certain amount of overlapping. Moreover, the people themselves are often in doubt as to which class a particular *akombo*
should belong. This grouping makes no distinction between the
rites connected with the fertility of human beings and those of the
crops, the two terms being interchangeable. This is quite natural;
but the same class also includes all those *akombo* which bring
sickness and misfortune, and though this is correct according to
present ideas, these, as already suggested, were probably once
distinct. The hunting *akombo* form a class by themselves, but
here also there is a slight overlapping of ideas, in that the word

[1] J. H. Driberg, loc. cit.

ikɔr, which doubtless at an earlier stage of development meant hunting and luck in securing game only, was later extended to success in any venture, and the functions of the *akombo* were accordingly given a wider scope. So that although in form they are still purely hunting cults, in function they may affect mankind in any of his activities, including those of bearing children or growing yams. They might equally well, therefore, now be called '*akombo* of luck', or more strictly, if one judges by their effects, 'of bad luck'. The '*akombo* of arrows', which Akiga takes as synonymous with the hunting *akombo*, should probably more correctly be regarded as a sub-division, as they have a more limited application, being only liable to affect those actually engaged in hunting or (formerly) war, whereas the other *akombo-a-ikɔr* are everybody's concern.

All the hunting cults, and most of the others, Akiga believes to have been acquired from other tribes, and it is interesting, in view of what has been said above of the apparent decay of the ancestor cults, to note that the rites which he puts down as indigenous to the tribe are just those which bear the most obvious marks of being of the ancestral type. The only serious omission is that of the very important *Biamegh-Poor* cult, which he considers to have been imported from the Dam people, but there is at present little evidence for this view. It may be added that when he wrote this about the comparative age of the cults he was, like the great majority of his tribe, profoundly sceptical of the ancestral theory, and has only lately, as a result of much questioning of the aged, come to believe that there is some foundation for it. With our present lack of data concerning the past relationships and interchange of ideas between the Tiv and their neighbours, it would doubtless be unsafe to place too much reliance on the chronological aspect of Akiga's record. The significant fact is that by giving these few rites a different date in the cultural history of the tribe, he, or rather his informants, have unconsciously recognized them as belonging to a separate category.

There is another important grouping of the cults which has been noted by Captain Abraham[1] and is implied, though not expressly stated, in the following extracts, namely the distinction between those performed for personal or family reasons and those carried out for the benefit of the group, or, as the Tiv say, 'for

[1] Op. cit., p. 131.

setting right the land'. The latter are the *Ilyum* and *Iwoyaŋgegh* (Guardian Arch), which were usually placed together on the boundary between two groups, but are now almost obsolete, the *Ingbianjor* (including the *Atsuku*), the *Biamegh-Poor*, and the *Imborivuŋgu*. This classification cuts across the other, as the *Biamegh* is a hunting *akombo*, whereas the others were apparently fertility cults, but all function in connexion with the general prosperity of the group. To these perhaps should also be added the *Swem*, which was originally a place, but is now a sacred object. The public rites were of great sociological importance, and, as shown above, the constitution of the kindred group was dependent largely on the existence of an elder who had the power to carry them out. All the rest of the cults are of the private type, and have no application outside the family of the man who practises them.

Although the prevailing conception of the *akombo* is that of evil forces, each liable to cause some specific form of ailment or misfortune, it must not be thought that all ills which come upon mankind are believed to be due to supernatural causes. The Tiv recognize three possibilities or stages in every adverse event. The first is that the thing may have happened in a quite natural way. If a man meets with an accident, or falls sick of some common disease of which the symptoms are obvious, he does not necessarily at first suspect supernatural interference, and treats his wound or ailment without recourse to magic of any kind. But just as it is natural for animals to be healthy and for trees to bear fruit, so it is natural for the sickness to run its course and the sore to heal up. If it does not do so, then it is time to suspect other agencies at work, and recourse is had to divination to discover which particular *akombo* is interfering with the normal course of nature. If the symptoms are obvious it is not always necessary, of course, to go to the diviner. If you have a cough, or pains in the stomach, which do not yield to normal treatment, any knowledgeable elder can tell you from the symptoms of the complaint which *akombo* is the cause. You then go to some one who is master of that particular *akombo*, who gives you the medicine which belongs to it, and for this you pay a nominal fee (*tɔndo ataa*). You do not need to go through the full ceremony of 'setting it right' (magically), unless the medicine is ineffective. At this stage, therefore, magic and medicine play an equal part. Finally, if all rites have been performed and there is still no sign of improvement, the cause must be witchcraft. The guilty party is discovered by divination, and steps are taken against him as described below (p. 326). If action is not taken then, the man may die, but he cannot be killed by the *akombo* alone.

There is another form of magic, also sometimes included under the same general term *akombo*, namely the charms. The above remarks do not apply to these, for they have not a negative but a positive function; moreover, they are not practised openly like the more reputable kinds of magic. But these are known to have been adopted from other tribes in quite recent times, and should not be considered as genuine Tiv magic. The fact that they may be 'bought' and that no initiation is required is an indication of their alien character (see p. 210 below).

T HE origin of the *akombo* practices amongst the Tiv is very old indeed, but only three were really their own from the beginning: the *Twel*, the *Ihambe-icigh*, and the *Ilyum*. When they had obtained a wife by exchange, it was the *Twel* and *Ihambe-icigh* that they set up at the door of her house, and performed the rites over them. But those who did this were very few. Sometimes there would be only one in a whole clan who had power over the *akombo* and could perform the rites. This man was called the Master of the *Twel*, because the *Twel* was the first and greatest of the *akombo*. The reason why there were so few was that no one could become an initiate and perform the rites unless he had reached a position of high seniority, an old man, filled with *tsav*, and held in great respect. Otherwise, if a man were still young, he would never dare to be initiated and to perform the *akombo* ceremonies as people do nowadays, however rich he might be. . . .[1]

Akombo are divided into two classes: the *akombo* of birth and the *akombo* of the hunt. The *akombo* of birth are also the *akombo* of crops, and the hunting *akombo* are also called the *akombo* of arrows. Besides these, there are also the protective charms, which were introduced very

[1] Here is omitted a story told to explain the origin of the word *akombo*, which Akiga derives from *a-kombo*, 'he hoards', said to be the nickname given to a miser who was finally induced to part with some of his money in order to have his sick child cured by magical means.

much later. Of the above two classes of *akombo*, only the first was originated by the Tiv themselves, the second class, and also the charms, were acquired from other tribes. Moreover, of the birth *akombo* only the *Twel* and (later) the *Ilyum* and *Ihambe-icigh* were originated by the Tiv; all the rest were brought in afterwards. Of all the hunting *akombo* there is not one which really belongs to them. To set them right they make an offering of *tashi*, as they have been taught to do by the foreigner, for *tashi* is the beer of the foreigner (Chamba). But if *tashi* cannot be got quickly, and they are in a hurry, they ferment some gruel and pour that out instead, or else simply use flour and water. The *Biamegh*, which is one of the hunting *akombo*, came from the Dam. The protective charm is an idea which they got from the Hausa. It is used chiefly by the Shitire, Ukum, Ugondo, Nɔŋgov and Iharev clans, and is not much known in Kparev. It is a thing which is bought, and no initiation is involved, as in the case of other *akombo*.

The birth *akombo* are set right when a woman is failing to bear children, in order to bring about childbirth; or when a man's crops are poor, to cause them to improve; or when many of his animals are dying or are unhealthy. And if one day a birth *akombo* seizes him and causes him to fall sick, he sets it right in order that he may recover.

The hunting *akombo* are set right when a man is having bad luck in hunting and failing to bring home any meat, in order that his luck may improve and he may kill much game; or if he is unsuccessful in making money, and people do not buy what he has for sale, he will set right the hunting *akombo* so that men may snatch up his wares and he become wealthy. At other times, if a man has been seized by a hunting *akombo*, he is continually meeting with accidents, or falling down, or being wounded by one of his own arrows.

Charms are used to protect a man from a variety of things and to prevent any harm coming to him. There is one type of charm with which you can tread on a snake without its biting you, or if you step over it without noticing, it will die at once. With another kind you can meet a wild beast, but it will not be able to harm you. If you go into battle no one will be able to shoot you, or if an arrow does hit you it will be harmless and not enter your body. Another charm enables you to ride any horse, and it will not be able to unseat you, however vicious it may be. This you can also use for the purpose of causing another man to fall off his horse. Then there is the charm which gives strength; if you have this no one will be able to throw you in a wrestling match. However many come out to challenge you, you will down them all. There is the charm which gives you invisibility, and the one by means of which, when men lie in wait for you on the road to catch you or kill you, you can vanish out of their hands. Another insures that you will always win your case in a court of law; let as many judges come together as they please, you will still be pronounced innocent. There is also the charm which makes you beloved by the white man, so that he will never find fault with you; even when you do wrong he will think you are right, and you can go on doing just whatever you like without his being able to touch you. Another kind again makes you popular with women; armed with this you may be sure of winning a woman's favour, even though she may have turned down every one else. Then there is the charm used when competing for office; with its help you will be able to get the better of all other claimants; you will get the chieftainship, and they will fail. Finally, there is the charm which gives you rapid promotion in the service of the European.

THE EMBLEMS

Every *akombo* has its own guardian emblems, and it is by these emblems that each kind of *akombo* can be distinguished. The guardian emblems of an *akombo* are the means by which it 'guards'; that is to say, by means of the emblems you guard your property, to prevent others from touching it. So when the Tiv wish to keep something safe, or if they are going to make a farm and are afraid that the *mbatsav* may damage it by witchcraft, they place an *akombo* there in order that the *mbatsav*, or thieves, may be afraid.

In addition to the guardian emblems, every birth *akombo* has also its magic cruse.[1] The emblems are leaves or some other symbol, and the cruse is a pot which is tied up to the roof by a piece of string in the *ate*, or the *dwer*. If you enter an *ate* belonging to any man of standing, cast your eyes up to the rafters and you will see many cruses there belonging to all the different kinds of *akombo*. The *Agashi*, however, does not have a cruse, but a wooden boat. Wherever you go in Tivland you will never hear it called the *Agashi* cruse, but always the *Agashi* boat. The word for cruse in the Tiv language means 'to join on to' or 'to fit in loosely', from which it can be seen that the cruse is not the actual *akombo* but something which is connected with it. Nevertheless, if you transgress against the *akombo* cruse you transgress against the *akombo* itself. It is an act of transgression to touch the cruse or to take something out of it; for it is the custom to keep things in it, and if you or anyone else put out your hand to steal anything which has been put there, you are committing an act of transgression against it. All the birth *akombo* have cruses, but the hunting *akombo* have only guardian emblems.

DEFINITIONS

If a man transgresses against an *akombo* and it seizes him, he 'sets it right' in order that it may leave him alone, and he be restored to health. The meaning of 'to set right' is the same as in the case of anything else which it is desired to make good again. For this reason the *akombo* practices are sometimes called the 'setting to rights'.

When you have committed an offence against the *akombo* you must first of all be 'gladdened', and if you wish to become master of it, that can be done at another time. The meaning of the word 'gladdening' is the same as in being glad when you are pleased with something, that is to say, you are glad because you know that the *akombo* is

[1] A small earthenware vessel with a wide open top.

being set right for you, and that you are going to be well
again.

What is meant by 'getting the mastery'[1] of an *akombo* is
the same as when you take hold of something in order
that it may become yours. In the same way, a man takes
hold of the *akombo* in order that he may have it for his
own, and can, in his turn, set it right for others.

If you are seized by an *akombo*, and a man sets it right
for you, either by gladdening or making you master of it,
you give him something in return for this service, and
what you give him is called 'the *akombo* fee'.

The 'striking by the sword-grass' is done only in
connexion with the hunting *akombo*, and not all of these.
In the case of others the rite is known as the 'blackening'.
The blackening and the grass-striking are carried out
when a man has had very bad luck in hunting. He goes
to a man who is master of all the hunting *akombo*, and
asks him to perform one of these two rites on his behalf.
The meaning of both these practices is that the man clears
the hunter's eyes, which had formerly been 'darkened'
by bad luck.[2]

To set right the *akombo*, both of birth and of hunting,
it is necessary to kill a chicken, and pour its blood over
them. Beer must also be poured out, or flour and water.
The shedding of blood is for well-being, and its purpose is
to give health to the man for whom the *akombo* is being set
right. Otherwise, if the rite be performed without the
shedding of blood, there will never be good health;

---

[1] Lit., 'seize' or 'take hold of'.
[2] The magic works as follows: In the case of the 'blackening' the master takes
a piece of charcoal and draws a line on the body of the unsuccessful hunter.
When the latter washes the black mark away the mental blackness, which had
formerly prevented him from seeing or hitting the game, goes with it. In the
case of the other rite, the sword-grass, which is perhaps symbolical of the
uncultivated bush, is an integral part of most of the hunting *akombo*, being
either bound round the emblems or used to thatch the roof over the 'bin' in
which the secret objects are kept. The master takes a bunch of this grass,
strikes the hunter on each side of the body, passes it behind his limbs and
breaks it, saying, 'I am purging you of—' (naming the various hunting *akombo*),
and finally tells him to turn his back while he throws it way. The hunter, that is
to say, has had the evil drawn out of him, but he must be careful not to see it
go. The rite is analogous to that already described in connexion with the
purging before circumcision.

however much meat may be provided for the ceremony, it is essential that a chicken be killed and its blood poured out if well-being is to follow. Health is in the blood of the chicken, or of the sheep or goat. As to the pouring out of the beer, or of flour and water, some of the old men say that the reason for it is to give the ancestors the produce of the land, that they may be pleased and grant you good fortune on earth; that you may be happy, and that all your affairs may prosper.

Below you will find a description of each *akombo*, its guardian emblems, how it is set right, and how the mastery of it is obtained. The protective charms are treated separately.

BIRTH *AKOMBO*

THE *IHAMBE-ICIGH*

The *Ihambe-icigh* of the father's group is set up at the door of the house, on the left-hand side as you go in. It consists of two emblems, fashioned out of wood, one of which is sharpened to a point, while the other has a rounded top. The one with the pointed head is called the *ihambe*, the other is called *mtam*. Round these are set the *akuve*.[1] Three things are planted inside the enclosure, together with the *ihambe* and *mtam*, known as *icigh*, *ikarika*, and *ator*. *Icigh* has nothing but a plain stem, on which grow a few thorns and long fleshy leaves. It is to this plant that the name *icigh* is properly applied. *Ikarika* has no leaves, but only branches; these branches are, in fact, its leaves. It exudes a resinous substance, which is very corrosive: if it gets into the eyes, and they are not properly treated, it will cause cataract. It is used by some as a purgative. If a man has stomach-ache and wishes to purge his bowels, you pour a little of the resin into a bowl, break in one egg, cook the mixture till it thickens, and give it to him to drink. A violent reaction follows, and the patient feels much better. *Ator* has not got thick leaves like the other

---

[1] This term is used for the whole of the enclosure, including the encircling stones or sticks, but is more properly applied to the two empty pots inside, one planted with the mouth upwards and the other inverted; see below.

two. It is used as a remedy in the case of wounds. First some copper is rubbed off on a grindstone, and then some leaves of the *ator* are picked and baked in the hearth. When they have withered they are taken out and their juice is squeezed over the copper dust; this is then applied as an ointment on the wound. It is also used as a lotion in the case of bad eye trouble.

The *Ihambe* of the mother's group is not set up at the same time as that of the father's group. When your mother's kinsmen come to set it right for you, they put it on a separate piece of ground, but quite close to the paternal *Ihambe*. You may also be initiated to the mastery of the maternal *Ihambe*, and are then able to set it right for the members of your mother's group. When you are initiated, exactly the same emblems are set up for you as in the case of the paternal *Ihambe*. So if any women belonging to your mother's group happen to be living in the district, they can come to have the rite performed for them, without the necessity of going to their parents' homes.[1] But if your mother's kinsmen merely come to set the *Ihambe* right for you, and not to give you the mastery over it, they put the emblems there only, and not the plants. The ceremony for setting right the *Ihambe* of the father's group and of the mother's group is the same; the only difference is that in the case of the paternal *Ihambe* a male beast is slaughtered, and of the maternal *Ihambe*, a female.

Transgression against the 'Ihambe'. If you transgress against the *Ihambe*, it will seize you. The way in which it does this is to attack and destroy all the crops on your farm, so that the leaves turn red and useless. When you see this happen you go to the diviner, and if the cause is shown to be the *Ihambe*, you go back and perform the gladdening rite. This in the case of the *Ihambe* requires

[1] The members of your mother's group referred to are the women who have married husbands of your father's group. (Only married women would need to set right the *Ihambe*.) E.g. A.'s father's clan is Shitire; his mother's clan, Ukum. He gets a man from Ukum to initiate him to the maternal *Ihambe*. B., an Ukum woman who is married to a Shitire husband, has been 'caught' by the *Ihambe*. She can get this set right by A., because he is master of the Ukum *Ihambe*. B.'s husband would prefer this, as being less expensive than taking her home to her father's clan to have it done there,

a sheep or goat,[1] and the payment of a 'twenty'. When these have been collected, you call together all the members of your household, each with a chicken in his hand.[1] The master of the *Ihambe*, whom you have called in to gladden you, fashions the emblems and sets them up by the door of your house. For this you pay him a 'ten', which in the case of the paternal *Ihambe* is 2*d.*, and of the maternal *Ihambe* is 1*s.* Then the man who has come to perform the rites takes some flour and sprinkles it over the emblems for you. That is all. Henceforth the crops on your farm will flourish. But because you now have been gladdened, this by no means gives you the right to go and set the *akombo* right for some one else. You are not its master. If you are so foolish as to do this, you are transgressing against it again. Your crops will be worse than before.

The Initiation to the Mastery of the 'Ihambe'. The initiation for the *Ihambe* requires a cow.[2] But do not let this astonish you. A 'cow' for purposes of initiation to an *akombo* means a bar of iron. This holds good for all the *akombo* of the crops. Thus if you are told to pay five cows, that means five iron bars. There are only two *akombo* whose initiation requires a real cow which flicks its tail, namely the *Biamegh* and the *Irkombo*. So you, the candidate for initiation, produce your iron bar and the chickens, and hand them over to the man who is initiating you. Thereupon he sets up the *Ihambe*, takes the chickens and kills them, pouring the blood over the emblems. Then he tells you to get your wife to make *ruam*, and cooks a chicken with which to make the passes.[3] He gives the guardian emblems into your keeping, and the

---

[1] For slaughter; see p. 208 below.

[2] To be given to the other initiates in the group: see p. 208 below.

[3] *Cia.* The master and the candidate or patient (as the case may be) stand on either side of the emblems, and the master passes the food backwards and forwards over the emblems in a circular motion, while the other goes through the same motions with his hands empty, but with less movement. The master then puts a little of the food into the other's mouth, and gives him the dish to go and eat with any who have already been through the same rites. There are some variations. In the case of the hunting *akombo* (see p. 211) the master holds out the food over the emblems, apparently as though to offer it, the other puts out his hands as though to receive it, then they both withdraw their hands again, and repeat this three times before the food is handed over.

power to set them up as you will. After that you can set right the *akombo* for others, and no harm will come to you.

❡ The *Ihambe-icigh* group seems to exemplify in itself the fusion of two ideas. On the one hand, the fertility aspect is represented by the genital symbols (*ahambe*), which are recognized as male and female, and probably also by the two pots (*akuve*), which are placed next to them, one with the mouth up and the other down, though the significance of this is not generally understood by the Tiv. On the other hand, its function in connexion with the healing of disease is represented by the plants, known collectively by the word for medicine (*icigh*), which forms the second element of the compound. Originally the two ideas were probably distinct, but now the group is treated as a single entity. Both aspects are shown in the maleficent influence ascribed to it, for it either attacks a man's crops, as mentioned above, or his person in the form of a skin disease or swelling of the testicles. Possibly the plants were originally placed round the emblems in order that their healing properties might be made more effective by contiguity to the sacred objects, and afterwards came to be regarded as an integral part of the group. *Ikarika*, a cactus, and the other plants all have a somewhat grotesque appearance, and this fact has doubtless as much to do with their magical effect as has their medicinal value. The subject is further confused by the nomenclature, because although *ihambe* is said above to be the name for the male emblem and *icigh* for one of the plants, *ihambe* can be used for either of the genital symbols, *icigh* for any of the plants, or for medicine in general, and the whole cult is called indiscriminately *Ihambe*, *Icigh*, or *Ihambe-icigh*. There are also local variations in the practices, some clans setting up only two emblems, a male for the father's group and a female for the mother's group, some a male and female for each group, others a larger number.

The most interesting feature in the *Ihambe-icigh* and *Twel* (for they are always placed together, and these remarks apply to both) is their connexion with exchange marriage, and, if our theory is right, with an even older system of mother-right. The Tiv custom is as follows: The two groups of emblems, representing the greatest of the family cults, are set up by the head of the household outside the house of a wife whom he has married by true sister exchange. It is not necessary for every member of the family who makes such an exchange marriage to do this, because the head of the household, that is the senior man in the *iŋgɔl* group, is responsible for the welfare of the other members, who go to him when necessary to have the *akombo* 'set right' by performing the preliminary (gladdening) ceremony over his emblems. (His younger brothers may, however, have their own emblems, if they have made true sister exchange marriages, and will in any case on his death probably divide up and set up the emblems in their own homes.) But when the old man dies, his eldest son by true sister exchange inherits his father's *akombo* and, having been initiated, performs the rites at the door of his mother's house as before. He continues to do this as long as his mother is alive, but when she dies he moves the emblems, or makes a new set, at the door of his own true exchange wife's house, unless his wife has already been living in his mother's house, in which case she inherits it, together with the emblems, and there is no need to move them. If he leaves his parents' home while they are still alive and founds a home of his own, he will still not set up new emblems, but will go back to the old site to perform the rites, as long as his mother lives.

The cult, therefore, is very closely bound up with the person of the mother, and the reason that it depends on the exchange marriage system will be made clear by a consideration of the Tiv exchange theory. For, as already shown, it is only the wife obtained by true sister exchange who is the true representative of the full sister, and carries on the line from the mother. But the circumstances surrounding the old custom seem most strongly to suggest that originally the fertility emblems were placed, and the rites performed, at the house of the daughter of the family, who bore children to the group in that house, and whose daughter in turn succeeded to the cult emblems when her mother died. The strength of the mother-daughter relationship which still survives is clearly shown by Akiga in his section on the exchange marriage *akombo*. They are placed on the left of the door so that the wife who sleeps on that side of the house 'may have good health and happiness through the mother, . . . to show that the man holds his mother in high regard', and that he may 'not be visited by bad dreams about his mother'. The case for mother-right, thus stated by one who does not believe in it, could hardly be put more strongly.

The reason that the emblems are not set up by a man outside his wife's house before the death of his mother is that while his mother is alive she forms the earthly link with her own mother, and so back along the maternal line of ancestors, who are called upon to increase the fertility of their descendants. It will be remembered that on the exchange theory this line coincides with the paternal line of ancestors, because the mother was herself a substitute for a true daughter of the group, and so through each generation. As soon as the mother dies she becomes the nearest in the chain of ancestors, and the living link in this chain then becomes her exchange 'daughter', who is her true representative in the group. It is true that the *Ihambe-icigh* is now divided into two parts, one for the father's group and one for the mother's group, but this may well be a later compromise, introduced at the same time as exchange marriage to reconcile the two conflicting systems of father- and mother-right. The Tiv still recognize that the cult is especially connected with the mother, and in clans which only set up one emblem for each side of the family, the female emblem holds the more prominent place.

It will now be understood why the abolition of exchange marriage struck such a heavy blow at the old structure of tribal beliefs. If a man could no longer take his sister by the same mother to exchange for a wife, when his mother died she had no representative to carry on her line, and the chain which bound the group to its maternal ancestors was broken. Nowadays, say the old men, the women do not bear big families as they used to do, and the yield from the crops is not what it was. How could it be otherwise, since the white man has spoilt the fertility of the land? Unfortunately there is some truth in what they say, but no arguments about the increase of venereal disease or over-cultivation of the soil will convince them, when they are satisfied that the true reason is that there is now no exchange marriage. Yet perhaps one may take the matter too seriously, because, after all, the old cults had already lost much of their meaning, and few understand *how* they are connected with the fertility of the race and the soil, or *why* the emblems must be placed at the door of a true exchange wife.

Some modifications had already been made, which show that the true nature of the rites had been partly forgotten. Sometimes a man could not make a true sister exchange, and had to be

o

content with an exchange made through another woman in the *iŋgɔl*
group, but since she was not mystically related to his mother he
could not in this case place the emblems outside her house. Feeling that possession of the *akombo* was essential to the well-being
of his family, he would then occasionally place the emblems outside his own house, that is the *ate*. This, however, was considered
very unsatisfactory, and indeed changed the whole purpose of the
cult, which had no longer the maternal association; but the true
reason why it was unsatisfactory was latterly not fully understood.
It has therefore been suggested by some that even under the new
bride-price system it might be possible to preserve the old cults
by some such compromise. Others have thought out another
solution by paying for the new wife in the actual coin or property
which was given as the bride-price for their *iŋgɔl*; by this means
they consider that they have made a true exchange, the money
being regarded as an intermediate carrier of the vital principle.
The majority of old men, however, take a more gloomy view, saying that without exchange marriage there can be no *Twel* or
Ihambe-icigh, and without these there can be no children or food,
so that the race will die out with the present generation. But the
fact that the more progressive are trying to find a compromise shows that, even if this indicates ignorance of the true
object of the rites, the Tiv mentality with regard to their spiritual
beliefs is more elastic than might be inferred from the conservative head-shakings of the older generation.

THE *ILYUM* AND THE GUARDIAN ARCH[1]

THE *Ilyum* is an *akombo* for setting right the land.
In former times, when everything went wrong,
when crops were bad, when the hunt yielded no meat,
and the women bore no children, the elders all met
together at the *Ilyum*. They spoke words to make the
land good; they killed a sheep and poured the blood over
it. The *Ilyum* itself was originally a tall stone, set up on
the road at the boundary between one clan and another.
Nowadays people no longer come together at the *Ilyum*.

After the Tiv split up into clans they used to meet
together at the Guardian Arch. This also, like the *Ilyum*,
was set up at the boundary between two clans, but

---

[1] *Iwoyaŋgegh.*

consisted of two forked posts planted on either side of the road, with a pole resting on the top. The people passed under it, in order that any one who had the evil intention of going to do harm to the land of the other clan would be killed by the Guardian Arch if he stooped to pass underneath. These were the only two *akombo* known to the ancestors for setting right the land.

⁋ 'Setting right the land', as explained above, is the expression used of those rites which are carried out on behalf of the whole group, as opposed to the personal or family cults. The *Ilyum* appears to have been a thing of great importance in the past, and the centre of the magico-religious life of the people. It was the meeting-place for the council of elders of the group, or of two neighbouring groups, for performing fertility rites, rain-making, or discussion of serious matters affecting the community (see p. 373). It is here described as a stone, but more exactly consisted of two stones, a male and a fçmale, like the other fertility cults described above. The *Ilyum* in Kusuv is said to have had as its emblems one tall (male)stone, and three hearthstones to represent the female principle. Neither of the two cults mentioned above are in general use to-day, but Captain Downes informs me that they still survive in parts of Turan, Ikurav South, and Utaŋge.

The *Biamegh-Poor*, which is described below, is another of the public cults. In origin it is a hunting *akombo*, but it also has general application, and is put here on account of its importance. Nowadays, however, the rites are seldom performed, and there is no one, so far as I know, who has a *Poor*—that is, the mud container built like a corn-bin in which the *Biamegh* mysteries used to be kept. The decay of the public cults is usually attributed by the elders, like other evils of modern times, to the white man, and it is true that the measures taken by us against those rites which were supposed to entail human sacrifice, though afterwards repealed, helped to bring them into disfavour, but this only hastened a process which had been going on for many years. The old men say that 'the land is not as good as it was', because those who knew how to set it right have all died off, and the present generation 'are only children'. In other words, those who ought to have succeeded to the position and inherited the mysteries have not enough faith or interest in them to carry on the tradition.

THE *BIAMEGH*

THE *Biamegh* consists of three parts: the preparation,[1] the initiation, and the setting-right.

The Preparation. When a man is ready to be initiated to the mastery of the *Biamegh*, he first makes a general proclamation that all who also wish to be initiated should make ready and collect enough money to pay the presents. At the same time he drags in a big tree-drum, and sets it down in his village. Every evening all those who are preparing for initiation come together to practise the *Biamegh* songs. During the whole of this time dancing does not stop in the village. All those who have set their heart seriously on the *Biamegh* are moving hither and thither,[2] and the boys and girls give themselves up to merry-making. When the time approaches, the man who made the proclamation sets out, taking with him a 'twenty', and goes to some one who can carry out the *Biamegh* rites, that is, a man who has been fully initiated, and has set up the *Biamegh-Poor*.[3] He tells him that he has announced a *Biamegh*, and asks him to come and perform the rite for him.

When he comes, the man who has proclaimed a *Biamegh* calls one of his female relatives, and gives a chicken to the master, who ties it round her neck. With this hanging down behind, she starts to pound the millet for the *Biamegh* beer, singing as she works. When she has finished, and the grain is ready for soaking, she first takes some in a basket and sets it on one side. The master puts in his hand, takes out a pinch of the pounded corn, and throws it into the water; then he gives his permission for the woman to put the grain in to soak. This is also accompanied by singing. During these days all the other candidates for initiation are also putting in their corn to soak, and the report travels round that the So-and-so's are brewing beer for a *Biamegh*.

When the day for the beer-drinking arrives, the man who has proclaimed the *Biamegh* pours some of the beer

[1] Lit., 'going round'.
[2] Collecting enough funds to pay the 'presents' (*nambe*).
[3] P. 199.

into a pot. Then he takes a dish and lines it with pieces
of buffalo hide, cooked with fermented seeds of the
locust-bean and palm oil. He gives the beer to his wife or
daughter, and goes with her to tell the master, taking
with him a 'twenty'. Then he returns home again, and
on the day on which the master is due to arrive goes out
to await his coming, taking some beer and the dish with
the buffalo hide. This is known as 'The Roadside
Watch'.

The Rite.[1] When the master arrives a fire is made by
the side of the road, and all the candidates for initiation
assemble there with chickens and beer and pieces of hide.
The master starts to perform the rites. He takes all the
chickens, cuts their throats and gives them to boys to
scorch. Then he cuts off the drumsticks, wings and head,
makes the passes while they are still uncooked, and then
gives some to each of the candidates. Having done this,
he gives the order for a screen to be put round the *ate*.
By the time they leave the place by the roadside night
has already fallen. They all go into the *ate* of the *akombo*.
The man who proclaimed the *Biamegh* brings out a huge
beer-pot which is known as the *wuna*,[2] and each of the
candidates comes with several chickens. A fool will
bring an absurd number, but those who have been
through the rite before take some from him and hide
them, saying to each other, 'See, the quarry has fallen
into the net!'[3] They also take in with them the pieces of
hide and locust-bean seeds, and knead them on a big
grindstone.

Now every one who is being initiated goes into the *ate*
surrounded by members of his own party, for this is the
moment of peril, and the time for his destruction.[4] The
master proceeds with the rites. He takes a chicken and
makes the passes six times for the man whom he is
initiating. Then he makes him hold the chicken by the

---

[1] This is for initiation. The measures taken to 'set right' the *Biamegh* are
not given here. They are similar to those carried out for other hunting *akombo*.
[2] 'Corn store'.   [3] I.e. the man's a fool.
[4] The man is not killed in the *ate* by physical means, but with so many elders,
powerful in *tsav*, collected in a small place the time is very critical for the
'empty-chested' (see p. 217), and especially favourable to the *mbatsav* for
bewitching their victim. He will not actually die till some time later.

head and cuts through the neck, pouring the blood into the beer-pot. He makes passes with the drumsticks, wings, and gizzards, and then gives them to the candidate. After this the master takes up some *ishuragh* grains.[1] This is when the trap is set for the weakling. He throws one grain into the pot and tells you, the initiate, to pick it out. If you have any sense, you will have some of the seeds with you, in your mouth or in your hand, and when he throws in the seed and tells you to take it out you will produce your own and give it to him. The seed is thrown in six times. If you do not have the sense to bring some seed with you, you will not be able to take it out when he tells you, and every one will laugh at you for a fool.

At the first light of day the people burst out of the *ate*, and run out shouting, 'The *dzembe* tree shall wither!' that is, 'The elephant has fallen!'[2] It is at this cry that the weak man is destroyed. So the dawn breaks. All who have undergone the initiation start to dance the *Biamegh* dances.

The Visit to the Wild Plum Tree. The master then takes all the new initiates to a wild plum tree, each carrying a chicken. There he takes up his position, and each initiate comes with his chicken and stands before him. The master draws out a knife, severs the chicken's head with one blow and casts it towards the rising sun. Thereupon the initiate starts to run backwards and forwards, crying, 'Mother, Mother, you have borne a son indeed! I have eaten hot peppers! I have taken women both dark and fair! To-day I have finished the *Biamegh*! I have come to the wild plum tree!' Meanwhile one of his female relations is uttering shrill tremolo cries, and rubbing him over with camwood. He runs out into the middle of the village, still racing round and shouting, and comes back

---

[1] *Ishuragh :* a small black pepper. The grains are part of the equipment of the *mbatsav*. When they are used for magic purposes they are given the special mystic name of *ikehegh*. This term is also used in several places, but has been transcribed *ishuragh* to avoid confusion. See p. 250.

[2] The first phrase is in the secret language of the *mbatsav*, and its origin is unknown. It means, however, that the weakling (in *tsav*) will be overcome at this moment by the power of his superiors. The origin of the second phrase is from the danger of dispute and bloodshed which followed on the killing of any large animal.

again to the wild plum tree where the master is standing. The master then fills his mouth with beer, and spits it out on to the initiate's chest, saying, '*Biam gagaga*! Lost on the farmland, lost in the village!'[1]

The *Biamegh* is finished. The initiate goes home and bathes. Then he dresses himself up, breaks into song, and comes out into the middle of the village, dancing the *Biamegh* dances, and throwing taunts at those who have not been initiated. He is now a master of the *Biamegh*.

THE *POOR*

Even when you have been initiated to the *Biamegh*, and have been to the wild plum tree, if you have not also been made master of the *Poor*, you are only a *Biamegh* initiate and have not the power to set it right for any one else. Initiation to the *Poor* is the final stage in the cult of the *Biamegh*. In former times a master of the *Poor* held equal rank with a drum-chief. Whenever a beast was killed in the hunt, a foreleg was given to the chief as 'the Arm of the Land', because the land was under the arm of[2] the chief. If a beast were killed, and the foreleg were not given to him, the land would be spoilt. The master of the *Poor*, on the other hand, was given the centre of the back, because he was the man who set right the *Poor* to give good luck in the hunt; for the *Poor* is a hunting *akombo*. If he were not given the back, his group would not have good hunting. Thus the master of the *Poor* and the drum-chief each had their own special portion of the same beast. Sometimes a man who was master of the *Poor* tried to get himself made chief, when the chief of his district died; but when he spoke of it, and the question of his suitability arose, some would say, 'No. A man cannot hold two chieftainships at once. He is master of the *Poor*, and therefore a chief already. What further chiefdom can he hold? Can he, alone, take both the things for himself— the Arm of the Land, and the Back of Good Hunting?

[1] If the *Biamegh* seizes a man he loses his way in the bush, and nothing goes right at home.
[2] Or 'in the hand of'. *Uwegh* is used for the hand or arm of a man, or the foreleg of a beast. Thus the 'hand' of the animal killed in the hunt is associated with the hand of the chief, as the symbol of his power.

Never! He is not the only free man amongst us'. So he
failed to get the chieftainship. Some one else was
appointed, or, if there were no one in his group of
sufficient standing, the post would remain vacant.

Initiation to the 'Poor'. When you are ready to obtain mastery of the *Poor*, you first summon a man who
has himself undergone the full initiation, and is qualified
to set right the *Biamegh* for others. When he comes, he
says that you must first 'consent', and when you ask him
what this consent implies, he tells you the price that you
must pay for it. In former times the cost of 'consent' to
the *Poor* was twenty-four packets of salt. When you have
brought this, the man who is initiating you takes it and
sets it on one side, saying that you have paid for the
'consent', and must now give the presents.[1] For this you
give a cloth of twenty-four strips. You also bring out one
feathered chicken.[2] This must be killed, and the blood
poured over the stake which supports the *Poor*. If you
have not been initiated, but are only 'consenting', you set
up only one stake, and when the chicken is killed the
blood is poured on to it, so that it runs down the side of
the post. That is the end of the 'consent'.

Unless you have the strength you will never get beyond
the 'consenting', and so will never be able to set right the
Poor for others, nor dare to look into the *Poor* bin. If
some one else is 'consenting' you may go and take part,
but if there is an initiation you will not venture to
approach, because you yourself have not obtained the
mastery, but have only 'consented'. But if you are strong
enough you will not stop at the 'consent', but go on till
finally you receive initiation.

For initiation you must give a present of a cow.[1] You
must also bring a chicken and a sheep to be slaughtered,
that their blood may be poured over [the stakes of the
Poor]; and at night you give a Night Sheep[3] for the same
purpose. When the blood has been poured out, the
initiate, taking the head of the chicken in his left hand and

---

[1] To those who have already been initiated; see below.
[2] I.e. a real chicken, not a human victim; see below.
[3] A human victim.

the *Biamegh* knife in his right, races round, calling on his group, 'Hey Itier!' (supposing that he is of the Mbatierev), 'What now remains?' 'The *Poor*!' they answer. This he does six times, and when all is over his kinsmen disperse to their homes. The initiation to the *Poor* is finished, and all that remains is to build it.

The place for the *Poor* is in the centre of the village. The choice of a builder is not restricted by any taboos; you can ask any man, who knows how to build, to come and do it for you. But special woods must be used for the uprights, the cross-bars, and the roof-poles, namely *mtselama* and *mtsakombo*. The stakes are planted exactly as for the small bean store, and the bin itself is also built on the same plan. When the building is completed, and it is ready for the designs and decorations to be put on, it is screened off by a circle of mats. The craftsman works alone inside the screen. He mixes the clay down by the stream, brings up a little in his hand with which to go in and work, and then goes back to fetch some more. Thus he continues for many days, until he has finished his task. He makes figures of men, snakes, monkeys, leopards, and lions. All the time that he is working he must eat meat sauce and no other kind. (This is the origin of the Tiv saying: 'So-and-so eats as much meat as a *Poor* builder.') When the work is complete he takes away the screen, and every one goes to look at the objects which he has fashioned on the outside of the *Poor*. As they gaze in admiration, they exclaim, 'He has moulded the figures by *tsav*! There is no one more *tsav* than the man who built this *Poor*!' The man who is called in to do the building is given a purely nominal wage; it may be only a 'twenty'. Six stakes are planted to support the building, and six main poles form the framework of the roof. But if you are frightened at having to kill so many people, you use only three main roof-poles.[1]

The Things kept Inside the 'Poor.' When a man ĥ finished building the *Poor*, he sets about procuring as things to put inside it. During that time every one who dies a violent death in the initiate's group is said to have

[1] Because each of the poles and stakes requires a human victim.

been killed by him to give for the *Poor*. A man dies from a snake-bite, and every one says, 'So-and-so killed him to give for the *Poor*!' Another is killed in the bush, and they say, 'So-and-so has killed again for the *Poor*!' Every case of death by drowning, by falling from a tree, in battle, as a result of pains in the head,[1] or any other violent death that occurs during that time, is attributed to no other cause but this, 'So-and-so has killed him on account of the things which he is trying to get to set right the *Poor*, in order that the land of his group may be good'.

When people die in this way, he is given the things for the *Poor*. These are: the skull of a manatee, the head of a Great Father, and the *Biamegh* knife. A Great Father means a man who was, in his time, a full master of the *Biamegh* and of the *Poor*, and who used to set right the *Biamegh* for all his group; who was also master of many other *akombo*, filled with the strongest *tsav*, a giant amongst men. A man who was wise, and feared by all his clansmen; who could say to one of his kinsmen, 'To-day you will die, young man!' and he would die. Ah! it was the head of a man like this that was put in the *Poor*, and called the head of the Great Father. There are not many men of this kind in Tivland.

Some clans keep in the *Poor* the head of a young cob, or the head of a boar. This is because the *Biamegh* rites are done differently in different parts of Tiv, some using the head of a manatee, others that of a young cob, and others of a boar. So the head which is kept in the *Poor* is that which was used in the rites. In no case is the *Biamegh* set right with the head of the Great Father, but only with the [other] objects which are kept inside. Nevertheless, the thing which invests the *Poor* with its peculiar awfulness is the head of the Great Father which it contains. It is this which brings so many men to their death. Sometimes a *Poor* has only one head, sometimes several, according to the number of great men in the group of the kind described.

Looking into the 'Poor'. When a man has built a

---

[1] I.e. when a man dies after a short illness, complaining of violent headaches, but with no other obvious symptoms.

Poor, given a feast, and put all the objects inside, he has reached the summit of power within his group. He can then go round performing the rites for the *Biamegh*, and after his death his head will be kept inside the *Poor*. It is because the *Poor* is such a big thing that it is the cause of so many deaths amongst the Tiv. This is how a man may bring about his own destruction through the *Poor*: If, after he has been initiated to the *Biamegh*, he goes round to attend the *Biamegh* rites in this place and that, boasting amongst those of his own age, then he is very near to death. Some day one of his age-mates will say to him, 'I, So-and-so of the So-and-sos, am not a man to fool with. Do you think you can catch a leopard by the tail and play about with it as though it were a civet-cat? Let me tell you this, I am a full master of the *Biamegh*; I have laid my hands on the *Poor*, and have held the head of the Great Father against my breast'. (This means that he is a candidate for initiation to the *Poor*, and has already reached the stage of 'consenting'. He has also looked into the *Poor* bin and touched the head of the Great Father.) When his age-mate hears this he goes back to his own group and tries to find means by which he can also look into the *Poor*. When he feels himself strong enough in his group, he goes to a master of the *Poor* and asks him to show him the *Poor* bin, that he may look inside it. When he has done this, the master says to him, 'No one may look into the *Poor* for nothing. Now that you have seen what is in it, you must give me a man to kill, that I may pour his blood over the objects'. If he is unable to provide a victim, the master of the *Poor* will kill him, and afterwards every one will say, 'So-and-so's uncurbed ambition has brought about his destruction'. (This is the meaning of the Tiv saying, 'You ate your yam so greedily that you have swallowed a bad bit!') But if he sees what will happen, and gives one of his children or kinsmen to be killed, then all is well. He will live to tell all the world that he is a better man than any of his age-mates, for he has looked into the *Poor*, and clasped the head of the Great Father. People speak of him with respect. 'So-and-so of such-and-such a group', they say, 'is a great man now. There is none in his grade to be compared with him. If he wishes to become master even of the *Poor* itself, there is nothing to stand in his way, nor will he lack a chicken[1] to kill.' When his age-mates hear this they, too, seek to look into the *Poor* bin and clasp the head of the Great Father, in order that men may esteem them, and this alone may cause many deaths in the clan. When it is said that there has been much killing on account of the *Poor*, the meaning is that men have met their death for reasons of this kind.

Chiefs who are also Masters of the 'Poor'. Although the *Poor* and the chieftainship are quite different things, you occasionally find amongst the Tiv a man who is both chief and master of the *Poor* as well. This happens in the following way: The Tiv elders have never chosen an old man to be chief, but always one of the younger men (see the section on the drum-chiefs). In this way, a man who becomes chief when he is quite young may still be alive when all the elders of his group are dead, including the master of the *Poor*. Having outlived them all, and being himself an old man, he may be given all the things [pertaining to the cult], because there is no one to set right the *Poor*, and the hunting has consequently become very unsuccessful. This is the only case in which you ever find amongst the Tiv a man who is both chief and master of the *Poor* at the same time; and even so, if one of the younger men in his section eventually becomes strong enough, the chief will hand over the *Poor* to him. Otherwise, if no one of sufficient worth is forthcoming, he will continue to hold both offices until the day of his death. The head of such a chief can be put in the *Poor* bin. In after years there may appear men in the group to inherit each of the two things which once were his, one taking the *Poor*, and another the chieftainship. Then their land will become good again, and every one will be glad, saying, 'Formerly our land lay idle,[2] but now it has come

[1] A human victim.
[2] I.e. without an owner, because no one had the power to take over the 'things for setting right the land', viz. the ancestral relics.

back into the hands of men!' Then the hunting will be good, the women bear children, and the beasts of the field be in fine condition.

As the Tiv introduced chieftainship from the foreigners, so they got the *Poor*, together with the *Biamegh*, from the people of Gbe and Dam.

¶. The Tiv idea of chieftainship is explained in a later chapter. It had, like the mastership of the *Poor*, a mystical rather than executive quality, and both offices were supposed to be acquired and held by sacrifice of human victims. The Tiv did not like both being combined, first because they were afraid of one man having too much power, and secondly because they recognized the two things as being quite distinct in origin and function, and thought that by dividing them they had a stronger control of the forces on which the prosperity of the land depended.

The question of the ritual murders is also more fully discussed later. It will have been noted that Akiga here approaches it in the rational way, when he says that whenever a man died a 'violent' death, whatever the cause, it was attributed to, and in fact claimed by, the man who required a certain number of victims for his initiation. It must also be understood, throughout the above section and in similar contexts, that 'killing' always means killing by magical means, and being 'strong' always implies being 'strong in *tsav*' and thus able to bring about the death of other members of the group for the purpose required. Speaking rationally, all that was necessary was for the elder to acquire sufficient reputation to be able to assume responsibility for these deaths as they occurred, but the Tiv certainly believed that he was the cause of them, and the alleged slaughter of human victims for the *Poor* and other cults was one of the immediate causes of the trouble which led to the witchcraft investigation of 1929.

The Tiv make a distinction between 'violent' death (*ku swen-degh*) and death 'on a bed' (*ku anaŋge*). Professor Lévy-Bruhl has shown that amongst many people the significance of violent death is that it reveals the anger of the unseen powers,[1] and this is partly borne out by the Tiv practice of burying a man who has died such a death away from the village, and performing certain rites to remove the blood taint (see under *Swende* below). But

[1] *Primitive Mentality*, p. 274 et seq.

the ultimate cause of death is now always attributed by the Tiv to human agency, and the distinction between 'violent' and 'natural' death forms a part of the belief that the victims are killed and eaten by the *mbatsav*. From this point of view the important thing is the condition of the corpse. A man who has died a sudden death would be a more acceptable victim, and more suitable (the Tiv say) for cannibalistic rites, than one whose body has become emaciated through a long illness. For this reason, although deaths 'on a bed' were also said to be caused by the senior members of the group, and could be counted for the *Poor*, they were not considered of the same value in reckoning the total. The general rule was that the elder who was seeking initiation could count one for a 'natural' death in his family, and for a 'violent' death two or more.

The following is a brief description of some of the other cults in this class. These are directed solely against ills and misfortunes and have no obvious connexion with the cult of human ancestors, but all are included by the Tiv under the heading of 'birth' *akombo*.

THE *SWENDE*

THE *Swende* seizes you with a cough. Sometimes it causes a woman to cough till she has a miscarriage. It is of two kinds: the wet *Swende* and the dry. It is an offence against it for a woman to step over the blood of a man who has died a violent death, or to look upon a dog which has been killed.[1]

Wet *Swende* is set right by means of a he-goat and a cock, and its guardian emblem is the fruit of an oil- or dum-palm. Dry *Swende* attacks a man with a dry cough. Its rites are performed by slaves of the Utyusha clans, but not by freemen. This also requires a he-goat and a chicken.

[1] That is to say, the *Swende* rites are performed to remove the blood taint. It is more liable to attack women than men, because (*a*) there are more ways in which a woman may offend against it, and (*b*) it attacks by causing miscarriage as well as the Cough (usually = tuberculosis). But men are also liable to be caught by it, if it is not set right when a violent death occurs. Moreover, the body of a person who has died in this way must not be buried in the village, as this would also be an offence against it. Hence the common name for violent death is *ku swendegh*.

THE *AHINA* [1]

The effect of the *Ahina* is to cause a woman to bring forth two children at one birth; any woman who bears twins must have transgressed against it. It is set right by means of a forked stick, a pair of chickens, or a pair of bracelets. The forked stick is also its emblem.

THE *IKUŊGU*

When the *Ikuŋgu* attacks a man he falls down in a fit. It may throw him into the fire or into water, and if it throws him into the water when no one is about, he will be drowned. To put it right only one chicken is needed. Its guardian emblem is a strip of raffia tied round a piece of cotton-wool.

THE *IWA* [2]

If a man is seized by the *Iwa* his skin peels off, or he is struck by a thunderbolt on his farm, or has pains in his loins; it also stops him having children. The *Iwa* is a big *akombo*. Its emblems are the clay nozzle of the forge and the slag from the furnace.

THE *WANAƆNDO* [3]

Wanaɔndo is the brother of *Iwa*, but is more powerful. When it seizes a man, it tears the roofs off his houses with the wind, and breaks down all the standing corn on his farms. It is put right with one chicken, and its emblem is the stone called the 'axe of heaven'. [4]

THE *DƆƆR*

The *Dɔɔr* causes sexual impotence. To put it right one chicken is required, and the man must be massaged in the

---

[1] *Ahina* means twins. These are not liked by the Tiv, but the reasons they give are unconvincing and conflicting. The true reason has probably been forgotten. If both live they say that their *tsav* is equal; if one dies they say that the other had the more *tsav* and killed his brother.

[2] *Iwa* also means blacksmithing.   [3] 'Son of heaven'.

[4] 'Axes of heaven' are stone celts, popularly supposed to be thunderbolts. There is a close connexion in Tiv magic between heaven (*Aɔndo*), thunderbolts, &c., on the one hand, and the blacksmith's craft on the other, said by some Tiv, probably rightly, to be derived from the association between the lightning and the sparks which fly from the anvil. For further details see Abraham, op. cit., pp. 139–140.

lumbar regions. He pays a 'ten', and recovers his power.

THE *IKƆƆR*[1]

If a woman is seized by the *Ikɔɔr* her menses cease, or after having a number of children she ceases to bear. If divination shows that the *Ikɔɔr* is to blame, she goes to her first husband and gets a hen from him. When she brings this home, one of the old women takes a snail and hangs it round her neck, thus freeing her from the *Ikɔɔr*. In return for this service she goes off with the hen. For the emblems, an old woman collects a number of snail-shells, threads them on a piece of string, and puts them on whatever she wishes to guard.

THE FEES FOR THE PRACTICE OF MAGIC AND MEDICINE

❐. The payments which must be produced by those who wish to undergo the magic rites are of three different kinds. First, there is the beast for the slaughter. This consists always of a chicken, and sometimes of a larger beast as well, a sheep or a goat, occasionally a pig, or (for the *Ivase* and *Ijɔv* rites only) a dog. The blood is poured over the emblems, and the meat is eaten (except in the case of a dog) by any one who has already had the rites performed on his behalf, though he may not necessarily be an initiate. Secondly, in the case of initiation to the more important cults, there are the 'presents' which must be given (*nambe*) to all those in the same *akombo* group who have previously been initiated. This payment is usually made in livestock, or its equivalent (see p. 190), and is given in the first place to the man who is conducting the initiation. He then divides it, or sells it and divides the proceeds, amongst his fellow initiates. Thirdly, there is the fee, a nominal amount paid to the master personally. A few notes on this are added here.

It has already been seen that in the case of certain operations, such as circumcision, it is an essential condition of success that the patient should give something to the practitioner, and also that the practitioner should have 'bought' the right to perform the operation. It is not enough for him to have learnt how to do it. The same applies to the use of most medicines and the treatment

---

[1] 'Snail'. This and the *Ingbianjor* are the only *akombo* to which women can be initiated.

of diseases. The healing properties of many herbs are well known to every one, but it would be useless to administer them without having paid a fee to some one who had already acquired the qualifications to do so in the same manner. The object of this is to protect the interests, not so much of the doctor, as of the patient, and the origin of the practice seems to lie in the idea that nothing is truly your own unless you have given something in exchange for it. The price given may be something of purely imaginary value. For instance, an old man who wishes to prepare a potion may send out a boy to collect the herbs or roots for him, but when he brings them he must lay them on the ground, and the older man must first 'buy' them by picking a blade of grass and dividing it with the boy.

The practice of medicine is closely associated with magic, but just as not every mishap is due to a supernatural cause, so not every medicine is a magic medicine. Medicines are divided into three classes: First, there are a few simples which can be used by anybody without formality, as for instance the *alufu* grass (see p. 35) used for stopping bleeding. These are called 'sword medicine' (*icigh ki shɔmough*). Secondly, there are some which must be 'bought', but are not connected with an *akombo*, such as certain herbs used to cure gonorrhoea. The third kind, and far the biggest, are the *akombo* medicines. These can only be applied by a man who has control of the particular *akombo* to which they belong, but even when he has been fully initiated he must pay a further fee for the right to administer them. This classification, however, is not based entirely on the type of medicine or treatment employed, but also depends to some extent on the nature of the disease and the circumstances in which it was contracted. Even the herbs in the first class can only be applied without original payment of a fee if used as a cure for simple cuts or wounds which a man may get accidentally in the course of his normal avocations. They cannot so be used in connexion with an operation like circumcision. In this case, as seen in the first chapter, the practitioner must buy the right, not only to perform the operation, but also to give the prescribed after-treatment, even though this may consist merely in the application of remedies which at other times he is in the habit of using without any such restrictions.

Thus for every *akombo* right, and for every kind of medical or

P

surgical treatment, except a few 'household' remedies in everyday use, there is a fee laid down, both that which the patient must pay the doctor and also that which the doctor must pay for the right to practise. This fee must be paid to ensure success, whether the treatment is purely pathological or whether it is wholly or partly magical. But there is an important distinction between 'natural' and 'supernatural' treatment (using the words in a European sense) with regard to the initial qualifications of the practitioner. The right to do operations, such as circumcision or teeth-cutting, and to use the non-magical medicines mentioned in the second category, has only to be bought (*yam*), but no man may perform the magic rites or apply the herbs or treatment of the third category unless he has obtained control (*kɔr*) of the particular *akombo* concerned by undergoing initiation. It is held by some of the Tiv, probably correctly, that the latter class of treatments is indigenous, whereas those which need only be bought have been copied from other peoples in comparatively recent times. It should, however, be emphasized that in every department of life, and more especially in the practice of medicine, the line between the natural and the supernatural is very faintly drawn, and that even in the case of those treatments and operations which have no especial magical significance in themselves, the unseen forces are felt to be very near at hand, waiting for a chance to make things go wrong. For this reason, no important operation is undertaken, or treatment applied, without every precaution being taken against their intervention.

The fees themselves are paid in recognized articles of small value, such as one strand of tobacco, an arrow-head, a little bag of salt made out of palm fronds (present value 1*d*.), or a single head of cotton. The larger amounts, which are laid down as additional payments over and above the nominal fees, are called 'five', 'ten', 'ten-twenty' (between ten and twenty) and 'twenty'. These may have been introduced later. The terms at least are not very old, as they are derived from the number of strips on a native cloth (*tugudu*), a full-sized cloth having originally consisted of twenty strips of woven material. Thus if the patient or candidate for initiation is told to pay two *akombo* fees and a 'ten', this means two arrow-heads (or strands of tobacco, &c.) and an article which is theoretically the equivalent of half a cloth but in practice may vary considerably in value. Even so, the full amounts are not always exacted, the important point in every case being not the value of the payment, but the fact that something is given.

HUNTING *AKOMBO*

In addition to the *Biamegh-Poor*, Akiga describes the rites of a number of hunting *akombo*, but only one representative example will be given here. They are all somewhat similar, and have certain characteristics in common, of which the following may be noted:

(i) The emblems are not put in the middle of the village (except the *Poor*), but usually just outside by the side of a path.

(ii) Sword-grass, or rope made from the leaves of the meni oil tree, is used in their construction, and 'grass-striking' or 'blackening' (see p. 187) forms a part of their rites.

(iii) There is much use of beniseed. A beniseed diet is supposed by the Tiv to make a man fat but not strong (cf. p. 253), and its purpose in connexion with the hunting rites is probably to have the same effect on the wild game.

(iv) They have certain taboos, most of which are associated with blood. A menstruous woman must not go into the *ate*, because here are kept the hunter's weapons with the emblems hung round them. Strictly speaking she should sleep in a special hut at the back of the village, and on a bed only used at this period. A man who has an *akombo* must not touch her or anything connected with her, nor eat food prepared by her, otherwise he breaks the blood taboo, and thereby loses his control of the *akombo*. To some of the hunting *akombo* the wood of the *ikpine* is taboo, doubtless because of its blood-red sap, and to others the copaiba balsam tree, which has a red core and exudes a crimson resin when cut.

THE *ITIMBE-MKU*[1]

WHEN a man is ready to set up the *Itimbe-mku* and perform the rites, he goes to some one who has it. The latter tells him to cut a length of *gbaaye* wood, pull

[1] *Itimbe* means a temporary grass hut, and is now represented by sword-grass bound round a piece of wood, which was once presumably the *Mku* emblem. *Mku* seems originally to have been an ancestral cult of some importance (see p. 95), but is now the name of a rite only observed on the occasion stated below. The *Itimbe-mku* is treated as though it were a distinct cult, and its connexion with the *Mku* rite is not always even recognized.

up some sword-grass, and get ready a chicken, some camwood, and some *ishuragh* grains. He returns home and follows out these instructions. The man who is to carry out the rite arrives in the evening; he ties the sword-grass round the piece of *gbaaye*, leaving one end uncovered, and at the other end the grass is made into two flat-sided plaits branching out on either side of the top. He plants the uncovered end in the ground, so that the part with the sword-grass on it is uppermost. Then he goes away. If his home is far, he waits in some other hamlet near by. When night has come, and the evening meal is finished, it is time to carry out the rites. The *Itimbe-mku* rites are not performed in the day-time, lest any one who has not got it should see its fire and have bad luck in consequence.

So when the time arrives, the man who put up the *Itimbe-mku* earlier in the day comes back again, and the man for whom he is setting it right gives him the things which he has put ready. The master takes the camwood, mixes it into a paste, smears some on the *Itimbe-mku* and some on the other's temples. Then he takes one of the *ishuragh* grains, bites it, and spits it out in the direction of the sunrise and of the sunset, and on to the *Itimbe-mku*. He gives another of the grains to the man for whom he is setting it right, and he does exactly the same. When this is done he kills the chicken and pours some blood over the emblem. Then he has it cooked on the spot, together with some other meat besides. The chicken and the other meat are cooked with beniseed. When they are ready it is time to make the passes. Some *ruam* is prepared and brought out, and the man who is performing the rite breaks off a handful of the *ruam*, makes a hollow in it,[1] takes out the liver, stomach, and head of the chicken, and makes passes over the *Itimbe-mku* three times. He tells the other to put out his hands on one side of it, and withdraws his own; then they do the same on the other side, and so on. When he has gone through this ritual with him he gives him the *ruam* with the meat on it. He eats this, and takes all the meat which is left over to

[1] To hold the meat.

divide amongst those who have already got the mastery over the *Itimbe-mku*. By this time people are asleep. When the passes have been made and the food eaten, the beer is poured over the *akombo*, and finally the man who has had it set right for him gives something to the woman who has cooked the food. If he fails to do this, she will certainly be seized by it.

THE *MKU*

The *Mku* itself you will not find inside its *itimbe*, but, nevertheless, there is such a thing, and its rites are carried out differently. The rite is known as 'Raising'.[1] You do not say 'I am going to set right the *Mku*', but 'I am going to raise the *Mku*'. Moreover, it is of quite a different character from that of its *itimbe*. The *Itimbe-mku* is a hunting *akombo*, but the *Mku* itself a rite which is observed by a person who has had a dream about some one who is dead, for instance, his father or mother.

But some people say this about the *Mku*: It is really a very big thing, and the elders of long ago who understood the true reason for raising the *Mku* used to say that its purpose was to give food to your forefathers who were dead, in order that they might be pleased with you; that they should not come and speak with you in dreams, but give you good luck and a life of happiness on earth, blessed with every good fortune.[2]

THE SOCIAL ASPECT OF THE CULTS

❡. As already mentioned in the note on age-grades, the latter stages in the life of a Tiv, as he grows in age and importance in his group, and after he has become a husband and a father, are marked by his gradual initiation to the mastery of the many *akombo*. His rate of advance depends to a certain extent on his wealth, because of the expense involved in providing the fee, the beast for slaughter, and especially the 'presents'. But this is not the only, or most important, factor which regulates the Tiv's social and spiritual progress. It depends primarily on his position

[1] Because the officiating elder raises a small mound of earth, and pours the blood of the chicken over it.

[2] The name '*Mku*' has been regarded as the equivalent of *mba-kúûv*, 'the dead' (from *kú*, death), but this derivation is not recognized by the Tiv themselves, and is hardly in accordance with Tiv etymology.

in the group and his relationship to the elder members of it. So long as the older generation is alive he would not presume to aspire to the higher offices, and for the others he is also dependent on the compliance of the elders. Because if a man has offended one of the senior members of his own group, or excited his jealousy, and particularly (I speak according to Tiv beliefs) if he has contracted a flesh debt, he would not dare to run the risk of drawing attention to himself and thus laying himself open to the maleficent magic power of his seniors. For it is the older members of his father's group whom the Tiv fears more than the *akombo* or anything else. If disease or misfortune befall him, he knows, after he has eliminated the *akombo*, that it is they who are the cause. The dangers of a man attempting to attain to a high position without the necessary spiritual power, and against the will of his betters, have been shown in the account of the *Biamegh* and the *Poor*. A man is also dependent largely on the position of his father. If his father is a powerful member of the group he will often initiate his son into many of the *akombo* while he is still alive. This serves as a kind of investment; it gives his son an assured position in the group after his death, and also material advantage in the shape of the gifts which must be paid by all who seek initiation to those in the *akombo* group who are already masters. While he is alive, a father will protect his son from the other members of his group if his *tsav* is strong enough to do so, and if he was respected by them during his lifetime they will usually extend their goodwill to his son after his death.

PROTECTIVE CHARMS

CHARMS have no magic cruses and no guardian emblems, neither are they acquired by initiation, but are bought for money. Everything connected with them is done in secret, and not openly as with the birth and hunting *akombo*. The visible signs by which you can tell that a man is dealing in charms are the wearing of phylacteries, the binding of leather girdles round the waist or bands on the arm, and the putting of antimony on the eyes. Antimony is used as a philtre.[1] Phylacteries

[1] A practice copied probably from the Hausa, by whom antimony is used as a cosmetic. The Tiv have attributed to it a magic potency, which originally was not claimed for it.

are threaded on to the belt and tied round the waist, or sewn into a cap and worn on the head. Some are worn for protection, and some for other reasons. Each phylactery has its own peculiar function, as I have already described, and the girdles are also of many different kinds. You cannot distinguish between the nature of a phylactery and of a girdle in the same way that you can say whether an *akombo* is intended for this or the other purpose. Only the owner can tell you the difference, unless you have at one time yourself been the possessor of the charm, in which case you would know it at once if you saw it.

Another sign by which you know that a man has a charm is the little horn vessel. In some cases this is a ram's horn, in others the horn of a duiker, or the tusk of a wild boar. The horn is filled with powdered medicine, and a piece of red leather is sewn over the opening. It is provided with a loop so that it can be threaded on to a girdle and worn round the waist. This charm is known as *madugu*, which is the Hausa word *mai-dufu* (also called *layan zana*), meaning 'possessor of darkness'. If a thief has stolen something, and a hue and cry is raised, this charm makes him invisible, so that his pursuers may pass quite close without seeing him. Another form of charm is made by Hausa malams, who write on their wooden tablets and then wash off the ink and give it to people to drink. Thus a man may appear to have neither phylacteries, nor girdles, nor armlets, nor horn boxes, but do not for this reason suppose that he is devoid of all protective charms—he may be going to the malams and drinking their potions.

If you know anything of the Hausa people there will be no need to tell you from whom these charms have come: you will recognize at once from this description that it was they who gave them to the Tiv. None of the things described here are peculiar to the Tiv; other tribes have them too. But amongst the Tiv, the people whom you would find to be making the most use of charms are those who hold high positions in European service and are drawing big salaries. For if you take all the things on which people generally spend their money—beer, women, gambling, and charms—more money is spent on charms than on any of the others, and every Tiv chief, holding a staff of office, who has Hausa settled in his district or living permanently with him, drinks the charms which their malams give to him.

In former days the Tiv used to buy charms to give them victory in battle. War, fought with arrows, is now no longer. To-day another kind of battle is waged, the battle to be made paramount chief. (Where can the Tiv have got this notion of a paramount chief?) For years past, some of the chiefs have been in the habit of buying charms from the Hausa—phylacteries to wear and potions to drink—in order that the white man may be favourably inclined towards them and make them paramount chief. Others buy Hausa charms because they are afraid that he will take their staff of office away, and depose them.[1] Moreover, not only the chiefs, but all sorts of people who have got posts under the European—messengers, scribes, teachers, and what not—have set their hearts on being made paramount chief. They say that the Tiv who live at home know nothing, whereas they can write and speak English, and are obviously the people who will in future be made chief by the white man. So they, too, are buying spells and drinking charms.

SWEM IKARAGBE

Every Tiv knows that the *Swem* is a very big *akombo*; it is the great *akombo* by which they swear. But in point of fact Swem is a hill in the land of the Ukwese and Undir, the Bush Tribes through which the Tiv passed on their way down from the hills, as described in the first chapter. It is a magnificent hill to look at; there is none finer in all Tivland or in the surrounding country of the Bush Men. In actual size it is no larger than the neighbouring hills, but it is formed of one huge piece of rock. It is not wooded like other hills, and little is to be seen growing on it. On the top is a great round boulder, and all the vegetation there is grows on the rock beneath. From a

[1] This was written previous to the re-organization; see p. 409.

distance it looks like the tuft of hair on the crown of a man's head.

I, who write this, went to Swem Ikaragbe with Mr. Brink and Mr. La Grange, and we saw it exactly as I have described it. We did not go up, but stood and looked at it from the bottom, and I wrote down my impressions at the time. I also made inquiries amongst the tribes who live there, in order to find out whether they knew anything fresh about Swem. But Samu, the chief of the Iyɔn, said that though Swem was in their country they knew nothing more about it than we did. At one time they used to kill elephants on the hill, but there were no elephants there now, and he did not know of anything else. It was only when they came down into Tiv country that they heard so many different stories about Swem.

The Tiv say that none of the empty-chested[1] would dare to go to Swem, nor, if they did, would they be able to see it. It is only the old men with *tsav* who can go there, in order to set right the land. People do not even know where it is. Some say it is in Turan, some Maav, and some Kunav; so vague are their ideas as to where Swem may be. They say that it is in a forest, and that Swem itself is a huge pot, buried in the ground with only the rim showing above the surface. Round it grows the *iyandegh* plant, and in the forest are all kinds of savage creatures—leopards, elephants, lions, snakes, and bees. These creatures drive away every one who approaches; only one who is truly *tsav* can go there, and nothing will harm him.

Many wonderful tales are told about Swem. At the beginning of the dry season, when the birds come out from the east and fly in great flocks across the sky, they say the elders of the Tiv have come together from all parts of the country and changed into birds; they are off to Swem to set right the land. (That is to say, those of the elders who are *tsav* above all others.) When they have set right the land and start again for home, they take back

---

[1] *Vaŋger gbilin.* I have adopted Abraham's translation of this term; but note that *gbilin* means 'empty' in the sense of 'ineffective', since every one has *tsav* of a kind, see p. 241 below.

to their own country all kinds of different things from
Swem. The elders who have evil in their hearts bring
back hunger for their people, the hunger which kills.
Others take smallpox or coughs, which bring their group
near to extinction. Others bring with them the birds
which eat the millet grains, and that year not one head of
millet will be harvested in their villages. But the good
elders bring back Prosperity. When they return from
Swem the land of their clansmen flourishes; in that time
the women bear more children, more game falls to the
arrows of the hunters, and not a single misfortune
befalls their people.

The Origin of the name 'Swem Ikaragbe'. Ikaragbe
was a man of Nɔŋgov who had eaten human flesh in his
father's group and had given all his family in payment of
the debt. When he had no one else to give, they told him
that he must himself lie down and submit to the knife.
In terror he fled and took refuge amongst the Utyusha.
There he lay in hiding, and though his kinsmen searched
for him everywhere they were unable to find him. After
a time, one of his group, called Kpamberakpa, went on
a journey to the Utyusha, and one day, while he was sitting
and drinking beer with them, he heard some one say,
'Take this cup to Ikaragbe'. So he asked who was this
Ikaragbe to whom the beer was being taken, and was told
that it was Ikaragbe of Nɔŋgov. Hearing this, he struck
his hand upon his chest and said, 'Is not this the man
for whom we have been seeking in vain through every
clan in Tivland?' Thereupon he rose up at once from the
beer drinking, and went back to tell his kinsmen. When
they heard the news they decided to send Kpamberakpa
and Anyamagere, two men noted for their strength and
daring, to go and seize Ikaragbe and bring him back to
be slaughtered. These accordingly set out, taking with
them one or two other Nɔŋgov men whom they had
chosen to accompany them, and in due course came to the
Utyusha. But when they stated their mission, the people
of Utyusha strove to prevent them, saying that they could
not give the man up. The Nɔŋgov men replied that if
they refused to hand over their kinsman, they must give

them one of their own people to kill instead of him. But when matters had thus reached a deadlock, Ikaragbe said to the Utyusha, 'Let be. I will go with my kinsmen and be killed'.

As the men of Nɔŋgov rose up to take Ikaragbe away, he said to them, 'Wait. I have a small thing to show you, and after that I will go with you'. So he went on ahead down the road, and they followed close behind him, till they came to a great forest. There he bade them sit down. When they were all seated, he took a pot and filled it with ashes. In the ashes he put some lengths of *gbaaye* wood and *iyandegh* plants, and on the top he set an Axe of Heaven. After he had finished this he lay down and rested his head upon it, and his wife sat down beside him. Then he told his kinsmen, 'Now take me away and kill me. If a Tiv does evil he shall not escape his fate, to whatsoever land he may flee'. So they rose up together and went on.

And as they brought him along the road, the men of Nɔŋgov sang, 'Kpamberakpa has caught a man for me!' and others took up the refrain, 'Hee-e-e! Anyamagere has caught a man for me, Hee-e-e!' This is the origin of the song which is known to every Tiv.

So they brought Ikaragbe home, and killed him.

Not many days later Kpamberakpa and Anyamagere fell ill with swellings on the legs, and died. When the Tiv saw this they said that these had been punished with death for their cold-blooded murder of Ikaragbe. For though Ikaragbe had done wrong, he had begged for mercy, and had 'dressed' the *Swem* and lain upon it, yet they would not spare him. Wherefore the *akombo* on the *Swem* had killed them. And so will the *Swem* destroy every man who kills without pity.

The Dressing of the 'Swem.' Since that time it has become the custom to dress the *Swem* in cases of crime or illness. A little pot is filled with ashes, pieces of *gbaaye* wood and *iyandegh* plants are put in it, and an Axe of Heaven is set on the top, after the manner in which it was first dressed by Ikaragbe. Moreover, nowadays every man who is initiated to one of the big *akombo* brings it and lays it also on the *Swem*. Afterwards a piece of raffia is tied round the neck of the pot with a knot at each side. That is how the *Swem* is dressed for use in courts of justice. For illness it is dressed in the same way, but in addition arrows are thrust into it, and a knife is laid on the top.

For judicial cases it is used as follows: If a man is being tried by the elders for some crime, and persistently denies it, they dress the *Swem*, place it on the ground in front of him, and command him to swear. They tell him that if he is guilty, and deliberately denying it, the *Swem* will seize him; but if he is speaking the truth, he will thereby obtain acquittal. Thereupon he pronounces this oath: 'If I, So-and-so, have indeed done this thing, and wilfully deny it, then will this *Swem* seize me, so that my stomach and my legs swell up and I die. But if I am innocent, I shall go forth a free man.' While he utters these words he places his hand on the *Swem*, or else takes it and sets it on his head. He has then taken the oath. If he has sworn what is true no harm will come to him, but if he has sworn falsely the *Swem* will seize him, his stomach and legs will swell, and he will certainly die.

This is how it is used in case of illness: If a man falls sick, and gets no better in spite of all efforts to discover the cause, he dresses the *Swem* and sends out his boys to call in his paternal kinsmen. When they have all assembled, he takes the *Swem* which he has dressed and sets it on the ground. Then he says: 'I have not summoned you without good reason. This disease is killing me, and I do not know what sin I have committed. So I have called you here that I may swear to you my innocence before I die. Since I came to boyhood in my father's group I have taken no man's wife; I have bewitched no one, nor eaten human flesh with any. I have done nothing but good to all my kinsmen, yet death is killing me for no cause. Therefore I say come, and I will declare to you my purpose: I will break the *Swem*! If the guilt is mine, it shall strike me down dead, and you shall go unharmed; but if I am innocent, and am being wilfully done to death, the *Swem* shall seize the man who is killing me. That is my oath. Let me then hear what you have to say, before I break it.'

To this his kinsmen reply: 'We have heard your oath. What you say is good. Yet you need not break the *Swem*; your illness will leave you of its own accord.' Then each in turn stands up and takes this oath: 'I know nothing of the death which is killing So-and-so. I protest my innocence with my whole heart.' When they have all spoken these words, they tell him to place the *Swem* on the ground and lay his head upon it. Thereupon he abandons his purpose and sets the *Swem* down without breaking it. He may subsequently die of the disease, or he may not. But sometimes a sick man dresses the *Swem* and breaks it, despite all the entreaties of his kinsmen. He lifts it up, and though they cry, 'No, no, let it be!' he dashes it to pieces on the ground. People then say, 'So-and-so has dressed the *Swem* to-day and broken it on account of his illness'.

If the man falls sick while he is staying in his mother's group, he pronounces the oath with these words: 'O my mother's kinsmen, when my troubles were more than I could bear I fled to you for refuge, that you might also see what wrong I have done that my father's group so persecutes me. But since I came to you it has fared no better with me than before. Therefore I have dressed the *Swem*, and laid upon it the arrow and the knife, and the *akombo* of my mother's people. And I have said come, that I may swear to you my innocence, then break the *Swem* and die. For if I die without your hearing what I have to tell you, you will afterwards say that I had eaten human flesh with my father's kinsmen, and that for this cause they dogged my footsteps here and killed me. Listen, therefore, to my oath: If I have come to you to seek refuge after eating human flesh in my father's group, and he with whom I shared the meat has come to one of you, my mother's kinsmen, and conspired with him to cast me out and give me up to him, then it is well, for it is I myself who have done it. So let me be killed by this very knife which lies here on the *Swem*, and do you live your lives in happiness, blessed by every good fortune. Or if it

be one of you, my mother's people, and not one of my
father's group, to whom I owe the debt, so let it also
happen. But if I have eaten no human flesh, either with
one of my father's group, or with you, my mother's kinsmen, and you are killing me without cause, your land shall
be brought to ruin, and when you go out to battle you
shall be utterly destroyed by the arrows of the enemy,
and die the violent death which you have prepared for me.'
With this he takes the *Swem* and breaks it. But sometimes,
being prevented by his kinsmen, he refrains, and, having
placed it on the ground, lays his head upon it.

Another case is when a man wishes to found a new
market. He calls together all the elders of his group and
explains his purpose to them. If they all agree, he dresses
the *Swem* and utters this imprecation: 'If any man spoil
this market by *tsav*, the *Swem* shall surely seize the
sorcerer!' Thereupon the elders all stand up and take
hold of the *Swem* together, then set it on the ground at the
foot of a fig-tree in the market-place. In former times,
whenever the elders made an agreement on any important
matter, they used to dress the *Swem* and take the oath, in
order that, if any one of them should afterwards break
away and act independently, the *Swem* might seize him,
and he would die.

To the Tiv in the past the *Swem* was a very big thing.
But nowadays they do not pay so much regard to it as they
did. They still take the oath, but it is only a formality;
they do not swear from the depths of their heart as they
did in the old days. In the courts of the white man, when
chiefs who are judging a case dress the *Swem* and set it on
the ground, as they used to do in the old Tiv courts, when
a case baffled them, to frighten a lying witness, now no
one is afraid at all. In Tivland to-day, when a man is
standing his trial for a grave offence, and the judges,
seeing that he is deliberately concealing his guilt, tell him
that if he swear to the truth of his denial he will be
acquitted, but that if he forswear himself the *Swem* will
seize him, the accused man stands up and takes the oath
without hesitation. Or a case may be brought by two
disputants, neither of whom will give way, both protesting

the truth of their statements. If the judges set before them a *Swem*, or some other *akombo* such as the Tongs or an Axe of Heaven, warning them that if they swear falsely they will be seized by it, they both swear in exactly the same words, and each leaves the court without any fear that he will be killed by the *akombo* for having taken the oath with full consciousness of his guilt.

When a man is summoned to court on account of a crime which he has committed, his people, who know perfectly well that he is guilty, give him every encouragement. 'When you go,' they say, 'keep on telling the same story. Whatever charge they bring against you, deny it. Don't contradict yourself. With the white man's justice it is merely a matter of keeping on saying the same thing and you get off. And if they dress the *Swem* and tell you to swear on it, swear. Don't be afraid. We, your people, are your *Swem*. Only we can kill you. A man is not killed by the *Swem*, nor by any other *akombo*; it is the *mbatsav* who kill him. And if we do not kill you, the *akombo* by itself can do you no harm. If you are such a fool as to be afraid of the *Swem* you will find yourself in prison!' So in the court of justice it is the guilty man who has the most to say. Sometimes, if the judges forget about the oath on the *akombo*, he remembers it himself. 'I am telling you the honest truth,' he says, 'but it does not satisfy you. Dress the *Swem*, and let me swear on it!' When it is brought, he is the first to take the oath.

The reason that the *Swem* is so popular amongst the Tiv to-day is because through it they can obtain acquittal when they appear before the white man, and not because they have any faith in it as a time-honoured institution. It has become nothing but a means of escape from justice. Tiv chiefs and judges know this, but they will not speak of it openly in such a way that a European would understand. And if any one were so to disclose the true state of affairs, they would not be pleased with him, for to them it is a way by which they can save themselves from the white man.

While other peoples of the world have been advancing

in knowledge of how to make all kinds of new things, progress amongst the Tiv has consisted in learning how to make more and more *akombo*. Yet their faith in the *akombo*, as a thing in which to place their trust, is growing less and less. Even at the present time people are still adding to the number of *akombo*. In the year 1930 a man invented one for himself. His name was Inya, and his father was Makwar of Mbagen in Kparev. He called his *akombo Icieshe*,[1] and went through a ceremony with a mouse. He made a clay pillar, broke off some leaves of the locust-bean tree and set them down close by, then caught a mouse and cut its throat, pouring the blood over the clay pillar and the leaves. Then he cooked the mouse which he had killed, together with many other mice, and performed the rites. All the people who were initiated with the inventor joined in the meal; if any one else were to eat of it, he would be seized by the *Icieshe*. The guardian emblem of this *akombo* is a hawk's feather, the idea being that if the *Icieshe* catches you you will have no more shame than a hawk. For a hawk is so lacking in decency that if you have a hen with a hatch of chickens it will not be ashamed to come and take one under your very eyes. That is why he based his *akombo* on the shamelessness of a hawk.

Inya also tells the following story: During the time when men were being made to throw away the evil instruments of the *mbatsav*, every one who produced something was much credited with *tsav*, and held in general respect as a dangerous man. Now people always said that Inya was *tsav*, and so the idea came to him that he would perform some great miracle that would astonish everybody. But as he did not possess a single article of the *mbatsav* equipment, he could not think how to do it. In due course he set out for Katsina Ala.[2] When he came to the place where the Dura flows into the Katsina River he saw two large black crabs, which he caught and put into his lynx-fur pouch. When the crabs moved, the pouch seemed as though it were alive. Seeing this, he was

[1] Shame.
[2] Where the witchcraft investigation was conducted (1929).

delighted, and said, 'Heaven has helped me to find what I have been seeking!'

So he crossed over the river with his pouch and came to Katsina Ala. There he found his group sitting in consultation about the *akombo* of the *mbatsav*. 'You are full of *tsav*,' they said to him, 'yet you have not brought out a single thing. Why is this? If you do not show us something, we shall take you to the District Officer to-day.' He replied that he had indeed an *akombo*, but its purpose was not to kill people, but to protect the land. He also used it, he said, to protect himself when he was asleep. If the *mbatsav* came to do him harm it woke him, and he got up and drove them off. The elders told him to show it to them. So he brought out the lynx-fur pouch with the crabs in it, and threw it down in the middle of them. The crabs began to struggle, and the bag moved about on the ground like a live thing. The meeting broke up in alarm. The elders told him to take the thing away. They said it need not be shown to the white man, as it was meant for protection and not destruction. So he took it away, and was acclaimed by all for having produced the best magic article! When he came on to the road he took out the crabs and threw them away, passed on, and returned home.

THE *IMBORIVUŊGU*

The *imborivuŋgu* is a very big thing to the Tiv; it is used for setting right the land and has a much greater value than you would judge from its appearance. It is a human bone: some say that it is a shin-bone, others that it is taken from the arm. It looks more like an arm-bone, as it is hardly big enough for a shin-bone, unless possibly that of a small child. When a man dies, his body is dug up by the *mbatsav*, who take one of the bones to make an *imborivuŋgu* for setting right the land. This is done as follows: The bone is cut down to about the length of a man's hand. (They are not all quite the same size, but all are made in the same way.) Then some rags are tied round the top and covered in wax, on to which is stuck some hair and sometimes also some red love-beans. Two

Q

cowrie shells are fixed in the wax to look like eyes, and some more red beans on either side for the raised face markings. It is also provided with a mouth, nose, and ears.

The *imborivuŋgu*. may also be made of metal. This kind is cast in brass, and is made after exactly the same pattern as the bone type, except that there is no wax on it, and its head is brass throughout. Some have male heads and some female, as in the case of those made of bone. When it is finished, a hole is bored in its chest, the bottom end is stopped up with wax, and on to this is stuck some spider's web. In recognition of its dignity, the *imborivuŋgu* is decorated with the best sort of beads.

There are two different kinds of *imborivuŋgu*, that owned by one man personally, and that belonging to the group. A private *imborivuŋgu* eventually becomes a group *imborivuŋgu*. First of all a man makes it and sells it to some one, who buys it for his own, in order that he may acquire honour, wealth, and good crops. He keeps it very secret and carries out its rites alone, because if his group were to know of it they would demand that he should give it to them, and that they should perform the rites together. It would then become the property of the group for setting right the land.

The Sale of an 'Imborivuŋgu'. An *imborivuŋgu* is not sold openly like a cloth or any other article; the transaction is kept secret. A man who has made an *imborivuŋgu* does not wander round aimlessly with the hope of selling it, but takes it to men of worth, whom he has already heard spoken of as being *tsav* and anxious to have these things of the land. For example, the seller is Agaku, the buyer Adugu: Agaku puts the *imborivuŋgu* in his bag, wraps it up carefully and arrives at Adugu's home in the evening. Sitting down discreetly, he places his bag by his side, or in his lap, and allows no one to touch it. Adugu, noticing how careful he is of the bag, perceives that there is something in it of value. So he fills a pipe for Agaku, and when he has made all the usual polite inquiries asks him where he is going. Agaku replies, 'I have only come to see you'. So when they have finished their conversation, they sleep, and the next morning, when the sun is up and every one has gone to the farm, so that quiet reigns in the village, Agaku calls Adugu to come with him into the house. There he unties his bag and takes out the *imbor-ivuŋgu* to show Adugu. Adugu is shaken, but keeps his head sufficiently to remain seated and inquire the price. Agaku says, 'It is not expensive; I am only asking six "twenties" for it. If you will buy it at this price, I will also show you how to carry out its rites'. Adugu buys it. Agaku tells him to go and catch a house-mouse. When he has brought one, Agaku cuts its throat and pours the blood over the *imborivuŋgu*, for that is how it is set right. He also teaches him how to blow it. It is blown at the bottom end, which is covered with spider's web, and to get a good note from it you must strain very hard. The piper does not stand in one place to blow it; he gives one blast, then runs a long way off before he stops to give another. That is all there is about a privately owned *imborivuŋgu*.

The 'Imborivuŋgu' of the Fathers. It is a personal *imborivuŋgu* that is converted into an *imborivuŋgu* of the fathers, for the group to set right the land. This con-version comes about when the group induces the owner to part with it for the common good; but if he is very evasive, they wait till he dies, and then the senior elder persuades his children to give it to him. The whole group then joins together to set right the land with it. The man who takes it over keeps it in his charge, but it belongs to the group, not to him alone. Moreover, when it becomes the concern of the whole group, its rites take on a more serious character; a human life is required, instead of the mouse which was used when it was the property of an individual. Some say that a man is killed, but those who know best say that it is not a man that is used to set it right, but a baby, or the fœtus procured from a woman who has aborted. But it must be a woman who has not previously given birth.

When the rite is carried out by means of abortion the procedure is as follows: If a young girl becomes pregnant at a time when it is desired to set right the land with an *imborivuŋgu*, the elders sit together and plot how to get

the child from her womb by stealth, in order to set right
the land with it. They determine to make her abort.
As soon as she feels the first signs of quickening, and
complains of sensations in her womb, aha! then the elders
who have been discussing her are pleased. One of them
fetches some medicine for procuring abortion, grinds it
up and gives it to her, saying that it will cure her. The
girl takes it without knowing, and has a miscarriage. Even
though this should occur during the daytime, the abortion
is not buried. Those who are in the secret tell the boys
to wait, as So-and-so has been sent for and they must not
bury it till he comes. They practise this deception in
order to make time and keep the fœtus till nightfall,
when they will set right the *imborivuŋgu* with it. They
delay until it begins to get dark, and then tell the boys to
bury it, as they have waited for So-and-so long enough,
but he has not come. But when the small children have
taken it away to bury at the back of the village, one of
the elders goes round quickly, takes it from them and
sends them away. 'Go home', he says. 'It is too dark for
you children to bury it. I will do it properly myself.'
The children, who are afraid of the darkness, run back
into the village. After they have gone, he takes it and
hides it. When every one is asleep the elders meet
together, the keeper of the *imborivuŋgu* brings it, and they
start to carry out the rites with the dead fœtus. The man
who has been hiding it lays it on the ground, and beside
it they place the *imborivuŋgu* and a calabash of water.
First they take the fœtus, make passes[1] with it, and cut its
throat with a knife. They take some of the blood and
smear it on the *imborivuŋgu*. When they have finished
they wash their hands in the calabash bowl, then take the
water and pour it into a well and over the farm of the
keeper of the *imborivuŋgu*. Thus the crops of the whole
group will be good, and the first woman to draw water
from the well the next morning will straightway conceive
and bear a son, even though she had hitherto been barren.

Others kill small babies by secret means, to set right
the *imborivuŋgu*. The *mbatsav* elders who wish to carry

---

[1] *Cia*, see note on p. 190.

out the rites decide on a woman that has recently given birth to a child, and one of them watches her. One night, while she is asleep, he takes some powdered camwood, bites it up in his mouth, and blows it up the baby's nostrils. The powder goes right up into the child's head, and it dies. When the mother wakes up and finds her child dead, she cries out in the night, and those who come in give her the blame. 'You must have lain on the child', they say. 'But do not cry. The oil is spilled, but the flask is not broken. You will bear again.' So they take the baby and bury it. Later, during the night, they dig it up again and set right the *imborivungu* with it, in exactly the same way as with an abortion. The land prospers. Soon after the woman conceives, and bears another child. The elders straitly charge that no harm shall come to it.[1]

The *imborivungu* is kept in a box, and everything else that is put in it receives virtue from it. If you wear a cloth [which has been in contact with it] for any occasion, you will certainly win the day. No one present at the gathering will be able to compete with you.

❡ The *imborivungu* or 'owl-pipe' was given much publicity at the time of the witchcraft investigation (1929), because it was a notorious article in the equipment of the *mbatsav*, and its cult was one of those which were believed to entail human sacrifice. The original type seems to have been, like the *Poor* skulls, a human relic, to which has been added moulding and decoration to represent a human figure. Presumably, therefore, the *imborivungu*, as well as the *Poor*, was intended to procure the co-operation of the ancestors, that is, in the first place, of the particular ancestor to whom the relic belonged. It is possible even that the two cults were once connected, since examples have been found of a human skull with the *imborivungu* pipe protruding from its base or mouth, or, looking at it in another way, a real skull has been fixed to the pipe instead of its head being fashioned from clay or wax. At the present time, however, they are regarded as quite unrelated, and the ancestral aspect of the *imborivungu* has been forgotten.

[1] I.e. they exert their authority over the supernatural forces, as a reward for the service rendered by the mother (unconsciously) in sacrificing her former child to the good of the community.

Functionally, the pipe presents some difficulty. I was privileged to see some unpublished work of the late Professor Henry Balfour on a class of voice-disguising instruments, which he had collected in various parts of the world. The common principle in these is a hollow tube provided with an aperture, into which the man speaks, and a membrane or spider's web which vibrates with a reedy tone. Their object, where the ritual significance has not been lost, is to create the impression of voices from the dead. Such instruments are actually still used for this purpose by the Gwari and other Nigerian tribes. Professor Balfour's collection proves beyond all reasonable doubt that the *imborivuŋgu*, of which some fine specimens are included, is a highly elaborate member of the same series. The difficulty, however, is that no Tiv has yet been found who understands its true function. The *imborivuŋgu* is always spoken of as being not talked into but blown into, and that with superhuman lung power, as the description on p. 248 implies. It does not even appear to be generally understood that it should be blown at the side hole, not at the end like an ordinary Tiv pipe. In some of the examples the end hole is stopped up, as in Akiga's description, showing that the original object of the spider's web or membrane had been lost. The conclusion must be, therefore, that the *imborivuŋgu* is in reality a voice-disguiser, made out of an ancestral relic, but that either in the process of developing into a conventionalized cult object its original purpose has been forgotten, or else that, like so many other of the tribal institutions, it is a foreign importation, of which the outward form only has been copied and adapted to suit local cultural and artistic fashions, without an understanding of its true nature and function.

AƆNDO (THE SKY GOD)

The following paragraphs were originally written as an introduction to the section on missionary work amongst the Tiv, which has had to be omitted together with most of the accounts of other European departmental activities. Aɔndo has been accepted by the Mission as the name for God, and Akiga's object is to define the concept as it existed before it was appropriated and converted to the Christian needs. If the definition is sketchy, so are the Tiv ideas on the subject. Aɔndo is, in fact, to the non-Christian Tiv of to-day a typical Bantu 'Supreme Being', conceived hazily as the

creator of the world and sometimes as the first ancestor of mankind; identified with the sky, and spoken of as raining, thundering,
lightning, and so forth; but otherwise taking no active part in
man's affairs, being beyond the range of everyday magic and
religion. If Akiga is right, and his views on this subject have not
been unduly influenced by his Christian upbringing, it appears
that Aɔndo was at one time considered to be subject to the influence of magic, perhaps even of prayer, particularly within his
own especial sphere of controlling (and being) the forces of nature.
At the present time, however, the practice of rain-making seems
to have almost died out.

IN very early times the Tiv used the name of Aɔndo
frequently. They knew that Aɔndo existed and was
nowhere else but above. They used also to speak of
Aɔndo giving and refusing to give. And they knew that
nothing was greater than he. With regard to this belief
in the supremity of Aɔndo, one can find examples in Tiv
speech and song, and in the fact that, though their understanding of the matter is very slight, you will never hear
any Tiv in his senses say that a thing is greater than
Aɔndo. However excellent it may be, they will say only,
'It is as Aɔndo', not that it is greater. Or if they praise
a man in song and wish to do him the highest honour,
they may say 'He is as Aɔndo', but say 'He is greater than
Aɔndo', no. Even when the white man came and was
above everything else, they never said he was greater than
Aɔndo. When they greeted him after their own fashion,
they pointed first to heaven, then to earth, then to the
white man. This meant Aɔndo, Earth, White Man;
these three are greatest. Nevertheless, in olden times,
most of the things they did were done for the sake of
Aɔndo. The earth was honoured by them, and still is so,
for two reasons. First, because food grows from the soil,
and secondly, because every man who dies is buried in it.
They said that there was a great town under the ground,
and every one went to live there when he died. For this
reason a man who was in misery would say that when he
died his troubles would be over. But of Aɔndo they said,
'Aɔndo sees, and sleeps not. If you cherish evil in your

heart against some one, Aɔndo will perceive it. Aɔndo hears; if a man does good and makes a declaration of his innocence,[1] he will accept it'.

The people who lived in those days had several great men who called upon the name of Aɔndo. In the whole of Shitire, Ukum, Ikurav, Toŋgov, Nɔŋgov and Iharev, Masev and Tɔmbo, there was one great and wise man whose name was Gbayaŋge, son of Ato, of the Ndzɔrov section of the Nɔŋgov clan. He had a brother called Akaakase. Of all the other clans there was none that did not know or that had not heard of Gbayaŋge Ato, as a wise man, who never ceased to utter the name of Aɔndo: till they came to call Aɔndo 'The Aɔndo of Gbayaŋge'. There have been four great men of this kind in Tivland: Gbayaŋge of Nɔŋgov, Ityevajir of Kunav, Ikeratar of Tɔmbo, and Abaverijuwa of Ukum. These four are the greatest that the Tiv have had, but they did not all appear at the same time. They were known as 'The Masters of the land[2] who called upon Aɔndo'. Aɔndo hearkened to their voice, and this is why he was called 'their' Aɔndo by the Tiv. What they did was to set right the land. When the land was becoming spoilt and no rain fell, the chief brewed beer, all his group assembled, and there came also one of these men who set right the land. He was clothed in the skin of the red-flanked duiker, bound round with leaves of the *iyandegh* plant. He stood up, and the people seated themselves on the ground. Then he began to speak. As he spoke he uttered the names of many things,[3] and when he had finished he sang:

'The Drum of the Dance I clasp to my breast',

(Answer) '*Hie!*'

'From the Drum of Death I draw aside, that it may pass by me, go down, and fall into the water.'

(Answer) '*Hie!*'[4]

---

[1] *Ta icia.* See p. 220. This is an essential part of Tiv ritual when removing a curse, taking precautions against intervention of malicious forces, &c.

[2] *Mbatarev:* the true meaning of this word implies magic control of the 'land', i.e. of natural forces, rather than authority over its human inhabitants.

[3] I.e. *akombo.*

[4] The dance drum is symbolic of happiness. For the idea of evil flowing away on water, see p. 32.

Then he dipped up some of the beer and drank it, leaving a little in the cup, which he poured back into the pot for the others to drink. Though till then no rain had fallen, it would surely rain that day.

Even when all these were dead, some of the older men who had held them in high regard did not forget them, but used their names continually. And when the sky was black with rain, and a terrible storm was blowing, an elder would rise up and cry, 'Ahe-e, Aɔndo of Gbayaŋge Ato! Aɔndo of Ityevajir! Aɔndo of Abaverijuwa! Aɔndo of Ikeratar! O be calm and stay still!' When the elder uttered this invocation, Aɔndo would stay his hand and send good rain without wind.

One day Gbayaŋge sent his brother Akaakase to fetch some human flesh for him from another section of their clan called Kaambe. This was given to him, and he put it in his bag. But while he was crossing the river, Aɔndo caused a great red storm-cloud to appear, and the wind caught the boat in which was Akaakase and his human meat. As the boat was about to sink, Akaakase began to sing, calling upon Aɔndo:

'O Aɔndo of Gbayaŋge, be still!
It was Aɔndo of Gbayaŋge that killed him,[1]
It was he that smote him, O!
O Aɔndo of Gbayagŋe of Nɔŋgov!
Thou Aɔndo of Gbayaŋge, be still!'

When Akaakase sang thus, Aɔndo made the wind to cease. They crossed in safety, and the storm dispersed.

Such was the belief in Aɔndo held by the Tiv of long ago. But in after years they gave all this up, and cared not to use Aɔndo's name for any cause, as did those men of old. Or if they did use it, they said instead, 'It is the will of Allah, as the Hausa man says'; and so eventually, 'It is the will of Aɔndo, says the Hausa'. This they learnt from the Hausa who were beginning to go amongst them, because whenever these are in trouble they say, 'Ba Allah ba?' Some of the Tiv even called their children Allah, after the Hausa name for Aɔndo. The father of Zaki

[1] Sc. the man whose flesh he was carrying.

Biam, who was chief of Ukum at the time when the white man came, was called Allah, and his grandfather was called Akugar. This name the Tiv got from the Hausa call to prayer, 'Allahu akbar'. This is Arabic and means 'God is great'; but the Hausa never divulged the meaning of their sacred learning to the Tiv, whom they called pagans. For they did not come among the Tiv to teach them religion, but to make what they could out of them. But it is characteristic of the Tiv immediately to seize upon anything new, whether they understand it or not, and if it please them to adopt it. This is how they acquired this name (Akugar) without knowing what it meant. In latter times the Tiv have not troubled to use the name of Aɔndo in sincerity, as did their forefathers, with very few exceptions, and as for calling upon him, no one does this now. It was at the time when the Tiv had ceased to regard Aɔndo in the way that their fathers did that the missionaries came. . . .

V.

TSAV

⚁ In contrast to the elusive and contradictory attitude of the Tiv to the supernatural forces examined in the previous section, the belief in witchcraft, that is in the malevolent use of these forces by human beings, is comparatively well defined, uniform, and little affected by the recent changes in social conditions. In what follows it is this belief which is discussed rather than the actual practice. It is almost impossible, even for an African, to study the question from the point of view of the witch, or to say how far the Tiv ever deliberately practise witchcraft, if by this is meant the conscious use of occult arts, spells, and so forth, calculated to do harm. Probably it is rare. It is true that a man will often admit that he is the cause of another's death or sickness, but this, as Akiga points out, is usually for one of two reasons: either he makes the claim deliberately in order to overawe the fellow members of his group, or else he is unable to maintain his innocence in face of public opinion. As an individual he cannot hold out against the decision of the group of which he is an integral part. It is a fact that a man tried and found guilty of practising witchcraft by the group council seldom denies it. Although he may not be aware of having or using the mysterious power, he accepts their decision without question, like a patient who is told by a board of experts that he is suffering from some malignant disease, of which there are no subjective symptoms. In some respects, indeed, the view taken of witchcraft is pathological rather than criminal, though not on this account any the less dangerous. It should also be remembered that ill-omened words, or even thoughts, are considered to be effective in themselves, whether there be conscious intention to harm or not, and this not only by the Tiv but also amongst such comparatively advanced peoples as the Hausa and Fulani. This idea is clearly apparent in the *hamber ifan* rite, where the man who has been the cause of misfortune to some one through his evil wishes ritually washes them out of his heart.[1]

Apart from this there are two practices associated with witchcraft

[1] Footnote on p. 298.

which are not imaginary, though probably infrequent: one is the use of poisons to produce the same effect; the other is the practice of causing terror to people at night by various tricks, noises, and so forth. But in these cases also, although it is easy to get second-hand stories, and even to meet people who claim to have been victims of such an experience, it is almost impossible to find any who would admit to an outsider that he had taken an active part in such doings. The whole subject is best approached from the other side, the view-point of the injured party. This aspect is also the most important, because the belief in human agency, working by means of *tsav*, as the ultimate cause of every death, and of much else, has a very profound influence on the social life of the people. Akiga says that he no longer holds this belief. His first paragraph, in which he makes this confession, appeared in the original manuscript, but he afterwards proposed to delete it, with much of what immediately follows, as being a record of purely personal experience. It has been left as originally written, however, in fairness to himself and his teachers; it is the only occasion in this work in which he obtrudes the convictions which are the result of his Christian upbringing.

Nevertheless *tsav* does not mean witchcraft. Or rather, witchcraft is only one of its manifestations. *Tsav* is the power by which a man can achieve that which is beyond his normal faculties to accomplish, and is thus equivalent in many respects to the conception which has become familiar under the name of Mana and other terms for similar ideas elsewhere. There are, however, one or two special features in the Tiv idea which need to be mentioned. First, *tsav* is not a general form of energy which can reside in inanimate objects or exist in a free state, but is a strictly personal and non-transferable force or quality possessed by human beings. In this sense it corresponds quite closely to our vague notion of 'personality', that undefinable something which enables a man to impose his will on others and succeed in whatever he undertakes. Like personality, it is a thing which is apparent in others but is not strictly applicable to oneself. This fact explains much in the Tiv attitude towards witchcraft. Akiga uses it as an argument to support his declaration that there is no foundation for the belief in *tsav*, but if *tsav* is regarded primarily as an abstract personal quality rather than a demonstrable fact, it is easy to understand its objective character. It is no more to be expected that a Tiv should recognize his own *tsav* than that a successful leader should understand the nature of the impression which he makes on the minds of his followers.

It is true that magic power is often regarded as having concrete existence inside the body of its possessor, which can be discovered by means of a post-mortem examination. In the case of the Tiv the strength and character of this power are shown, respectively, in the size and shape of the fatty tissues surrounding the heart. *Tsav* has therefore been defined as a physical condition, indicating occult power. But, strictly speaking, this is an inversion of the logical sequence of Tiv reasoning on the subject. First is the observed fact that some men are better craftsmen than others, grow bigger yams, or have more influence over their fellows. Why? It must be due to some hidden virtue which they possess in a greater degree than other people. This is *tsav*. Lastly the conception is rationalized by an organic explanation, which provides after death a means of discovering the true nature of a man's behaviour during his life, and of confirming or refuting the suspicions which may have been held about the way in which he was employing his magic power. The practical implication of this test is described on p. 241.

Tsav itself, considered in the abstract, is of a neutral character, and varies in intensity rather than in quality. Fundamentally there is no distinction between good *tsav* and bad *tsav*; the difference lies in the use to which it is put. But since there is no other word in the language for witchcraft, and the maleficent attributes of the supernatural have always a more prominent place in the Tiv mind than the beneficent, the word has taken a somewhat sinister meaning, particularly in its compound *mbatsav* (witches), which is now always used in a bad sense. Thus, to be specific, witchcraft must be called *kwagh u mbatsav*, 'a thing of the witches', and a witch *or u mbatsav*, not *or-tsa(v)*, which has no evil implication. It may also be noted that the word *tsav*, like mana, may appear to act as more than one part of speech, according to the grammatical context in which it is used. But it would be wrong to draw from this any conclusions as to its nature. Parts of speech are not rigid in African languages, and the distinction between them is often undefined. Thus it may be said that a man 'is' *tsav*, 'acts' *tsav*, or does something 'by' *tsav*. Basically the word in each case has a neutral significance. Only in the expression *a duwe tsav*, 'he went (out) *tsav*' (see p. 248 below) has it very definitely a bad flavour.[1]

The degeneration in the meaning of *tsav* has come about partly through its supposed abuse by seekers after power described in the final chapter, and partly through the loss of faith in the efficacy of the ancient rites. For *tsav* was that power by which the elders were believed to control the supernatural for the benefit of the community, or, as the Tiv say, to 'set right the land'. It used to be thought essential that every kindred should have at least one senior man (formerly called *tee*) of sufficient *tsav* to do this effectively. To perform the more important of the public rites a human sacrifice was said to have been required, and the victim had to be the child or near relation of the officiating elder. This condition of sacrifice is too well known to need discussion here. Its interest in the present connexion is that it may very probably give a clue to an understanding of the present Tiv beliefs in witchcraft. These beliefs are, namely, that every death, in theory at least, is ascribed to the elders of the group in which it occurs; conversely, that a man can only bewitch a kinsman, and that an older man can only bewitch a younger, not vice versa. (With regard to the last condition it should be mentioned that a man may be the cause of a senior being bewitched by complaining (*vaa*); for example, a young man who considers himself unfairly treated by an older brother over a matter of the *aŋgɔl*. In this case divination will indicate him as the guilty party. But this does not affect the principle, since the actual bewitchment can only be carried out by an older man.)

Whether human sacrifice was ever actually practised in connexion with the rites is a matter of doubt. It seems reasonable to suppose so; and also, in view of the charges of cannibalism commonly levelled against the elders, and on analogy with the practice observed in other rites, where a beast is killed, that the flesh of the victim was ceremonially eaten. But it does not appear that this custom has been observed in recent times. Under the Tiv code there is no necessity. Sooner or later some one in the group will die, and the elder is then said to have killed him by *tsav*, and can claim him as a victim for the public rites. Doubtless, when a man found that his *tsav* was not strong enough by itself to effect the death of his kinsmen as quickly as he wished, or (as

[1] Cf. Marett, op. cit., p. 112.

we should sceptically put it) they failed to die of their own accord, he sometimes assisted its efficacy by means of poison. But whether he killed the man by *tsav*, or by more direct methods (from our point of view) was to the African mind only a point of technical detail. The poison, in any case, could not be effective without the power of magic to make it work.

No harm was done so long as society as a whole recognized the necessity for these imaginary ritual killings, but later the object of them was to some extent forgotten, and the public cults fell into disuse. The theory that every death was caused by the *tsav* of the elder kinsmen, on the other hand, was held as strongly as ever, and the reasons attributed to them for killing their children or younger brothers were lust of power (because the holding of high office required a certain number of victims), the necessity of paying off a flesh debt, or pure malice. Thus did the whole idea of *tsav* fall into general disrepute. The leaders of society, instead of using their supernatural power in the interests of their people, had allowed it to degenerate into the worst form of witchcraft. The ceremonial eating of human flesh was pictured by public imagination as taking the form of ghoulish midnight orgies, at which old men and women who had acquired a taste for human meat greedily preyed on each other's families. The very name *mbatsav*, originally an honourable title, came to signify the most hated and feared members of the community.

It is not suggested, of course, that there was ever a golden age in which *tsav* was only used for good causes. Doubtless there were always evil-intentioned persons who turned the power to their own illegitimate uses. But at one time, when its value to the community was more clearly recognized, it certainly held a more honourable place in public estimation than it does now. It was indeed largely on the belief in its efficacy that the authority of the elders rested, and the group was held together. The lack of confidence in the old rites, and in the ability or willingness of the old men to use their supernatural powers for good purposes and not solely for bad, is one of the main causes for the loosening of the family ties and lack of discipline, of which the older men complain so bitterly to-day.

Therefore, although the *mbatsav* have been regarded by some as a criminal secret society, of which both the qualification for membership and its main object were the eating of human flesh,

and although this view of the matter appears to derive support
from the description in the following pages and from popular Tiv
belief, it is founded on a misconception. It was this mistaken
attitude towards *tsav*, held by the younger members of the tribe,
and by us until we discovered the error, which gave rise to the
movements against it, particularly that of 1929, recorded at the
end of this section. Those who had the power of *tsav*, and used
it, were originally not a secret society outside the social structure,
but the central pillar of it on which the tribe believed that its
continued existence rested.

NOTHING in Tiv is so illusory as *tsav*.[1] There is
no reality in it whatever, nor in any of the ideas
associated with it; yet it is of all things the one in which
every Tiv places the most implicit belief. From the time
when a child begins to understand what is said, he listens
to people around him talking about the *mbatsav*. He is
continually hearing about them till he himself is old
enough to talk, and starts to go about with other children,
speaking to them of the *mbatsav* in the way that he has
heard from his elders. So it has come about that this
thing lies at the very root of the Tiv's life, and is bound
up with all his activities. Fear of the *mbatsav* has taken
hold on the people like a persistent and incurable disease.
Even those who have been educated, and have travelled
abroad, too, have not learnt enough to show them that
tsav is nothing; because all their thought and all their
learning are on the surface, and cannot teach them the
difference between what is black and what is white. It
gives them a knowledge of material things, but does
not penetrate to their immortal souls. I, Akiga, who
to-day no longer believe in *tsav* have come to this only
through the mercy and power of God, the Giver of Life.
Otherwise, there would to-day be no more fervent
believer in *tsav* than I, nor any in Tivland whose beliefs
were more debased than mine. So it is that the man
who stands close to the house cannot see in what
manner the roof is crooked. It is only when he goes back
and stands some distance away from it that he gets a true

[1] Lit., 'That which is not in Tiv, as *tsav*, is not'.

view, and can tell the builders how to set it straight.

According to the Tiv, *tsav* has actual material existence, and is a thing which can be seen and touched. The place where it is found is in a man's heart, and it can also sometimes be seen in animals, both domestic and wild. In appearance it is like the liver, but is not so broad or so thick. In man it is of two kinds. In some it is large and its edge is finely notched. This is the bad kind, the *tsav* of killing men and eating human flesh. In others, though it may be big, its edge is not notched, but rounded. This is the good kind, the kind for protecting the land; it is not the *tsav* of eating men, but the *tsav* of wisdom. As to its exact position, it is attached to the base of the heart. During youth it is quite short, but separates off when a boy grows up. In some cases it becomes detached while a child is still young.

In the days before the white man came, if a man died the members of his age-grade cut open his chest and examined his internal organs. If he had the serrated type of *tsav*, they said that he had brought about his own death, for with this kind of *tsav* he would not fail to be an eater of men. But if when they opened him up they found only the rounded type of *tsav*, they said that he had been killed out of malice, and that they would not let the matter rest. So they went to the diviner, and, having learnt who it was that had killed their age-mate, they called together all the members of their grade and subjected the man named to the *hoyo*.[1] The knife which had been used in cutting open the body of the dead man was stuck into a tree by the side of a path along which many people would pass. Every one who saw it expressed his approval. 'So-and-so belonged to a fine age-grade', they said. 'His death is not being left to go unavenged. His age-mates have cut him open to examine him, and though he is dead they are fighting his battles.'

Many are the stories told by the Tiv about the *mbatsav*, some of which are recorded below. They are all figments of the imagination, and there is not a particle of truth in any of them. If a Tiv tells you all these things, and you

---

[1] P. 329.

ask him if he is *tsav* himself, he will deny it. There is not a man in Tiv who will honestly admit to it. If he professes that he is *tsav*, it is for one of two reasons. Either he is lying, and says that he is *tsav* in order that men may respect and fear him (for they say that the word of a man who is not *tsav* carries no weight, and he is disregarded as being of no importance), or else he admits it of necessity; that is to say, no one will believe him when he denies that he is *tsav*, and he is therefore compelled to suffer the name against his will.

That the doctrine of *tsav* is a myth, which men are forced to accept whether they wish it or not, I know well from my own experience. Many years ago, when I lived in close companionship with my father, Sai, all my group said that I was *tsav*, but there was never any truth in it. My reputation for *tsav* was acquired in this way. My mother left me when I was a child, and my life was a very hard one. But my father took great care of me, and did all he could to find means to feed me. For this reason he used to perform the rites of the *akombo* of the crops in the farm of his chief wife, the daughter of Turan, called El. The *akombo* was in the field at the foot of a shea tree, and *iyandegh* had been planted round it. Whenever the time came to perform the rites my father woke me at cock-crow, before it was light, caught a cock and gave it to Hilekaan, his eldest son, to carry, filled a gourd with water for me to take, and he himself carried the fire. Then we went out to the farm. My father carried out the *akombo* rites, we killed and ate the chicken, and returned to the village in the early morning. Seeing this, people said, 'Hilekaan and Akiga are *tsav* beyond all measure. There is no one in these parts to be compared with them. They are eating human flesh with their father'. But for my part, I knew that it was not so; my father was only seeking an opportunity to give me something to eat. Yet when I heard that people interpreted the affair in this way, and that it seemed to them the work of the *mbatsav*, I was not content to let the matter rest there, but did everything I could to play up to my reputation for *tsav*, in order to attract attention to myself and make people afraid of me.

There was another incident. An agent of the firm of John Holt at Ibi gave my father a large iron box. This was very highly prized, for at that time iron boxes in Tivland were rare. The key was kept by Hilekaan, and he alone used to open the box; no one else touched it. At the time when the daughter of Buriya, one of my father's chief wives, was being brought home as a bride, and the marriage dance was in progress, I went into the house of the daughter of Adamu, where the box was kept, this being also the house into which the bride had been taken.[1] I sat down on a bed, on which were several boxes, including the iron box in question, and began to play about with it for amusement. While I was engaged in this, I noticed that the iron hasp into which the padlock fits was raised, by which I knew that it was unlocked. So I went out and told my father that Hilekaan had opened the box, and had forgotten to lock it again. My father asked me how I knew this, and I told him that I saw that the hasp was pointing upwards. So he called Hilekaan and questioned him. Hilekaan replied that he had locked it quite securely, and that I had opened it by *tsav*. Thereupon my father seized hold of me, and undoing the girdles round his waist, set about beating me. To every one who came to stop him he said, 'No, leave me alone. Akiga's *tsav* has passed all bounds. Look at my iron box that he has opened by *tsav* in order to see the *imborivuŋgu* inside!' When the other heard this he was seized with fear and backed away, saying, 'Beat him! If so small a child has this much *tsav* in him, what will he not do with it when he grows up?' My father beat me till my body was covered with sores. In the end I broke loose from him, and ran away and hid. But for the love which he had for me he sought me out, and when he had found me in the house of the daughter of Adzande, he took me in his arms and soothed me.[2]

The next morning my name was in every one's mouth. They all spoke of my *tsav*, and many things were invented

[1] The bridal chamber is filled with drummers, &c., for several days.
[2] The father beating his favourite son is genuinely frightened, for to see another man's *imborivuŋgu* means to incur a flesh debt.

to add to the story. Some said that yesterday I had opened the box and put my head and shoulders inside, so that the sweat poured from me. Others said that I had taken out the *imborivuŋgu*, and was looking at it, when Hilekaan found me and went to tell Sai, who came and caught me with it in my hand, and beat me. 'With this sort of *tsav*,' they said, 'Akiga, when he grows up, will surpass Hilekaan.' When I realized that every one admired me for my *tsav*, I was much flattered, and began to tell people all sorts of lies about the *mbatsav*. In this, moreover, I was never contradicted. They said I was so full of *tsav* that anything I said about the *mbatsav* was not to be doubted. I was delighted at this, and thenceforth set my whole heart on *tsav*, so that people came to marvel at me. And I was only a very small boy.

There was another reason why people called me *tsav*. In those days, when I was still a child, I used to follow my father about like his shadow. Day and night I never left him; only when he went a long journey did we part company. So it happened that being always with him I had the chance to see and hear much. For he was a man of high standing, and the head of his group. Now he had many wives, and in the house of whichever wife he was spending the night I would sleep, too. And if in the night I felt the need to relieve nature, I went outside to do it; I was never afraid of darkness like other children. Moreover, it was a case of necessity; I was afraid to make water in the house, lest, if I did so, the wife to whom it belonged would rate my father on the morrow for having brought me in to make a mess in her house, and when she came to cook the meal she would refuse to give me any.[1]

One night when I had gone out, according to my usual custom, I saw two little black pigs which scampered away from me, one this way and one that. Now there were two people who owned pigs in our village, Akure, my father's sister, and Gata, his wife, and as each of their

[1] It is not only unnatural for a child not to be afraid of the dark, but definitely sinister, in view of the connexion between witchcraft and darkness. He is already well on the way to become one of the 'People of the Night'.

pigs had litters I concluded that the young pigs belonged to them. When I went back into the house my father was awake, so I told him about it. 'When I went out just now', I said, 'I saw two little black pigs. I wonder who has left his pigs out like this for a hyena to take?' My father asked me whether they were both black, or whether one was not white, and I answered that in the darkness they both seemed to me to be black.[1] The next morning he told Hilekaan. Hilekaan called me and asked me what I saw when I went out in the night, and I told him that I had seen two little pigs. When I said this Hilekaan answered angrily that I was to stop lying and tell him exactly what happened; otherwise he would give me a thrashing. Even so I did not at first understand what he wished to hear, and so when he asked me again I repeated exactly what I had told him the first time. Thereupon he picked up a stick to beat me for not telling him the truth. I had not the least idea what to do, and the thought passed quickly through my mind, 'I have told the truth, and Hilekaan is not satisfied. I will tell him a lie and see whether perhaps he will believe it'. So I turned round the story as though it were the work of the *mbatsav*. 'I will tell you the truth', I said. 'What I saw last night were the owls of the *mbatsav*. There were two of them, and they had indigo cloths wrapped about their bodies. When I came out they scuttled away along the ground flapping their wings.' Hilekaan said, 'Ah, now you have told me the truth!' When the story got round, my reputation for *tsav* was much enhanced. 'Last night', they said, 'the *mbatsav* appeared in Sai's village, and Akiga came out and drove them off.' For many days people talked of nothing else. Kɔhɔ, a kinsman of my father, gave me the name of Ipemke, a name connected with the *mbatsav*, which means a pepper that is different from all other peppers; that is to say, the *mbatsav* were hot as red pepper, but I was hotter than they, and had driven them off. The people at my home still remember this name, but I do not like to be called by it now.

[1] Black is the colour associated with witchcraft, and white with the People of the Day; see under *Ijɔv*, p. 270, and sasswood, p. 321, below.

The Tiv say that every one has *tsav*, and that this, as already stated, is of two kinds, the *tsav* which preserves the land, and the *tsav* which destroys it. It is the *mbatsav* who kill people. No man ever dies a natural death, it is always the *mbatsav* who have killed him; and if any man falls sick it is often the *mbatsav* who have bewitched him. 'Bewitching' means the process by which the *mbatsav* bring about a man's death, or give him a disease. The Tiv do not bewitch people indiscriminately. You only bewitch a near relative, on your mother's or your father's side, who has done you some wrong. The bewitching is not always intended to kill; sometimes it is used by a grown man against a child who has been very impudent to him. The child lies on the ground in considerable pain, but eventually recovers. Another time he will not be so disrespectful to his elders. Sometimes an older man will bewitch a child with stomach-ache, or will give him such a headache that he spends a sleepless night. Another will cause a child to have eye trouble or give him sores on the body, which only heal up after an exhaustive inquiry.[1] All these kinds of witchery are intended only as punishments. Most commonly it is over the question of a woman that an elder bears a grudge against a youth and bewitches him, or because the younger man has seduced one of his wives.

If one of the *mbatsav* wants to frighten some one he goes by night and takes up his position by the side of a much used road, having with him a long stick or raffia pole, and a big cloth covering his body. There he waits in silence. When a man approaches, he rises to his feet and pushes up the pole inside the cloth, lifting it high above his head. When the man sees this he runs for all he is worth, yelling at the top of his voice. He flings himself into the village, and on being asked what is the matter recounts his terrible experience with a witch on the road. 'I was going along', he says, 'when suddenly one of the *mbatsav* rose from the ground and grew to such a height that he almost touched the sky! My hair stood on end, and as I ran it seemed that my legs had grown to an

[1] P. 326.

unnatural length.' 'Oh! that's a bad road', says every-body. 'It simply swarms with *mbatsav*.' After this every one is afraid to pass that way by night. At other times when the man approaches the place where he is crouching, the witch covers his head and body with a large cloth, bends down, and runs along with his head near the ground and arms spread out on either side. The victim takes to his heels, and runs back screaming to the village. Gasping for breath, he tells his audience how the witch turned into an elephant and chased him all the way home. . . .

The *mbatsav* also give people bad dreams. The witch waits till every one is fast asleep, and then goes to the house of the person to whom he wishes to give the dream. Standing in the doorway, he clutches his own throat, and goggles at him with his eyes starting out of his head. The sleeper cries out loudly in his sleep. On being awaked he says, 'It was a nightmare. I dreamt that a man pinned me to the ground with his hands round my throat, and was killing me. I am always being visited with dreams by the *mbatsav*. I go to bed, but I cannot sleep'. 'It is one of your relatives', says every one. 'Who else would keep on giving you bad dreams? These terrible *mbatsav*! We empty-chested are nothing but their slaves. They can do whatever they like with us.' Sometimes the witch, having crept under the eaves of the house, takes hold of one of the roof-poles and twists it round with a creaking noise. The man asleep inside cries out, and when the people run in he tells them that the *mbatsav* had lifted the roof off the house and were peering down at him. 'Amazing!' they say. 'The *mbatsav* are as Aɔndo. There is nothing beyond their powers!'

Often, when one of the *mbatsav* has given some one a bad dream, he goes to his house early the next morning in order to overhear the conversation and find out whether the man has recognized who it was. Conse-quently, the Tiv always say that if you have a dream, and the next morning some one pays you a visit very early, you may be quite certain that he was the cause of it.

GOING *TSAV*

'Going *tsav*' means going out in the night and doing the deeds of the *mbatsav*. It does not happen only at night; in the day-time, too, if *tsav* strongly impels[1] him, a man will go out and so obtain relief. But the night is the real time for going *tsav*. The hours in which the *mbatsav* are most active are, in the day-time, when the sun begins to show his strength, and in the night, either at dusk or after men have had their first sleep.[2]

It is said that for everything that is owned by men the *mbatsav* have their equivalent. They have a lamp, which they call *ishan*,[3] and the oil which is burnt in their lamp is human fat. They have a horse which is cast out of copper. It is quite small, but in the night-time they enlarge it by *tsav* into a great steed on which they mount. Or sometimes one of them seizes a brother who is not *tsav*, changes him into a stallion, and rides him. And since the white men came, and the *mbatsav* have seen the bicycle, they have made bicycles for themselves to ride by night, and motor bicycles too, and cars—nothing is beyond the power of the *mbatsav*.[4] The *mbatsav* also have a pipe. It is called the *imborivuŋgu*, and it is this which is used to set right the land. The *imborivuŋgu* pipe is very difficult to play. It is not played in the same way as an ordinary daylight pipe, nor does the piper stay still in one place. While he is blowing he must press his heel tightly against his fundament.[5] He may blow the pipe in one place, and then if you listen you will hear him blow it again about a league away.

THE DANCE OF THE *MBATSAV*

When the *mbatsav* hold a dance, the old men and women assemble at the dance place on the night that the

---

[1] Lit.: 'lifts him up'. *Tsav* is spoken of almost as if it were a natural instinct which must be satisfied.

[2] There are two 'sleeps'. The first till about 2 a.m.; the second from 2.0 a.m. till cock-crow.

[3] ='Star'.

[4] New ideas are grafted on the old without any sense of anachronism or inappropriateness. The same applies in other departments of life. Cf. Junod, *The Life of a South African Tribe*, vol. ii, p. 219, on new ideas in folk-lore.

[5] To prevent his intestines being forced out by the strength of his blowing!

beer is ready, riding on their night horses and cars. The old women put on their best clothes. Round their necks they wear strings of dead men's teeth, and over their shoulders they sling a human skin[1] as though it were a leopard-skin kaross. The old men dress themselves up, too. They carry human skulls in their hands, and when their host serves out the beer these skulls are the cups out of which they drink. As soon as the beer is all finished, they get up to drum and to dance. The *mbatsav* style of dancing is not like that of the empty-chested. When they are about to begin the dance they stand well apart, and do not go close to one another. If one were to touch the other both would die.[2]

When the dance has been going on for some time, the host commands every one to sit down, as he is about to serve the meal. When all are seated, he goes and fetches the member of his family whom he is providing to feed his guests at the dance, and throws him down on the ground. All this time the victim is asleep and knows nothing. He is quite unconscious of everything that happens, because he is one of the empty-chested. The host, then, having produced his brother or sister for the feast, says to his *mbatsav* kinsmen, 'This is the food which I wish to prepare for you'. Sometimes the *mbatsav* refuse, saying that So-and-so is not ready to be killed yet, and in this case he is spared. He is taken, still sleeping, and thrown down in his house. As he has been asleep the whole time he knows nothing at all of what has been going on; but in the morning he says, 'I had a very bad dream last night', and does not feel well. Sometimes, on

---

[1] *Ikpaor*, the skin of a dead man flayed complete. This is a famous article in the *mbatsav* equipment, but it is doubtful whether there are any in existence to-day; see p. 279.

[2] The reason for this is said to be that the participants, after 'going *tsav*', are no longer living a normal corporeal existence, but are in an attenuated, quasi-astral condition, which gives them certain supernormal powers but is also attended by considerable risk to themselves. It is held by some, but not all, that the witch leaves his empty shell (*ifeesegh*) behind on these occasions, asleep in the house (cf. Junod, op. cit., vol. ii, p. 508). It is possible that it is this idea which is implied in the expression '*duwe*' *tsav* (go 'out' *tsav*). But the Tiv have no very clear ideas on this subject, and no word for the man's soul, as distinct from his body. In any case the idea of the witch being in two places at once would present little difficulty to them (cf. Lévy-Bruhl, op. cit., p. 101 et seq.)

the other hand, they accept the proffered meal, and take the victim which has been given to them.

The *mbatsav* do not kill a man in the same way as the People of the Day. When a man has been handed over to them for some purpose[1] they kill him in that night, and afterwards treat him with *ishuragh*, so that he comes back to life and seems perfectly well again. But at the same time they doom him to some fate, and when in due course this befalls him he must die, and no remedy on earth can save him. People then say, 'It is an old wound which has been opened'.

Ishuragh, which is used by the *mbatsav* to bring a man back to life after they have killed him, is a drug which is applied to the nostrils. It is, in actual fact, the name given to the seeds of a small shrub which grows in forest country. This shrub bears an egg-shaped fruit, not very long, and about the thickness of a man's finger. The seeds are like grains of guinea-corn, but smaller. If you split open the fruit and eat the seeds, you will find that they are hot and somewhat pungent to the taste, and cause a tickling sensation in the throat. These seeds are chewed by the *mbatsav*, who then put them into the nostrils of the man they have killed. This acts as a stimulant, and he comes back to life again. The *ishuragh* treatment, however, cannot be carried out by every member of the *mbatsav*, but is the duty of a special official. This man must always be present when the victim is killed, or if not, the corpse must be hidden in the bush, and one of the *mbatsav* placed on guard over it, until such time as the man who administers the *ishuragh* can be found and brought to the spot, to revive the dead.

To 'doom'[2] means to decide the fate which shall afterwards kill the person who has already been killed by the *mbatsav*. The things which may be decreed to be the man's doom are of different kinds: for instance, it may be a snake, lion, leopard, buffalo, or some other wild beast. But none of these is able to kill a man, unless the *mbatsav* have already killed him by night, and afterwards doomed

---

[1] I.e. to provide a feast, discharge a flesh debt, &c.
[2] *Vende.* Cf. Lévy-Bruhl, op. cit., p. 39 *et passim.*

him to be the victim of one of them. Only then can they kill him; of their own accord they have no power at all to do so. A man may be shot in the chest, and the bullet enter his heart, but if the *mbatsav* have not already killed him by night, and decreed that he shall afterwards be killed by a bullet from a gun, he will not die. Though a man climb the highest mountain and fall from the top to the bottom, yet unless the *mbatsav* have already killed him, and doomed him to die this kind of death, he will still be alive. Illness is also sometimes due to the *mbatsav*, but in this case the *akombo* are partly involved. Yet the *akombo* by themselves cannot kill a man. A child, as soon as he can walk, is past the age at which he can be killed by them. They can kill him while he is still a baby in arms, but after this it is always *tsav* which is the cause of death.

THE EXHUMATION OF THE DEAD

When a person has died and been buried, the *mbatsav* assemble at the home of the dead man and send the Exhumer to disinter the corpse. The exhumation, as in the case of the administration of the *ishuragh*, is carried out by a man whose especial duty it is. He has a hook which is attached to a long chain. Taking up his position a league or so away, he casts the hook, which catches the corpse by the throat, and the dead man leaps from his grave and falls in front of them. The *mbatsav* raise a shout, and call the Reviver of the Dead to come and bring him to life. The exhumation may be done in a number of different ways. Sometimes the Exhumer stands a long way off and calls the dead man by name. The dead man answers the call from his grave, then gets up and comes to the man who has summoned him, to the great delight of the *mbatsav*. Another time the Reviver catches a white cock, which has not a single black feather, swings it over the grave, and the dead man comes out.

If, when a man has died, his people keep a very close watch over the grave, in order to discover who have killed him, the Exhumer brings him out in the evening before it is quite dark,[1] and the watchers know nothing about it.

---

[1] I.e. earlier than expected.

Another time he causes a drowsiness to overcome the
watchers, and brings up the corpse while they are all
asleep. If the cause of death is in dispute, each party
saying that it was not they who killed him, the Exhumer
may bring up the body and then hide it. When the
people who have killed the man come to get the corpse
they find it gone. So they secretly make discreet inquiries
from their *mbatsav* confederates, who tell them who it is
that has exhumed the corpse and hidden it away. But
when they go and beg him to give them the meat which
belongs to them, he replies, 'Was it not you who the
other day denied having killed this man? How is it
then that you have come to exhume him? Very well, I
will not give you your meat unless you pay me for it'.
So they go home and collect a large sum of money, and
bring it to him in exchange for the corpse. By concealing
the body in this way the Exhumers make a great deal of
money.

The next day the Exhumer lets it be generally known
that he disinterred the corpse and hid it, and that the
So-and-sos, who said before that they had nothing to do
with the death, have just come to redeem the body. All
the people round hear this, and say, 'The So-and-sos have
been found out'. And if it is a woman who has died, and
the men who killed her are those who owned her as their
iŋɔl, her husband gets up and prepares for a fight. He
goes to their clan, and demands the return of his *iŋɔl*.
Originally, he says, they gave him their *iŋɔl*, but since
they have now taken her back again, they must return his.
So they give her to him, and he takes her back to his
home. But if they are fond of the woman they ask the
owner to leave her, and say that they will find another
woman for him instead. Thereupon he goes home and
tells the elders of his group, who usually raise no objection. So in due course he comes back again and asks for
another wife in exchange for his *iŋɔl*. This is given to
him, and he goes home and settles down again. A woman
who is given to replace a wife who has died is called 'a
wife by the old contract'. Women do not care much for
this type of marriage.

⫶, If a man's wife dies, the people who would naturally be suspected are the members of her father's group, since the *mbatsav* always kill their own near relatives. It is therefore most probable that the people that killed the woman were actually her own family, who originally owned her as their *iŋɔl*. When this suspicion is confirmed by the evidence of the Exhumer, the aggrieved husband demands that the exchange be adjusted, either by the return of his own *iŋɔl*, or by the substitution of another wife in return for the one which they have eaten. This explains why it was necessary to send your wife home to her father's group if she fell ill, and why, if she died, it was considered quite legitimate to reclaim the *iŋɔl* which you had given in exchange for her. If your wife is sick, and you have tried first pathological, and secondly magic, treatment without effect, she must be bewitched. You naturally suspect her relations, and divination corroborates this. If you keep her in your home, and she dies, you have only yourself to blame, so you send her back to her own group. If they do not remove the spell, and she dies there, you are perfectly justified in demanding the return of your *iŋɔl*, since they have 'taken back' the one which they gave to you.

THE body, then, having been exhumed, is not allowed to remain dead, but is brought back to life. When the man is alive again he is taken and tied up in a wood, and one of the *mbatsav* is set to guard him. The food for a dead man is raw beniseed. This is ground up and given him to eat continually, so that he shall grow large and be well fattened before he is killed.[1] He is fed on beniseed until the day when he is ready for the slaughter. Then they torture him, drive him round the village with a huge grindstone on his head, and finally kill him.

After the killing comes the cutting up. The *mbatsav* find a big green tree which has plenty of leaves on it, bend it over on to the ground, and cut up the corpse on the leaves. Then they tell the tree to stand up again as straight as it was before.[2] The business of cutting up the body is also delegated to a special member of the *mbatsav*,

---

[1] Cf. Hunting *akombo*, p. 211 note (iii).
[2] This explanation is probably given to account for the fact that no traces of the cutting up are ever found.

who alone carries out this duty. This official is called the *Haabuar*, and it is he who also distributes the meat. The name *Haabuar* is used only by the *mbatsav*, and is unknown to the empty-chested.

If the dead man was some one of great importance, he is not killed again at once. When they have brought him to life they first ask him many questions, and if he has any secret thing which he has been hiding from them he must declare it.[1] If he was a composer in his lifetime, they tell him to compose a chorus for them to learn and sing by day; or if he sang solos, or played the pipe, or did anything else whatever, they force him to perform for them, before they kill him and hand him over to the *Haabuar* for cutting up. For the cutting up of human bodies only one knife is used throughout the whole group. The *Haabuar* shares out the meat, but gives the head to the man who provided them with the victim, because 'The killer eats the head'.

If a man has a very handsome child and is anxious always to take the lead at the nocturnal meetings, he will kill and flay the child, in order that he may wear the skin round his shoulders and so outshine all his companions.[2]

THINGS WHICH THE *MBATSAV* FEAR

The things which the *mbatsav* shun are fire, earth, slag from the furnace, the Tongs, the Axe of Heaven, and the

[1] E.g. an *imborivuŋgu* or ancestral relic, which he buried or gave away to some one else before his death, because he knew that his group had bewitched him and wanted to be avenged on them by 'spoiling their land'.

[2] The following account was given me by a young Tiv who has been to school: 'My father, who was a fine-looking man, was killed for the sake of his skin. I was quite young when it happened, but the story was told to me afterwards. There were two brothers, Ator and Gyuve, my father. When Gyuve died, Ator cried bitterly, and swore that if he could find the man who caused his death he would kill him. Now he had a young slave, who, going one day into the forest to cut wood, came upon my father's skin laid out to dry, guarded by some of the *mbatsav*. The slave, who himself was *tsav* and so able to see this, came back and said to Ator, "You said that you would avenge Gyuve's death, if you could find out who had killed him. To-day I have seen his skin in the forest!" Thereupon Ator armed himself, and told the slave to lead him to the place. When he came and saw the skin of his brother, his grief knew no bounds. Drawing his knife, he slit the skin from top to bottom. At this the guards of the *mbatsav* fell upon him, and they fought together until they had killed each other. After this his group said that Ator should not die in his home, but doomed him to be killed by the Dam. . . .' I.e. the fight in the forest was fought with *tsav*, and though all combatants were 'killed', they did not die, physically speaking, till later.

Igbe. If a man goes *tsav*, and you, one of the empty-chested, hold a lighted brand in your hand, he will run for his life when he sees it; for if he bewitches you with fire in your hand he will become a leper. Or if he goes *tsav* in the night-time, and while he is sitting down you take up some earth and throw it over him, he will die, killed by the *Swange*. If one of the *mbatsav* bewitches a man who has tied some slag round his neck, he will be struck dead by lightning, and the same death will befall him if he bewitches any one who has the Tongs, or the Axe of Heaven.[1]

It is the *mbatsav* who bring the birds which eat the millet, and the red monkeys which destroy the crops in the farms, and the beetles which eat the yams.

THE FLESH DEBT

If you eat human flesh with some one, you may flee to the land of the white men, yet he will follow you there from Tivland in a single day, and kill you. It may be that you have shared a meal with a man who has killed his brother, or who has been given a portion of the body by night, and has cooked the meat and is eating it. If you do this, you are bound to repay him. If you do not pay him, and try to escape, he will follow you and kill you wherever you may go. The debt of the *mbatsav* is very evil; it is called the 'flesh debt'.

A man may incur a flesh debt in different ways, sometimes with one of his own age, and sometimes with an older man. If you have a friend, or if you are a young man in the service of an elder, beware. Otherwise, you may unwittingly contract a flesh debt with him. The *mbatsav* do not offer a man human flesh and say, 'Have some of this. You can pay me back some other time'. It is not done in this way at all. The man who incurs the debt usually knows nothing about it. For it is not necessarily over an important matter that he becomes involved in it. Perhaps your friend, or some older man,

---

[1] Taboos of this kind are not peculiar to those practising witchcraft. All charms, and many other forms of magic, including 'white magic', have their own especial taboo; cf. p. 266.

has noticed that you have a large number of children, or brothers and sisters, and so tricks you into contracting the debt with him. He invites you to eat food in his house alone with him, and when you begin the meal he sets before you two dishes of sauce, one of which contains cooked human flesh. You do not know this, but suppose it to be just ordinary meat, and he does not tell you. You, his guest, stretch out to dip into the gravy. But as soon as you start eating, if you are not *tsav*, you will go out and be very sick. Thereupon you go and tell the head of your family that So-and-so has tricked you into eating human flesh with him, and when the older man questions you about it, you tell him the whole story. The elder then sets out and goes to the witch, prepared for a fight. 'Why', he demands, 'have you been trying to entice my boy to get into a flesh debt, and break up my home?' A dispute ensues, and the matter becomes known to every one round. In this case no harm is done, because the man will never dare to claim the debt.

But sometimes the man who dips into the human fat is also *tsav*, and will not withdraw, although he knows what he has done. He says to his host, 'I have fallen into the trap, but I will not turn back. Give me the rest of the meat, and I will finish it'. Then his host cuts off some meat and gives it to him, and they go on eating it together every day until it is finished. Some time later the man who cooked the flesh goes to the man with whom he shared it, and says, 'I have come. It is now for you to kill a man and give him to me'. The debtor may say, 'Yes, I will also kill, and give you the gravy and a small piece of the meat, since that is what you gave me before'. But the other replies, 'Certainly not! You must give me the whole body without fail. "He who eats a child must pay back a full grown man" '. So the man who ate the flesh is caught in the toils.

After a short time the man to whom the debt is owed begins insistently to demand that which is his due. This is an example of how a flesh debt is claimed: Ityɔvenda has killed his brother Aba, and while he was eating him Amopav came and dipped into the sauce. In other words,

Amopav has eaten Aba, and Ityɔvenda is about to come and demand payment for his brother.

On the first day that Ityɔvenda comes to claim the debt, he does not come alone, but sends out to collect all his *mbatsav* companions. Not one of these comes in his own shape; each takes on a different form. Some become *mbaakiki*, some great owls, some little owls, and some witch-cats.[1] They form a long line, and set out for the home of Amopav, the man who owes the flesh debt. When they arrive at his home it is about the time of night when men have had their first sleep. The *mbaakiki* and the owls perch on the fig-trees in and round about the village, hooting, while the witch-cats fight amongst themselves and bump against the door of Amopav's house. Every now and then they stop and place their forepaws on either side of their heads, wailing like a child. At this cry every one's hair stands on end. Meanwhile Ityɔvenda, the man who is actually claiming the debt, sits with the chief men of the *mbatsav*, who are smoking their pipes and talking quietly together. That night the air is full of strange noises, and no one dares to go outside his house into the darkness.

Amopav knows well what this means. He comes out and asks them, 'Why have you come?' Ityɔvenda answers, 'Don't ask foolish questions. When I recall with sorrow how I killed Aba, my brother, and how we both ate him together, and when I see all your brothers and sisters alive here and working for you, is it not enough to make me want to kill myself?' And all the *mbatsav* elders who are sitting with him join in denouncing his debtor, 'Your question is not good', they say. 'Do we seem to you such fools, that you think to eat Aba and spare your own brothers to work for you? To keep your home standing after your death, while his falls in ruins? No, no. You have sought for trouble, and trouble has come upon you. Come and lie down on the ground, that we may cut your throat'. 'Spare me!' cries Amopav, 'I

---

[1] The *akiki* is a black crested bird with white wings, mostly seen at night. All these creatures are associated with the *mbatsav* because of (*a*) their nocturnal habits, (*b*) their strange appearance, and (*c*) their weird cries.

S

will give you the "dew" '. (He means by this that he will recompense his creditor for his trouble in coming to claim the debt, and for the dew through which he has walked.) Saying this, he goes back and fetches one of his brothers or children, and gives him to them. Ityɔvenda takes him, and says, 'I accept this. Take him and put him back now; I will come and kill him when I am ready'. At this the *mbaakiki*, the owls, and the witch-cats are silent and disperse.

Some days later a little owl comes and utters his cries outside the house of the person who was taken in his sleep and given as the 'dew', and the next morning a *kpile*[1] also comes and cries under the eaves, or on one of the trees in the village. Or else while he is walking along the road a *timekumun* bars his way.[2] (The *timekumun* is a little white insect which crawls on the ground and has a very hard shell. .Many of the Tiv have never seen it, but only know it by name.) This means certain death. When all these things happen it is time to go to the diviner. You ask what is the interpretation of the omen or bad dream, and are given the answer that your brother, So-and-so, is giving you in payment of a flesh debt, in fact, you have already been delivered up and accepted. Though you are still walking about, you are like a bird in a cage.[3] When the victim hears his death sentence he is broken-hearted. Some, on being told this, sit down and weep; others try to escape death by fleeing to their mother's home. And since the white man has come, they often run away to some distant country and live amongst the foreigners in the hope of saving their lives. A large number of the Tiv whom you see living amongst foreign tribes to-day have left their homes for this reason. Some, even though they have not yet been handed over in payment of a flesh debt, hear rumours that they are about to be given, and go to the diviner, who tells them that they are hedged about by death. So they go and take refuge

---

[1] Another bird of ill-omen.

[2] I.e. if a man sees this ill-omened insect in the middle of his path he will usually turn back.

[3] The word (*mgbe*) means a trap made of corn-stalks in which small birds are caught alive.

amongst the foreigners, instead of fleeing to their mother's home, as they used to do in the old days.

Nevertheless, if you have been given to the *mbatsav* in payment of a flesh debt, and have been accepted, do not, in the bitterness of your spirit, think to evade your fate. Wherever you may go, you are caught in the cage. On the day when they are ready to kill you they will take the winnowing mat, the calabash scoop, and the forked stick.[1] Holding a bunch of leaves on one side, and the winnowing mat on the other, they utter the following incantation: 'If it be we, the Tiv, who gave you birth, and poured the water into your mouth in accordance with our own Tiv *ityumbu* rite, wherever you may be, return. But if it be not we, the Tiv, who bore you, and performed the *ityumbu* rite for you, go in peace.' Saying this, they jerk the mat as though winnowing.[2] Then, though you may be in your mother's home, or living amongst the foreigners and holding a high position in the white man's service, perhaps even drawing £10 a month, yet when the *mbatsav* jerk the winnowing mat you are seized with a great longing to return home. You think and speak of nothing else but the affairs of your own village, till finally your work goes to pieces, and you are dismissed by the white man. (It is the white man to whom the Tiv nowadays apply the name of 'foreigner'—the white man and all those who work for him. In former times this used to be a term of derision, and if any one called a Tiv 'foreigner' he regarded it as the greatest of insults. But now it has become a title of honour, and is the name at which the chiefs slap their chests with pride.)

As soon as you arrive back at your home the *mbatsav* bewitch you and you die. People then· say that you returned from the land of the foreigner 'with death upon you'. After your death you are buried, and in due course the same *mbatsav* bring up your body by night, cut you

[1] These utensils are for the preparation of food (the scoop is for dishing out the *ruam*, and the forked stick for holding the pot on the fire), and all, including the bunch of leaves, are used in the *ityumbu* rite, performed soon after a child's birth (see p. 304). By repeating the ritual used at this ceremony the absent relative is recalled to his birthplace.

[2] The mat is held horizontally in front of the body, and jerked upwards with the wrist. The idea of beckoning is also present in this case.

up, and give your head to the man who is paying the debt. This he is entitled to eat, as the rightful owner. But if he accepts it, the flesh debt goes on and on. The creditor keeps on coming, and each time the debtor has to give him the 'dew'. Unless he has men behind him who are very strong in *tsav*, he cannot free himself from the flesh debt until he has given up all his people, and his family is finished. Then he goes himself and lies down on the ground to be slaughtered, and so the debt is finally discharged.

But if he who has contracted the flesh debt is wise and of a stout heart, and if, moreover, he has kinsmen who are powerful in *tsav*, he will not let the debt go on, but will settle the matter at the first demand. He can free himself in this way: Having given the victim to be killed, he and all his brothers go out fully armed, and stand by while the body is being cut up. When they have finished cutting it up, and take the head to give to him, he refuses it, telling the man whom he owes to take everything, including the head, in full settlement. If he objects, the debtor gets ready for a fight. The creditor is frightened, and takes the head as well, whereupon the flesh debt comes to an end.

A man who has incurred a flesh debt goes in abject fear of his creditor. He gives him whatsoever he asks. He pays him the greatest deference, and does not dare even to raise his voice in his presence. If he were to defy him, his creditor would come by night and demand payment. When the *mbatsav* have encompassed a man with death, all sorts of things happen to him. He puts a cloth into a pot, and rats eat it. He goes on a journey, but a chameleon bars his way. He sits down, and an *iguigu*[1] crawls up on to him. Such things are called 'visions' or 'omens', and are described later in the section on Tiv customs.

POISONING

In former days the *mbatsav* did not kill men for no reason, as they do now. However *tsav* a man might be,

[1] A small red insect with a black band round its middle. The black band is compared with the cloth bound round a man's stomach in times of crisis or emotional stress, and so is an omen of coming disaster.

he would not kill except for some definite purpose; for instance, if he were performing some rite for which a human victim was essential, he killed his own son, or the son of his sister.[1] But later the Tiv started to buy poisons from the neighbouring Bush Tribes and from the foreigners. Those from whom the Tiv chiefly acquired the poisonous herbs were the Gbe, Dam, and Akporo tribes, the people of Wukari, the Chamba, the Gbur, and the Mbafum; but the most deadly of all were those which they got from the Gbur and the Mbafum. When the Tiv got these poisons, they spared no one. They tried them on any one they could, and even killed their own guests.

There are several different ways of administering poison. The poisoner either buys the herb from some one who already has it, or asks one of his *mbatsav* companions to give him some. Then he proceeds to kill the man who has wronged him. A Tiv may have many motives for poisoning a man, but the commonest of all, to-day as in the past, is an affair over a woman. Here is an example: Iyaŋge has seduced Ihande's wife, Wantor. Ihande knows this, either because he has caught them together, or has been told by some other person who has seen them. Perhaps he calls Iyaŋge and asks him why he has been seducing his wife.

IYADGE: Have you been told this, or did you see it yourself?

IHANDE: What has that to do with it? I am asking you. If it is true, stop it. If there is nothing in it, very well, the matter is finished.

IYADGE: Don't talk such nonsense, Ihande. I am very annoyed at your ridiculous suspicions.

IHANDE: Indeed! Ridiculous, are they? I don't like the tone of your remarks.

IYADGE: You don't like it? Well, what are you going to do about it?

IHANDE: Put your hand on mine, then, if you say that I can do nothing to you![2]

[1] N.B.—His nearest matrilineal descendant.
[2] *Ta hwande.* The two strike the palms of the right hands together. The one who is afterwards proved right then says, '*Hwande wam kɔr u ve!*' (My *hwande* has caught you).

Iyaŋge may actually do so, or he may only defy him by word of mouth.

It sometimes happens that a husband accuses some one of seducing his wife without making quite certain, and the man who has been accused, although he has not seduced the woman before, thereupon sets about doing so. He says that he has not slept with her, but since the fellow has made up a foolish tale about him with no foundation, he will now see if he can give him a real cause for complaint. So possibly Iyaŋge is innocent of any relations with Wantor, but when Ihande questions him, he tries until he succeeds in seducing her. Or he may have already done so, and on being asked by Ihande does not give a satisfactory answer. In any case, the result is that Ihande starts looking round for a poison with which to kill Iyaŋge. Now sometimes when a woman is carrying on an intrigue with a man, she will secretly set aside for him some of the food she has made, that is, a little which he can eat by himself, without any one noticing. So Ihande proceeds with cunning, and when Wantor puts aside a little food to give Iyaŋge in secret, Ihande creeps round and puts the poison into it. Wantor, not knowing, gives it to Iyaŋge, who eats it and is lost!

Sometimes, if Iyaŋge has seduced Wantor, Ihande's wife, or is trying to do so, Ihande may know it, but does not confront him with it. Instead of this, he looks for some poison, and when he has found it lies in wait for Iyaŋge. He never on any occasion opens his mouth to tax Iyaŋge about the matter, but keeps on good terms with him; for the hunter does not whistle while he is stalking his quarry. One day Ihande fills his pipe, and passes close to Iyaŋge, smoking. Iyaŋge believes that Ihande is well-disposed towards him, and asks him to give him a pull at his pipe. Ihande is inwardly pleased. He slips a pinch of the poison quickly into the pipe, and hands it to Iyaŋge with every show of friendship. When Iyaŋge takes it and smokes it, he has taken his death.

Another common medium for giving poison is beer. Two men go to a beer party together, one of whom bears the other a grudge, either because of an affair with his wife, or on account of an *iŋgɔl* (as, for instance, if you and I are brothers with the same father and mother, and are disputing over an *iŋgɔl*, I may decide to kill you in order that the *iŋgɔl* may become mine). For example: Two brothers, Ijɔhɔ and Atav, have a dispute over an *iŋgɔl*. Atav, who is very *tsav*,[1] obtains some poison, and on the next occasion on which they go out to a beer party together he takes it with him. They start drinking in company with the other guests. Atav waits until Ijɔhɔ has drunk a quantity of beer and is no longer sober. As soon as he begins talking nonsense, Atav asks him to pass him a little more beer. Ijɔhɔ gives him the cup, and he puts it to his lips as though to drink, but does not do so. As he lifts his head from the cup, he pours a little of the poison into it, and gives the doctored beer back to Ijɔhɔ. Ijɔhɔ takes it, quickly drains the cup in his ignorance, and dies. The poisons which are given in beer and tobacco are the most deadly of all.

Women are the cause of many murders amongst the Tiv. In some cases it is the woman's paramour who kills the husband. For example: Korgba has an intrigue with Wanmue, the wife of Aga. One day he buys a deadly poison, and treacherously gives it to Wanmue. 'Take this medicine', he says. 'It is called "Blindheart". If you put it in Aga's food and he eats it, he will love you more than all his other wives. Whenever he kills some little creature he will give it to you alone, and not to any of the others. You will get all the presents, and all the attention.' Wanmue takes it. She prepares a meal, and cooks some good meat. She puts the herb in the meat, and places it inside the house. Then she calls her husband Aga, who goes in and eats it by himself. A few days later he is dead.

Sometimes when the woman sees that her husband is dying she becomes distraught, whereupon people know that she is guilty. The older members of the dead man's family exert strong pressure on the woman until she confesses. When the man who gave her the poison hears

---

[1] Note that just as *tsav* is closely bound up with healing medicine, and no treatment can be effective without it, so the bad type of *tsav* is associated with the administering of poison. The poison by itself has no effect without *tsav*, and the poisoners are practically synonymous with the *mbatsav*.

that she has divulged the truth, he takes to the bush and goes to seek refuge amongst his mother's kinsmen. There he remains, in some cases till the day of his death. The woman is well beaten by her husband's relatives, who send to the man through whom the marriage was formerly arranged, and tell him to take her back to her family and demand the return of their own *iŋgɔl*.[1] If, however, she has borne children, they let her stay to look after them, and leave her to mourn her loss and to envy other women who have husbands.

These things still go on amongst the Tiv to-day. Many chiefs and important persons meet their death in this way. It is indeed the fear of death which stops some chiefs and elders from giving other men access to their wives. If there is a strong man who is feared by everybody, and the elders wish to do away with him, but cannot find a way, they enjoin a young man to go and seduce his favourite wife, and give him a poison by means of which he is to entice her into killing her husband without any one knowing. Afterwards people say, 'No man is invulnerable'. The Tiv do not usually bring these matters to the notice of the white man, or, if they do, they do not explain them to him in a way that he can understand, but state the facts in a fashion which misleads him.

ANTI-*TSAV*

When the land has become spoilt owing to so much senseless murder, the Tiv have taken strong measures to overcome the *mbatsav*. These big movements have taken place over a period extending from the days of the ancestors into modern times. One was called the *Budeli*. Many years later came the *Ijɔv*. The *Ijɔv* appeared during the time of the white man, in the year 1912. Since this there have been the *Ivase* and the *Haakaa*. The *Haakaa* was started under the control of the white man. Some of these movements have spread over the whole of Tivland,

---

[1] The negotiations for a marriage are always carried out through a third person (see p. 112), who acts as a mediator between the two parties in case of any subsequent trouble. This was particularly necessary under exchange, because, if the marriage was unsatisfactory for any reason, it always involved the other party as well, and a dissolution meant two dissolutions.

but others are only known locally. People have heard of them, but have not taken part in them, because some of the chiefs refused to allow them in their districts. Sometimes, on the other hand, a movement has been started and made some stir, but has not lasted long. It has received no support, and become ineffective. The most important of these movements, and those which especially pleased the Tiv, were the *Ijɔv* and the *Haakaa*. These were so popular that the Tiv did not wish them to come to an end, but after a short time they both died out.

THE *BUDELI*[1]

A man who was going to use the *Budeli* took a small gourd and bound it tightly round with cotton. He killed a red cock, and put one of the tail-feathers into the mouth of the gourd. He cut off the skin from the cock's neck with the red feathers on it, and drew it over the neck of the gourd. Then he attached a string to the gourd, and went about with it hung round his neck. When he came into the village he sang: 'Budeli-o! The rack is piled up with meat!'[2] And all the empty-chested gathered round and joined lustily in the chorus, hurling abuse at the *mbatsav* in the Hausa language, '*Dan kashi! Dan kare!* What will you dare do to us? If you come here with *tsav* the *Budeli* will kill you!' That night the *mbatsav* would decide to test it, and find out whether it was true or not. So they sent a mouse to go to the home of the man who had the *Budeli*. The mouse died, and the next morning the owner of the *Budeli* showed it to everybody. 'You see,' he would say, 'yesterday the *mbatsav* sent a mouse, and the *Budeli* killed it.' At this every one declared that the *Budeli* was genuine. The *mbatsav* then sent a skink, and the *Budeli* killed this too. After this they were very much afraid of it. But it did not last. Not long after, men who had hung the *Budeli* round their necks were found dead with it clasped to their

---

[1] We have not been able to discover the origin of this word, but it is certainly foreign, probably Hausa. The only similar Hausa word known means a species of wild-cat, which is not recorded as being used in the ritual. It may, however, be a corruption of some other Hausa word or proper name.

[2] I.e. everything is all right again.

breasts. People then said that the *mbatsav* were too strong, and that they had discovered its taboo, by which it could be overcome.[1] So they gave up the *Budeli* as a useless thing which had no power at all over the *mbatsav*, and the movement collapsed.

THE *IJƆV*

At a time when the *mbatsav* were very active, and were killing many by poison, the *Ijɔv* came to put a stop to evil practices. The *Ijɔv* appears in human shape. But no one who sees it knows that it is the *Ijɔv*. You think it is some one whom you know. But when you speak to it, it never opens its mouth, but listens in silence. Even if you abuse it, it will not answer you back. It lives in the woods or in the hills, and does whatsoever it pleases, good and ill. The good that it does is to give men good things. If you are in the direst want, and have had to struggle hard to get some little thing, yet when some one asks you for it you do not refuse him, one day the *Ijɔv* will come and beg something of you. You do not know that it is the *Ijɔv*, but suppose that it is your brother whose need is as great as your own, and wish to help him. So you give it what it asks, and it departs. But some other day it will come and meet you in the bush and put something small into your hands, telling you how you must use it, and showing you exactly what is its taboo.[2] If you do as it says, you will be wonderfully lucky. Sometimes it gives riches, and the man becomes the wealthiest in the country round. He tells every one that it is the *Ijɔv* who has given him his prosperity. Whenever he sells anything small he gets something big in exchange. Sometimes the *Ijɔv* gives a man success in hunting, and then no one in the land can shoot so well as he; in one year alone he will kill twenty beasts. Another receives from the *Ijɔv* a fine crop. Though he only hoes a tiny plot, the yield is so big

[1] *Akombo* and charms can be rendered ineffective by breaking their taboo. This can be done by another person, who is not the owner. E.g. if you have a charm whose taboo is water, and you leave it about, your enemy can render it ineffective by sprinkling water over it.

[2] I.e. tells you what you must avoid, to keep the virtue of the charm unimpaired; see above.

that it cannot all be carried home, and part is left to rot on the farm.

The *Ijɔv* also does ill, visiting men with afflictions. If the *Ijɔv* asks for something, and the man refuses, believing it to be merely a fellow human being, he has brought trouble on himself. The *Ijɔv* will 'afflict' him. The affliction may be of different kinds. Sometimes it takes the form of importunity. The person always wants whatever any one else has got, till people say, 'So-and-so is afflicted by the *Ijɔv*. He keeps asking for things, as though he were out of his mind'. At other times it may be a pregnant woman who is very mean, and, when the *Ijɔv* asks her for something, she denies it, and so becomes afflicted. When her child is born it is a monstrosity with its mouth on one side, or a weakling. Or it may be dumb, or may never learn to walk but always drag itself along the ground. People say, 'His mother was afflicted by the *Ijɔv* for her meanness, when he was in her womb'. A man sometimes becomes afflicted by the *Ijɔv* over a woman. He goes after the same woman continuously, and never gives up, however often she may have refused him. In his songs and in his conversation the woman is his only theme, and he talks about her even while he is eating his food. 'He is afflicted by the *Ijɔv*', says every one. Sometimes, also, if a man does a wrong which angers the *Ijɔv*, it beats him and raises weals all over his body, without being either seen or heard. When he is asked how he got his marks, he does not answer, and every one concludes that he has been beaten by the *Ijɔv* in the wood.

'*Begetting*' *the* '*Adzɔv*'.[1] A man who is going to carry out the *Adzɔv* rites brews beer and invites all the elders amongst his kinsmen, who assemble at his house on the day that the beer is ready. The man who prepared the beer for the *Adzɔv* rites is known as the 'begetter' of the *Adzɔv*. They start drinking. No one is refused the *Adzɔv* beer; every one may draw off and drink what he

---

[1] *Adzɔv a maren*. *Adzɔv* is the plural of *Ijɔv*. They are also called *Mbakúv*, not to be confused with *mbakûuv*, 'the dead', with which they have probably no connexion. The word *mar* (to give birth) is only so used in reference to this cult.

pleases, without any daring to stop him. If any were to do so, the *Adzɔv* would be angry with the man who had begotten them, when the people went down to them. They would not answer when he called them, and would appear hostile. When he asked them, 'My fathers, what have I done?' they would say, 'Why did some one deny people our beer, as if it were his own? We are not pleased at what he has done. We shall not listen to you unless you propitiate us'. So the begetter of *Adzɔv* goes home and catches a white chicken which has not a black feather on its body, some pearl millet, koko yams, *alev* beans, guinea-corn, ground-nuts, and a strip of indigo cloth. These things are put down at the foot of a tree. The trees at which the *Adzɔv* are begotten are the copaiba balsam, *haa*, and *hurugh*, and at no others, because it is these trees alone in which the *Adzɔv* live. When the begetter has set down the presents, he calls on the *Adzɔv* by name. The names of the *Adzɔv* are Lim and Ageraiber. Lim is a woman, and Ageraiber a chief. After this the land prospers. Crops are good, hunting is successful, and the women bear children.

Initiation to the 'Adzɔv'. For initiation to the *Adzɔv* you need a dog, six 'twenties', eight 'twenties', and a cow. These are all taken by the man who initiates you, but before he goes he distributes shoots of *iyandegh* amongst all the elders who are present at the beer-drinking, to take away and plant on their farms. He also makes a pronouncement that all pots must be cleaned out that night, and that no woman is to throw the slops outside the house, because if she does so she will throw the water over the *Ijɔv*. Furthermore, no menstruous woman must wash in the river-bed, and no woman must take herbs for sauce from another wife's field. A woman who goes to the farm must not refuse to share her meal with any one who asks her. If the maize is ripe on the farm and some one comes and picks it, the owner must not cry 'Thief!' and no dog must be beaten that night in the initiate's village.

Drinking the 'Ijɔv'. The *Ijɔv*[1] appeared many years

---

[1] I.e. the anti-*tsav* movement called by this name and the rites connected with it, described below.

after the *Budeli.* It originated in Iharev, and from there spread into Nɔŋgov. All who were much troubled by *tsav* went to get it, and brought it back to suppress the *tsav* practices in their own clans. The *Ijɔv* was obtained in this way: The man who wished to acquire it for use in his own group listened for news of some place where the *Ijɔv* was being brewed,[1] and when he learnt of some one who was doing this, he went and stayed with him and took note of all the details connected with it. On the day that the *Ijɔv* was to be drunk, he asked the man who had brewed it to give him the *Ijɔv*,[2] that he too might brew it, and with it chastise the *mbatsav* of his own district. The other poured some of the beer into a square black bottle,[3] and gave it to him together with some *iyandegh* leaves.[4] Having received this, he set off by night, for he was afraid to travel by day, lest the *mbatsav* should lie in wait for him on the road and kill him. On the day that he arrived at his home he stood in the middle of the village, when the sun was well up, uttering cries of triumph and singing the song of the *Ijɔv*. Then he made known to all the commands of the *Ijɔv*, that is to say, the things which were not to be done during the days that he was bringing it in. These commands are sometimes called taboos. The taboo decreed for the day of brewing the *Ijɔv* was this: that no man must kill a monitor, skink, or any creature that came into the village.[5] Strange things happened in those days. Many people might be sitting in an *ate*, and a monitor come in amongst them and stay there, yet no one would put out his hand to touch it. Skinks and other creatures became very tame during that time.

---

[1] I.e. where beer was being brewed for an *Ijɔv* meeting; see below.

[2] I.e. some of the *Ijɔv* beer, in order that he might impart the virtue contained in it to his own brew, in much the same way that the Muhammadan pilgrim brings back a bottle of the holy water of Zemzem for sanctifying the water in his home town. As in other rites, the beer has a strong ritual significance, and in the language is identified with the *Ijɔv* itself. *Mir Ijɔv* means to 'brew' the *Ijɔv*, *ma Ijɔv* to 'drink' it. But these expressions should not be taken too literally as having a sacramental implication; see note on *nyia Ijɔv* below.

[3] These were the old 'square-face' gin bottles, and probably the only kind known at that time.

[4] The *iyandegh* plant is the sign of goodwill, used as a badge by any one bearing a peaceful message.

[5] Because it might turn out to be the *Ijɔv* in disguise. Cf., also, the taboo on beating a dog.

On the day that the man started to brew the beer he
caught a white ram and took it to the *Adzɔv*, telling them
that he was brewing the beer for them, and asking them
to come and succour his land. The *Adzɔv* consented,
and every time a meal was prepared and a beast killed
some was taken to give the *Adzɔv* in the grove. The male
Adzɔv who were the fiercest were called Gudanasila and
Wanikpughulkapa; their mother was Myam, and their
father Agaishuwa. The land was quiet in those days.
No one went *tsav*; if any did so, his bowels would become
loose, and he would die.

On the day of drinking the *Ijɔv*, the group of the man
who had brewed it assembled in his village. When they
were all seated, he brought out a great pot of beer, and
set it down in the centre of the open space. He himself
sat on an inverted mortar. Then he stood up and commanded silence. The people stopped talking, and not
a bird twittered, while he took the bottle with the little
beer in it and held it up for all to see. 'My kinsmen,' he
said, 'do you see this?' 'Yes,' they replied with one voice,
'we do indeed.' 'This is the beer', he said, 'which the
Ijɔv has given me, that with it I may come and set right
the land. I am going to mix it with the beer in this pot,
and if any one drinks without having first thrown all his
medicine or *akombo* for killing men into the basket which
stands here in this place, and confessed the evil deeds
which he has already done in the past, the *Ijɔv* shall cause
his bowels to gush out,[1] and he shall die.' With this he
poured the beer in the bottle into the beer which was in
the pot, and the people began to drink the *Ijɔv*. If there
were any man there who had no medicine for killing, he
stood up and swore that never in his life had he bought
any magic thing with which to kill men, nor any evil
medicine. He said, 'If I have done this, and am denying
it falsely, let the *Ijɔv* kill me. But if I have spoken the
truth, I shall drink and pass it out again freely'. After

---

[1] *Nyia Ijɔv :* Lit., 'defecate the *Ijɔv*', but this does not mean that he will pass
the *Ijɔv* in his motions, or even the *Ijɔv* beer (see below). *Ijɔv* is used adverbi-
ally, and the meaning is that he will be seized with that form of diarrhoea which
is the result of an offence against it. Cf., also, *nyia Igbe*, to have diarrhoea as
a consequence of transgressing against the *Igbe*.

he had taken this oath, the man who had brewed the beer gave it to him, and he drank. Then he went and sat down again. Some said, 'Well! We quite thought that So-and-so was *tsav*, but to-day he has absolutely denied it!'

Another, who was *tsav* and in the habit of killing people by poison, would stand up and confess his crimes of his own accord, without any compelling him, knowing that were he not to make a full confession his bowels would be loosened by the *Ijɔv*, and he would die. Another would bring out the medicine with which he killed people, and, holding it up that every one there might see, disclose the names of those whom he had killed with it. He said, 'I killed So-and-so of such-and-such a family. He quarrelled with his brother, and was getting the worst of it, so he came to me and asked if I would help him.[1] I did so, and killed his brother, who had been too strong for him'. With these words he threw the medicine into the basket. A cry of praise was raised by some woman of the village, and every one admired him for a brave man. Some confessed to having killed as many as five people. One man might stand up and, displaying a charm, declare that when he got into trouble he turned himself into a leopard. Another said that he escaped by changing into a mongoose, and asked whether he need throw away his charm, as it was only used in self-defence. If every one agreed that his charm need not be put into the basket, he took it back again. Even if a man had an *imborivuŋgu*, he brought it out that day. If it was an *imborivuŋgu* of the forefathers, he was told to throw it away, because men were killed to set it right. But if it was an *imborivuŋgu* for making the crops good, it was not put into the basket, because people said that he must not throw away the crops. My father threw away an *imborivuŋgu* on one such occasion, after he had brought it out and crushed it.[2]

[1] See note on *vaa*, p. 238.

[2] This shows how confused the whole question had become in the minds of the people. The *imborivuŋgu* 'for making the crops good' was a personal matter; the victim used in its rites was only a mouse, and therefore there seemed to be no harm in it. But the *imborivuŋgu* 'of the fathers' was for the whole group, and its rites involved the shedding of human blood (see p. 227). Nevertheless, it was done for the benefit of the community, and if the throwing away of the

But although people threw away all manner of things in this fashion, no one ever brought out a human skin. Yet many asserted that this had been done. When my sister, after whom I came next in age, died in Mbaiyɔŋgo, people always said that she was such a handsome girl that my father had killed her and given her to his eldest son, Hilekaan, to skin, in order that he might be the smartest at the night dances. At the coming of the *Ijɔv*, therefore, I was deeply interested to see whether Hilekaan would bring out the skin of my sister, Kasevevduwe, and when my cousin Ndeer brewed the *Ijɔv*, on the day of the drinking I took up my position next to the man who was dispensing the *Ijɔv*, in order that if Hilekaan brought out my sister's skin I should be sure to see it. There was no one who stood nearer to him than I. The only things that Hilekaan displayed openly were our father's *imborivuŋgu* and some woman medicine.[1] Every one saw these, and I, too, saw them quite clearly, but he never brought out a human skin. Yet when the people went back to their homes they spoke everywhere of how Hilekaan of Sai had that day done a thing which was not good; he had brought out the skin of Kasevevduwe in the public place.

The *Ijɔv* movement made a great stir in Tivland at that time, and was known to every section of the tribe. The power of the *mbatsav* languished, and since going *tsav* was forbidden by the *Ijɔv* every one in those days went about freely. The things which were thrown away by people at the drinking of the *Ijɔv* were gathered up by the man who had brewed it and thrown into the stream. But after a while the *Ijɔv* movement came to an end. People began again to buy *akombo* and medicines for killing men, and the land went back to its evil state.

❡ It will be understood that nothing which has been said on the subject of Tiv magic in the section dealing with the *akombo*

---

lesser *imborivuŋgu* harmed the crops, much more damage might be expected to result from the destruction of the sacred objects belonging to the group. In short, the people had lost faith in the beneficent power of the relics, and saw only their destructive side.

[1] I.e. a philtre.

applies to the *Ijɔv* cult. In fact, the idea of an anthropomorphic, or zoomorphic, spirit, of a distinctly ethical and disciplinary character, has no parallel in the Tiv magico-religious code. In many ways the cult represents the antithesis of normal Tiv magic, and it was doubtless for this reason that it was practised as an antidote to witchcraft. The *Ijɔv* is regarded as a personal being, which has, on the whole, a benevolent disposition, and must be approached with prayer, and a certain humility. It is spoken of as being propitiated (*wam*), a word of very different meaning from *sɔr*, 'set right', used for the other cults. All the beasts slaughtered must be pure white, to counter the black magic of the People of the Night.

The cult is spoken of as having 'appeared' in comparatively recent times, and it would seem natural to suppose, in view of its exotic character, that it was introduced, like the other anti-*tsav* measures, from foreign sources. It will be shown below that there is good reason why this should be so. But although some of the ideas about the *Ijɔv* may have been grafted on to it in recent times, the conception of the *Ijɔv* as a spirit which lives in the woods is old. It appears in folk-lore. Apparently this being was invested with a special significance and function at the time of the anti-*tsav* movement which bears its name, and a ritual and terminology, copied largely from current magic practice, was invented *ad hoc* to counteract an alleged outbreak of witchcraft and restore public equanimity. These rites were only carried out during this time, and have not been practised since.

THE *IVASE*

AFTER the *Ijɔv* had come and failed to put an end to *tsav*, there came the *Ivase*. The *Ivase* started in Utaŋge; any one who had been to buy it set up an *Ivase* enclosure in his own village, consisting of a well-made stockade of stout posts. In the centre of the enclosure he planted a three-forked pole, on which he placed a covered pot containing hens' eggs. To set it right he caught a cock, swung it round over the pot, and then struck its head against the palm of his hand. The cock's head, which broke off, he took and put into the pot; the rest of the bird was cooked and eaten, but only by those who had bought the *Ivase*. Sometimes a dog was killed,

T

and its head cut off and put into the pot; but, as the Tiv do not eat dogs, they gave the body to the Utaŋge to eat.

A man who wished to be initiated went to some one who had an *Ivase* in his village, and gave him some present. The owner of the *Ivase* took a piece of leopard's skin and bound it round a stick, broke an egg over it, and gave it to the man who had come to buy it. When the latter arrived back at his home he proclaimed the *Ivase*, speaking an unintelligible jargon in the Utaŋge language mixed up with Tiv: 'Ho *Ivase*, of the savage heart! of the *bele bele inko, we biano we biano, we shi mbembe. Ivase,* fight the *mbatsav*, fight furiously, furiously. If any become an owl, you are an owl also; if any come on the water, you too are water. Let no one use you to savour his food, as you use no man for yours!' When he had finished speaking in this manner, all those who had bought the *Ivase* came together and in the evening danced the *Ivase* dance to the accompaniment of a small tree-drum. The *Ivase* dance was similar to the dance of the *mbatsav*. The dancers did not touch each other, and while they danced they sang, '*Wo wo, woro wo wo, Ivase* of the *wororo wo wo*'. If any one brought the *Ivase* into his village, no one in the whole of the group would go *tsav*. If any did so his feet and stomach would swell up, and he would die.

The *Ivase* taboos were as follows: No one must plant an iron weapon into the ground (as, for instance, a broad-bladed or barbed spear) inside the village of a man who had bought the *Ivase*; if he did so the weapon would be seized, and he must redeem it by payment of a penny. No *ruam* must be brought out uncovered; and any one who threw water out from inside a house would get a headache.

When any one died, wherever he might be, it was said that the *Ivase* had killed him. On that day a red cloth was hung over the entrance to the *Ivase* enclosure. Those who had bought the *Ivase* again spent the day dancing, and the *mbatsav* were afraid, believing that if they went *tsav* they would die as this man had died. When a man brought an *Ivase*, the *mbatsav* would send a mouse to test him. The mouse died as soon as it came into the village.

The End of the 'Ivase'. The *Ivase* spread rapidly, and the Dam in their turn began to buy it from the Tiv. One day a man of the Dam people came to see a Tiv friend of his, who had the *Ivase*, and asked him if he would bring it to his home, that he might buy it. So the Tiv made ready to go. But before he left he killed a number of mice, put them into a bag, and took them with him to his friend's village. After dark his friend the Dam came out of his house and hid, in order that he might see whether there was any truth in the *Ivase*. When every one was asleep the Tiv got up, and taking the mice quietly out of the bag threw them down here and there between the huts. Then he went back to bed. All this time the Dam had been watching him. The next morning, when his friend came to ask how he had slept, the Tiv said, 'The *mbatsav* who are in Dam country last night sent some mice to test you, and they have all died'. 'Stop lying', said his friend. 'It was you yourself who took out the mice and put them down in between the huts. I saw the whole thing. If you deny it, come and I will show you your footprints which you made last night while you were doing it.' The Tiv was very much ashamed, and the Dam took back off him all the money which he had paid to be shown the *Ivase*, saying that the thing was obviously a hoax. When news of this spread round there was general disappointment. All those who had bought the *Ivase* lost their confidence, and the movement was much discredited.

THE *HAAKAA*

A long time after the *Ivase* had proved worthless, there came another big movement, which shook the land of Tiv to its very foundations. It was called *Haakaa*,[1] or, by some, *Pasepase*,[1] and began in this way: There were two brothers in Shitire-on-the-farms, Kpela and Aganyi. When Kpela died Aganyi took his wife, Dzuŋgu, according to Tiv custom. But Nyikaan, a kinsman of Aganyi, started a story that Aganyi was killing his wife; he also went to Mbaakande and told Iganden, the

---

[1] *Haa-akaa* = 'throw things away'. *Pase* = 'confess' or 'reveal'. The meaning of the terms will be clear from what follows.

owner of Dzuŋgu, to come and take away his *iŋgɔl*, for otherwise Aganyi would kill her.   Dzuŋgu, while on a visit to her home in Mbaakande, heard what Nyikaan had said, and came back and told Aganyi. When Aganyi heard this, he went to lay a complaint before Tordwem[1] that Nyikaan was seeking a quarrel with him.   Tordwem summoned them both to his village, and questioned them. When he and his council had heard the story they said that it was just malicious gossip, and since it was purely a family matter they had better go back and settle it at home; it was not a case to bring before the court.   So they went home and held a discussion. Amu, chief of the Mbaseer division, and the other elders of their district, Ihɔɔn, Agishi, and Torciembe, held that Aganyi was to blame. They said, 'When you hear something about your brother, you ask him first if it is true. But Aganyi went straight to Tordwem and made a complaint without questioning his brother at all. That was not good; he must not do it again'. When Aganyi heard this he was angry, and said he would take his complaint against them even to Katsina Ala.[2] But they took no notice of this, knowing him already for a man who harboured resentment for no reason, and a fool.

So Aganyi set off for Katsina Ala, and told the District Officer that Amu, Ihɔɔn, Agishi, and Torciembe had killed his brother Kpela. They had brought him the head, but he refused to accept it,[3] so they had taken it away and given it to Dzegeate, who had eaten it. The *akombo*, which they had killed his brother to set right, was the *Fe* of the People of the Night.[4] The District Officer, hearing this, sent Tordwem's messenger, who happened to be in Katsina Ala at the time, to tell Tordwem to bring in the people who were accused by Aganyi of killing his brother Kpela to set right the *Fe*. When Tordwem arrived with the elders whose names had been given by Aganyi, the District Officer took them into his house and questioned them. They, on being asked, denied all knowledge of the

---

[1] Chief of Shitire.   [2] I.e. to the District Officer.   [3] P. 260.
[4] A hunting cult whose rites were said to necessitate human sacrifice; see Abraham, op. cit., p. 124.

matter. So the District Officer asked Aganyi what he had to say. Aganyi replied that they knew all about it, and were wilfully concealing their guilt. When they still persisted in denying it, the District Officer asked Aganyi whether he would recognize his brother's skull if it were brought to him. Aganyi said that he would know it, because his brother had one molar missing on the right-hand side. Then Dzegeate said, 'Aganyi has spoken the truth. Leave me alone, and I will go and bring Kpela's head'. The District Officer gave him leave to go and fetch it. When he arrived at his home he dug up the grave of a woman who had lately died in their village, called Kwaghtagher, and brought in the head to show the District Officer. The District Officer saw no missing tooth, and when he asked Aganyi whether it was Kpela's head, Aganyi said that it was not. He accused Dzegeate of hiding it, and of bringing a woman's head instead. So the District Officer punished Dzegeate and the elders for deliberately hiding the truth.

At that time the whole land of Tiv was shaken. When the Tiv saw that the Shitire elders were severely dealt with by the District Officer they were glad, for they were given a great chance to avenge themselves on their enemies, by falsely accusing them before him. One would come and say, 'So-and-so killed my brother to set right an *imborivuŋgu*'. When the District Officer heard this he would send to the chief to have the man brought in. The policemen[1] went to fetch him, and before they even started from his home they would give him a thorough beating. When they brought him in, the white man asked him where was the *imborivuŋgu* for which he had killed the man. When he began to deny it, the District Officer violently upbraided him and accused him of hiding the truth, until finally he admitted his guilt and asked to be allowed to go and fetch it. Policemen were sent with him. In some cases, when the man arrived at his home he would ask to be allowed to go into his house, and when he found

[1] *Dugwer* (= Hausa *dogari*) means a Native Administration policeman. It is translated as policeman throughout, as the government police are not mentioned in this book.

nothing which he could give up, took an arrow and
stabbed himself, saying that death was better than so
much undeserved misery. Another would enter his house
and set it alight, thinking to be burnt to death inside, and
had to be dragged out by force. Some had a real *imborivuŋgu*, or medicine, and brought it in; others, being
unable to find anything, took a bone or some other thing,
covered it with wax, stuck hair on it and red beans, and
said that it was an *imborivuŋgu*. By giving this up they
obtained relief from their troubles. Some who said they
had nothing were lying, but after they had been well
punished they cunningly went and found something quite
different to bring in. This they said was the medicine
which they had for killing men, and the District Officer
and the chiefs accepted their story. (At that time many of
the chiefs were assembled at Katsina Ala.) The chiefs, of
course, were perfectly aware of all this, but they wanted
to find favour with the District Officer; so even when
people brought in what was quite spurious they said it was
the real thing.

Sometimes a man was said to own a *Poor*, and to be
tsav, but when the white man told him to bring the
human skulls which he was keeping he was unable to
produce any. When he failed to find any skulls the police
gave him such a beating that even if he returned home his
strength was exhausted, and he died. But if a man was
wise, when the white man told him to bring the skull of
the man he had killed he did not deny it, but set off at
once to go and dig up the grave of some one who had died
many years ago. Taking out the head, he brought it back
in an old sack, gave it to the white man and the chiefs, and
all would go well with him. But the man who had no
sense, and truthfully protested his innocence, brought
enough trouble on himself to last him his lifetime, and
often did not survive it. The people who suffered most
were the two sections of Shitire and Ikurav, Ugondo,
Kunav, and Turan.

The white man knew little of the suffering which occurred
in the clans affected by the *Haakaa*. The trouble was
made much worse by the mutual incriminations that

took place when he first called in all the chiefs to Katsina Ala. Every one who was indicted for having instruments of the *mbatsav* turned round and accused his enemies, so that in any one case five men suffered. The thing which the white man was most anxious to get was a complete human skin.[1] He said that a human skin must be brought, but no one could produce one. When the District Officer went on leave, and another took his place, Tseva, of Ikado in Ukum, said that if the white man would give him the chieftainship of Ukum on condition that he brought him a human skin, he would find one. The white man agreed, and Tseva sought with all his power, and all his knowledge, but he never found one. People in the end began to laugh at him, saying that he was looking for a thing which did not exist.

At the time when the white man and Tseva were making every effort to find a human skin, there was a certain man and his wife who perhaps suffered worse than any one. The man's name was Atserve, his wife was called Tuŋgwa, and their son Agundu, who was a very beautiful child. Agundu died, and about the time of his death it was said that Tsofo, the son of Zaki Biam, had in his possession a human skin. So the white man ordered Gana, his foreign messenger, and a policeman called Igbudu to go and arrest Tsofo, and make him give up the human skin. Tsofo denied having one, but asserted that Atserve had killed his son and skinned him. Gana stayed at Zaki Biam, and sent policemen to seize Atserve. Atserve was then beaten till he could no longer cry out, and his whole body was covered with sores. They told him to bring the skin of his son Agundu. When he saw no escape he lied to them, and said that he had indeed killed Agundu, and would bring his skin. So they untied him and told him to go and fetch it. Every one was glad, thinking that at last they were going to see a human skin. The police went with him, but nothing was found. So they brought him back again, beating him as they went. When they came back, and Gana questioned him, he put the blame on his wife, Tuŋgwa, saying that he was actually fetching it, but

[1] Footnote on p. 249.

she had prevented him. So Gana sent them to arrest Tuŋgwa and bring her in. They beat Tuŋgwa till she screamed and could scream no more, while her husband lay on the ground and watched his wife's sufferings. Then they caught hold of him and started beating him again. When they had beaten him for a long time, he said that if they would let him go he would fetch the skin, and fool no longer. So they untied him and took him back again. He told the police to wait outside while he went into the house to get it. So they waited. He entered his house, took an arrow, and stabbed himself in the thigh. Then he sat down to await the death which seemed to him a better thing than the trouble that had come upon him without cause. The policemen, having waited in vain for him to come out, went into the house, and there found him on the point of death, with the arrow stuck in his thigh. They took him, and quickly applied remedies, and sent word to Gana. Gana was afraid, and released his wife, who was still lying bound in the middle of the village. The man did not die, but he and his wife still bear the marks of their beating. A few months after this Gana gave up his post, but I do not know the reason. I afterwards, however, met him in Abinsi, and he told me that he would rather be left to live in poverty than undertake *mbatsav* work again.

At that time all the officials working under the European claimed to have a good knowledge of the Tiv, and the white man acted on their advice without question. In this way they had great opportunities to hoodwink him, and many obtained promotion in consequence. One day the white man sent his policeman, Abaivo, to Chief Yaakur in Ugondo, telling him to go with him and seize the *mbatsav*, and to take their bad things from them. Abaivo went, and they came and stopped at Ugba's old village. (Ugba was then living at Kaduna.) Ugba's brother, Igase, was away at the time, but the labourers who were working on the road from Zaki Biam to Tombo were staying in his village and going to their work from there. The name of their headman was Korinya of Akaa in Kusuv. That day, as they went to work, two eagles were fighting in a tree, and they saw them fall off into the grass at the side of the road, on the site of the present Ugba market. The road workers ran to the spot. One of the eagles got up, but the other was caught by one of the young labourers (his name was Uwogba of Ugondo), who took it to Korinya, his headman. Korinya handed it over to Yaakur, who was drinking beer together with his chief men and Abaivo. Abaivo took the eagle and said, 'I will go and tell the white man that I took Igase's box with the instruments of the *mbatsav* in it, and that I caught this eagle as it came to take it away from me'. Chief Yaakur agreed to tell the same story if he were asked by the white man. So they tied a string to the eagle, and three days later, when Igase returned, they told him that they were waiting for him to give them the box in which he kept the bad things. Igase denied having any *mbatsav* instruments, but they beat him, went in and took one of his boxes by force, and put into it some *mbatsav* instruments out of another box which they had previously confiscated. Then they set out for Katsina Ala to give their evidence. When they arrived, Abaivo told the white man his story, and Yaakur, on being questioned, supported him. Every one praised Abaivo for the power of his *tsav*, by means of which he had been able to catch the eagle. The white man plucked the eagle's feathers and put them in the place at Katsina Ala where the bad things were kept. Abaivo's fame spread to all parts of Tivland. Men came from a distance to see the eagle, and, having seen it, paid homage to the greatness of Abaivo. This pleased Abaivo beyond measure.

Then there was the case of the human slaughter-slab.[1] The Tiv originally knew nothing of a slab for cutting up human flesh; they always said that the *mbatsav* found a big tree, bent it down to the ground and cut up the meat on its leaves. But when the *Haakaa* came, Ukum started the idea of the slaughter-slab. This was sewn like the cloth which is put over a horse's back. It was made of

---

[1] *Kpande* is any board, bed, &c., cut out of a solid piece of wood, which is used sometimes for cutting up the meat when a beast has been slaughtered or brought in from the hunt. But the *mbatsav* article was made of cloth, and was therefore called *kpande* only by analogy.

black material, at the corners of which were attached
human hair and phylacteries, and it had blood on it
which, they said, was human blood. Every slaughter-
slab, moreover, had a small butcher's knife attached to it.
This thing also at first caused the Tiv the greatest suffering, until they discovered a way out of the trouble. Afterwards, when a man was seized and told to bring a
slaughter-slab, he did not argue, but asked to be allowed
to go and fetch it. Then he went and sewed together
an old black blanket and a strip of cloth, and attached to it
all the things which he had seen on another one. For
blood, he squeezed out some juice from the bark of the
ikpine tree and let it dry. Then he took it to the white
man, and said it was a human slaughter-slab.

The following account was given me by my cousin,
Wangba: While he was at Takum one of the older men of
his family, called Shishi, was arrested and told to bring
in a human slaughter-slab. Shishi denied all knowledge of
this, and the policemen started to beat him. Wangba,
seeing this, went quietly and squatted down close to
Shishi. He told him to send him for the slaughter-slab,
and said that he would bring it. Shishi asked him, 'Where
are you going to find one?' 'It is quite all right', he
answered. 'Just tell the white man that you have sent
some one, and he is bringing it along.' Thereupon he got
up and went to his home, where he took an old blanket
and sewed it in exactly the same way as one which he had
seen given to the white man before. He tied on all the
things he had seen on the other one. Finally he killed a
small goat, and put some of the blood on it, to serve as
human blood. Then they ate the goat, and the next
morning he set off, taking the cloth with the goat's blood
on it, carefully rolled up in an old sack. When they
arrived, the open place in the centre of the village was full
of people, and the white man and the chief were there too.
As soon as he brought out the cloth, every one asked how
it was that the day before Shishi had denied having a
slaughter-slab. Shishi said that he was confused by his
beating. Thereupon he was released, and thus Wangba
saved his father.

Those Tiv into whose districts the *Haakaa* came say
that it was the worst trouble that has ever befallen them.
Some, indeed, died as a result of it, for during the investigation there was none amongst the elders of the tribe who
did not suffer. Some came into such distress that they
took their own lives, and others survived only after undergoing the greatest hardships. Much of this suffering went
on unknown to the European, and the men who were the
chief cause of it were the *ugwana*.[1] These *ugwana* were
employed by the policemen and messengers. When a
policeman was sent out by the white man or a chief, he did
not go by himself, unless it were some small matter. If
it were anything of importance, such as an arrest, or the
collection of labour for some purpose, and he knew that
he would have trouble with the people, as soon as he was
out of sight of the white man or the chief, he found ten or
twenty young men to go with him. These he called 'my
ugwana'. The type of men whom he chose to carry out his
purpose were those whom he knew to be of a violent disposition and strong physique, ready to say anything, swear
without compunction, and completely shameless. When
they reached their destination he did not do much himself,
but left it all to them. If some one were to be arrested it
would be they who caught him and tied him up, and if he
happened to be a man against whom they had some
grudge they treated him very badly indeed. But when
they had brought him back nearly to where the white man
was, they left the policeman to bring him into his presence.
Moreover, it was not only the man in question who was
maltreated, but any one else in the village who opened his
mouth, or even looked at them too hard, was accounted
to be seeking a quarrel with them and beaten to within an
inch of his life.

It was these *ugwana* who brought the people most of
their troubles. The white man did not know, but the
chiefs knew. It was over the *Haakaa* that the chiefs
finally became so unpopular in Tivland. The Tiv asked,

---

[1] This is a corruption of the Hausa term *sojan gona* ('farm soldiers'), which
was the name given to the men who in the early days of the British occupation
went round the countryside extorting from the people, under the guise of having
been sent by the European.

'Why is it supposed that the chiefs themselves are not
tsav ? Is it only we that are *tsav*, who are not chiefs ?' If
any accusation connected with the *mbatsav* were brought
against a chief, the other chiefs gave evidence in his
favour, and he was acquitted. Nor was any one *tsav* who
was a favourite of the chief. The chiefs who were most
hated at that time were Jato Aka and Tordwem. Because
Turan, Jato Aka's clan, being strongly defended by their
chief, escaped all the trouble, whereas every one said they
were the worst of all. Yet at that time neither he nor his
people were *tsav*! They were only slightly affected in the
later stages, when rumours reached the ears of the white
man. There was so much ill feeling about this amongst
the Tiv that if they had been allowed to give their opinion
about Jato Aka they would certainly have demanded that
he should be deposed; but they were afraid, because the
white man said that he was the greatest of their chiefs.
Tordwem, on the other hand, oppressed his clansmen with
the greatest harshness, and without pity. He spared his
own near kinsmen to a large extent, but vented his hatred
on the rest of his clan, till they cried bitterly.

The End of the 'Haakaa'. The *Haakaa* came to an
end in this way: Saama and Oralai were two brothers by
the same mother, of the clan of Shitire-on-the-farms.
Their section was Tɔmbo, Mbaagia, and their family-
group Mbaidyo. Their clan chief was Tordwem, and the
section head of Tɔmbo, to whom they paid tax, was
Agishi.

At the time when the *Haakaa* was at its height, Saama
went down to Akwana to drink *tashi*. On his way back, as
darkness was falling, he stopped for the night at the village
of Ibumun, of Anengena in Mbavihi. In that night he
died, and they sent to tell his brother Oralai to come
and bury him.

After Oralai had buried him, word was brought to
Tordwem that it was he who had killed his brother Saama.
When Tordwem heard this, he sent a policeman to seize
Oralai and bring him to his village. Tordwem and the
elders asked Oralai why he had killed his brother. Oralai
protested that he had not killed his brother, and that his

accusers were lying. He said, 'I am much distressed by the death of my brother, and feel his loss deeply. Why do you add to my grief? There were only two of us, and why should I kill Saama, to be left alone in the world?' Tordwem and the elders told him not to tell deliberate lies. But if he persisted in denying that he was guilty, they said that Agishi, his section head, should go with him and a policeman to open up the grave. For if it were indeed Oralai who had killed his brother, the corpse would not be there; but if he had not killed him, they would find the body in the grave. (Because, amongst the Tiv, if a man kills some one, he afterwards exhumes him in order to carry out the purpose for which he killed him; but if a man who makes a habit of practising *tsav* buys some medicine without understanding how to use it, and is killed by it in consequence, his body, having been buried, is left in the ground, and not eaten by any of the *mbatsav*.¹)

So Chief Agishi set out with the policeman and the *ugwana*, and Oralai, who was accused of killing his brother. When they arrived at the grave they stood round it in a circle, while some one took a hoe and opened it up. When they had opened it they saw the dead man, Saama, inside, as plain as could be, and quite untouched. 'You see?' asked Oralai. 'Is this not Saama lying in the grave?' When he said this, Agishi slapped him across the mouth. 'Don't tell lies!' he said. 'Saama is not in the grave.' 'Good Heavens!' cried Oralai. 'You can all see Saama as well as I can.' The policeman and the *ugwana* then started to beat Oralai, telling him to stop lying, and filled in the grave again with the body inside. They brought Oralai bound before Tordwem. Tordwem asked them what they had seen, and they all replied with one voice that Saama was not in the grave. Thereupon, since

¹ This does not necessarily mean that he poisons himself accidentally with his own medicine. Its noxious principle (magically speaking) may recoil on the user if he fails to observe its taboos. If it seem that even this must be a somewhat rare contingency, it must be remembered that, since there is no such thing as death from natural causes, this is practically the only way in which a man can be killed without the direct intervention of the *mbatsav*. The argument then is this: No one kills people except the *mbatsav*. Every one killed by the *mbatsav* is dug up and eaten. If some one dies, and his body is afterwards found intact in the grave, he cannot have been killed by any one else. Therefore he must be the cause of his own death.

Oralai again asserted that he was in the grave, and they strongly affirmed that he was not, Tordwem sent some more of the elders to go back with them, and open up the grave again.

So they rebound Oralai, and set off. They again dug up the grave and saw Saama in it, and Oralai again said, 'You see? There is Saama in the grave'. But they replied, 'Don't talk nonsense. You're a confirmed liar. We do not see Saama in the grave'. At this Oralai's heart began to fail him. They came back to Tordwem, and he asked them, 'What did you see this time?' They said, 'Saama is not in his grave'. When Oralai made as though he would contradict they all shouted him down, saying that he was wilfully lying. So he admitted that Saama was not in the grave. The chief asked him whether it was he who had killed him, and he said 'Yes'. Tordwem then asked him for what purpose he had killed him, and he answered that he had killed him to set right an *imborivuŋgu*. The chief said, 'Who else was with you when you killed him?' He said that beside himself there was an older man called Agbega. So Tordwem told his scribe to write down, 'Oralai has killed his brother Saama, assisted by Agbega'. When this had been done they told Oralai, 'Since the scribe has put it in writing the matter is closed. Wherever you go, from now on you must say exactly these words and no others, namely that it was you and Agbega who killed Saama to set right an *imborivuŋgu*. If you say anything different from what has been written in the book the white man will not spare you, for the written word cannot lie'.

Tordwem then sent a policeman and *ugwana* to seize Agbega and bring him in. Before they brought him they first tortured him almost to death. When they came the chief asked him, 'It was you, was it not, who together with Oralai killed Saama to set right an *imborivuŋgu*?' Agbega said that he knew nothing about this, but Oralai told him to stop trying to hide his guilt by deliberate lying. Indeed, he said, it was to set right Agbega's *imborivuŋgu* that they had killed Saama. When Agbega still denied it, one of his own sons, called Dauda, gave evidence against him. 'On the night that Saama died,' he said, 'Oralai brought his flesh to Agbega in a basket. I saw this quite plainly, because that night I was sleeping in the *ate*. Why is my father wilfully denying it?' Agbega said, 'You are right, my son, I admit it'. Then he asked Tordwem to send some policemen with him, and he would go and fetch the *imborivuŋgu*. So the chief sent policemen, some *ugwana*, and Agishi, and they took him to his home, beating him as they went. When they arrived he told them all to wait outside while he went inside the grass-mat enclosure to fetch the *imborivuŋgu*, for them to take to Tordwem. So they all waited outside. Agbega then went inside, sat down in a dark corner, and stabbed himself with an arrow. There he remained while the others were still awaiting him outside. As he was dying he called Agishi and said to him, 'Agishi, come, take me and bury me. Dauda, my son, has killed me. May he live happily'. As he said this the others came in, and he died. They took him and buried him, and brought back word to Tordwem. Tordwem and all the council said, 'Now there is no doubt that he was guilty. He was afraid that the white man would kill him, so killed himself instead'.

At that time the District Officer had not yet returned from leave, and the District Officer at Wukari was acting in his place. There was an Assistant District Officer at Katsina Ala, and another was in Ugondo at Ugba's old village. So Tordwem sent Oralai bound to Wukari in charge of policemen, with a letter to the District Officer. The District Officer read the letter, and asked Oralai, 'Is it true that you killed your brother, you and the man who has killed himself?' Oralai admitted that it was true, and said that they had killed him to set right an *imborivuŋgu*. The District Officer was much surprised at this, and ordered him to be taken to the Assistant District Officer at Ugba, to help him get to the root of the matter. The Assistant District Officer questioned Oralai, who continued to stand by his statement that he had killed his brother Saama to set right an *imborivuŋgu*, and that he had been assisted by Agbega, who had been afraid and

killed himself. So the Assistant District Officer sent him
back again to Wukari. The District Officer asked him,
'As your brother's body is not in the grave, did you eat
it up entirely when you performed the rites?' Oralai
said that they did. The District Officer then called his
chief messenger, Ibrahim, and said to him, 'Take this
man who has killed his brother Saama, together with
all the elders of the clan, straight to Saama's grave.
Dig it up, and if you find his body inside, bring it to
me here at Wukari. And if you do not find the body,
but only bones, then collect these together and bring
them'.

So Ibrahim set out with them, and they went on ahead
and led him to the grave of the dead man, Saama. All
the elders stood in a circle round the grave. Ibrahim
told a man to dig, and there they found the body of
Saama, absolutely untouched. It was quite complete,
and had only just started to decay slightly and turn black
at the navel. Ibrahim told them to bring a bed, lay the
corpse on it and take it in to Wukari. A large crowd
looked on with horror. When they arrived, the District
Officer asked Oralai, 'Is this not your brother, who you
have continually asserted was killed by you and Agbega
to set right an *imborivuŋgu*, and whom you said you had
entirely consumed?' Oralai remained silent. The white
man asked him again, 'Oralai, is this the body of your
brother Saama, or is it the body of some other man?'
Oralai said, 'It is no one else; it is my brother Saama'.
Then he burst into tears. 'I told them that I had not
done it,' he said, 'but Tordwem and the elders forced me
to say that I had. I could hold out no longer, and agreed
to what they said.' Yet he did not disclose the whole
matter in detail to the white man, fearing lest if he told
him everything, he would be angry with the elders, and
they would kill him by *tsav* for exposing them before the
European. But as for Dauda, the son of Agbega, who
said that Oralai and his father had killed Saama, when he
saw that Ibrahim had dug up Saama's body he took to
the bush and fled.

From that day the Europeans made no further efforts

with the *Haakaa*, nor did the District Officer go on with it when he returned from leave. What can have been their views about it?

❡. A detailed report of the final case recorded here appears in R. C. Abraham's work, *The Tiv People*, pp. 97–105, and it is interesting to compare the two independent accounts, the one written by a European, the other by an African. The two versions agree quite closely as regards the facts, but there is a slight difference in interpretation. Akiga implies that the charge was framed by Agishi and his followers. Abraham considers that they were acting in good faith, and believed that they actually saw that the body had been tampered with. 'All were convinced that Arayi [= Oralai] was guilty, and so strong was this conviction that, when the body was exhumed, no less than fourteen individuals, against the evidence of their senses, were certain that the body had been dismembered and the burial-cloth removed; the concrete evidence of vision had no weight against their inner conviction; even when it was demonstrated to them that the body was intact, their belief was not disturbed and they thought this perfectly natural, as the body had been reconstructed.'[1] Such cases frequently occurred during the investigation of the *mbatsav* practices. Those accused of taking part in the cannibal rites would not only confess to the charges brought against them, but give minute details of the share which they had taken in the affair, and the parts of the body which they had eaten, although it was afterwards proved, on exhumation of the corpse, that the whole thing was entirely imaginary. Another case of the same type of group hallucination is described by Akiga earlier in this chapter (p. 272), when all his relatives believed that they had seen the skin of his dead sister brought out during the *Ijɔv* rites.

I will now try to answer Akiga's last question. The causes which led to the events described in the last section have already been mentioned. Public feeling against the *mbatsav* had been growing for many years, and the need for action had already been expressed in a series of local anti-*tsav* measures, of which the *Haakaa* was the last and by far the most rigorous. The incentive came not from the European Administration, but from the people themselves. Fundamentally, however, it was the outcome of factors

---

[1] Op. cit., p. 100.

introduced by the new régime, chief of which were the growing independence of the younger generation, the weakening of tribal authority, and particularly the loss of faith in the old public cults. The more immediate cause was the abolition of exchange marriage, which brought home to the elders in a very concrete form the fact of their declining power over the young, and impelled them to buttress it up by increased insistence on the more terrifying aspect of the tribal rites of which they had control. It even led them to claim that they could and would use their supernatural powers for maleficent and anti-social purposes, and to boast of the possession of articles used for the practice of black magic, which in other days they would have indignantly denied. Meanwhile, the younger sections of the tribe, though in no way losing their respect for the magic powers of the old, were gaining confidence in the belief that they had found an ally in the white man.

It is interesting in this connexion to note that every anti-witchcraft movement has a foreign, that is an extra-group, element in it. It will be realized from the nature of the Tiv beliefs that this must be so. Since the danger comes always from within the group, protection against it can only be sought outside. Thus the oldest anti-*tsav* organization, the age-grade, cuts across all family ties; the victim appeals for help from his age-mates in other groups. An important point in the *Ijɔv* movement was that the sufferer should learn the ritual, and bring back the sacred beer, from another clan to 'chastise the *mbatsav* in his own district'. In the case of the *Budeli* and *Ivase*, help was sought even further afield, and one can hardly doubt that the foreign origin of these cults, and the foreign language that was used in the incantations, Hausa in one case and Utaŋge in the other, was deliberately welcomed by the afflicted Tiv, who here recognized a force which might save them from the baneful activities of their own kinsmen, and help them to shake off the old order and all the terrors which it implied. This, in fact, was the beginning of the modern movement, tending towards the introduction of foreign ideas, which is now splitting the tribe in half.

Similarly, the movement which occasioned the *Haakaa*, or witchcraft investigation (as it was called by us), originated in a cleavage inside the family-group which led to a rising against the alleged evil power of the elders, and was made possible by the presence of an outside influence, namely the European Administration. Touring officers first began to receive complaints of murders and threatened murders, and on investigation it appeared at first sight that there existed a secret society, called the *mbatsav*, of a cannibalistic nature, with branches in every district. The evidence was that each senior member of the society possessed some cult object to which the victims were sacrificed. Afterwards they were said to be eaten by members of the society at the gruesome night-time feasts which have already been described. When the first complainants had been heard, more followed in increasing numbers, all telling the same type of story, and it is not surprising that the first impression received by the Administration was that ritual murder and cannibalism was being practised on a large scale, especially as the elders, when questioned, often admitted the charge of having killed and eaten the members of their own groups. Here is an account of the affair from the administrative point of view, written by K. Dewar, one of the officers engaged in it:

'The general opinion was that if the cult objects were surrendered the witch societies and the evil practices associated with them would die a natural death. The District Heads of the clans in which the cult seemed most prevalent were accordingly ordered to call in all known possessors of cult objects; the intention being that investigation should be made into the practices that were alleged to be associated with them.

'As soon as this action was taken it became evident that practically every elder in Tiv country was a suspected witch. Anti-witch feeling rose to a very high pitch and many young men, losing their heads, resorted to traditional and violent measures against them, e.g. "hoyo". Very exaggerated rumours were spread by both parties. Every death that occurred at this time was attributed to the witches—and there were never lacking youths who would give vivid details (which they often genuinely believed to be true) of the methods a particular witch had employed in compassing the death of a particular victim. Similarly elders would bring in tales of how they had been beaten severely by the young men of their village; and on investigation it would transpire that the accused youths had merely "lashed them with their tongues"! A number of cases of excessive violence did, however, occur. District police and messengers who used to gather bands of young men about them to assist them to bring in the witches were among the worst offenders. If a witch refused to produce the fetish object he was alleged to have they would say that he was concealing it in order that when the investigation was over and the white man had gone he might avenge himself by killing them. They would then resort to force to induce the unfortunate old man to produce some article he possibly never had possessed, despite the fact that he had often foolishly boasted that he had.

'Besides many genuine and spurious fetish objects many alleged poisons were surrendered by the elders. Of twelve sample "poisons" collected by me, only one on analysis at Yaba proved to be poisonous. Numerous poisoning devices were also produced, e.g. dummy snakes, metal claws, &c.'[1]

When the extent and gravity of the affair became known, Mr. H. H. Middleton, Resident Plateau Province, and Mr. E. S. Pembleton, who had just been appointed to take over the duties of Resident Benue, were sent by Government to hold an inquiry into the nature and truth of the charges. By this time, however, several important facts had come to light. First, that the whole belief in ritual murder and cannibalism was largely imaginary; but that if the issue was less serious than at first supposed, it was more abstruse. Secondly, that the so-called *mbatsav* society consisted of the true leaders of the community, whose possession of *tsav* and the rites which it gave them authority to perform were in essence legitimate and intended for the public welfare. Moreover, that shortly before the arrival of the British a new motive for ritual murders had arisen owing to the introduction from Wukari of the magico-religious office of *Tor-agbande* (Drum-chief),[2] the holder of which was supposed to provide a certain number of human victims for the elders who appointed him. It was suspected that poisons had actually been employed to satisfy the requirements of this cult, and that the source of the poisons was Wukari. The following were some of the conclusions reached as a result of the inquiry:

'It may also be regarded as inevitable that the modern Tor u

---

[1] Examples of the *mbatsav* equipment, including the *imborivuŋgu*, ornamented skulls, instruments for making eerie noises, and so forth, collected at this time, can be seen at the British Museum and in the Pitt Rivers Collection at Oxford. There are also some good photographs of these in Abraham's *Tiv People*.

[2] P. 363 et seq.

Gbanda has prostituted the "Tsav" to his own ends, rejecting all that was beneficial and retaining only the inhuman orgies and rites which were once purely sacrificial, but have now lost their religious significance and are chiefly acts of lust and vengeance.

'I use the word "vengeance" advisedly as this is probably an important key to the present position. Civilization, with its external attractions and the opportunities it offers to see something of the world in safety, has tended to break up the family ties and to diminish the respect previously shown to the elders by their juniors. The former, therefore, have allied themselves with the spurious Tor u Gbanda and are willing to sacrifice their own children and nearest relatives to the mercies of the cult rather than allow the younger generation the chance of becoming more powerful than themselves. So impressionable and superstitious is the Munshi that every death and every accident is now attributed to the Tor u Gbanda and mbatsav, against whom they feel themselves powerless; a few of the younger men have migrated elsewhere while the majority who remain are living in a "Reign of Terror". . . .

'A further point of interest is the apparent satisfaction and pride with which these old men enumerate the number of persons they have killed (and eaten). In this connexion, however, we must not forget the original position of the Tor u Gbanda as sole trustee for the lives of his clansmen and it can hardly be expected that he would now be willing to undermine his own power by shelving that responsibility. All of which goes to show how difficult it is to get at the real facts and much corroborative evidence would be required before legal action could be taken. . . .

'If it is true—and I see no reason to doubt it—that the number of deaths amongst the Munshis has been abnormally high during the past decade or so, we must bear in mind that those years have themselves been abnormal from the epidemiological point of view and that influenza, cerebro-spinal meningitis, and relapsing fever have taken a heavy toll of the population. Under the circumstances, it is natural that the uninitiated should place the responsibility for this mortality on the mbatsav and that the latter should only be too glad to maintain their power and influence by accepting that responsibility. Nevertheless, the fact remains that these orgiastic rites still exist and we must, therefore, steer a middle course between the Scylla of entire disbelief and the Charybdis of blind credence before taking any drastic action to cope with the situation. . . .

'It is obvious that there can be no clear case of murder or manslaughter, but it is more than probable that sufficient evidence will be forthcoming to try some of the leading members of the cult under . . . the Criminal Code. If one conviction in each District were obtained, it should (and, I think, would) have a salutary effect on the others as well as imbuing the uninitiated with a certain amount of self-confidence and determination to resist the evil influence of the mbatsav. . . .'[1]

Every effort was accordingly made to obtain the necessary evidence, and a large number of alleged murders were closely investigated by the local administrative officers: but the only result was to strengthen the conviction that the belief in the existence of cannibalistic rites, held by the whole tribe, was entirely illusory. 'It has not been possible to prove ritual killing or eating in a single case and this leads us to believe that these ideas are a memory of what was done in the past but has now been abandoned.'[2]

In a sense, therefore, the *Haakaa* was a false alarm. But not from the Tiv standpoint. The fear of witchcraft was very real. In view of the strength of public feeling the Administration was forced to take action, and if the initial action taken was based on a misunderstanding as to the identity of the offenders against whom it was directed, and of the function of the cult objects which they were told to surrender, the misunderstanding was on the part of the people themselves. (By cult objects are meant the ancestral relics, &c., used in the public rites. Some of the other objects brought in, poisoning devices such as the *mbatsav* snake, the 'monkey's head',[3] and other evil-working charms, had no social justification at all, and were as well destroyed.) As soon as it was known that all the most prominent and influential elders of the tribe were involved, the Administration perceived that it must retrace its footsteps. The arrest of suspected 'witches' and confiscation of their equipment were immediately stopped by the new Resident, Mr. Pembleton. But by this time the younger section of the tribe had got somewhat out of control; hence the excesses described by Akiga. In some cases these may, as he says,

[1] Report by H. H. Middleton.   [2] Abraham, op. cit., p. 73.   [3] P. 376.

have been actuated by a desire to pay off old scores, but in many the young men acted out of pure fright in a desperate attempt to defend themselves against the unknown powers of the old.

The events described above helped to widen the rift between the old and the young, and drove another nail into the coffin of the ancestral cults, but they had one very good result. They showed that the existing type of administration was unsuited to the Tiv, and led to a period of intensive investigation, including study of the language, which produced, amongst other useful material, two monographs on the tribe, and finally gave birth to the reorganization policy which is described in the final chapter.

VI.

THE INDIVIDUAL AND THE GROUP

❡ This section deals with birth, childhood, death, and some miscellaneous matter, most of which was originally collected under the general heading, 'Tiv Customs'. It has been slightly rearranged for the sake of clearness.

THE *IDYUGH* RITE[1]

THE *idyugh* is carried out after conception. It takes several forms, of which the following is an example: The husband buys sixteen chickens and a he-goat. The elder who is performing the rite cuts a post of the wild apple tree, sharpens it at one end, and plants it in the doorway under the eaves of the house. Round the base of the post he makes six little cones of mud, called the 'sherds', and on each of these he places a small piece of broken pottery. When this is finished the husband dresses his wife in her best clothes, and she comes out and kneels in the doorway near the post of wild apple wood. The elder takes two leaves of the same tree, lays one on this side and one on that, mixes some soil with water and places a lump on each. Then he takes a little of this mud and smears it on the woman's navel. After this she moves back, and some one else comes and sits in her place. He holds a chicken, while the elder cuts off its head and lets the blood drip on to the sherds. Fifteen chickens are killed, but the sixteenth is tied up by the legs to the roof-poles over the doorway, and left to hang head downwards. This is called the 'suture-closer':[2] it is not killed, but taken away alive by the man who conducted the rites.

[1] *Idyugh* means 'taking out'. The origin of the term is obscure. Explanations offered by Tiv elders were (*a*) bringing the woman out of the control of evil influences, (*b*) 'bringing forth' the woman from the house (because she is taken by the wrist and led out over the threshold). The obvious interpretation that it refers to the 'bringing forth' of the child was not accepted, but it seems likely that the ritual referred to in the second explanation (*b*) is, in fact, symbolical of this process, and is intended to assist it by sympathetic magic.
[2] I.e. to enable the sutures in the baby's skull to close up properly.

When this is finished, the woman is called up again, and kneels down in the place where she knelt before. The elder pulls a hair out of the he-goat, adds it to the ritual clay, and again puts some on the woman's stomach. The goat is then slaughtered and its blood poured over the sherds, after which the woman gets up and goes away. The chickens and the goat are cooked, and when the time comes to make the passes the woman returns and kneels down again in the same place as before. The elder then takes all the drumsticks, the heads, and the wings of the chickens, and puts them into the lid of a calabash together with *ruam*. He tells the woman to make the passes with her hands [empty], and then gives her the food. She takes this away with her, and others then come round to eat the rest of the meat and *ruam*. But one chicken is cooked separately. This is called the *Swende* chicken, and may only be eaten by a man who has mastery of the *Swende*.

When all the food has been eaten, the husband brings a woman's loin-cloth of fourteen strips and gives it to the man who has carried out the rites. The latter also makes fourteen lines in the dust to indicate the number of small articles which must be given by the woman, slabs of camwood, strands of tobacco, or such-like. When she has given as many articles as there are marks on the ground the fee has been paid. On the following morning the husband takes his wife to the officiating elder, bringing with him a little meat and oil. The elder takes this to a place between the houses, puts the meat into an earthen bowl, and makes pretence of laying a fire and lighting it. Then he puts the vessel on to it, mixes in a little flour and oil, and takes out the meat and eats it.

That is the way the *idyugh* is done in Kparev. In Iharev they bring a ram, five chickens, and a basket of meat. The man who performs the rite lays five grass-stalks on the ground, cuts the chickens' throats and pours the blood over them. There is also one forbidden[1] cock. The elder makes a little mound of clay under the eaves, sticks into it

---

[1] Lit., 'bad', i.e. *sacré*, not to be eaten by the initiated.

a small piece of wood which he cuts for the purpose, and kills the cock over it. When the chickens and ram have been killed, and the woman has undergone the *icegh* rite,[1] all the chicken and the other meat is cooked, and the passes are made. The special cock, however, is only eaten by those who have the mastery of the *Icigh*, *Swende*, and *Hikumun*, and as to the rest of the meat, when the passes have been made with it and it has been put into the hands of the woman, she does not eat it, but gives it to her husband. The fees are sixteen brass rods for the special cock, six for the rest of the cocks, and five for the hens, according to the marks which the elder makes on the ground, and, in addition, a strand of tobacco and one brass rod. When this is finished, they wash the evil from their hearts.[2] An egg is put into a pot and cooked. When the water boils, the egg is taken out and some flour is put in and stirred into a paste. This is then served out on to a piece of bark from the copaiba balsam tree, and after some passes have been made it is given to the woman, who places it on the ground. An elder takes a little water in a wild apple leaf and sprinkles her back with it: this act is called the *Hikumun*.

In Turan and other clans the husband takes his wife to her home as soon as she is pregnant, in order to have set right the *Aku*, an *akombo* of arrows, to be purged from

---

[1] The smearing of mud on the woman's stomach described above. See also p. 91–2.

[2] The Tiv expression is *hamber ifan* (*hamber*, 'squirt out': *ifan*, 'curse'). All those present take some water in their mouths and blow it out again. The theory is this: If a man bears you a grudge, the ill which he wishes is liable to take effect and bring you sickness or misfortune, although he may not have deliberately laid a curse upon you. His unspoken thoughts are enough to set in motion the inimical supernatural forces, even without his conscious intention. This is why the rite is used in the present connexion. If any of those present are ill-disposed towards the woman who is undergoing the *idyugh*, the measures taken to insure a successful delivery cannot be effective until all evil thoughts have been ceremonially washed away. It is customary to use the same ritual on all occasions when two or more people come together to carry out some important business which concerns them all, especially if it is of a magico-religious nature.

The spraying of water from the mouth is used in other parts of Africa in connexion with rain-making, and it is probable that it once also had this meaning amongst the Tiv, as is shown by the words which often follow the above formula (e.g. on p. 370): 'that moisture may fall (*mdolom m gba*)', which is a way of saying 'that good may come'. Nowadays, however, it is only used for the purpose indicated above.

the *Twel*, and to have the *akuve* of the *Twel* and *Igbe* inverted for her.[1] When these rites have been carried out, and evil has been washed from their hearts, the girl is sent back home with her husband. Every woman who has not previously undergone the *idyugh* rites must be purged of the things I have mentioned as soon as she becomes pregnant. But in any case a woman who has already had a certain number of children and then ceases to bear must have the *idyugh* carried out for her by her own group.[2] Her husband buys a he-goat, and also takes with him a 'dry twenty'[3] as the fee. On arrival, he shows these to the owner of his wife, and the owner shows them to his group as the things which his sister has brought for the *idyugh*. The man who is going to conduct the rites cuts a sapling of the meni oil tree, and one of *gusa* and of *ishough*. (But Turan is the only clan that uses the *ishough* in their rites. Wherever you may go in Tivland, if you enter a village and see an *ishough*-tree growing in front of a house you may be quite sure that one of the inmates is a member of Turan.) He sharpens one end of these and plants them in the ground, the *ishough* being placed apart from the other two. Chickens are then killed over each of the posts. The woman's children hold the chickens, while the officiating elder cuts their throats and pours the blood over the emblems: this closes the sutures.[4] The goat is also slaughtered, and the meat, together with that of the chickens, is cooked. *Ruam* is prepared, and the passes made. But first a piece of *ruam* is broken off, and on to it is poured a little of the chicken's blood, which has been previously collected in a snail-shell and set aside for the purpose. This is rolled into a ball and given to the woman to swallow. The chickens 'for closing the sutures' are taken out, and the passes made with them. The meat is put on to her *ruam*, but is not given to her. It is handed over to be eaten by the men, excepting the husband. Then

---

[1] Note on p. 188.

[2] Sc. whether she has had it done before, or not.

[3] I.e. the equivalent of a 'twenty' (see p. 210), but not a chicken or anything that has blood in it.

[4] See above. This has no special application to the case under reference, viz. a woman who has stopped bearing, but is a necessary part of the *idyugh* rite.

they bring the *mtam* drum, the emblems of the *Twel's*
children, and those of the *Cirate* and *Lough*. (The *Cirate*
is an earthen vessel with a cup tied to its neck.) They
take the drumsticks, wings, and head of a chicken, put
them on the *ruam*, make the passes, and give it to the
woman. This she may eat. Then every one else starts to
eat the meat. The *idyugh* meat is not taboo to any one.
Hence the saying, 'Let a great one be not the meat of
Swende but *idyugh*, that the children may also live'.[1]

This is the conclusion of the rite. The husband pays a
fee for each of the members of his family for whom the
rite has been performed.[2] Water is brought, and they
wash evil from their hearts. The people disperse, and
the woman also goes home with her husband.

THE PURGING

When a woman conceives, her husband buys a he-goat
and six chickens, and takes them to his wife's home. She
also goes with him. When they arrive he gives the things
to her owner, and tells him that he has come to have the
idyugh and purging rites performed. The owner brews
beer and invites all his kinsmen, who come in on the day
that the beer is ready. When all have assembled, he
brings out the presents and lays them on the ground, then
cuts off a corner of his cloth and gives it to the husband in
'payment' for them. Having bought them in this manner,
he takes them and gives them to the elder who is to do the
purging, and the latter starts to carry out the rite. He
takes the chickens and purges away all the lesser *akombo*;
then takes the goat and carries out a general purging from
the greater, such as the *Swende* and the *Twel*. The reason
why the woman has to be purged of all these *akombo* is
that when she was a child she would not have refrained
from eating any of the *akombo* meats. This is why it is
called the 'purging'. Kparev leave the purging and
idyugh till after the woman has given birth,[3] but all others
carry them out before the child is born.

---

[1] I.e. impartiality is expected from those in authority.
[2] Viz. his wife and the children already borne by her.
[3] Even here it should probably be done before if possible. It is sometimes
left over owing to lack of funds.

¶, In every case the *idyugh* and the 'purging' are performed in the group of the woman and not of her husband, and this, as already suggested in connexion with the purging rite practised in Masev (p. 124), is probably a relic of the time when marriage was matrilocal. The husband has to take his wife back to her own people, and provides the necessary chickens and so forth for the purpose, but the fact that the woman's kinsmen must make a pretence of buying these from him is an indication that they were once responsible for providing them. For the same reason, probably, in the account of the *idyugh* rite, the elder in the woman's group must make a show of preparing the food brought by the husband, although this has in fact already been cooked or dried before being given to him. In later times, according to the ideas which were evolved under the system of exchange, the woman became a member of her husband's group as soon as she had borne a child. But still, until there were children, the exchange marriage had not achieved its object, and so was considered purely conditional. The woman still belonged to her owner's group, and could theoretically be recalled at any time. It is therefore quite logical that the rites performed before birth should take place in the woman's group, whereas those carried out after the birth of the child, such as the *ityumbu* described below, should be done by the group of the husband.

BIRTH

WHEN a woman has conceived, and her husband has had the *idyugh* and purging done for her as already described, her pregnancy develops. When her time is near she begins to groan in the pangs of childbirth. These may last for two to five days, but if they go on for many days there must be some reason for it. In this case the husband goes to the diviner. Having been shown which *akombo* is the cause, he comes back and pays the nominal fee.[1] This act does not involve undergoing the full *akombo* rites. The husband merely sends for an elder who is master of a large number of *akombo*, and when he comes he cuts off a piece of tobacco and touches the woman with it on the back of her hand, while he utters an incantation absolving her from each of the

---

[1] *Tɔndo ataa*, see p. 182.

akombo.[1] When he has done this, it is all over; the woman immediately proceeds to give birth.

When the woman is about to give birth, an old woman is sent for to carry out the duties of midwife. When she is called in to where the woman lies in labour, she tells her to sit up straight and strain. She also rubs the woman's stomach in order to cause the child to turn round and come down. When the child descends and tries to come out, a boy is sent to fetch a fig-leaf, and the midwife puts this in a position where the child will fall on it. When it falls on to the leaf it cries. If it does not cry, the midwife throws some cold water on it to make it do so. When the afterbirth has also come away, the mother comes outside and washes the vagina with hot water. The midwife first cuts off the umbilical cord with the cuticle of a corn-stalk, then binds it up with a small piece of fine thread. She comes outside and starts to bathe the child in hot water. A boy takes the afterbirth and digs a hole for it at the entrance to the woman's house on the left side as you go in; he buries it there, covers it well over with earth, and lays a stone on the top.[2] When the midwife has finished bathing the child, she starts to massage its navel. She does this by warming her fingers over a glowing ember and then gently pressing the navel with them. After this she lays the child by its mother's side, and leaves. Her work is finished for that day. The mother bathes and massages her breasts, using hot water. She also rubs camwood on them to make the milk come. With some women there is no flow of milk for as long as two days, and the baby must be fed by other women. At first the child drinks nothing but milk and cold water.

The child is not taken outside until its umbilical cord drops off, but remains in the house for about three days. When the cord drops off, the midwife is again summoned, and given a ball of camwood, a little oil, and a few grains of salt. She puts the salt into a calabash cup, adds a little camwood, and mixes it with water into a paste. She rubs

---

[1] The formula is of the kind recorded on p. 30.

[2] If the placenta were to be taken by a dog or other animal, the child would suffer (*tsee*); but it must not be buried too deep, as in that case the cord would fail to drop off quickly.

the oil over the child's body and puts on the camwood. Then she gives the baby back to its mother and goes to bury its umbilical cord. The cord is not just buried anywhere. In the case of a boy it is buried under a red pepper shrub or *gbaaye*[1] tree, in order that he may be brave, of fierce temper, and a dangerous man. But if it is a girl, the cord is buried at the foot of a pawpaw, silk-cotton, or fig tree, that she may have a gentle nature. When the midwife has buried the cord, she takes the rest of the camwood which was used to rub on the child, and goes home. If she has been called in from a distance she is also given a chicken. Her part is finished. The child may then be brought out without danger. But if it is taken outside before the cord has dropped off, it will become sickly. The mother washes her baby at the entrance to the house in the place where the afterbirth was buried. When she has finished washing it she takes a little of the water remaining in the vessel and pours it on to the stone which was placed there, over the afterbirth.[2] Then she tosses up the child two or three times and catches it again, to cure it of dizziness and fear, and holds it head downwards by the feet. She does this every time she washes it.

THE *ITYUMBU* RITE

All the Tiv practise the *ityumbu* rite, but it is not everywhere done in the same way. Kparev, Turan, and Iharev each have their own way of conducting the ceremony.

The Turan rite is somewhat similar to that of Shitire. It is carried out as soon as the umbilical cord drops off. A boy goes early in the morning, and in silence, to draw some water. He sets it on the ground, and the elder who is to carry out the rite brings a snail-shell,[3] and performs the *ityumbu* in respect of each of the *akombo*. He scoops up some water in the shell, pronounces an absolution[4]

[1] Footnote on p. 27.

[2] In order to 'refresh' the placenta, whose well-being at this time is thought to be intimately bound up with that of the child with which it has been so closely connected.

[3] At the rite of which the photograph (plate xvii) was taken about a dozen shells were used in succession.

[4] For the form of this absolution see p. 30.

from the *Wanishima*, and puts it to the baby's mouth for it to drink.[1] Then he scoops up some more water and does the same for the *Twel*, the *Cirate*, the *mtam* drum, the *Abumkpekpe*, and the *Wanimunda*. The child drinks a little each time, or if not it does not matter. When this is finished he lays the shell down, takes up an adze, and taps it to detach the blade. This is in order to *tumbu* the *Kwenihundu*.[2] He dips up some water in the socket of the handle, and pours it into the child's mouth, saying, 'I *tumbu* you to-day on account of the *Kwenihundu* and of the *Ihundu*'. After this comes the 'fanning'. The elder takes some copaiba balsam leaves in his hand, a winnowing-mat, and a chicken. He makes certain motions[3] with the mat, first on one side of the entrance, then on the other. Each time, as he does this, he drops the winnowing-mat on the ground, then stoops down and picks it up. He does this six times. Then he stretches out his hand, takes hold of the woman with the child at her breast, and leads her out through the entrance. He pours some water on to the roof, and the woman puts out her foot and draws it back again three times.[4] At the fourth time he brings her out into the middle of the village. He takes a chicken, and is also given one fee.

In Shitire also the *ityumbu* is done as soon as the umbilical cord drops off. The father, having told the elder and obtained his consent to carry out the rite, brings his wife to him with the child at her breast. But the things that he must bring with him are cotton and a chicken to kill for the *Icigh*; except in the case of a daughter, when he must bring corn instead of the chicken. The elder tells a boy to draw water and bring it to him in silence. He must set this down, and watch that no chicken drinks it. If a chicken were to drink of the water which was afterwards used in the rite, the child would become very ill indeed. The elder then picks some leaves of the copaiba balsam, bauhinia, and *irkwargbande* trees, and also prepares a flask with a piece of raffia tied round the neck

---

[1] The word used is *tumbu*, viz. the verb from which *ityumbu* is derived.
[2] *Kwen*, socket; *ihundu*, madness.
[3] *Cia*, in this case the jerking motions of winnowing; cf. p. 259 and footnote.
[4] Sc. under the water as it flows off the roof.

(that is the *Cirate*), a calabash scoop (the emblem of the *Ikòmbo*), and some Akwana salt. The elder puts the water by him, the woman sits down in the doorway, and he sits on the outside, facing her. He takes a knife and draws a line on the ground between them. The water is on his right. Then he takes the shell, puts out his hand and grasps the woman with the child at her breast. She stands up. He scoops up some water in the shell and pours it back again, saying, 'This is for the mothers of our line',[1] then takes some more and puts it to the child's mouth, and again scoops some up and pours it back again, saying, 'This is for the mothers of our line'. After this the woman steps over the line and touches the other side with her foot, then steps back and touches the ground on her near side. This she does six times. The elder then gives her some water with which to bathe the child. The father gives six fees in respect of each *akombo*, and the ceremony is over. This description is typical of the rite as it is practised in all Tiv clans, except that some have added things to it.

CHILDHOOD

If as the child starts to grow he becomes weakly, the reason is discovered by divination, and some of the smaller things are set right. But in a very short time he has outgrown the power of *akombo*, and this fact is recognized if anything happens to him. Then, even though he may be seized by an *akombo*, it is not the *akombo* alone that are doing it, but also *tsav*.[2]

When the child is about three months old, he begins to sit on the ground and soon afterwards to crawl. Some time later he is able to stand up by holding on to something, and eventually, with some trepidation, by himself. When he can do this his mother or father or his nurse says, '*Jiji ya kuaa!*' and, holding him by the arms, starts to teach him to walk. '*Taata*', they say, and the baby answers '*Taata*'. Soon he can walk a little without being

---

[1] *Jimeti*: lit., 'back-name'. This expression is almost obsolete, except in this connexion. It means the female line of ancestors from the great-grandmother backwards.

[2] Cf. p. 251.

X

held by his nurse, falling down every few steps, and people say, 'He is beginning to find his feet'. Finally he starts to run about and moves surely.

The first word a child learns is *de* (don't!), and after that *taata* and *nam* (give me). Then he learns swear-words like *iwa*! (dog). When he says this his mother laughs delightedly, and calls some one to hear what a clever child she has got; he can swear like anything ! 'Swear at him !' she says. The child does so, and every one is amused. The mother teaches him some more, and he grows up with a good stock of swear-words. He starts to go about with other children, killing crickets.

It is in killing crickets and lizards, and in hunting birds, that the Tiv child first shows his mettle. Crickets come first, when children are very young. They go out in the sun to hunt them with sticks round about the village. If one settles on the ground, the child creeps up and hits it with a big stick, and does not care if he crushes it so badly that the earth gets into it. They also catch them by another means. They tap a fig-tree with a stone till the gum comes, and smear a little on the midrib of a raffia frond. With this they stalk a cricket which has settled on the ground and lime it. Then they catch it and bake it, and eat it with their *ruam*. In former times, when children were at the cricket-hunting stage, they were not considered old enough to use arrows.

After they have finished with crickets, they turn their attention to killing lizards. It is at this stage that they begin to learn the use of arrows. But they do not have real arrows. They string a bow with raffia twine, and for arrows they sharpen a midrib of the raffia leaf with which to shoot lizards. They go down into the spinney, and when they put up a lizard give chase. The sturdy child will make a kill, while the weakling may spend the whole day looking for lizards and come home empty handed. . . .

When boys have grown out of lizards they start to go after birds. Their fathers then make for them a bow with a thong, but not one that it would be difficult for them to string. By this time they are no longer very small—about thirteen or so, and in the past, even at this age, children would not consider they were capable of anything at all. Their arrows are not made of iron. Their fathers sharpen some small pieces of wood and insert them in shafts made from corn-stalks. With these they go out bird-hunting, and it is here that they learn to shoot well. A boy who is a good shot can bring down a bird with his wooden-headed arrow at long range. They eat the wings with their friends. This is done as follows: Ayaor and Adɔr eat birds' wings together; Ayaor kills a bird and gives a wing to Adɔr; Adɔr must give him a wooden arrow in exchange. So the boy who kills the most birds collects from his friends the largest number of arrows.

If a boy sees a bird's nest he says, 'I know where there's a bird-o!' and another who is standing near touches him with his hand and says, 'Bags first share!'[1] So they climb up and rob the nest. If there are eggs inside, the boy who made his claim is given one, and the boy who discovered the nest takes the rest. So also if there are young birds. This is where the children first learn something of bush-lore. Some time later their elders begin to let them have blunt arrows, not poisoned, for fear that they may fall down and wound themselves. Nor is a child allowed to have a knife lest he should cut himself. In former times a boy was not considered old enough to have a knife till he was about fourteen, but would have to use a blunt knife belonging to his mother. In the evening, when they have come back from bird-hunting, the boys engage in a shooting match with blunted arrows. When a boy is circumcized he stops hunting birds, and goes about with bow and arrows, killing game. He is then no longer a child, but a young man.

In the past a boy did not start work at an early age. He would be quite grown up before he could finish making a yam-heap by himself. He followed his mother round, begging for yam-tops. All he did was to carry his father's hoe to the farm. If he were an intelligent child, in the evening he would get some wood and light a fire for his

---

[1] *Hambe* means to claim first share of the kill, and is applied to all kinds of hunting; see p. 97.

father in the *ate*. Or if his father had some one to see him, he would tell his son to fill a pipe for his guest. The boy filled a pipe, and first pulled at it till it was going well, before giving it to the visitor to smoke. When the visitor had taken a pull the boy handed it to his father to smoke, then took it and put it out. All the Tiv used to smoke more heavily in former times.

When the day was over none of the children might wander about, lest they be bewitched by some one. As soon as it was dark they lit a fire in the middle of the village, and the children, the older men, and the women all gathered round it to spin cotton and tell hare-stories. But before they began the story-telling, they spent a long time asking each other riddles. This is a game played mostly by children. They played it by the fire, made of *mbohom* wood to give light for the cotton-spinning, but as soon as the older people came they told the children to stop asking riddles, as they were going to tell hare-stories. I will here give a short example of a riddle:

Ishɔm is asking the riddle. Adamgbe has to answer it.

IsHɔM: A riddle !

ADAMGBE: Scour it out.

IsHɔM: The elephant fell on the rock, but they did not finish cutting up the meat.

ADAMGBE: The answer is 'Water'.

IsHɔM: Give me a man.

ADAMGBE: 'Bush', then.

IsHɔM: Give me a man.

ADAMGBE: I give you Agaku.

IsHɔM: I have washed it clean and given you the scourings. Have you drunk them?

ADAMGBE: No.

IsHɔM: I shan't tell you unless you do.

ADAMGBE: All right, I've drunk it.

IsHɔM: Here it is then! 'Beniseed.' If grains of beniseed fall on rock or soil, can you ever pick them all up?

Hare-tales are fictitious stories told in company for amusement. The story-teller opens by saying, 'I can tell you some lies too. So-and-so thinks he is the only person who can tell good ones, so just listen to mine!' Then he starts off. If the hare is not one of the characters in the story, it is not called a hare-tale, but a fable. Story-telling at one time became a big thing in Tivland. Sometimes an elder would even hold a beer-feast for the purpose, and people would go and compete for the honour of being the best story-teller.

¶ In the original manuscript, a considerable amount of folk-lore was included here. Unfortunately it has had to be omitted, for lack of space.

CONCERNING WOMEN

MOTHERS in the past used to take great care of their daughters, and never allowed a chance for them to be seduced. When a woman saw that her daughter's breasts were beginning to appear, and that the young men were paying attentions to her, she became very worried about her. She took her off to an old woman who had the mastery of the *Ingbianjor*, and asked her to tie a snail-shell round her neck to prevent any one from violating her. The old woman accordingly threaded a shell on to a piece of cotton, and tied it round the girl's neck, thus putting a guard upon her. The young men would fear to have intercourse with her, and she would come to full puberty without any boy touching her. In the days before beads were known, a girl would reach the age of puberty without tying anything except a cotton cord round her waist, and she would not dream of wearing a cloth before she was married and had a house of her own.

When she became a housewife[1] she would start to wear a cloth, and carry out her womanly tasks, as she had already learnt to do while she was with her mother. She would go early to draw water, sweep the house clean, make the fire, cook and peel a yam for her husband to eat, then go out to work on the farm. On the way home she would collect some firewood. Having brought this in, she would pound up the corn, fetch a grindstone and grind it to flour, singing as she worked. When she had finished

[1] *Kwase u iyoughough*, as opposed to *wan-ya*, 'daughter of the family'; see p. 125.

she cleaned the grindstone, and cooked the *ruam* for her husband and others. When they had finished their meal she collected and washed up all the utensils. Then she went down to the stream to bathe, drew water and brought it back with her to the village. After this she rubbed some camwood on her body and lay down on the ground to rest. But another, when she came back from the stream, would set to work to pick out the seeds from the cotton. When evening came she put this away and made some more *ruam* for her husband. By the time she had washed up everything it was dark, and time to sit round together. So she took the cotton and began to spin, till drowsiness overcame her and she fell asleep. This is what good wives used to do in the past. With the cotton spun for him by his wife a man might weave cloths, and with these buy many cattle. Sometimes a poor man would become rich entirely through his wife. Another virtue possessed by the women of former days was that when the men were sitting talking they would never open their mouths unless they were asked. But the women of to-day will interrupt their menfolk in the middle of a sentence, whether their opinion has been asked or not. The Tiv say that women nowadays are on a complete equality with men, and the country has gone to the dogs.

Female Taboos. The head of the ox is taboo to women, but not entirely. When an ox is killed, and it is particularly desired that the women should partake of it, the bad parts, which are forbidden to women, are picked out, that is to say, the adrenal glands, the tongue, the back of the head, the forehead, and the throat. In former times these parts of the ox were very strictly taboo to women. In some clans—Kparev, for instance—a woman would never touch the ox after slaughtering, as long as the blood were in it, and the men put all the meat into boiling water before they gave it to the women to cook. Originally this practice was universal. Nowadays, however, the Tiv make a distinction. If the ox has been slaughtered by a foreign butcher, the women eat the meat without observing any taboos at all. The taboos only apply in the case where a Tiv has killed for a marriage feast.

It is taboo to all Tiv women to look into a grave, and to bury a frog, or to step over one.[1] They must not see the *Igbe*: formerly, when occasion arose to blow the *Igbe*,[2] it was given out that all women must remain in their houses. Hens' eggs are taboo to the majority of Kparev women, particularly those of the Mbainyam section, but not to the daughters of Ukan. Gav women do not eat eggs, and they eat the *ifam* but not the *atuŋɔ*.[3] The chaffinch is not eaten by any women of Usar, a subsection of Nanev. Ukum women all eat the *indiar*[4] while they are at home, but not after they have married outside the clan and had children. They also eat eggs. Shitire women, on the other hand, eat both the *indiar* and hens' eggs as well.

If you marry a Maghev girl, you will find she has dozens of taboos. Eggs are especially tabooed, because if a Maghev woman eats one she will have a miscarriage. This gives them cause for considerable annoyance with Turan, whose women are not bound by any such restriction. The *atuŋɔ* frog is also taboo to them for the same reason, but they have no rule against eating the *ifam*. They may not eat skinks, either the small or the large variety. The men of Maghev, on the other hand, observe no taboos at all.

Ugondo women of the Mbayam, Mbamar, and Iyɔnov subsections do not eat eggs if they bear their first child in Ugondo, but only if they have first had a child elsewhere and subsequently married an Ugondo husband. . . .

℟ The food taboos recorded here apply only to women because their observance is believed necessary to successful childbirth.

---

[1] The place held by the frog in Tiv beliefs is apparently due to its resemblance to a human being, or, possibly, to the human foetus. If a man starts to dig a grave, and cannot finish it owing to the hardness of the ground, he buries a frog in it before covering it up. The frog in this case acts as a substitute for a human corpse, thus avoiding the sinister suggestiveness of an empty grave in the village. But if a woman were to bury a frog she would be offending against the *uwarkombo* ('grave *akombo*'; see p. 332), just as though she had looked into a grave or handled a dead body.

[2] A noise made by hooting into the mouth of a pot, intended to terrify the uninitiated.

[3] Species of frogs.   [4] A black fish.

The only taboos observed by men are those imposed by the possession of *akombo*, charms, &c. The rule governing women's taboos is as follows: A woman observes the taboos peculiar to her own clan or group, as long as she remains at home, and after she is married, until the time that she bears her first child. She then takes over the taboos of her husband's group, in place of her own. The reason for this is that until she has borne a child the marriage is not ratified, and she is not a true member of her husband's group. If, however, she afterwards leaves her husband and marries one from another group, she continues to observe the taboos of the group to which she bore her first child. If she had no children by her first husband, she naturally keeps the taboos of her father's group, until such time as she bears a child to a second or subsequent husband.

POLYGAMY

THE Tiv practice of having several wives may be due to a variety of causes, but there is one main reason, namely the desire to found a family. However successful in life a man may be, if he has no heir to his house, to the Tiv he is a useless person and a standing butt for their scorn. 'What sort of a man is So-and-so without children?' they sneer. 'Who is there to carry on his line when he dies?' So also a woman, if she does not bear children, falls in Tiv esteem, however excellent she may be in other ways. And she herself is never happy, though she may be very well treated by her husband, because when she dies there will be no one to mourn for her. It is for this cause above all others that women desire a child. They are not so concerned as men about the founding of a family.[1]

If it were not for the family, many men would not marry at all; their relationships with women would be entirely promiscuous. But because of it, every Tiv when he reaches manhood sets his heart on taking a wife and producing a son to carry on his line, that his heritage may not pass to another. If a young man reaches puberty and

[1] Here follows a discourse on the habits of the field mouse (*san*) from the name of whose burrow (*tse*) the Tiv word here translated 'family' or 'line' is said to be derived, and a comparison of the life of its family with that of the Tiv.

is not concerned about getting married, but prefers to wander about, sleeping with women who do not belong to him, his elders speak to him severely. 'You are quite grown up,' they tell him, 'but you have no sense. Instead of making it your care to marry and found your own family, you are founding families for others.' When he hears this, the boy will give up his dissolute mode of life and try to find a wife.

In former times the Tiv did not have so many wives as they do to-day. Most of them had one wife. A very important man or a chief might have two. They said that the reason for having several wives was that even if the children by one wife were foolish, those by another would be wise, so the family would survive, whereas if they were all failures the line would die out. Nowadays, however, people do not marry only for the sake of the family, but also to acquire prestige. A young man who is getting on well in his group may marry five, six, or even ten, wives. A man of standing may have ten, or, if he is a staff-chief, as many as forty. Whether they have children or not matters to them less than it did in the past.

There is nothing on earth that the Tiv esteems so highly as Woman, but he does not treat her as though she were his most valued possession. A man may have a large number of wives, as we have said, but they are not happy with him. He makes farms for some, but others are left without and must beg. Even so they have to give their husband of the food which they have got by begging, otherwise he will beat them. A man with many wives may have only one honoured wife, and the rest are all uncared-for.[1] The honoured wife is referred to as 'So-and-so, the chief's wife', or the wife on whom he 'rests his head' or 'hangs his bag'. She is never allowed to want for anything. Her husband makes a big farm for her, and is constantly giving her cloths and ornaments to wear. Some may have two, three, or four, honoured wives, but there is only one 'rest for the head'. She is the wife in whose house the husband keeps all his belongings

---

[1] *Mbaatsanev* (sing.: *cankwase*), a regular term for all wives except the favourites.

and most frequently sleeps, and it is she who has an intimate knowledge of all his affairs. When a chief or big man dies the responsibility is usually laid at her door. This is indeed the disadvantage in being a favourite wife, she is always suspected of being the cause of her husband's death.[1] Not much attention is paid to the uncared-for wives when their husband dies. They have their share of trouble during his lifetime. They may not even have a cloth to wear. Sometimes one will spin some cotton and give it to a friend to weave for her, but if it wears out and she has no more cotton she goes about naked again: yet she is still known as 'the wife of So-and-so'.

Women are of the utmost value and help to the Tiv. They cook the food and work on the farms, as described above. With regard to sexual intercourse, it is impossible for a Tiv to remain continent for a month or so, unless he is prevented by some serious illness or other unavoidable cause. Otherwise, though he may be an old man, he will continue trying to have relations with women until the day of his death. Death itself seems hard to the Tiv chiefly because they are sad at leaving their women. And being deprived of sexual intercourse is for them the most disagreeable part of going to prison. Women and food are the two things about which a Tiv will boast.

INHERITANCE OF WIVES

The Tiv custom of inheriting wives dates from very early times and is still practised to-day, but since they have been helped by the advice of administrative officers at each of their council meetings they have made some slight modifications. When a man dies and leaves his wife, she is taken by his brother or his son, and is then said to be a 'woman in trust', 'widow', or 'inherited wife'. When a man is about to take over a wife of this nature, he does not act alone, but calls together all his senior kinsmen. When they have finished dividing the inheritance, the woman stands up to take her husband. Here is an example:

[1] Cf. p. 263.

The man who has died	..	..	Asɔm
Asɔm's wife	..	..	Wantor
Asɔm's son or brother	..	..	Awua
The senior elder in Asɔm's group	..	Maisho

After Asɔm's death a long time elapses before the inheritance is divided and his wife taken over. Then Awua summons all his kinsmen who are members of the same *iŋgɔl* group. When all are seated on the ground, he says to them, 'Asɔm is lost to us, and his goods are standing out in the rain. I have called you, kinsmen, to come and take charge of them. Or if you think that the property of Asɔm, your kinsman, should rot, it is as you wish'.

THE ELDERS: No, we will not leave a kinsman's possessions to spoil in the rain. Rise, Maisho, and give these goods to those who are able to look after them, that we may see and depart.

(His 'goods' really mean the dead man's wife or wives. Perhaps he had a number of wives, all of whom will take husbands on this day.) So Maisho stands up and divides the inheritance, both the non-human estate and the *aŋgɔl*. When this is finished he comes to the wives. Now, from the time that her husband dies a wife knows the man whom she will take, but she keeps this to herself. It is not any one who would dare to take her, but only her husband's son, or his brother by the same mother, or at least a kinsman belonging to the same *iŋgɔl* group. Suppose that in this case Awua, Asɔm's son, is the man who is to take over Wantor, his father's wife. Maisho asks Wantor whom she wishes to look after her.

WANTOR: It was Awua here, who even during his father's lifetime cared most for me, his mother,[1] and now that his father is no more, it is he whom I should like best to look after me.

MAISHO: You have well spoken. What do you say, Awua?

AWUA: I also have no objection.

MAISHO: Good. Go and bring the chicken for 'straddling the *Megh*'. (He fetches a chicken.) Stand up,

---

[1] In the classificatory sense. A Tiv does not inherit his own mother.

Wantor, and do each of you place one of your legs against the leg of the other.

So Wantor and Awua stand up, side by side, with their inside legs touching. Then if Maisho is a master of the *Megh* he will 'straddle' them himself, otherwise he will ask some one else, who has the mastery, to do it. The ritual consists of passing the chicken between the legs of Awua and then round through the legs of Wantor. To 'straddle', in fact, means to set right the *Megh*. If Awua took Wantor without doing this, she would bear no children. It is therefore essential that any one who inherits a wife should have the *Megh* 'straddled' for her. When this has been done, and they have all sat down again, Awua brings out a she-goat to give his kinsmen. They slaughter it, divide the meat, and go home to eat it. The man who carried out the rite takes away the *Megh* chicken alive. Wantor has become Awua's wife: yet he will never call her his 'wife', but always his 'mother'. One man who has inherited a wife may be kind to her, so that she forgets her sorrow, and her former husband remains only a memory; another will not treat her well, and the woman mourns her loss continually.

Widows are of two kinds: those who have already borne children to their first husband and those who have not. If you inherit a wife who has already had a child, any children that she may afterwards bear to you, however many they may be, do not belong to you, but to her first husband. When they grow up they will go and work for their elder brother—that is, the son of their mother by her former husband. Their names will always be coupled with that of their former father,[1] and they will be reckoned as his descendants. Further, if you have children by your father's wife, you never dare to call them your children, but speak of them as half-brothers.[2] And if some of them are daughters, and you take them to exchange for wives, you are merely adding to your father's family, and will still have no child to carry on

---

[1] E.g. 'Akiga Sai.'
[2] *Anterev*, i.e. 'father's children', cf. note on p. 107.

your own line. When you die, your father's son, whose mother you inherited, will take all the daughters to be his *aŋgɔl*, and the sons to work for him. Only if you marry a wife by means of an *iŋgɔl* who is your true sister, or who was originally given to you by your father, can you beget a son to call your own, and to carry on your line. But if, on the other hand, you inherit a wife from your father or brother who has never had a child, then in this case she becomes your true wife; all her children will belong to you and be counted as your descendants.

In a few Tiv clans, such as Ikurav, a son does not inherit his father's wives. And in those clans where inheritance is the rule there are occasionally instances where a man does not comply with the custom; but any one who refuses to take the wife of his father or brother lays himself open to much adverse comment. People say that he is a poor sort of man to leave the wife of his father or brother to wander about with no one to care for her. Others say that it is on account of jealousy that he refuses to raise up seed to his brother.[1] Sometimes also a woman, whose husband has died, does not consent to take any one else there, but wishes to go home to her father's group and find another husband elsewhere. Her owner may object on the grounds that he has already many children by the *iŋgɔl* of the dead man, but if he is a man who considers the feelings of his *iŋgɔl*, and does not wish her to suffer, he says, 'Very well. We will transfer the agreement to the children'.[2] If, on the other hand, he is a hard-hearted owner, he does not care. His *iŋgɔl* may be ill treated and run away home, but he beats her and sends her back again to her husband's people, where her lamentations are wasted on deaf ears.

This is how women who were left 'in trust' suffered in the past. But nowadays, since the white man has begun to understand these things, women's troubles are becoming lighter in this respect. They have made an announcement that when a woman's husband dies, she has a free choice. If she wishes to take another husband she may do so. If she does not like to stay there, she may go away

[1] Cf. Gen. xxxviii. 9.   [2] P. 154.

and marry any one she pleases. So, as far as that is concerned, the women have obtained some relief from their
worries, but some are still no better off in relation to their
owners. If a widow is unhappy and says she will go back
to her owner, he threatens her: 'If you come home, I
shall certainly kill you. See, —— ·forbade exchange
marriage; but if you think you are going to lose me my
wife whom I got by exchange before he stopped it, and
so bring about my ruin, your grave shall be the same as
mine!' If the wife then runs away and brings her case
before the court, they give their decision with one voice:
'Young woman, do you want to destroy your owner's
house? This exchange was made back in time of ——,
and are you going to break it up now? Look at the way
you women are ruining the country! Aren't you pleased
that the white man has given you claws to scratch with!
Get along with your owner!' So the owner takes her back
to her husband's people, there to bewail her lot. If she
plucks up enough courage to take her case before the
white man, her owner says, 'If you bring a complaint
against me, I shall bewitch you without fail!' So she is
afraid.

A man never cares so much for an inherited wife as
for one whom he has married himself. If he brings home
a cloth he gives it to his own wife, or, if meat, he gives her
the larger share. To the other he gives only enough for
an oath on the sasswood.[1] The land cleared for her farm
is always too small for her, and her house is built without
care. Only if a widow has grown-up children will she not
suffer anything at the hands of the man who has taken
her, because her children will do this work for her. And
if her children are very powerful indeed, the man who
has taken her may, in his turn, be quite under her thumb.
They will see that no harm comes to her.

❡ The rules governing the inheritance of wives are based on the
exchange marriage system, and will be seen to be quite logical in
the light of what has already been said on this subject. Marriage
is not complete until a child is born: therefore, if a man dies

---

[1] Sc. if he ever had to take one.

leaving a wife who has not yet given birth, and she is inherited by his son or brother, she is treated, for purposes of inheritance, exactly as though she had never been married. But if she has once borne a child to her husband, she is then his full wife, and has become, by the exchange theory, the true representative of his *iŋgɔl* for the purpose of bearing children to him and carrying on the line from his mother, as already explained. Moreover, the status thus acquired by virtue of childbirth is not lost on the death of her husband. She continues to bear to him posthumous descendants, though the actual duty of their procreation on the part of the male is performed by a deputy.

In theory this rule should hold good whether the children borne by the woman before her husband's death are sons or daughters, but in practice, under the present patrilineal system, it only applies if one of the children is male. Because if there is a son, he is the heir and direct lineal representative of his father by that wife, and inherits not only the *aŋgɔl* who are already in existence, but also any that his mother may subsequently bear while she is living with his father's kinsman. But if there is no male issue, the brother or son of the dead man who takes over his wife succeeds to the ownership of his daughters, because there is no one else with a prior claim.

THE SASSWOOD ORDEAL

AMONGST the Tiv the trial by sasswood ordeal was a means of killing men in the past, and was instigated by a man who was deeply distressed over the death of one who was near to him. Here is an example:

Afa has died, and his father, Iker, is overcome with grief. He consults the oracle, which convicts the members of his father's group. So he goes to tell the maternal kinsmen of his son Afa, or more particularly, the owner of Afa's mother. He says, 'Afa, my boy, is dead. And I have come to ask you to kill me and bury me by his side, for I do not know what use my life is to me now'. Afa's owner, who is called Ayɔ, replies, 'I had heard the news of his death, and am very distressed about it. I have been thinking that I would not bury Afa alone in his grave, but would provide him with a shroud.[1]

---

[1] I.e. the man who killed him.

But tell me what was the outcome of your search'.

IKER: The divining chain pointed very strongly to my own group—Nako, Yaor, Adamako, Iyarakɔ, Imor, Ajen, six persons in all were shown as guilty. I also tested them by giving the poison to chickens, and all their birds died. See, I have brought you the wings.

AYƆ: Very well. Go and fetch some money for me to pay the sasswood man.[1]

IKER: Right!

Iker goes back and collects six 'twenties'—that was the regular fee of the man who administered the sasswood in former times—and one 'twenty' for 'stripping the bark', making seven 'twenties' in all. When Iker has brought the full amount and given it to Ayɔ, they set out together and go to the sasswood man, who agrees to carry out the trial, takes his fee, and appoints a day. Iker goes home and waits.

When the time comes, Ayɔ goes round and summons all the elders of his group—that is, the maternal kinsmen of the dead man, Afa. They make ready and set out in a long line, with their cloths tied round their waists[2] and their arrows slung over their shoulders. They arrive when the sun is well up in the sky, uttering the loud sasswood cries. As for those whose names have been mentioned for the trial, their hearts beat faster and they roll their bloodshot eyes. Those who have come to give the sasswood seat themselves on the road, and a crowd gathers round. Fear sits in every one's eyes. Some are singing the songs of the sasswood. When all the people are seated here and there, the senior elder of the party which has come to administer the sasswood summons the head of Iker's group to a conference in a place between the huts. Then the elders of each group get up and go to one side. No one else goes except the elders, Afa's father, his owner,[3] and the sasswood man. The elder of Afa's maternal group calls the elder of his father's group, and

---

[1] The right to administer sasswood has to be 'bought'. There are said to have been not many so qualified, often only one in the whole clan, and sometimes not even that.

[2] A sign of their distraught and angry mood.

[3] I.e. his mother's owner.

takes out a number of grass-stalks, one for each man's name. 'Take this one', he says; 'that is Nako's chicken which died. This one is Yaor's, this Adamako's, this Iyarakɔ's, this Imor's, this Ajen's. So choose those who are to drink.' The elder of Iker's group says that he has three who will drink; for the sword does not kill all the workers in the fields. 'I will pick out the men who are spoiling this place', he says, 'and put an end to them with sasswood, that all minds may be set at rest. It shall be Adamako then, and Iyarakɔ, and Imor.' The sasswood man is also listening while the names of those who are to drink are being mentioned.

The elders then come back to the sasswood court. The men named for trial tie only an *akpem*[1] round their waists. Any one who has not got a white cloth borrows one, for no cloth of any colour except white was ever worn while drinking the sasswood.[2] The sasswood man starts pounding. He takes some of the bark and holds it up, telling the elders to come and look well whether it be sasswood or no. All the elders go and stand round, inspecting it. 'We see', they say. 'It is sasswood. Pound!' The sasswood man starts pounding. He throws the bark into the mortar, lifts the pestle and brings it down with a thud. Thereupon he falls backwards on to the ground, as though overcome by the poison. He rises to his feet, lifts the pestle and brings it down, then falls to the ground again. He does this six times. At the seventh he starts pounding fast, sneezing hard the while. This he does whether the sasswood tickles his nose or not, in order that every one may say how strong it is.

When he has finished pounding, he announces that the sasswood is ready. The senior elder of the maternal group that has come with the sasswood man calls the leader of Iker's group. He tells him that he has prepared the draught, and wishes that Iker shall first take the oath of

[1] A white cotton cloth woven in strips.

[2] Two reasons are given for this: (*a*) White was the original colour of cotton cloth, and of bark-cloth before cotton, in the days when dyeing was unknown; (*b*) white is the colour always associated with anti-witchcraft measures. See p. 245.

Y

denial, before the others. The other elder agrees. 'That is quite right', he says. 'Iker, come and deny that you are guilty of the death of your son Afa, and drink the sasswood that all may see.' So Iker comes near and declares his innocence in these words: 'Touching the death of my son Afa, if I have eaten the flesh of any man's child, taken my son to redeem my life, and sought to lay the blame on others, let me fall a victim to this sasswood. But if I am innocent of my son's death, then let me vomit it out again.'   So saying, he clasps his hands behind his back, and holds his mouth ready for the sasswood man to pour in the draught. (He does not stand face to face with him, but a little to one side; because in the past it sometimes happened that a man who very strongly resented being made to drink the sasswood would take it into his mouth and then spit it into the face of the man who gave it to him, thus damaging his eyes.)

When Iker has drunk, he goes and steps over the sasswood fire, and his companions then lead him away. The others are called up, and each in turn rises, takes the oath, drinks, steps over the fire, and is led away by his companions. Those innocent of Afa's death vomit the poison; the guilty succumb. The dead are laid out on a wooden platform, and left to lie uncovered throughout the day. Every one who passes by heaps abuse upon them, saying, 'They revelled in the practice of *tsav*, and have died on account of it. The world is happier without them'. So they are buried, and when night has fallen the *mbatsav* dig them out again, and cut up the meat. The right arm they take off to give to the sasswood man (so the Tiv say). Any one who has vomited the poison is very pleased with himself. He is visited by his companions and female relations, bringing presents of chickens. He goes to see his mother's kinsmen, who also kill a chicken for him. Some time later Iker is ordered by his group to provide the dregs of the sasswood[1] as the price of instigating the trial. So if after a while a death occurs in his family, it is said that Iker has given the dregs.

[1] I.e. a human victim.

THE CHICKEN ORDEAL

We have already seen in the section on *tsav* that no one ever dies unless the *mbatsav* kill him. Therefore when a man falls sick, his brother or his father goes to the diviner while he is still alive, and finds out who it is that has bewitched him. Having learnt this, he comes back and first of all tells the elders of his group in secret the names of those who have been shown as guilty. (Because bewitching is never the act of one person alone. There are always two, or perhaps three, people concerned. Women are often indicted as well as men, particularly old women who have no husbands, such as 'women in trust'.[1] The elders, having heard all the facts, tell the sick man's relative to keep it a secret. . . . They also ask him if he has obtained his information from the divining chain only, or whether he has also tested the result on chickens. If he has not yet carried out the chicken ordeal they tell him to do so.

The chicken ordeal consists in making the birds drink sasswood, and this is the final test of divination. For it sometimes happens that a man is repeatedly shown guilty by the divining chain, but when the sasswood is administered to a chicken on his behalf it vomits the poison. The following is an example of the chicken ordeal:

Ityɔvenda	..	The sasswood man.
Taiyol ..	..	The man who is sick or has died.
Yaga ..	..	Taiyol's brother.
Abaŋger	..	The man who is said to have bewitched Taiyol.

YAGA: Ityɔvenda, Taiyol is very ill; indeed, at death's door. I have been often to the diviner, and each time Abaŋger, my kinsman here, has been shown to be the guilty person. But he has continually denied it, and has now declared that he will take the oath here before you in my presence. We have therefore come to you.

(Before you go to the trial you buy some young chicks,

[1] P. 314 above.

about four markets old,¹ to give to the sasswood man.)
So Ityɔvenda gets up and takes a little sasswood bark
from a pot in the *ate*, together with a small grindstone.
Taking these, he goes with Yaga and Abaŋger to a place
at the edge of the village where the chicken ordeals are
always held. There he rolls up a bunch of leaves from
the meni oil tree, and places the grindstone on it. He
pours a few drops of water on to the stone, and grates
some of the sasswood bark on it, so that a little fine
powder is mixed with the water. At the place where the
ordeals are carried out Ityɔvenda will have set an *Igbe*
potsherd to prevent any of the *mbatsav* from spoiling his
sasswood by witchcraft. When he has finished grating up
the bark, he calls Yaga and Abaŋger to tell him the words of
the oath on which he is to give the sasswood to the chicken.
Abaŋger thereupon gives him the chick and the fee (this
used to be an arrow, but now, since the introduction of
currency, is one penny), and says: 'Touching this illness
of Taiyol, if it be indeed I who have bewitched him, may
my chicken die of the poison; if not, may it spew it out.'

Meanwhile Ityɔvenda has put some *ishuragh* seeds into
his mouth, bitten them, and spat them out on to his hand.²
He has also taken the chick, put its feet together and
fixed them in the space between his big toe and the one
next to it, holding it tight in this way. Then he pronounces this injunction: 'If Abaŋger is responsible for
Taiyol's illness without question, let this chicken die.
If not, let it vomit the poison.' So saying, he folds a leaf
into a cone, scoops up into it a little of the sasswood
water on the grindstone, opens the mouth of the chick,
and pours it down its throat. Then if it is Abaŋger that
has bewitched Taiyol, the chicken will die at once. If,
on the other hand, Abaŋger himself has not bewitched
him, but is the victim of *mjiir*,³ the chicken will die
slowly. *Mjiir* is the process by which a man who has

---

¹ Twenty days.
² The *ishuragh* seeds, in addition to their use already mentioned (p. 250,
&c.), have a magic cleansing property, and he does this to purge himself of
evil influences. Otherwise, if he is under a spell, or has accidentally broken one
of the taboos imposed on the administration of sasswood, the trial will not work.
³ The verb is *jiir*, meaning 'to victimize' in the manner explained below.

done wrong contrives that an innocent person shall appear guilty at the sasswood ordeal. It is a word in the vocabulary of the *mbatsav*, and is only used in connexion with witchcraft and the drinking of sasswood, either in person or by substitution of a chicken. Nowadays when you hear the word *mjiir* it refers to the chicken ordeal. So then, if the poison is given to a chicken and it dies after an interval of time, this means that the man is under *mjiir*. He did not actually go and bewitch any one in person. For this reason it is sometimes the custom to have two chickens, one to show whether the man has actually bewitched some one himself, and one to test for *mjiir*. In the case of the latter, the sasswood man uses this form of incantation: 'If you have been caught by a spell which has been set at the cross-roads, this shall be accounted as *mjiir*, and your chicken shall not die unless you went [to bewitch] in person. If a cockroach or a house-cricket has been sent to you,[1] it is *mjiir*, unless you went in person. If you have been seized by an *akombo*, that also is *mjiir*, unless you went in person.' Then, if the chicken succumbs, the man who has brought it in order to undergo the ordeal is guilty; but if he is innocent of causing the sickness, or death, it will not die, and it is then said that So-and-so's chicken has vomited.

So if, in the case of Abaŋger and Yaga, Abaŋger's chicken vomits the poison, that is conclusive. Nevertheless, Yaga will not let matters rest there, but will try the result of divination on other members of his father's group whom he considers must certainly have bewitched Taiyol.[2] If, however, Abaŋger's chicken dies, Yaga cuts off the wing, fixes it into a piece of split raffia cane, and thrusts it into the roof-poles of his *ate*. He goes, probably the same evening, to his elder kinsmen, whom he secretly consulted about the result of the divination in the first place, and who told him not to take any steps until he had carried out the chicken ordeal. When he tells them that he has also given the sasswood to a chicken on behalf

---

[1] Sc. 'to cause that you shall appear guilty'.

[2] Divination is not an inquiry of a general nature, but is strictly limited in its scope to one or two likely people whose names are given. Thus if it gives a wrong answer the first time, it must be done again.

of Abaŋger, and that it has died, they say, 'In that case
it is now time to go into this matter. To-morrow we will
meet in So-and-so's village to try the case'. The next
morning, accordingly, Yaga goes round to summon his
elder kinsmen who belong to the same *iŋgɔl* group, and
when they have all assembled the trial can begin.

INVESTIGATION INTO A CASE OF ILLNESS[1]

Suppose then that a man has discovered by divination[2]
who is the cause of his brother's sickness, and has called
in the elders of his *iŋgɔl* group. He greets them, and fills
a pipe for them. When they have all smoked, the senior
elder asks him, 'So-and-so, why have you summoned
us?' He replies, 'My brother is very ill. I could not sleep.
And as I rose and wandered, an evil dream came to me.[3]
I dreamt that if you were too late, you would find nothing
but his mortal clay. So I have called you here, to come
and ask him, before his voice is silenced for ever, whether
he has himself eaten of human flesh, that you may know;
but if not, and he is being wilfully done to death before
his time, you may know this also'.

The elders ask him, 'In your wanderings did you seek
and learn the cause of his sickness?' 'Yes', he answers.
'When my brother became very ill, I asked him, seeing
that his disease was too serious to be caused by an *akombo*,
to tell me whether he had either himself eaten [human
flesh], or had bought some medicine to kill some one, and
it had turned upon him because he did not understand
how to use it,[4] in order that if he died I should not be
angry with my kinsmen, knowing that he had brought it
upon himself. But he denied it, saying that he had neither
eaten, nor had any given him cause to seek medicine for
him. So having this assurance, I went to seek the cause,
and on my return spoke privately to my family.[5] They
told me to go again; so I have been twice before calling

---

[1] *Ijir*: or 'trial'.

[2] The word *ishol* may also include the ordeal.

[3] 'Wander' (*dzende*) in this connexion implies visiting the diviner, and
'dream' includes all omens and manifestations.

[4] I.e. its taboos; see note on p. 285.

[5] *Anterev*. Here it means his very close relations, inside the larger *iŋgɔl*
group which has now been summoned.

you here, that you also may hear the result of my journey.'
One of the elders says, 'When the dance has begun, there
is no need to hide the song' (meaning that when the case
is tried the name of the man who was pointed out by the
oracle is no longer kept secret). So the brother of the sick
man, Yaga in this case, takes out from his bag the wing of
the chicken on the raffia cane and gives it to Abaŋger, the
man who bewitched Taiyol and was shown guilty when
they went together to the chicken ordeal. This giving
of the chicken's wings to Abaŋger is tantamount to an
open accusation. A hush falls on the assembly. Then
one of the elders asks Yaga, 'Did you go alone, or did
Abaŋger know that you had gone?'

YAGA: We went together. The chicken died under his
very eyes. Do not imagine that I merely came back
afterwards and told him about it.

THE ELDER: Abaŋger, for what reason are you killing
Taiyol?

ABAŊGER: It is a question of an *iŋgɔl*. I could not
stand the way he was collecting all the *aŋgɔl* for
himself, and decided to kill him, so that I might have
a chance to get some of them. From the insolent way he
behaves you might think that there was no one else in the
family!

THE ELDERS: Did you tell your elder kinsman, Agɔr,
that he was taking all the *aŋgɔl* for himself?

ABAŊGER: Yes.

THE ELDERS: What did he say?

ABAŊGER: Why not ask him?

ADAMGBE (an elder): Agɔr, when Abaŋger had this
dispute with his kinsman, Taiyol, over the *iŋgɔl*, did either
of them speak to you privately about it?

AGɔR: Abaŋger told me about an *iŋgɔl* that Taiyol had
given in exchange. He gave her in compensation for a
wife whom he had previously obtained by capture from
Ukan, and who has borne children to him. I called them
both to my home one evening, and told Abaŋger to let the
matter drop. Had it been that Taiyol had only pointed
out the girl to the Ukan people, and that they had not yet
taken her away, I should have told Taiyol to stop this, and

give her back to Abaŋger; then the other young girl who is growing up could have been given to Ukan as soon as she reached puberty. But as he had already given the other girl as compensation, and had actually handed her over for them to take away, I was ashamed to go and fetch her back again, so told Abaŋger to leave her, saying that when her younger sister grew up she should become his *iŋgɔl* instead. That was what I said, and we afterwards took water to wash any resentment from our hearts before we parted. I thought that everything was settled. Was it necessary that any one should suffer? Well, now it has become a matter over which the group must help me.

ADAMGBE: Agɔr's decision was very fair, Abaŋger. Why were you not satisfied?

ABADGER: Confound you! Is this the first time that Taiyol has taken the *aŋgɔl*?

YAGA (who has the same mother as Taiyol): You may well bluster. You hold the handle of the knife, Taiyol has the blade!

ABADGER: None of your impudence! Do you imagine that your side of the family is to go on taking all the *aŋgɔl*?

ADAMGBE: That is not the way to go about it, Abaŋger. There is no need to kill a man to get an *iŋgɔl*. It should be done with peace and goodwill. If you obtain *aŋgɔl* by killing, what is to prevent another from doing the same? No. Talk the matter over, wash the evil from your hearts, let the sickness depart, and Taiyol arise. Share the *aŋgɔl* with mutual good feeling. Build up this house of Atim; let it not fall in ruins.

Thereupon all the elders agree with one voice that Adamgbe has summed up the case very well, and that all evil thoughts must be washed away before parting, that the sickness may leave Taiyol. A boy is told to bring water in a cup, and the elders all cleanse their hearts of evil. Then one of them takes the water that remains in the cup and pours it on to the roof, over the door of Taiyol's house, that the sick man who lies there may feel relief.

He will dream that he is bathing in a running brook, and the sickness will leave him.[1]

HOYO (OR DANKOL)

In the days before the white man came the Tiv had a very terrifying custom called *hoyo*. (*Hoyo* or *aguda* were the names by which it was known in Shitire, Ukum, and other clans. Kparev called it *dankol*.) When a man fell sick, his brother, having discovered the culprit by divination, told some one else, who called together all the members of his age-class in the group. Or sometimes the sick man himself, being in great pain, would send for one of his companions who had partaken of the same age-feast,[2] and say to him, 'I am very ill, and expect not to recover. Go, therefore, and learn what meat has passed my lips. If I have indeed eaten human flesh, and am being killed by him with whom I have eaten, it is enough; let me die, and let him live on in happiness. But if I have eaten no man, do you, my age-mates, all assemble and ask him, while I am still struggling here, and before my voice is mute, that I also may bear witness; for I know nothing of the People of Darkness. This is my sasswood oath I give to you. When I die, cut open my body and learn the truth'. So his companion rose up and went to the diviner. When he had learnt who it was that was bewitching his age-mate, he called in all the other members of his age-class, and they went together to the home of the sick man. There they summoned all his kinsmen, and pointed the accusing feathers at the man whom the oracle had pronounced guilty. Sometimes he would deny it, and if he were insistent they would take him to the diviner in person. If he were then shown guilty, he would confess. Whereupon they told him to put an end to their age-mate's illness, for if he did not, and their age-mate died, they would not spare him. He could die too, and they would be well content.

Sometimes the accused person would then cure the

---

[1] To dream that you are bathing is a sign that you will recover, but to dream that you are farming means that you are digging your grave.
[2] *Ya kwagh*, see p. 42.

disease, and the sick man would recover.   But if he were
unable to do so, and the man died, he had to answer for it
to the dead man's age-class.   They came together, each
armed with a stick cut from a thorn-bush, *ikpine*, or
ihuerdza (in Kparev they also carried machetes), and
entered the village singing loudly in unison.   Their
leader, who was chosen for his strength, went in front
carrying an ox-halter or stout rope of hemp. He tied this
round the neck of the witch who had killed their age-
mate, dragged him out and threw him on to the ground.
Then they set upon him and beat him unsparingly. They
pulled the roofs off the houses and scattered the thatch
round about. The inmates fled into the bush, the women
and children screamed.   None of those who were left
dared to open his mouth; if he did so they would turn
upon him, saying that he was also one of the *mbatsav*.
They dragged the witch into the bush, beating him with
their sticks, so that the thorns pierced his skin and his
body was covered with white weals.   Sometimes he died
there in the bush, and his young men took him up and
buried him.   Sometimes when they had finished mal-
treating him they let him go, and he went back to die in
his home. This was how the *mbatsav* used to suffer from
the *hoyo*, exactly in the same way as they afterwards suffered under the *haakaa*, as you may see in the description
of it in the section on *tsav*. The Tiv say that the white
man has spoilt the land, because he has forbidden the
trial by sasswood ordeal and the *hoyo*, so that the *mbatsav*
now kill people without fear that anything may happen to
them, and have got quite out of control. In the old days
it was the sasswood and the *hoyo* which, more than anything else, held them in check.

BURIAL

If a man dies young, he is buried without the performance of any *akombo* rites.   But if he is an elder, and
initiate of many *akombo*, he is laid out in the house, and
not buried until every one of the *akombo* has been set
right of which he had the mastery during his lifetime.
For example, if the dead man had been master of the

Iwa, on the day of his death his son, or one of his brothers, would buy a chicken to set it right. Similarly for all the other *akombo* which he had. If the dead man had been master of ten or more *akombo*, his son would have to buy a chicken for each. If he had not enough money to do so, his father would remain unburied. Sometimes the corpse would be left for a day and a night, while the son was still looking for chickens. If he were to be buried without the *akombo* being set right, the land would be very un-lucky. For this reason, a man of high standing who was master of many *akombo* would say to his children, 'I shall cause you much trouble when I die. I shall lie unburied, while you seek for chickens with toil and trouble, and the women go hungry'.

So when the son has bought a chicken for each of his father's *akombo*, he summons all the elders who belong to the same *akombo* group, and they come in and sit round on the ground. One of the initiates rises, takes some of the chickens, carries out the rites for each *akombo* of which he is master, and ties up his chickens to take away with him. Every one who has *akombo* does the same for those which belong to him.[1] When all are finished, it is time to bring out and bury the dead. The site for the grave has already been chosen by one of the elders, and the digging com-pleted before the *akombo* are set right. It is given out that the women must go indoors, and they run into their houses, together with the small children, leaving only the older men outside. When the body has been brought from the house and buried, the women come out and utter loud cries of lamentation. There is, however, a slight variation in Tiv practice as regards the bringing out of the dead. In some clans the women do not go into their houses. They remain outside, and may even go as far as the grave, so long as they do not look in. Women never look inside a grave. They stand at a distance and mourn.

A lament for the dead is called *kwegher*. This is not the

---

[1] I.e. any of the *akombo* over which the first man has no authority. Each *akombo* is only set right once, and the elder who does this divides the chicken among the other initiates, if any.

same cry as a man makes when he is being beaten, but is
a mixture of wailing and singing. The woman weeps and
then sings, but she is crying all the time and uttering words
which tell of her sorrow. After wailing and singing she
sobs, 'Aye-he-he! Who will care for me now that my ——
has left me? What shall I do with my life? Ayu! ayu!
My woes are too heavy for me to bear. What shall I do
when the birds laugh at me as I pass along the road?'
That is a lament. But children merely weep for the
dead, and use no words; songs of mourning are only sung
by old women. The bringing out of the dead is a moment
to make the blood run cold. It is then that a piercing cry
goes up from the women. But after the body has been
buried only the actual woman who is bereaved continues
to mourn, that is to say, the mother of the dead man or
his wife, and she mourns at two definite times, in the
evening and just before dawn.

The reason why a woman never looks into the grave is
that if she were to do so she would transgress against the
Uwarkombo. A man whose wife is pregnant may also not
look into the grave, otherwise his wife will have a miscarriage.

When the corpse has been buried, those who have taken
part in the burial fetch some hot embers, pick a handful of
sword-grass, blow on the embers till they glow, then light
the grass, swing it round their heads, and finally push it
into the grave. There are two reasons for doing this:
first, in order that their hunting may not be spoilt, and
secondly, that they shall not be visited by dreams of the
dead man.

The dead man is laid with his face toward the rising sun,
his feet pointing to the south and his head to the north. If
he is a man of importance he is buried with many cloths,
and a roof is made over the grave, covered with a good
thatch. Cloths are also spread over the roof, but these
are pierced with a knife. If this were not done, thieves
might come by night and take them away to sell.

A chief is buried in the same way as other men of
standing, with certain additions which are not observed in
the case of important commoners. On the death of a

chief, when all the death ceremonies have been observed and he is about to be carried out to burial, they dress him up in his chiefly clothes and place a blue cap upon his head. Then they set him on a bed and carry him round the village, drumming and singing, 'Ruwan Katsina'.[1] Then they bury him, first taking off some of his clothes to lay over the roof of his tomb. The best burial is given to a chief by the Iharev clan. They first spread out a leopard's skin, cover it with a mat, and lay the chief upon it. Then they cut logs of timber to put over him, cover them with earth and beat it well down. The Tiv do not usually bury a chief behind the village but in the central space, or in an *ate* or *dwer*.[2] But if they are afraid that he will be brought out,[3] and that this will frighten the women in their dreams, they bury him at the edge of the village and build a *dwer* over his grave. They call this an *ityar*.

'*Ityar*'. In former times, when a man of high standing died, his son or brother, if he had the means to do it, would give him an *ityar* funeral, saying that his father was worthy of something better than plain burial. First he cut down a silk-cotton tree, hollowed out the bole into the shape of a boat, and bored a hole in the bottom. In this he laid the body of his father, taking out the intestines. He planted two forked posts in the floor of the *ate* [to support it], and lit a fire underneath. There the corpse continued to drip. Then he went to drag in a big tree-drum. He took with him a cock, some prepared locust-bean seasoning, and a leg of meat, to give to the owner of the drum. If the drum got stuck on the way as they were bringing it along, those who were pulling it sat down and washed away evil thoughts[4] before proceeding further. When they arrived at the village the man who was giving

---

[1] The reference is to the 'drum-chiefs', described in the final chapter. This song was also sung at their accession, originally in Katsina Ala. The custom of dressing up the chief's body and carrying it round is taken from the Jukun of Wukari, from whom the whole idea of chieftainship was borrowed, see p. 371.

[2] P. 64.

[3] Sc. by the *mbatsav*.

[4] *Gber ifan*. The formula is of this kind: 'If ever I said that when So-and-so died I would not bring in the drum for him, I now put such thoughts away. Let it come on.' Every one does this, and the obstructive intention which had been holding up progress is thereby removed.

the funeral killed a chicken for the workers. The whole of his group came and sat round, till the place was packed with people, and he gave a beast to every section before they returned to their homes. He then started to brew beer. . . . When the beer was ready, the funeral drumming continued for two days, the host then again slaughtered beasts, and those who had come from a distance departed.

This took place in the rains. When the dry season came the *dzer* dance was held. The *dzer* was also accompanied by a beer-feast, but in this case beer was also brewed by the whole of the rest of the group. The people assembled, and there was drumming and dancing. The *Akume*, the *Ibaa*, and the *Ivughur* came out, and all women remained indoors.[1] When the funeral drumming had continued for a long time, every one sat down and the host led out an ox. At this his female relatives and his friends brought money to give him, and went on giving him presents till the evening came. The next morning he gave them the ox to kill. At the distribution of the meat the man who had brought the most money was given a leg and the head, the one who brought the next largest sum got a part of the other leg, and the rest were given smaller pieces. After this all the female relatives had *akombo* tied round their necks, and departed.[2]

When night fell the elders all assembled together. This was a time to make men's flesh creep. The big tree-drum tapped: '*kili-kili-kili*', and the smaller drum was beating: '*tigben-tigben-tigben*'. The great drum answered: 'Meat! *gede-gede*, go tell the *mbatsav*! Meat! *gede-gede* go tell the *mbatsav*!' As the dawn was about to break the body was

---

[1] These cults have apparently all been borrowed from the Jukun or kindred peoples. The *Akume* (Jukun *Akuma*) and *Ibaa* are represented by masked dancers, of the type known by the Hausa as *dodo*; the *Ivughur* by an instrument consisting of a notched stick which makes a rasping noise when another is drawn across it. In their land of origin they represent spirits whose function is largely of a disciplinary nature, directed against the women. The *Akuma* cult is described by Meek in *A Sudanese Kingdom*, p. 272

[2] So that the *mbatsav* should not bewitch them on the road. Akiga explained that a witch would be able to do this without fear of detection, because every one would conclude that it had been done at the funeral dance where there was a big crowd of elders present. The female relatives referred to here and above are members of the dead man's group who have married outside and come home for the occasion.

taken out of the boat and buried. A wailing cry arose. The elders rushed out in a body, gave chase to one of the beasts and killed it with their spears, crying, 'The leopard has caught it!'

Such was the *ityar* of former days. It is still done by some of the Tiv, but not all. It is chiefly found in Kparev; other clans do not set much store by it, and consider that they have carried out an *ityar* funeral if they bury the dead man and spread his cloths over the roof of his *ate*.

¶ It appears that the original practice of preserving the body in the manner described is no longer observed, and has not been done, as far as I could ascertain, for the last thirty or forty years. All the accompanying rites are still carried out as Akiga says, including setting up the posts and keeping the fire burning in the funeral chamber. But the actual 'boat' has no corpse inside, and now consists of a solid tree-trunk, not hollowed out. These funeral rites have no fixed period of observance; they may be kept up for two years or longer, according to the wish, and means, of the dead man's son.

MOURNING

WHEN a man died his relatives used to go into mourning, that is, they adopted certain signs by which you could tell that a death had occurred in the family. They let the hair grow and refrained from rubbing camwood on their bodies. Kparev also wore bark-cloth as a sign of mourning, and other clans tied raffia string round their bodies. . . . The Tiv do not keep so many months or days of mourning, as do some other peoples. One man will be in mourning for ten days only, and then start to rub camwood on again. Another will mourn for a year; there is no fixed term. Nowadays the Tiv do not express their grief outwardly as much as they used to do; they keep their feelings to themselves. But you may still see a few wearing the signs of mourning.

OMENS

If a man is going on a journey, and a francolin flies up in front of him, he stands still in his tracks in a state of doubt and fear. He may go straight home and give up his journey, or he may be brave enough to go on. But sometimes when this happens things turn out well for him, and in that case he makes a note of it. Similarly, for one person it is a bad sign when a dove flies past his face with a whirring sound, but for another it means good luck, and he goes on. The Tiv also fear the crab, and a man who meets one will go home and tell the people that he has had to return because the crab stopped him. But the thing they fear most is the chameleon; any one who finds one of these in his path will certainly turn back. Other bad signs are the snapping of a twig in front of a man's face, and the twittering of a small bird called *kpancɔkolaya.*

The Tiv also find an omen in the stink-ant. If a man meets a line of these on the road he looks to see whether they are carrying termites in their mouths. If so, he says that his journey will be fortunate, and that he will get *ruam* to eat; but if their mouths are empty he believes that he will go hungry that day.

If a python comes into a house it is a very bad sign. The owner of the house will leave the place and go to live amongst his mother's kindred, saying that the *mbatsav* are killing him. And there is another snake called the *iverivese* which is chiefly nocturnal in its habits: if a Tiv sees this on the road in the daytime he goes to the diviner, or sometimes runs away to his mother's home. If a man picks up a dead Nile perch in the water he eats it sorrowfully, because it forecasts his own death. Or if he goes into the bush and comes across some guinea-fowl's eggs, he knows that death is near, and goes round visiting diviners in very low spirits. On account of these things the minds of the Tiv are never at rest.

DIVINATION

If a man is continually worried by omens of this kind he goes to a diviner to find out the reason. There is more than one kind of divining apparatus. One type is the horn of a reed-buck, with the mouth either closed up with meni oil leaves, or left open. Another is a chain made of *iyiase* and *ive* pods threaded on a string, alternatively with snakes' bones. A third kind consists of a number of short rods of *dzelagba* wood. But the chain of pods is the most important.[1] Here is an example of a visit to the diviner. The diviner is Wantsa, and Asarya the man who has come to consult him. Wantsa is here taken as an example, because he is the most famous diviner in Tivland at the present time. He makes use of [second] sight, as well as divination. He is of the Ishaŋgev clan, but has left them to go and live in Iharev, and refuses to go home.

Faishima, Asarya's son, had died, and Asarya was accused by his mother-in-law of killing him to set right an *akombo*.[2] Asarya was angry about this, and demanded that they should both go and swear their innocence over Wantsa's oracle. So he and his mother-in-law and the man who acted as go-between when the marriage was made set off together, making three in all. They arrive at Wantsa's house, and before they have said a word about the object of their visit he greets them all by name: 'Asarya, son of Asuga, welcome! Welcome, Igba son of Wanishase, and you too, Ashighe daughter of Taraga. So your son has died, Asarya? It is too bad that your mother-in-law should blame you for his death.' He adds, 'That was a sorry business about the leopard that was killed at your home last year; I mean the one that caused the quarrel in which the *mbatsav* were also involved, and was afterwards confiscated by the chief'. Then he tells Asarya to pay the fee. Asarya brings out one brass rod (this was worth sixpence at the time that this happened), and adds one penny. When this has been paid Wantsa says that, since they have come to consult the oracle with such angry looks, Asarya must buy the water which stands in the divining place.[3] Asarya pays a halfpenny for the water. Wantsa laughs. He takes

[1] The chain is worked by throwing it on the ground, and observing the position in which it falls. The other two are grasped in the hand, which moves backwards and forwards of its own accord, somewhat after the manner of dowsing. The movements can only be interpreted by the diviner himself.

[2] This is an actual case.

[3] The water is for crystal-gazing, and is only used for more important cases. The diviner sees that feelings are running high, and so increases his charges.

Z

the divining chain and throws it on the ground, picks it up again and throws it down, then stays quite still. Finally he tells Asarya to hold out his hand. He takes a lump of charcoal and draws a line on the skin[1] by the side of the divining chain, then gives the charcoal to Asarya.[2] Then he tells him that it is his brother who killed his son, and not one of his wife's group. Asarya asks, 'What reason can my brother have had for killing my son?' Wantsa throws the chain again, and says, 'Your brother had been trying to seduce your wife, and when she refused him he bewitched the child. Actually, he did not mean to kill him, but only to make him ill, and the child died in consequence'.

Asarya tells me that when he went home and questioned his brother privately about this, he admitted to every detail. Nevertheless, the oracle tells lies more often than not. Sometimes, when you go to find out something, it is you who have to tell the diviner everything that has happened. Even then it does not tell you anything true, and you may never get a conclusive answer to your question, however many oracles you consult.

JUSTICE

℄. An example of how disputes were settled between members of different groups in the days when the kindred was the largest unit which recognized any common authority.

IN the old days the Tiv did not steal from each other indiscriminately. Often there was only one thief in a whole clan. He used to steal cattle and livestock, and was known to every one in the district. If some one owed a debt, for example a cow, and did not pay, his creditor went to the thief and said to him, 'So-and-so owes me a cow, and refuses to pay. Go and untether one of his cattle, bring it to me, and I will give you a "twenty", or two "twenties" '. The thief accordingly went by night

---

[1] The skin of a cob, already laid out on the ground for the purpose.
[2] The act of giving the piece of charcoal to Asarya is to indicate that the guilt lies on his side of the family (*a na un ishol*). The accusation by the oracle is always accompanied by the giving of a tangible object, cf. the feathers in the chicken ordeal.

when every one was asleep, fetched a cow from the debtor's village, received his pay and went home. The next morning the owner, being unable to find his cow, would start off on its trail, and track it to the home of the man to whom it had been taken. On being asked the reason why he had taken the cow, he would tell him. (The thief himself was not mentioned. People were afraid of him and called him the 'invisible one'. They said he was a dangerous person, and could even carry you off while you slept.) So the man whose cow had been taken went to the head of the other's group and said, 'So-and-so has untethered my cow. I tracked it here, and have asked him to give it to me, but he refuses. So I have come to ask you if you will also hear the facts of the case. Because I am not in his debt, or, if I am, I should like him to come and tell me about it'. (This might be true. The man who owed the debt might be some one else in his district, not necessarily the owner of the cow.) The elder then sent for the man who had had the cow seized and brought to him.

The name of the actual debtor is Afera. The owner of the cow is Adɔgɔ, a kinsman of Afera, both being of Ukum. Afera's creditor, who sent to seize his cow, is called Adamako, a man of Ugondo. Afera had previously bought a slave from him and given him one head of cattle, but has still one to pay. The head of Adamako's group is Ipera.

ADɔGɔ: Ipera, last night one of my cattle was missing, and I set off to track it. The trail led me to Kibough's home, and there I saw it tethered to a fig-tree in the middle of the village. On inquiring, I was told that Adamako had tied it there. But when I went to ask him he did not give me a satisfactory answer, so I have come to you.

IPERA: Oh. But did I not hear rumours yesterday that the cow had been seized over some question of a debt in payment for a slave?

ADɔGɔ: I know nothing about that.

IPERA: Agase, go and call Adamako here.

AGASE: Adamako, Ipera wants to see you.

ADAMAKO: Good morning, Ipera.

IPERA: Good morning. Adamako, this fellow from Ugondo has come here to say that you have seized his cow.

ADAMAKO: That is so. I did.

IPERA: Why?

ADAMAKO: It is a matter between me and his kinsman Afera. Some time ago I bought a slave-girl from the Utyusha. Later, being hard put to it for a long time to find means to pay for the *Biamegh*, I offered her for sale, and Adɔgɔ bought her. But he did not complete his part of the bargain; he gave me one head of cattle, leaving one still unpaid. Whenever I went to him afterwards he just talked nonsense. And the fellow could not take a cricket off me.[1] So I paid the 'invisible one' to go and seize his cow. These Ukum neighbours of ours are becoming too uppish altogether. The other day a bull belonging to Ajav that had strayed into Ukum came back with an arrow in its body, and died.

ADɔGɔ: Well, who said I killed it? That's just like you people. When a fellow asks you about something, you go right off the point, and rake up all sorts of things which have nothing to do with it.

IPERA: That will do! No need for incriminations. Adɔgɔ, you know now why you have lost your cow. Go and tell Afera to come and redeem it for you. He is your kinsman.

ADɔGɔ: Yes, I understand. I will go and see him about it.

* * * * *

Afera, I tracked that cow I lost yesterday into Ugondo, and found it in Kibough's village. They told me that Adamako had caught it. I talked to him about it, but was none the wiser, so went across to tell Ipera, his kinsman. When Ipera asked him he brought up the matter of your debt. He said he had taken my cow as hostage for it. Ipera told me to go back, and said that he would give me my cow when he got yours.

AFERA: Yes, it is true that I owe him a cow. He offered me a slave-girl, saying that he was trying to get

[1] P. 93.

the *Biamegh*. I told him that I could not help him, as I was short of money myself at the time. But as he was very insistent, I said I would let him have one bull, and a cow some other time. He agreed to this and took the bull. When he came to ask for his cow, did I not tell him I was looking for one? Did I threaten him with violence? However, since it is causing trouble, I. will try to find a cow at once and redeem yours, or else I will take him a 'twenty' instead.

* * * * *

Adɔgɔ, I have got a 'twenty', and am going to Ugondo about your cow.

ADƆGƆ: Good. I need not go then.

AFERA: Not go? Why not? You told me the other day that Ipera said we were to settle the matter between us, and that then you were to go to him and he would get back your cow for you.

ADƆGƆ: All right, in that case I must go and tell the head of my family, Iyongoigba. I spoke to him before, when I came back, and as we are to go again I must tell him.

* * * * *

Iyongoigba, that cow I told you about the other night—Adɔgɔ has got the money, and we are going now.

IYONGOIGBA: Good.

(They set off for Ugondo.)

ADƆGƆ: We have come, Ipera.

IPERA: Who are you?

ADƆGƆ: Well really you old folks are baffling! Ipera, don't you remember it was I who came and told you about my cow which was taken by your kinsman Adamako?

IPERA: Tut, tut. I had no idea. We are getting old, you know, and our sight is gone. How could I know without your saying so? Now that you tell me, I remember perfectly. Well, did that kinsman of yours acknowledge the debt or not?

ADƆGƆ: He did, and he has brought the money to redeem the hostage.

IPERA: Very well, go and sleep now. To-morrow

morning I will send some one to call Adamako, and we will talk it over.

(The next day he sends for Adamako, to finish the case.)

IPERA: These people arrived yesterday, but as it was late I told them to wait till the morning, when I would call you, and we could talk over this business.

ADAMAKO: Welcome, Afera. How are the crops?

AFERA: No harm done, unless something has happened since I left.

ADƆGƆ: Nothing wrong here, I hope?

ADAMAKO: No, quite all right.

IPERA: Afera, let me hear about this affair.

AFERA: Is there anything more to say? I have brought you the money to give to Adamako, in order that he may hand over the cow to you, and you may give it to me. I can then give it back to my kinsman, and be rid of the matter.

IPERA: Show the money. . . . Adamako, you see the money; what do you say?

ADAMAKO: What can I say, Ipera? It is for you elders to decide everything. If you say it is enough, the matter is finished.

IPERA: We and Ukum are close neighbours. It is not good that we should do this sort of thing. Go and bring me the cow, that I may give it to them.

ADAMAKO: Take it, Afera. I am content. I have no wish to cause trouble between you and your brother, otherwise I should not give it to you. 'If you eat a man's small child, you must pay him back your full-grown son.'

AFERA: Ipera, that is all settled then. I am going now.

IPERA: Right. I wish you a good journey.

AFERA: Adɔgɔ, take the cow, and let us be going.

MANNERS AND MORALS

The Tiv are good workers. There are no better farmers in this part of the world. They know well how to sow crops in their season and in regular rotation, as we have already shown in the second chapter. In former times any man of standing would himself alone harvest at least 200 bundles of guinea-corn, and many score sheafs of millet beside, while an honoured wife filled two grass stores with yams. Beer never failed in the home of such a man. He became as the great stem of a mighty tree, and a haven of refuge to the fatherless.

The Tiv build fine villages, too. From the oldest times until the present day they have always built their homes on a definite and well-ordered plan. If the village belongs to the sons of one man, the eldest lives at the bottom end[1] and his younger brother at the top, while the other brothers and relatives who are living with them occupy the houses on either side. If any evil thing should occur, the elder brother gets up and stands in the centre of the village after dark, at the time when people sit together. He calls to his younger brother at the other end. Every one else stops talking, and a great hush falls on the homestead, as though not a soul were there. For instance, if an *akiki*[2] has been uttering its cries near the village by night, Iju, the elder brother, calls to Ityovenda, the younger, and asks, 'Is Ityovenda there?'

ITYOVENDA: I am here.

IJU: What have you been doing with your people, the Mbasombo, without telling me, that an *akiki* should come and beat its drum-note here? If it has come to claim a flesh debt from you, go and lie down for the Mbasombo to cut your throat, and do not come here to destroy the home of Adi, our father, who has gone beneath the soil and left us to carry on his line. Why has this *akiki* come, I ask?

ITYOVENDA: Iju, I know nothing of it.

IJU: Then let it be silent. For there are but two of us, and neither of us is guilty of dealings with our kin, the Mbasombo. But if it be that a man has come for Ivogba, our *igba*[3] who is staying with us, and is seeking help from some one in our group, let no one here take a murderer's hire to kill his sister's child.

Cotton was the origin of all wealth amongst the Tiv. In olden times both the head of the house and his wife would spin, and if they had five children they would each

---

[1] I.e. nearest to the stream.   [2] P. 257.   [3] Footnote on p. 112.

have cotton in their hands. When they had spun all their
cotton, the thick thread for the weft and the thin for the
warp, they put it together and gave it to the head of the
family to weave into cloth. With this he bought cattle and
looked after them in his village; for in the past an elder
did not travel about here, there, and everywhere. The
young men went out to the farm, while he stayed at home,
spinning unceasingly, till such time as he had enough to
start weaving. He would go out only when he was
summoned to perform some rite. But when the day was
over he sat with his children, and admonished them in
this manner: 'Sleep with no man's wife. If you commit
adultery with another's wife, you become his flesh-
debtor; one day he will take you and use you when he has
need. Do not dip into the sauce that is set before an
elder: if you do so, some day you may dip into human
fat, and he will order you to kill a man, too, that he may
also taste the gravy. And do not chide your elders; age
is *akombo*.' Such were the words that an older man would
speak to his children when they sat together in the evening,
and the young folk paid heed to them.

A Tiv woman would never pick herbs or gather wood in
another woman's farm without her knowledge. If she did
so, the elders would call her to account and order her
husband to pay a fine of a she-goat, which they would
divide amongst themselves. In former days theft was the
most shameful of all crimes, and is, indeed, even now
amongst some of the Tiv. Telling lies, on the other hand,
was always considered a fine thing, and still is. They say,
'O man, never speak the truth. If you do, you will not
escape the sword. A man should be quick to answer'.
Nevertheless, truth was also esteemed by the Tiv of old.
If they went hunting, and a dispute arose over the kill, the
elders asked for a lad whose word they knew could be
trusted. And if they were told that he had been there at
the time, he was sent for and questioned. 'You are the
ordeal chicken for such-and-such a group', they said.
'Tell us what happened, as you saw it.' Thereupon the
lad would give a true account of the matter, and the elders
would decide the case on his evidence. It was boys of this

kind who eventually grew up to be protectors of the land.

A good point in the Tiv character is their hospitality to strangers. This is what happened in the past, when people did not travel about as much as they do now: A traveller from another clan would first place his arrows on the roof of the house before entering. Then he went into the *ate*, and remained standing until the owner set a chair for him. When he was seated the master of the house greeted him and filled a pipe for him to smoke. After he had finished smoking, he asked him, 'Where have you come from?' The other might say that his home was in Ukan. 'Who is your father in Ukan?' 'Abar.' The master of the house would then call out to his wife that he had a guest, and she would come to greet him. She fetched his arrows, hung them up in the sleeping-house, and then went to prepare a meal. When this was ready, she came round quietly behind the guest, knelt down, and whispered to him to come into the house. But he would not get up immediately, lest it should be thought that he was over-eager for the food. He waited a little, then rose up quietly and went into the house. The woman set the food before him, but he would not eat it all, even though there might not be much of it, fearing to be laughed at for eating such a lot. After this the householder's brothers would invite the guest to eat with them, one after the other, treating him with the greatest consideration, and when the day came for departure his host would escort him on his way. If he were a guest for whom a chicken would be killed[1] the bird was caught and shown to him first, before killing. When it had been cooked, it was brought to him in the pot and served out on a plate in his presence. He began to eat the *ruam*, but did not take much of the chicken. Most of it he divided amongst the people in the village. The head, the drumsticks, and the wings he put back into the pot and returned to the house-wife. The neck was the portion always given to the person who cooked the chicken.[2] Chicken holds the place

---

[1] I.e. some one you know, or with whom you have common friends.

[2] Meat is cooked by men on two occasions: (1) for a guest (usually); (2) for the *akombo* rites (always).

of honour amongst Tiv dishes. You may cook a leg of
beef for your guest, but he who kills a chicken for him
pays the higher compliment.

It is a characteristic of the Tiv to prefer everybody else's
things to their own. For their own chiefs they have no
respect whatever, but any other chief wins their admiration, however useless he may be. They will honour any
important foreigner, but despise their own elders. If they
wish to compliment one of their chiefs, they compare him
to the chief of Shogodo,[1] who seems to them to be the
greatest of all foreign rulers, and if any one is wearing fine
clothes they say, 'He is dressed like a son of Shogodo!' If
a Tiv knows some English he uses it on all occasions. He
speaks it whenever there is a large number of Tiv present,
not caring whether they understand or not. Even those
who do not understand what he is saying will admire his
knowledge of the language. So also with Hausa. Nowadays, moreover, the young men who have gone to live
away from their country, as well as those at home who
run after everything foreign, no longer speak Tiv properly,
but mix in Hausa words. They say, 'I shall do whatever
I *gan dama*. I don't want any of your *rigima*, so stop your
wasa-ing with me!' Most of the Tiv who live among
foreigners corrupt the language in this way; they are
chiefly of the labourer and 'boy' class.

Another trait in the Tiv character is their lack of perseverance. They can never keep on doing the same thing
for any length of time. If you take a Tiv and a man of
another race, and set them both together at the same task,
you may find that the Tiv is better at it than the other and
at first makes good progress; but after a while the Tiv will
fall back, the other man will pass him and go on, and
finally the Tiv will drop out altogether. You may see a
Tiv who knows English thoroughly, wears European
clothes, and is very good at his work under the white
man. But do not think you have found the man you want.
If you watch him closely, you will say that you would
rather have a Tiv who had never seen a white man. You
can find Tiv who once went to live amongst the Hausa,

---

[1] The Sultan of Sokoto.

learnt in their schools, and finished reading the Qurān. They gave a ram for their names to be changed to Musa, Ibrahim, or Yakubu. They became Muhammadans, and did not eat from the same dish as pagans. But if you meet them now, they are wearing nothing but a camwood duster round their waists, carrying out *akombo* rites, and abusing the Muhammadans. And it is the same with us in regard to Christianity.

The Tiv have no care for the future. Being farmers, they laugh at the foreign traders. 'The foreigners don't know how to farm', they say. 'While people are working, they waste their time wandering about.' But when their crops are ripe, they sell the produce foolishly to foreign traders in the markets, a bundle of corn for twopence or threepence, and a full calabash of grain for a penny. The traders buy it up quickly at this price, and store it. When the Tiv, in their hurry to realize a few pence, have sold it all, they find themselves in want. As soon as this happens, the foreigners put up the price of a bundle from threepence to ninepence. The Tiv have no corn and no money, for the money which they got for their produce they have already spent on acquiring wives. So they go to beg from the foreigners, or work on their farms, in return for which the foreigners give them cassava, or gruel made from the corn which they originally bought from the Tiv. When the famine time comes round again, you may see Tiv women laboriously collecting wood to sell to the foreigners living amongst them, in exchange for cassava which their husbands grew for the same foreigners during the time of the previous food-shortage.

That is how the Tiv suffer from their improvidence. Some day they will look further ahead. Some day they will gain self-respect, and respect for their language and for the customs of their fathers that are of value. Some day they will learn perseverance and courage. Then the Tiv will be a fine people, for they are by no means lacking in ability. But at present these defects in their character hamper their advance amongst the peoples of the world.

VII

DISEASES AND THEIR TREATMENT

THE Tiv say that sickness does not come of its own accord, but is caused either by an *akombo* or by the *mbatsav*. Thus the name of nearly every disease, and of almost every medicine for curing disease, is coupled with that of an *akombo*. And whenever the *mbatsav* bewitch some one, they invariably use the *akombo* to carry out their purpose. Diseases are treated in three ways: by killing something, by simply giving medicine, and by washing away evil thoughts. In each case the nature of the treatment required may be determined by divination. Some ailments can be diagnosed by merely looking at the patient; he is told to carry out the rites and, if only the *akombo* is the cause, the sickness will leave him. But in the case of more obscure diseases the *akombo* must be properly revealed by divination before it can be set right. The divining chain will show whether it is necessary to kill a victim, as well as applying medicines both internally and externally, in order to cure the disease, or whether all that is needful is to wash away the curse, in order that the medicine may be effective. (The practice of divination is described in Chapter VI.)

There used not to be so much sickness amongst the Tiv as there is to-day, and plagues did not afflict the land as frequently as they do now. The old men say that their land has changed since the white man came.

SMALLPOX

This is a terrible scourge in Tivland. It is known by a number of names. . . . In former times smallpox did not come so often as it does nowadays. My father was about forty years old when the white man came, and during those forty years he saw only two epidemics. It began in the days of Ayeŋge, the first drum-chief of Shitire. At that time Cire, son of Tali of Mbagen, was one of the elders who used to go to Swem, and the old men say that it was he who brought back the disease from there.[1] This happened before my grandfather, Deekpe, was old enough to wear a cloth. It was he that told my father about it. Neither Akpaye of Mbaduku nor Acii of Mbala, who were born a few years after the Chamba had driven the Tiv off Ibenda Hill and were old men when the white man came, so that they held chieftainships under him only for a short time before they died, nor Asela of Sherev and men his age, nor any of that generation saw more than three smallpox epidemics before the white man appeared. It did not come in every generation, as it does now; perhaps it would come only once in every three.

When, however, an outbreak did occur it killed off a very large number of people. It is for this reason that the Tiv know so little about their past history. It was also due to smallpox in the first place that they grew accustomed to having a large number of wives. At first, before they knew about inoculation, the number that died was very great. In some villages no one was left to tell the tale; in others only one would survive, perhaps a young man. When he found that he was the only man left in the village, he took to himself all the women who had been left destitute, and begat children by them to carry on the line of their fathers.[2] He might not wish to have these women at all, but took them perforce, not knowing what else to do. Sometimes a few of the men who had survived in the surrounding hamlets (for it is said, 'The sword never kills all the workers on the farm') went to live with him and share his duties by the women, and this made things easier for him. But in some villages there were no men left at all, and the women in desperation had to go themselves to look for husbands. Sometimes a woman would slaughter a beast and give to a man to eat in payment for sleeping with her, so scarce were husbands at that time. Silence was over the land. The number of deaths was so great that the old men were wiped out, and there was no one left to pass on the ancestral traditions, except the few young men who survived to live with the

---

[1] Sc. deliberately. See p. 218.
[2] For the meaning of this phrase, see p. 316.

women. If the Tiv had been a people that knew how to write in the first place, and the elders had recorded the ancient lore before they perished from smallpox, then it would have come down to us, their children. But since they did not do so, it is difficult for us to get any accurate information about the men who lived in former times.

It was through ignorance that the Tiv were almost exterminated by smallpox. When an epidemic broke out they said that some one had brought it from Swem to destroy the people. So they merely continued to hold inquiries, saying that the disease would do no harm. When the day was over every householder called all his family together and charged them not to go *tsav*, for so long as no one went *tsav* the smallpox would not hurt them. But as he had nothing else that he could do, everybody succumbed to the disease. After a time, however, they discovered that smallpox was infectious, and acted differently. As soon as any one caught the disease they moved him out of the village and put him in a shelter far away in the bush. There he remained, being treated by some one who had already had smallpox and recovered from it. When the morning began to get warm the sick man went out and sat in the sun. He was never allowed to sit in the shade. Sitting out in the sun caused the disease to ripen quickly. If it failed to do so, the man who had had it before, and was looking after the patient, put a potsherd on the fire and filled it with sand. When it was hot, he placed it on the ground and the sick man lay on it, so that the heat should bring out the disease. When it was fully developed, and the pocks suppurated, he took some dry powdered camwood and rubbed it on them. After some days the scabs peeled off, and that was the end of it. But if the disease was going to be fatal, the spots did not come out well, the struggle with the disease continued out in the bush, until the man became delirious and died. When he died no one wept for him. People do not mourn death from smallpox; if they did, it would kill every one. There are two kinds of death which the Tiv do not mourn, death by smallpox and death by the sasswood ordeal. With regard to the latter the reason that there is no mourning is that it is a violent death;[1] if you mourn for a man who has died under the sasswood trial you will be seized by the *Swende*.[2] If smallpox attacks a man and does not kill him, it scars his face, making him for all time repellent to the women. And since epidemics used to come at very long intervals, a woman would refuse a suitor who had the pock-marks, saying, 'He's quite ancient. He has even got smallpox scars!'

After a time they began to practise inoculation. When a case of smallpox occurred, some one who had already had it took a razor and made an incision in the body of a healthy person who had not yet been infected. When the blood flowed he took a little of the pus from the pocks of the man suffering from the disease and rubbed it in the wound. The man who was thus treated with the pus would suffer from a headache, or sometimes a few spots would come out on his face, and that would be all. He would never get the disease again. This was a great help in keeping the disease dormant for long periods. But nowadays, since the time of the white man, smallpox has become a thing which recurs year by year and no longer appears in regular cycles. It may have appeared more than ten times in the lifetime of a youth aged between ten and twenty.

The White Man's Serum. When smallpox became so prevalent amongst the Tiv, the European doctors, both Government and Mission, made strenuous efforts to save the people. They helped in two ways: by segregating those who had the disease, and by inoculating those who had not. But the white man's serum is slightly different; it is taken from the lymph of a calf that has died of smallpox, collected in small glass phials, and applied to scratches made on the skin. Another way is to take a little

---

[1] *Ku swendegh*, see p. 205.

[2] This explanation was given to Akiga by an informant, but he agrees with me that it is not, as it stands, very satisfactory. If this were the true reason for not mourning deaths by ordeal, it should apply to all other violent deaths, and this is not the case. But it seems hardly necessary to look further than the obvious reason for not mourning a witch's death. With regard to smallpox, the reason for not mourning may originate simply in the fear of bringing on oneself the malicious attentions of the *mbatsav* with whom the disease is directly associated; because smallpox is not an *akombo* like most of the others, but is supposed to have been brought by the *mbatsav* from Swem.

of the pus from the arm of a man who has been already vaccinated, as soon as it begins to fester, and use this for the vaccination of some one else. The patient suffers from a headache and that is all. After this, if an epidemic breaks out, he will not catch the disease. But if he does not get a headache as the result of the vaccination, he is liable to be attacked by smallpox at some other time.

Sometimes the after-effects of vaccination are very serious, and may bring a man near to death. The Tiv, having seen this, will not now willingly submit to it. When the doctors get news of an outbreak of smallpox in some section of the tribe, they either go themselves or send their medical assistants to vaccinate. But when the Tiv see them they run away and hide, saying that vaccination is a bad thing and that they do not want it. When a white man is going round vaccinating, the Tiv are all in a state of apprehension. Every time they see one of his officials, they cry out in alarm, 'It's the vaccinator!' Nowadays they call it 'lamba'.[1] Many markets have been broken up from terror of the 'lamba'. If some employee of the European appears while a market is in progress, at a time when there is smallpox about, every one scatters; vessels are broken, money is lost, and some are injured in the general stampede.

❡ Inoculation by direct arm to arm infection was known to many tribes in Nigeria before we came, and is said to be still practised in some districts in spite of attempts by the British Administration to discourage it. Although it is undoubtedly attended by grave risks, and is, in fact, tantamount to the deliberate transference of the actual disease, the native view is invariably to the effect that a person who is thus inoculated gets the disease in a far milder form than if he were to catch the disease from a chance infection. How far this belief is justified on scientific grounds is a question outside the sphere of these notes.

It might be expected that where the people were already well acquainted with the practice of inoculation, they would have

[1] From English 'number', through Hausa. The old word for serum, which is pre-European, is *iwambe*, a singular form of *awambe*, 'blood'.

little objection to the same precautions when carried out by European doctors. In the case of the Tiv the fear of vaccination does not arise from the principle or the methods, which after all are not very different from their own, but from the circumstances in which the vaccination is done. It is unnecessary to look further than Akiga's description of circumcision, to infer that such an operation as this, offering exceptional opportunities to maleficent forces and human enemies to do harm, would naturally be done only by one well qualified to combat them by counter-magic, a man with 'good blood' and plenty of *tsav*. The operation would probably be done in the privacy of the man's home, and every possible magical precaution taken against disaster. But our vaccination is carried out by a stranger, the quality of whose blood and disposition is unknown, the danger of magic interference is apparently disregarded, and, worst of all, it is done in the presence of a large crowd of people, a circumstance notoriously favourable to the *mbatsav*. It is not surprising that the Tiv shrink from an operation carried out under such dangerous, and magically septic, conditions.

THE INFLUENZA EPIDEMIC

THERE was another kind of disease that visited the Tiv in the year 1919 and killed a very large number of people. Some called it *Ndovorkpoo*,[1] others 'the Cough'.[2] Its effect was so serious that a hush fell on the whole countryside. But after a short time it passed. If it had stayed for long the human race would have perished. No one knew its remedy. Those who caught it tried all sorts of medicines: some recovered, others died. But of those who had it more died than survived.

Smallpox, locusts, caterpillars and the Cough are all brought by the *mbatsav*, according to the Tiv.

GONORRHOEA

There is another bad and shameful disease which has been spreading recently amongst the Tiv, during the time of the white man. It has several different names. . . . Gonorrhoea is of two kinds, the one accompanied by a

---

[1] A name indicating the suddenness of the attack.
[2] *Hough*. This is a general term including influenza, chest troubles, &c.

discharge of pus and the other of blood.[1] It is an extremely bad complaint, and, if a man neglects it, it will
cause him to cry out in pain every time he goes to pass
water. It may even prove fatal if not treated in time.
I knew a man called Civir at Zaki Biam who died in 1925
from the effects of gonorrhoea. To-day if you took twenty
men in Tivland you might find only five who had not got
it: and the same with women.

The old men say that gonorrhoea was known by the Tiv
even in former days, but it was not so common as it is
now. They used to call it *coughikula*, the name of the
akombo. If any one caught it, he drank the medicine of the
Coughikula and was cured. It was never regarded as such
a serious complaint, and the cases that occurred were few
and far between. The women brought forth an abundance
of children. But when the white man came, the Tiv began
to travel about and mix with the Chamba, Dam, Hausa,
and Akporo peoples, amongst whom the disease was rife,
and not only to mix but also to intermarry with them.
Those who lived next to the Chamba took Chamba
women, those bordering on Dam country took Dam
women, while Iharev and Masev married wives of the
Akporo tribe. When the Tiv intermarried with their
neighbours they also copied their promiscuous habits.
For in the old days irregular intercourse with women was
regarded by the Tiv as a very serious crime. But they
became so accustomed to seeing it practised by these
tribes that they ceased to trouble much about it; and the
same with the women. In this way the disease began to
spread, as when a man fires the bush, and the grass catches
light as he goes from place to place, thrusting in the
burning brand. But where it was most common was in
the villages of the chiefs, and in those which were near to
Hausa settlements; and the people who more than any
others were the cause of its spreading were the white
man's carriers and road workers. These were young men,
the great majority of whom were unmarried. When they
received their pay, they spent it on food and women.
Moreover, they were not content to keep to the same

[1] ? Bilharzia.

woman; a man would sleep with this one to-night and that one to-morrow, passing the infection from one to the other. Another man would come after, catch the disease at once and give it to a third woman, just like men firing the dry grass.

If gonorrhoea takes a firm hold on a woman, she complains continuously of pelvic pains, and the parts become much inflamed. Moreover, she ceases to bear, and though her husband set right every known *akombo*, no more children are forthcoming. Even if he be lucky enough to have a child, it will be a weakling. If you travelled in Tivland in the days when the white man first appeared, in every village that you entered you would find large numbers of children, both boys and girls. It was extraordinary to see the crowds which followed you and pressed round you, if you happened to have something which they had not seen before. Nowadays, if you travel about, you will not see so many. Only in villages away out in the bush, where the white man's followers do not often go, is the number of children still on the increase. But if you go to a chief's village, or to places where the Tiv are living in contact with the foreigners, you will notice how their numbers are diminishing. In the past one woman would bear from ten to twenty children. To-day five is a large family for a woman. Often she has only one child, or perhaps two, then starts to complain of internal pains, and that is the end: she will bear no more. People in these days do not have families like Ikobo Agena of Ukan.

YAWS

This disease is indigenous to the Tiv. Every one of them gets it. Any one who has not yet had it is always afraid that, having escaped it in his youth, he will get it when he is old. And he is right; this is what happens. For every five who have never had yaws you can find perhaps a hundred who have, and those five are quite certain that one day they will get it too. The first symptoms are cramp in one of the limbs, with pains in both knees and all the other joints. Some time afterwards it begins to affect other parts of the body, first appearing as small local sores, later as evil-smelling ulcers in different places, a very unpleasant sight. If a boy gets it, the others make up mocking songs about him. It is better to have yaws while you are young. If you get it later in life it saps your strength. Even though you get rid of it, you will never be the same again till the day of your death.

The Tiv have a remedy for yaws. It is not a fatal disease, nor does it cripple a man, unless the *mbatsav* take a hand in it, in which case he may die, or unless it is complicated by the *akombo-a-dam*,[1] which may cause a deformed nose or mouth. 'Ancestral'[2] yaws does no harm to any one. But if you do not take the trouble to wash the affection and treat it carefully, even though it may be only the 'ancestral' kind, it will give you *indior*. (*Indior* means yaws between the cheeks of the buttocks.) This is a shameful complaint, and takes a very long time to cure. Yaws may heal up everywhere else on the body, while *indior* still persists. In the case of a child, if the parents do not bathe it early for fear of making it cry,[3] it will grow up with the disease, and get the insulting name of 'Indior-bottom'. In the days when the Tiv used to capture women under the *iye* system, this was often the means of spoiling a courtship. A young man would be courting a girl, and some one else would go to her and poison her mind against him. 'That young fellow who is running after you', he would say, 'is no good. He has got *indior* in his buttocks. Can't you see the way he walks?' The girl, hearing this, would say that she was not going to marry a man with *indior*, and the affair would be broken off. The youth would feel very sore with his father for having allowed him to grow up with the disease, so that the women would have nothing to do with him.

In this connexion the Tiv have a wise saying: 'Let not pity stay your hand from bathing the *indior* of your son

---

[1] An *akombo* associated chiefly with syphilis.

[2] This apparently does not mean congenital yaws, but yaws unaffected by syphilis, with which it is easily confused owing to symptomatic similarities.

[3] The treatment is said to be very painful. It consists of a poultice made of the leaves of certain small plants found in marshland, ground up with lemon juice and plastered over the wound.

while he is still a child, so that he come to puberty with it
still upon him. Lest, when the women refuse him, he
give you the blame for your neglect.' This means that if
a child do wrong, you should not hesitate to correct him,
even at an early age, for fear that he may cry. Punish him
well, and stop him. Otherwise, if he form bad habits, he
will not be able to give them up and, growing up dis-
graced among his fellows, will say that it is your fault for
not punishing him while he was still young, when his
faults could have been cured, instead of allowing him to
become set in his evil ways and suffer shame for the rest
of his life.

There is another form of this disease which takes a long
time to heal; it is called crab-yaws. Crab-yaws affects
only the soles of the feet and the palms of the hands, but
especially the soles of the feet. After a man has suffered
from yaws, and it has disappeared from every other part
of his body, it may then attack the soles of his feet, where
it becomes a chronic condition. He cannot walk properly,
but moves with a lop-sided gait. Crab-yaws is exceedingly
painful, especially during the rains; in the dry season it is
not so bad.

Sickness attacks the Tiv in periodic outbreaks. Sometimes the disease runs through the whole tribe, but may
not be serious enough to cause death. At other times it
does not spread everywhere, but only appears in certain
districts and comes to an end after a short time. The
beginning of the dry season is the worst time. When the
dry weather comes it brings with it colds and stomach
troubles, and, although not many die from these ailments,
the old folk grow weak and many of the young people
have coughs.

THE *IDYO*

The Tiv have a hospital of their own, which dates back
to early times: it is called the *idyo*, and a man who buys the
right to take patients into it is known as the man who
admits people to the *idyo*. Here is an example of a man
who wishes to buy the *idyo*, in order to admit others and

cure them in return for a fee: Ikaave is the man who already has the *idyo*, and the right to admit others. Ikpa is the candidate for initiation.

IKPA: Give me instruction in the *idyo*, Ikaave. I want to buy it, so that I can admit people.

IKAAVE: All right, I will. But it is not an easy matter.

IKPA: Never mind, I will buy it. I have set my heart on it.

When Ikaave sets out to go and give Ikpa his lessons in the *idyo*, he takes with him his lynx-fur pouch containing the *idyo* medicines, which he is going to teach him to use. In the pouch are: a flint and steel, some grains of *ishuragh*, a hen's egg and an *agyanku* fruit. He announces his arrival and proceeds to tell Ikpa what to do: He must put up a shelter between the houses, or, if he has already a small *dwer* for storing yam seed, that will do. He must also make some unfermented beer. When Ikpa has done this, Ikaave goes through the ritual, showing him what to do. He plants some posts round the door of the *dwer* and ties some string across, so as to form an enclosure. Round this he draws a line and pours some wood-ash on to it. Then he takes the pot of beer and places it inside the circle, on a pad of sword-grass made for the purpose. Ikpa and all those who have already been admitted to the *idyo* then enter the circle and start drinking. Those who have not previously been admitted dare not go in, but sit outside the circle, and the beer is passed out to them.

When all the beer has been drunk, Ikaave shuts Ikpa into the small *dwer*; there he remains for that day and the following night. The next morning, when the sun is up, Ikaave comes back and lets him out. He tells him to go and bathe: this he must do in absolute silence, and on no account speak to any one. When he comes back, Ikaave makes arrangements for him to have something to eat. He tells Ikpa's wife to cook *ruam*. Then he takes a little of each of the things which are taboo to a master of the *idyo*—potash, beniseed, red pepper, and pumpkin seeds— places them on the ground, and calls Ikpa to come and sit down. He takes a pinch of each of these things and touches Ikpa with them on the mouth. That is all that is necessary; Ikpa may then eat them without ill effect. After this they eat the *ruam*, and Ikaave proceeds to prepare the medicine. This consists of red sorrel and *aka*,[1] which he cooks together in a pot. When it has thoroughly boiled, he takes it off the fire and decants the liquid into a potsherd which he has placed ready on a grass pad. He puts this liquid back on to the fire. But before he puts it on to boil he must first rub it across the hearthstones on which the medicine was originally cooked, and so also when he takes it off again. Having taken it off the fire, he dips in a feather, stirs it round and wipes it on the sole of his foot, in order to show Ikpa what to do when he admits a patient to the *idyo*. He also teaches him some other medicines, which he must apply in the event of the first treatment proving unsuccessful. These are the shoots of the wild plum and sword medicine,[2] mixed together and rubbed up in the hands, then applied to the wound and covered with leaves of the meni oil tree.

That is all of that. Ikaave tells Ikpa what to pay. This will be three 'twenties' and a further four brass rods as the fee for taking the medicine out of the pot. Ikpa must also pay one brass rod to redeem the pot in which the medicine was cooked, and another to the woman who prepared the meal. If he gives her nothing, she will be afflicted with sores on her body. To the boy who drew the water for him he must give a chicken. The fees which he pays to Ikaave are the same as those which he will himself collect from any patient whom he may subsequently admit to the *idyo*.

Admission to the 'Idyo'. The *idyo* treatment is not intended for every kind of illness. You may go into it on account of sores, or if you are suffering from the *Wayo* in an acute form, resulting in a bowed shin-bone or flattened fore-arm, but not for stomach troubles, headaches, or eye complaints. If the disease is very persistent, and all attempts to cure it by other means have failed, then it is time for you to enter the *idyo*. You go to the master, who tells you the fee which you must pay. This is four brass

---

[1] A dark coloured clay dug up in small quantities and used medicinally.
[2] P. 209.

rods (formerly six 'twenties'), a chicken, and a hoe on which to sit in order to take away spells.[1] When you have given him these, he takes off the handle of the hoe, leaving the blade, which he lays on the ground, back-side uppermost, for you to sit on. Then he transfers[2] the spells into the chicken which you have brought. When this has been done, you pay him one brass rod to redeem your hoe, but he keeps the chicken for himself. Then he admits you. People say, 'So-and-so has gone into the *idyo*'. There you drink the medicine which has been set aside for you. The *idyo* medicine is called *kpaasu*; its ingredients have already been mentioned. On the day that you are admitted the *kpaasu* is put on the fire and remains there from morning till evening. Then you draw out the embers, leaving only one in the hearth. When the brew has cooled, you pour off the liquid into a small vessel and drink it before food, and again later in the evening. Every morning early you go out to bathe, and when you come back you squeeze on to the wound the medicine prepared for this purpose as described above, covering it over with leaves of the meni oil tree. This you do continually. You may get well, or again you may not. Some, when they come out of the *idyo*, go away and die. If you recover, the master of the *idyo* brings you out, and you give him a chicken, which he kills and cooks. Then he makes the passes with it and you eat it together. After this he dismisses you, and you must depart in silence, and not take leave of him, for this is taboo. If you say good-bye to him, the disease will come back. The *idyo* has a large number of taboos: when you are admitted, you must refrain from sexual intercourse and from eating black fish. No one must speak to you while he is eating sauce made from beniseed or potash. Nor must you speak to any one when you go to collect the wood for cooking the medicine, or the ingredients for making it. You must use only a Tiv flint and steel to light the fire for boiling the medicine or for cooking your food, and you must not eat any sauce that contains potash.

[1] See below.
[2] Or 'collects': sc. by swinging it round your head. Cf. p. 32.

The *idyo* is very profitable. In former days it enabled men to make money and build villages, too. If a man bought it and it worked well with him, so that he could cure people quickly, he had an abundance of patients, both men and women. If a patient who had been into the *idyo* had nothing with which to pay when he came out, he would go and work on the master's farm. Sometimes a man would farm for the master for two seasons, and do all other kinds of work beside. Another who had not been happy at home would settle down with him permanently as his servant. If the patient were a woman who had been brought in by her husband, and he were unable to find the money to redeem her, she would remain there indefinitely. One would try to pay, another would leave his wife so long that the owner of the *idyo* lost patience and had connexion with her, so that she became pregnant. When the husband saw this he would come and take her away, saying that she had redeemed herself. When the child was born it would belong to the husband. But if, on the other hand, the master seduced a woman who had been admitted to his *idyo*, after having received payment from her husband, he was guilty of an offence, and would be liable to a fine of a she-goat and six 'twenties'.

℃. The rest of this section in the original is devoted to the local medical work done by the Mission and by the Government. The following extracts, dealing with the native attitude to European medicine, are of some general interest:

THERE are medicines at every Mission station, and treatment is given to the sick. Of all the work which the Mission does this pleases the people most. Nevertheless, when for some reason or other they are angry with the missionary, they belittle his medical work, too. 'The missionary', they say, 'is of no significance. All he does is to cure people's ailments. The Governor has given all the other white men work, but to the missionary he gave the task of washing sores, saying, "Go, wash the Tiv and pray!" No one who is given mission teaching can do anything with it, except clean wounds and say prayers.

He can never get any useful work'. On these occasions they refer to the missionary as the 'Wound-washer'. But when the quarrel is over, they say that of all white men he is truly the one that brings deliverance to the people, and any one who slights him is slighting a fine man. . . .

Notwithstanding all the work which has been done by the doctors on the healing of sickness, the Tiv say that no doctor can cure a man's disease by his own knowledge of medicine. He can only cure him if the *mbatsav* give their consent to his recovery. So sometimes when a patient has been brought to the doctor for treatment and does not get well for some time, he is taken home again and carries out the preliminary rites[1] before coming back to the doctor. Often, too, when a person falls sick, they do not take him to the doctor at once, but first consult the oracles, set right the *akombo*, and hold lengthy investigations. Meanwhile the disease is getting a firm hold, but all they say is, 'We shall not kill our So-and-so. He will recover; he is not going to die. Don't take him to the doctor; it is all right'. After a time the man dies. Or if he gets over the disease, he is lucky. But sometimes, after they have been going on like this for a long time and the man is on the point of death, they take him to the doctor to be cured. If the doctor can do nothing and the patient dies, they say that it is the *mbatsav* who have killed him. In the same way, if the doctor performs an operation and the man dies under it, they say that it is not the effect of the operation but the *mbatsav* that have brought about his death. In no single instance do the Tiv blame the doctor in a case of illness. If things go well, they say, 'It is all right, because the *mbatsav* have said that it shall be so'. If they go wrong, they say that the *mbatsav* have so decreed. The doctors know all this, but they go on doing their medical work, without paying any heed to it.

[1] *Tɔndo ataa.* See p. 182.

VIII.

CHIEFS AND ADMINISTRATION

THE DRUM-CHIEF (*TOR-AGBANDE*)

¶ The conception of executive chieftainship is foreign to the Tiv. It is not suited to the tribal temperament or social organization. Yet when the British first took over the control of the tribe, and prepared to divide it up into administrative units each under a district head, according to the policy of that time, they found the idea of chiefs already in existence. This idea was, in point of fact, of recent growth, and was the outcome of contact with other races at a different stage of political development, whom they found living in the plains of the Benue valley when they came out of the hills. It has been suggested that the demand for some sort of political authority was created by the unsettled conditions which followed upon the Chamba invasions.[1] Attacked on their borders by tribes possessing a more advanced political and military organization than themselves, and harassed by inter-clan quarrels arising out of disputes over their newly acquired territory and the forcible capture of each other's women, it would not be surprising if the Tiv felt the need for leaders with wider and more dictatorial powers than the elders of the tiny independent units into which the tribe was divided. One type of chief, the *kur*, copied from the Donga section of the Chamba people by some of the south-easterly clans, had certainly a semi-military origin and function. But if the germ of a clan consciousness was ever born of the necessity for showing a united front and submitting to the commands of a single military or political leader, it did not survive long after the immediate danger of foreign invasion was removed. Even the name *kur* is now almost forgotten.

As regards the *tor-agbande* or 'drum-chief', at least, it is more probable that the office came into existence, not because it was felt by the tribe to fill any real constitutional need, but as a result of the people's inveterate love of imitating any new idea or institution

---

[1] Cf. *Intelligence Report on the Ukan District of the Tiv Division of the Benue Province*, 1935, by K. Dewar, p. 8.

which they have seen practised by their neighbours. Like
the Israelites, in very similar circumstances, they demanded a
king that they might be like all the nations. Of the 'nations' round
about them there was none which had a more impressive king
than the Jukun, a people with a long history behind them, whose
kingdom, under the name of Kwararrafa, had at one time extended over a large part of what is now Northern Nigeria. The
atmosphere of mystery and supernatural power which surrounded
the Aku Uka, the divine king of Wukari, appealed to the imagination of the Tiv, and it was to him that they first went for authority
to make chiefs of their own and for instruction in the art of
chieftainship.

In recent years (1927–34) an attempt was made by the British
Administration to revive this historical connexion between the Tiv
and the Jukun kingdom by putting the seven most easterly Tiv
clans in Wukari Division, with the intention of eventually bringing
them under the jurisdiction of the Aku Uka. This experiment
proved unworkable in practice, and was indeed, in theory, based
on a misconception of the nature of the relationships which
existed between the two peoples. The Tiv tribe of half a million
people never owed any political allegiance to Wukari. The
homage which the Tiv deputations paid to the Aku Uka was
derived from the respect which in Africa is commonly accorded
by new-comers to the older inhabitants of the country, however
virile the invaders may be, however weak and degenerate the
indigenous tribes. It bears a close analogy to the personal relationship between youth and age, and is founded, in general, on belief
in the superior magic power and knowledge of the old, and, in
particular, that supernatural knowledge by which man may
control the unknown local forces which inhabit a strange country.
By the time the Tiv came into their present territory, the political
power of Kwararrafa was already a thing of the past, and at the
period of which we are speaking the Jukun had dwindled to a
small and somewhat decadent tribe,[1] highly proficient in all
manner of occult arts, but little else, possessing an impos-
ing hierarchy of titled priest-officers: a ruling race without
subjects. Though the spiritual power and prestige of the
king was acknowledged by many people who were once his

[1] The 1931 census gives their total strength, including the Jibu and Rindre,
as just under 32,000.

dependants scattered over a wide area, his temporal kingdom was little more than the town of Wukari itself and a few outlying villages.

Afterwards some sections of the Tiv, who wanted one of the new chiefs, but who, according to Akiga, were afraid to make the hazardous journey to Wukari, conceived the idea of applying to the headman of the old village of Katsina Ala, a small settlement of the Abakwariga. These Abakwariga are a tribal remnant, now consisting of a few hundred members only. They have long lived in close association with the Jukun, and the village head of Katsina Ala was nominally a vassal of the King of Wukari. Others applied to the Utur (Turu), another tiny tribe of fishing folk living on the banks of the Katsina River, who were probably isolated by the Tiv invasion from kindred peoples further to the south. Even if some of the Tiv ever acknowledged the political sovereignty of the Jukun, they can certainly never have been under the control of either of these two insignificant remnants of tribes, and it must therefore be supposed that in each case the act of applying to them for the appointment of a chief was not a gesture of submission, but a recognition of their longer residence in the district, and superiority in this particular branch of supernatural knowledge.

Akiga's account emphasizes the fact that the idea of chieftainship was not indigenous to the Tiv,[1] and that the function of the chief, in the first place, was magico-religious rather than executive. The elders having decided on a suitable person, who was usually a comparatively young man, invited him to a general meeting of the group, and told him that they wished him to accompany them to Wukari. The preparations were kept secret from the rest of the group, and even the man who had been chosen was not openly told the true purpose of the journey. He was made to understand that he was acting throughout under the authority of his seniors:

[1] The name *tor* he derives from the Hausa *toron giwa* (bull elephant), which the Tiv first acquired from stray elephant hunters and later applied to the Aku Uka, whom they called *toro Waka*, and finally to their own chiefs who were copied from him. The expression *toron giwa* is used by the Hausa as a form of address to an important person, and it is possible that the Tiv may have heard it used by Hausa hangers-on at the Aku's court. Against this it should be noted that Abraham compares the Tiv *tor* with the Bantu *tware*, thereby implying that it was known by the Tiv long before they came into contact with the Jukun (op. cit., p. 12).

HE rose up, and took the elders' loads. Even though he might not carry them on his own head he gave them to his servant or his son, so that it was he, in fact, who took them.

⁋ They took with them presents of corn, and approached the Jukun king with great humility. After he had kept them waiting a long time 'while he thought the matter over', he finally summoned his council, and asked them through his chief officer of state (*Abɔ̃ wa chiho*) what they wanted.

THEY replied, 'We have brought this man to give to you, that you may appoint him to be guardian of our land'. 'I do not refuse,' said the king, 'but have you well considered whether this man of yours has the power to guard the land of the So-and-sos?' The elders answered that they were quite certain of this. Now what the foreign king meant when he asked whether the man was strong enough was whether he held sufficient authority amongst his people, and had the power to check wrong-doing and command obedience; but what the Tiv thought that he meant by this question was whether the man had the power of *tsav*.

⁋ This was the crux of the matter. The Tiv elders did not really want a chief in the sense which the term implied amongst the Jukun or other neighbouring states. They had no intention that he should usurp their authority, but simply that he should be the instrument by which this authority would be enhanced. Such a system of indirect rule, leaving power in their hands without responsibility, had obvious advantages for the elders, and they took pains to ensure that their protégé should not lose sight of his true position as a comparatively junior member of the group, who held office only by their grace, and whose behaviour was strictly subject to their control. It was only in after years, when the young drum-chiefs had outlived their electors, and themselves attained the status of elders, that they were able to wield any real power. Then the influence which they would normally have had in view of their age was much increased by the title, insignia, and esoteric rites, which attached to the office of *tor*, and being men chosen in the first place for the strength of their *tsav*, or, as we should say, personality, they contrived not only to rule their own groups with some show of despotism, but to extend their authority even over the neighbouring clans. There were several outstanding men of this kind living at about the time when the Europeans came into the country, and their names are still spoken with bated breath. Such men were Cia of Mbagen, Kibo of Mbakor, Aba of Shitire, Akaa and (later) Abul Abaŋga of Ukan. But all these inspired respect or fear in their clansmen by the sheer force of their own will-power, or reputation for *tsav*, which means much the same thing. Authority rested in the individual, not in the title. The British Administration was quite wrong, as events proved, in supposing that even the thirty-four separate clans, into which the tribe was somewhat arbitrarily divided, would each recognize a single leader for their component groups, far less a paramount chief for the whole tribe, as was later proposed.

However, the white man demanded the election of clan chiefs, or 'district heads', as they were called after the pattern of the northern emirates, and chiefs were elected. It was quite in accordance with precedent that the elders should appoint a younger man of no especial standing to carry out the administrative duties required by the white man, and not one of the men who wielded the real authority, that is to say, a senior elder, who was master of the *Poor* and other great *akombo*, and had all the power of supernatural sanction behind him. This fundamental difference in conception of the nature of chieftainship caused much misunderstanding between the Tiv and the British Administration. The men who were put forward by the elders to be the 'white man's chief' (*tor u Butel*) often were not backed by the consent even of their own group, far less of the clan over which they were supposed to rule. In consequence, they either completely failed to fulfil the function for which they were appointed by the Administration, being mere puppets in the hands of their seniors, as indeed the latter intended them to be, or else they used the power given them by us for their own ends, and defied the authority of their natural leaders, bringing down much odium upon themselves and the new régime. As Downes says, 'We cannot escape our share of the responsibility for the position as it exists now, and it is, to a large extent, our fault that the Tiv

authorities have remained in the background. We have seen that
many of the real authorities are not capable of carrying out the
duties of village head, supervising the census, collecting the taxes
in the way we would like to see it done. We have not liked their
arrogant claims to supernatural powers and we have ignored them,
and they, not understanding, have preferred to be ignored and
have elected a man of no importance to be the "or kohor kpandegh"
(tax collector) and to take the kicks of a District Head who, in
many cases, they consider to be inferior to them in position'.[1]

To return to Akiga's account of the appointment of the drum-
chiefs. The King of Wukari, having ascertained that the Tiv
elders were satisfied with their candidate, gave them the
insignia of office, which consisted of a cap and a cloak,[2] and they
then returned to their own country for the ceremonial investiture.

THEY told the chief elect to brew beer. When it was
ready he tied a piece of raffia round the neck of the
pot,[3] and took it to give the senior elder of his group. He
also took with him a 'twenty'. When the sun rose in the
heavens, the people of his group came in to the beer-
feast, and those in his village began the dance. (All the
time that the beer was fermenting, he never appeared in
the open, because he had become a male elephant, and
might be speared.) The day wore on, and the drumming
for the dance grew more furious, while the old men sat
drinking; for in the old days beer was only drunk by the
elders. When evening was come the chief elder stood up
and ordered all the people to sit down on the ground.
Then amidst dead silence, in which not a cough was
heard, he addressed them as follows: 'O my kinsmen,
people of So-and-so, know that we are not met here
without purpose; a matter of great moment has brought us
together. When I saw that the land was becoming spoilt,
I arose and said, "It is better that I should go out into the
bush and die". And when I set forth, the son of So-and-so
rose up also and followed me; and we said, "Let us go into

---

[1] Op. cit., p. 33.
[2] This applied also in the case of the Katsina Ala and Utur appointments,
though the details varied in each case. A full description is given in the original.
[3] One of the emblems of the *Igbe*, tied round the pot to prevent any one
putting a spell on the beer.

that other land, and pass into silence". For all the elders of our people are dead, leaving only me, who am a man of no worth. No one heeds my warnings. The people are dying, as though none will be left. The crops have failed. So in my despair I said, "Let me perish in the wilderness, and leave you to live your lives as you will". But when we came thither, and I had spoken to the king of the foreigners on this wise, he questioned me concerning the young man who was with me, and asked whether, if he were to appoint him to the work, he would be able to do it, with me to support him. I replied that the lad had indeed a stout heart.' (He would be referred to in this way, even though he were quite senior.) 'So after he had called together his own chief men and taken counsel with them, he gave me these things and told me to summon you, the elders who still are left, and speak to you of the matter, and, if you agree, to give them to him, that he may take care of the land and become the chief of all our kindred. So, now that you have heard, give me your answer.'

❡ This speech was received with general acclamation; the chief was clothed in the insignia brought from Wukari and carried round the village on a bed of raffia fronds, while the people sang one of the songs reserved for these occasions. The night was spent in feasting and dancing; but the chief himself took no part in the festivities, 'for a beast of prey lies hidden'.[1]

THE next morning the elders all came to the chief, and all those who had stayed there through the night also assembled. The chief slaughtered for the elders a cow, which, in accordance with the custom of former days, was left to swell for some time before it was cut up. Then they all went and sat down, and, having dressed the *Swem*, spoke thus: 'We appoint So-and-so chief with one mind. May no harm come to him, not even a headache. May he live to set right our land, and to take care of the fatherless, that the women may bear children, the hunting be good,

[1] A period of seclusion imposed on kings at the time of their investiture is a Jukun custom, though not, according to Meek (*A Sudanese Kingdom*, p. 135), actually practised at Wukari.

B b

and the crops flourish.' While they were saying this, the elders all placed their hands together on the *Swem*, then took it and placed it on the ground at the foot of a fig-tree in the middle of the village, and planted *iyandegh* shoots there. After this they took some water in a drinking-cup and washed the evil from their hearts, that the earth might be refreshed,[1] their land prosper, and the people take [even] snakes in their hand [without harm]. Then they rose and cut up their cow. When this was done they went to the chief and said, 'You have given us the day-feast; there remains that of the night. This is where we shall finally learn what sort of a man you are'. Thereupon they broke off a number of grass-stalks and gave them to the chief to indicate the number of persons whom he must kill for them as the price of his chiefdom.[2] After this they departed to their homes. During the days which followed, when people started to die in the group over which he had been made chief, every one said, 'So-and-so is killing the men required for his chieftainship'. But however many victims he provided, they did not consider that he had done enough until he had killed his own favourite son for them to eat; only then, they said, would their hearts be content, and they would respect and obey him. Sometimes a chief actually gave permission for his group to kill the child, but sometimes he refused, saying that, if this were the case, he would rather that men should not fear him.

℘. Here follows an account of the election of the sub-chiefs (*ati a tor*), the great *abɔ*, the lesser *abɔ*, and the *kinda*. This took place a few days later in the chief's village, and was celebrated with more feasting and beer-drinking. The arrival of the chief was announced by the blowing of a wooden trumpet and the beating of cone-shaped drums (hence the title 'drum-chief'). The chief was not allowed to sit down until a specially appointed official had 'set him down', which meant the payment of a 'twenty'.

[1] Footnote on p. 298.
[2] *Nuŋgwa tor :* i.e. a kind of election banquet, though the victims were not all supposed to be killed at the same time. Cf. *nuŋgwa kwase*, to slaughter (a cow or other beast) for the wedding feast given to the bridegroom's group. The corresponding term used in the *akombo* rites is *nambe*, see p. 208.

A bed was then set for him, on which was spread a leopard's pelt.

All the titles of the lesser officials and the ceremonial details are copied straight from the court of Wukari. The divine king is not allowed to touch the ground with his bare feet, as this would damage the crops. The leopard is a royal animal amongst the Jukun, and other neighbouring tribes who have chiefs. The idea of choosing a comparatively young man as chief is also probably derived from the same source. The Jukun king held office only so long as his health and bodily strength remained, and was in any case ceremonially killed at the end of seven years. The object of this was in order that the divine essence of kingship should not become damaged by residing in a weak vessel, but it is doubtful whether the Tiv understood the significance of this rule. However, the practice of electing a young man, who would normally have little influence, suited the elders very well, for reasons already indicated, while the high-sounding titles and elaborate pomp and paraphernalia appealed to the impressionable minds of the rest of the tribe.

But the Tiv introduced a more sinister element into their own version of the chieftainship, by grafting on to it a principle which was already associated with the existing gerontocratic system. This principle was, namely, that an elder could not attain to the highest office in his group, that is, become master of the *Poor*, except by killing a number of his own kinsmen. Their death was encompassed by *tsav*, and so was itself a sign of strong personal power. Now, as already emphasized, the killing of human victims was not in itself anti-social. In origin it was beneficial and necessary to 'set right the land'. Although Akiga's description of the *Poor* may give the impression that people were killed mainly in order to satisfy the ambition of an elder who wished to be initiated, in another place he emphasizes the fact that in former times a man who had *tsav* strong enough to kill only used it, when absolutely necessary, for the good of the community, and then provided a victim from his own family.

The inference that killing meant power was a perverted corollary of a salutary principle. If only the strong could kill, then, conversely, it was necessary to kill in order to become strong. Thus it came to be believed that a certain number of deaths, brought about by witchcraft, were a necessary condition of election to any important office. Even after the office had been attained, the holder, in order to maintain his influence and reputation for *tsav*, had from time to time to provide victims from among his near relatives, who were supposed to be ceremonially eaten by himself and his confrères. The effect of the new cult is aptly summed up by Mr. Dewar: 'To the Jukuns this spurious title (*tor-agbande*), with its sensational trappings, was simply a device for raising much-needed funds, but to the Tiv it was the central feature of a cult of incalculable potency. Moreover, by legitimizing, as it were, the use of destructive magic as an aid to constitutional authority, it introduced a foreign principle into Tiv politics. Hitherto all legitimate authority had been based on consent; not merely the remote and often fictitious consent on which many so-called democratic governments in practice rest, but a real and living consent continually ratified by the uncompelled obedience of the whole community. Into this, from the isolated point of view of political theory, Arcadian system the *tor-agbande* cult introduced something of the spirit of Hobbes's Leviathan.'[1]

As *tsav* is a force of neutral quality, the use of destructive magic means, strictly speaking, the use of *tsav* for destructive purposes. Although the killing of human victims in connexion with the *Poor* and other rites was originally recognized as a measure necessary to the public welfare, killing purely for the sake of enhancing personal power, as believed to be practised by the drum-chiefs, was an anti-social act, contrary to the wishes of the people as a whole. In consequence, the popularity of the new experiment was short-lived. The bad features which it contained, and the despotic leanings exhibited by the chiefs as soon as they were able to shake off the control of the elders, soon proved distasteful to the independent temperament of the people. The cult fell into disfavour, and had practically died out by the time of the British occupation. But its effects are still apparent; for the *tor-agbande* cult, with its anti-social practices and supposed abuse of supernatural power, was one of the factors which eventually brought about the rebellion against the authority of the elders. From this time the resentment of the younger section of the tribe against them gradually increased, till, becoming more articulate under the British régime, it culminated in an outburst of public feeling in 1929.

[1] Report cit., p. 9.

THE ADMINISTRATION OF JUSTICE BY THE DRUM-CHIEF AND ELDERS

Example 1: *A Case of Witchcraft.* In former times the chief did not try cases, but only gave the final decision. When occasion arose, the chief brewed beer, and all the elders of the district assembled in his village on the day that it was ready for drinking. He served out the beer to them, and, when they had all drunk, one of their number, who had the chief in his charge and looked after him, stood up and commanded silence. When all were quiet, he asked the chief, 'Chief So-and-so, have you invited us here to drink beer merely to quench our thirst, because you wish to show the hospitality which befits your position, or have you some other cause?'

THE CHIEF: Yes, it is as you say. But there is another reason beside. I have called you here to tell you about a bad dream, which came to me whilst I slept. I wish you to share it with me.

❡ Prompted by the others, the elder who put the first question then induced the chief to speak a little more plainly:

IT might be that a monkey was spoiling the crops, or the birds were eating the millet more than usual, and the chief, having resorted to divination and learnt who was the culprit, had called them in to tell them about it. However, he did not mention the man by name there in the public meeting-place, but alluded to the incident in general terms. If the matter was not at all clear to some of the elders, the chief, and the others who understood, drew them on one side and explained it to them. When all the elders had heard about it, they said, 'This matter is urgent. To-morrow without fail we must meet at the *Ilyum*'. (The *Ilyum* was the council at which the elders met to set right the land; but the word originally meant the big stone which was placed at the boundary between two main divisions. When occasion arose, the elders of both sections would meet at the *Ilyum* for discussion.)[1]

So on the next day all the elders assembled at the

[1] Cf. p. 195.

Ilyum, and then the matter was no longer kept secret.
They revealed the name of the witch to whom the
monkey, or the birds, belonged, and told the head of his
group, 'It is So-and-so amongst your people who is
spoiling the land'. In former times,[1] when the elders met
for some purpose, it was not the custom for all to give
their opinions; there was only one man to whom the
people and the chief listened. But when the matter was
concluded, his words were taken to express the general
view of the council.

Here is an example of the procedure:

The Chief	Akaanya
The Spokesman	Mjila
The Elder in whose group the witch is	Sabe
The Witch who is spoiling the land ..	Afena

CHIEF AKAANYA: It was you, O elders, who once met
together and said, in jest, that you would give the land
into my charge. I have therefore called you here to say,
if you have found that I am not worthy of this trust, then
take it back and give it to whomsoever you deem fit. For it
is no longer in my hands.

MJILA: Chief Akaanya, this is foolish talk. Did we not
appoint you with one mind? Any one who trifles with us
shall lose his head! Is it not so, you elders?

ALL THE ELDERS: It is indeed as you say, Mjila.

CHIEF AKAANYA: Well, as Sabe has assumed control of
the land, I thought that you must have all decided to
depose me and give it to him.

MJILA: Is this true, Sabe? I, at least, knew nothing
about it, and have been denying it as openly as the
sunshine on the goat's rump. Perhaps some of you
other elders know of this, and I am speaking in ignorance?

THE ELDERS: Mjila, who in this country would dare to
do anything without your knowledge?

CHIEF AKAANYA: At least, when the land was mine, I
cared for the crops of my people, but ever since Sabe took

---

[1] And to the present day.

it into his own hands, the crops have been eaten by birds and monkeys.

MJILA: Speak, Sabe. The chief keeps on returning to this theme, and the matter can only be settled by discussion.

SABE: After we had talked it over yesterday I went home and pointed the accusing feathers[1] at this young man [Afena]. He made as though he would deny it, but could not, and his contradictory statements proved him guilty. So I told him that we were meeting here to-day, and that he was to come too.

THE ELDERS: Sabe, you have well said. You then, Afena, do you know about this monkey and these birds?

AFENA: Yes, I do.

THE ELDERS: What induced you to commit such an act? How did you get them?

AFENA: I bought them from one of the Mbaiyeŋge.

ONE OF THE ELDERS: You evil-looking scoundrel, with chest stuffed full of *tsav* for spoiling the land, I should like to draw my sword and put an end to you here and now! Look at the wretch sitting there with his foul grey skin!

MJILA: Steady, So-and-so. Cases of witchcraft need careful handling, if they are to be settled satisfactorily. Spare his life and reason with him, for he is a free man. Do not be content to recompense evil by evil. Let him pay the fine of a female animal, and we will consider what warning to give him.

AFENA: Take this she-goat, then.

ONE OF THE ELDERS: Is witchcraft to be punished by a fine, as though it were a case of stealing?

MJILA: No, we will eat the comb first, before coming to the honey.[2] He is now to pay a day-fine; but if he does not stop at once he shall pay a fine of the night,[3] for his crime is a very serious one.

---

[1] Trials by ordeal were sometimes held without the suspected parties being present. The poison was administered to chickens, each one being given the name of one of the people who was on trial. When one of the chickens succumbed, its feathers were taken to the man whom it represented, as evidence that he had been proved guilty by the ordeal. The expression, however, can also be used metaphorically, as, probably, in the present case.

[2] I.e. this is only a caution for a first offence.

[3] =Provide a human victim.

THE ELDERS: Finish off the case, Chief, and let him go. It is getting late.

CHIEF AKAANYA: Since you have made me chief, it is my intent to keep the land safe from harm. You, Afena, let this matter go no further. Let the monkey feed on the fruit of the wild plum, and the birds on grass seeds, as is their nature. If you do not stop your evil practices, we shall cut your throat here at the *Ilyum*, as we are doing to this she-goat of yours.

Thereupon they slaughtered the goat and poured the blood over the *Ilyum*. They divided up the meat amongst the elders and the chief, after which they returned to their homes. In the old days the elders and their chief were of one mind.

❡ The allusive language and indirect approach are typical of the counsels of the old men, especially when dealing with a ticklish problem, such as a case of witchcraft. The above, indeed, is a very condensed example of the devious paths which the discussions would normally take, and which are so extremely difficult for the European mind to follow. The object of the conversations is not to determine the facts of the case, which are already well known to all present, but to shift the responsibility from the leaders of the people to the individual culprit. Until this is done the chief is held responsible for the appearance of the pests which are damaging the common food supply. He therefore accuses the head of the witch's group, who in turn becomes responsible until he has officially exposed the criminal, who was, of course, known from the beginning.

In the present case there are really two separate counts, both included in the general charge of practising witchcraft to the public harm: (i) turning into a monkey; (ii) sending birds. The fact that the witch is actually accused of becoming the monkey himself is shown (*a*) by the use of the singular, and (*b*) by the reference of the elder to the grey colour (*puŋŋ*) of his skin. A man who wishes to change his form cannot rub camwood on his body, like a decent member of society, as this would prevent him from regaining his human shape. This is one way of detecting a witch. The 'change' is said to be effected with the aid of a monkey's skin and skull which the changer, or were-monkey, puts on himself.

Several magic articles of this kind were surrendered during the *Haakaa*. The sending of birds is a different branch of the Black Art. It is done by stripping the leaves from a *gbagbongom*-tree and blowing them towards the crops which you wish to harm, uttering an appropriate spell. In both cases the power to do this has to be 'bought' in the same way as the use of drugs and the practice of medicine (see p. 209). That is, the intending witch goes to some one who shows him what to do, and pays him the fee without which the knowledge would be useless. This also pays for the use of the charm, which plays a necessary part in the performance. He is not, however, usually given the actual charm, but only the formula for making it.

Example 2: Theft. In former days men did not wilfully deny their guilt as they do nowadays. Moreover, theft was not common, and was regarded as a very shameful thing amongst the Tiv. The worst type of theft was that of farm produce, and the most heinous crime of all was to steal yam seed. A man who stole seed or guinea-corn was a social outcast. Theft of a beast, or of brass currency, was not considered so serious, though the thief would not dare to raise his head again amongst his age-mates. I have already referred to cattle-stealing in the section on Tiv customs. In the case of a goat or a sheep, if the thief were discovered, the owner of the beast would go and ask him to give it back to him. If he adopted a threatening attitude, the owner went to one of the thief's kinsmen, and said to him, 'So-and-so has taken my sheep. I traced it to his house, but when I asked him to return it he said he would fight me to the death. So I have come to ask you to get it back for me. If it is a question of a debt, let him tell me and I will pay him'.[1] The thief's kinsman called his brother and asked him if it were true that he had taken the sheep. When he admitted it, he told him to give it back.

THE THIEF: I have not got it; I have sold it.

HIS KINSMAN: Then bring the money which you got for it.

THE THIEF: I have spent it all.

HIS KINSMAN: Well, So-and-so, you will have to go to

---

[1] This is only a polite figure of speech, to avoid a direct accusation.

the chief. The land is his, and he will know what to say about it.

So the man whose sheep had been stolen went and knelt before the chief, throwing dust over his shoulders. The chief acknowledged his greetings in the foreign fashion,[1] and asked him what was the matter. Having heard his complaint, he sent a man to call the thief and his kinsman. . . .

❡ The charge having been corroborated, the chief pronounces the following sentence:

'YOU will provide two sheep in compensation for the one which you stole, and in addition pay a fine of one she-goat. On the tenth day of next month I want to see you here with all these beasts. You, the owner of the sheep, come back as well, and I will also call in the elders.'

❡ The council meets on the appointed day, and the elders, having confirmed the judgement of the chief, kill the goat paid as a fine and divide the meat between them. The complainant takes one of the sheep in return for the one he lost, and the chief takes the other, unless the complainant pays him his due of a 'twenty', in which case the chief allows him to take both.

Here follows a digression, in which the author explains that another fruitful source of income for the chiefs was a levy on other aspirants to the chieftainship, who had to pass through their territory on the way to Wukari. It was at this time that the head of old Katsina Ala village, seeing a chance of diverting some of the revenue of Wukari into his own pocket, persuaded the Tiv clans who lived round about him to save trouble and expense by coming to him to get the insignia. This brought a strong protest from the Aku Uka. The chief of Katsina Ala, being faced with an awkward situation, then invented a rule that, although he was still prepared, for a consideration, to dispense chieftainships to any who needed them, the office would not inspire the maximum terror (*ihindi*) unless the candidate afterwards had his appointment ratified at Wukari. By this happy compromise he avoided a

[1] P. 383 below.

break with his titular suzerain, without serious damage to his own interests.

Reflexions on the difficulty of travelling to Wukari owing to the unsettled conditions lead to the next section:

DEBT AND SLAVERY

AT that time the Tiv were in a constant state of war with each other. The small man could not travel about openly, and there were no roads. A man who wished to visit another clan might have to make a wide circuit, spending five nights on the way, where, by the direct route, he need only have spent one. If he were so foolish as to travel in broad daylight, he would soon find himself in slavery. He would be caught by some one, and sold for a price in a distant market.

A question of debt was not to be settled by sitting down and talking it over. The only way was to capture a hostage. Here is an example:

Ibo has contracted a debt with Adagu. Adagu is a man of Ukan, Ibo of Ipav. The debt is a cow, or it may be only a goat. Adagu has been to demand a settlement, but Ibo has not paid him.

ADAGU: Very well, I shall take steps myself to obtain repayment of this debt.

Adagu returns home, and some time later Ɗgibo, son of Dam, from Igɔrov,[1] sets out to visit his brother-in-law in Kunav. On his way he stops at Adagu's home. Adagu fills a pipe for him, and when he has finished smoking asks him to which clan he belongs.

ƊGIBO: I am of Ipav, and my father is Dam of Igɔrov.

ADAGU: Do you know Ibo?

ƊGIBO: Ibo, the son of Orga? Yes, but he is of the Mbakpegh.

ADAGU: That's all right, so long as you know him.

Adagu then gets up and gives secret instructions to his brothers, who sling their quivers over their shoulders and go and wait on the road by which Ɗgibo must pass on his way to Kunav. Adagu goes back and sits down, and engages Ɗgibo in friendly conversation. When he gets

---

[1] A sub-division of Ipav.

up to go, Adagu says he will escort him along the road.
So they start off together. But when they reach the place
where his brothers are in hiding, Adagu makes the first
move. 'So the meat has walked straight into my mouth!'
he says.

ÐGIBO: What do you mean?

ADAGU: What a stupid question! What is the difference
between Igɔr and Kpegh? Aren't they both Ipav? I have
got you now; the blind man has caught a locust against his
chest.[1] Back we go, and into the stocks with you!

ÐGIBO: Stop talking nonsense, Adagu.

ADAGU: Nonsense, is it?

He seizes Ðgibo by the arm, and when they start to
struggle his brothers come out of their hiding-place, and
set upon Ðgibo. They tie him up tight and take him into
the village, where he is pinned into the stocks and thrown
down on the floor of Adagu's *ate*. Adagu goes at once to
the chief of Ukan, taking with him a 'twenty', and tells
him the whole story. 'You are quite right', says the chief.
'We are not slaves of Ipav, and they had better stop this
nonsense. If they don't pay a ransom, sell him!' Adagu
goes back and guards his hostage. Ibo may hear of it, but
if he is unable to find a cow with which to ransom Ðgibo,
Adagu will keep his prisoner for a long time in the stocks,
and then take him out and sell him in some remote district. Ðgibo, son of Dam, has become a slave.

This was the origin of slavery. There was no hereditary
distinction between bond and free; men were born free
and afterwards became slaves.

Sometimes, even if there were no question of a debt,
a number of warriors from one clan would lie in wait for
some members of another clan who were passing through
their territory and attack them without any provocation at
all, killing some and capturing others. For instance, if a
man wished to be initiated to the *Biamegh*, but had no
money to pay for the presents, he would lay an ambush by
a road that was much used by travellers. If he saw a strong
party of strangers he remained hidden, but if they were
small men, accompanied by women, he fell on them,

---

[1] I.e. this is a windfall.

seized them, and sold them to buy the presents for the *Biamegh*, so that he could be initiated and boast amongst his age-mates.

My father, Sai, was once nearly killed by the foreigners over an affair of this kind. He used to say that he did not make his money out of cotton, but by catching and selling slaves. He did not know how to spin or weave; men were his stock-in-trade. It was the Hausa who suffered most at his hands. But another source of his wealth was black-smithing. A foreign chief would give a slave for one of his spears. (I can bear witness to the truth of this: I saw him once forge a spear for Garbushi, chief of Takum, who gave him in exchange a female slave, called Nyandi. I was a child at the time, and we were living by the Atu stream, where the Mbaaputor of Ukum are now.)

At the time, then, that my father was seeking initiation to the *Biamegh*, he found himself short of funds. So he set out with his friend Gba of Mbaityula, and they went about together, making attacks on foreign traders. One day they lay in wait by the side of the great road from Wukari to Takum, which used to be called the Kola Road, on account of the number of foreigners who passed along it on their way to buy kola-nuts. There was a place where the travellers used to rest, just at the spot where the Dutch Mission afterwards built their first station in Tiv country. Here they crouched in the grass, in the shadow of an *iyiase*-tree, waiting to catch the foreigners. Presently four travellers approached, and set down their loads. They had bows and arrows, but had tied them on to their bundles. So my father and Gba rushed out, and my father struck one of the foreigners on the leg with a club, threw him down, and tied him up. Gba seized another and pinned him to the ground, but as he was about to bind him a third hit him on the head with a club, and knocked him over. My father was left alone, and gave himself up for lost. However, he had secured one, and the others fled. He chased after them and caught the man who had been rescued from Gba. He also caught a woman, so that only one man escaped. When he returned to the spot he found that Gba had recovered consciousness, and gave him the man whom he had caught before he was struck down,[1] keeping two for himself. My elder brothers acquired a large number of slaves that were caught by my father.

How can I tell of all the heroes of old? Such men as Gire of Diiv and Ge of Adudu in Mbaigen, warriors of the Farm Ishaŋgev, whose names were used by the Dam as a warning to their children!

THE *KUR*, A WAR-CHIEF

The Tiv used to have another kind of chief, known as *kur*, who was of a different type from the *tor-agbande*. The name is derived from the Chamba word for chief, *kuru*, which corresponds to the Jukun *aku*.[2] The Tiv received the title of *kur* from Takum and Donga, in the same way that they got the drum-chieftainship from Wukari, from the Abakwariga and from the Utur. The kind of man suitable for election to the office of *kur* was a brave warrior who had a following of good fighting men.

When a man was in a position to become *kur*, he approached all the elders of the district with presents, and also the chief,[3] to whom he gave a cow. Then he took a slave or a cow (if he were a man of moderate wealth), and set off for the land of the foreigners, either Takum or Donga, escorted by some of the elders. On their arrival, the elders showed him to the foreign chief, who gave them a cap, or a straw-hat, to put on his head, also a white gown and some broad-bladed spears, or a sword to use in battle. These were the insignia of the *kur*. If a chief[3] died he would be succeeded by the great *abɔ̃*, or, if the great *abɔ̃* were not powerful enough, by the lesser *abɔ̃*: but a *kur* never succeeded to the office of chief, because the *kur* was himself a chief, and had sub-chiefs under him. The sub-chiefs of the *kur* were called *irmo* (*yerima* in Hausa), and *gagum*.

---

[1] According to the hunter's rule that the quarry belongs to the man who first hits it.

[2] It is the same word; i.e. not Chamba, but Jukun, as spoken by the people of Donga and other towns of Chamba origin.

[3] I.e. *tor-agbande*.

SALUTATIONS AND BEHAVIOUR IN THE PRESENCE OF CHIEFS

The form of salutation for a chief was different from that for a *kur*. When greeting a chief the Tiv used to kneel on the ground and throw dust over their backs, in exactly the same way as the people of Wukari approach their king, the Aku Uka. But the *kur* was saluted by a clapping of hands, after the fashion which they had seen practised by the Chamba at Donga and Takum. These were the first forms of salutation that the Tiv saw amongst the foreigners; but later they learnt the word *Zaki*[1] from the Hausa who began gradually to travel amongst them, and from the fighting men of Dankoro,[2] and used it as a form of address to the *kur* and other chiefs. The Tiv still greet a chief in this manner.

In former times, when the Tiv came before the chief, they all sat on the ground, and no one sat on a seat except the chief himself. The chief's seat was called *kwav* or *dogo*, and consisted of a couch about three feet high, made of raffia, with a small stool attached to the side, on which the chief could step when he mounted on to the *kwav*. But all this display of deference was not much known outside Shitire, Ukum, Nongov, and a few other clans, who had learnt it from the foreigners. Kparev knew little of these things, and paid scant respect to a chief, unless he were a man of very strong character, in which case they feared him on this account. Sometimes when the chief was seated on his throne they would say to him, 'Move along a bit, Zaki So-and-so, and let me sit down!' And if they greeted him they did so standing up. To the sub-chiefs they paid even less regard. They called them chiefs by name, but certainly never treated them as such.

THE WHITE MAN'S CHIEF

The system of obtaining chieftainships described above continued until the coming of the British. When the white man first appeared, the Tiv did not understand his

[1] Hausa: 'Lion'.
[2] A notorious Hausa warrior and adventurer who attained some influence amongst the Tiv and Jukun at the end of the last century.

ways and did not like his idea of chieftainship. Some who
were appointed by him refused on the ground that there
was no honour in being a white man's chief. People paid
no heed to the men who were first given the post. 'What
sort of chief is this,' they asked, 'who goes round to this
place and that, trying cases in the heat of the day?' They
made all kinds of derogatory remarks about the white
man's chief, with many jokes and insults.

Nevertheless, it was they who had the power. A drum-
chief would be sued for debt, and the white man's chief
would send an underling to pass judgement on him. But
even so the Tiv did not take much notice. A man who
was sent out by the chiefs to try cases they called the 'head
soldier'.... The 'soldiers' were the agents whom the chiefs
sent to call in the witnesses in any case which might
occur; for the Tiv knew nothing of policemen[1] at that
time. But the man who was actually put in charge of the
district by the white man they called the 'black European'.
Some of these 'black Europeans' had formerly been drum-
chiefs and were given extra powers by the white man to
administer the land; others, though not chiefs, were men
of some standing, whom he appointed after ascertaining
that they were suitable for the post. Nevertheless, they
did few of the duties given them by the white man; all they
did was to sit down and extort money from the people. It
was the 'head soldiers' who went round doing the work,
and it was they who had access to the white man. But
even these did not always obtain audience with the
European in person, but only got as far as his foreign
subordinates.[2] Having spoken with them, he then went to
his clan with imaginary instructions, which he said came
from the white man, that the people should fear to disobey. When the white man first came, these 'head
soldiers' had more influence than the 'staff-chiefs'.[3]

[1] Dogarai.
[2] The Hausa-speaking political agents; see below.
[3] This is not a recognized term, but an exact translation of the Tiv (tor-tɔ).
Those who hold staffs of office under the British Government are independent
or paramount chiefs, who owe allegiance to no one except the King of England.
In Nigeria these are divided into five grades, and those in the fifth class may
be very small chiefs with only a few hundred subjects. The Tiv chiefs were in
this class, and though they had comparatively large districts they had very

After a time the white man started to give out staffs of office. He included the whole of one clan under the jurisdiction of one man. To this man he gave a staff, and said that all his group must fear and obey him. He also set court members[1] over each of the sections of his group, who should sit in council with the chief. But the chief who held the staff of office was to be the head, in the same way that the Governor was the head of all the white men. When the Tiv heard this, at first they called all the council members chiefs, and the man who had been given the staff they called the *'gomna'*. And as if this were not enough, they added the title *Zaki*, and called him *Zaki Gomna*. (One day the District Officer resident at Katsina Ala, whom they used to call Dantsofo, went into Ukum, and Afegha, the first staff-chief of Ukum, sent his policeman to wait for him on the road. On meeting Dantsofo the policeman greeted him and said, 'The great Governor has sent me to meet you!' Dantsofo told Gbandepev, his interpreter, to ask him what he said. The policeman repeated it. Dantsofo asked, 'What Governor?' 'Governor Afegha', said the policeman. This so annoyed Dantsofo that he ordered that the policeman should be put down on the ground and given twelve strokes with the whip. When he got up again, he told him never again to refer to any Tiv as the Governor. A Governor was a big thing, not to be treated lightly. He then issued an order to this effect to all Tiv, and from that time they were afraid to use the term before the white man, though they still did so in secret.)

The white man, having appointed staff-chiefs and council members for all the Tiv clans, then gave them policemen. This was the beginning of the Tiv's troubles. After that it was not only staff-chiefs who beat the people and seized their possessions by force, but also council members, policemen, and messengers. Their greatest aim in life, then as now, was to acquire women. As soon

little authority over them. At the time they were actually known as 'district heads', but this term, in Northern Nigeria, is more usually applied to those who receive their appointments from a higher Native Authority.

[1] *Mbaajiriv*. Or 'council' members. There is no distinction between administrative and judicial functions: the council is the same as the court.

C C

as they obtained posts under the European, this was the object on which they first set their hearts; the work for which they had been appointed held little interest for them.

ACQUISITION OF WIVES BY THE CHIEFS

There were many ways by which the staff-chief used to get women. If his agents saw a particularly good-looking girl of a suitable age they went back and told him, 'So-and-so of such-and-such a group has a very pretty daughter. She is too good for an ordinary man, and ought to be the wife of a chief'. Then, if she were in the chief's clan, the matter was as good as settled. The woman was already his, and nothing could prevent him from taking her. He sent out to have her brought in, and she became a chief's wife.

Sometimes a man would bring a complaint to the chief against some one who had taken his *iŋɔl* without giving compensation. The chief sent policemen to bring in the girl and the man who had married her. He put the husband in fetters, and the woman into a house in his own village. The owner he told to go home, and said he would find some money for him; but later, when he came back to get it, he drove him away. Thus the man lost his *iŋɔl*, and the chief got her for nothing. If he were exceptionally bold and took his complaint to the European, the white man would send him back to the chief with a policeman or messenger and tell this official to find out from the chief what were the facts of the case. The chief said that the whole thing was a pack of lies, and this was confirmed by all the court members. The chief was shown to be in the right, and the complainant was convicted of lying. Sometimes he would be punished. At other times the chief would say that, although he had brought a false accusation against him, he would forgive him; but that if ever he did such a thing again he would tell the white man, who would put him in prison, and this would be the end of him. By this means some chiefs got as many as five or ten wives without giving anything in return.

Perhaps the case was one of long standing, and the

iŋɔl had already borne many sons and daughters to the defendant. Her owner, having decided, after unsuccessful attempts to get satisfaction from his brother-in-law, that it would be better for the chief to have the advantage, laid his complaint before him (not omitting to bring some money to support his claim). In this case the chief took the best looking of the daughters for himself and returned the *iŋɔl*, with the rest of her children, to her original owner.

If a case of debt were brought before the chief, he would send a policeman to seize the debtor. If the man had no money, he might offer to pawn his *iŋɔl* to the chief, on the understanding that the chief should pay the creditor, and that he himself should redeem his *iŋɔl* as soon as he had found the money. The chief would agree to this, and once the girl had been given into pawn the matter ended there. The debtor would never find the money to redeem his pledge, and the chief would not pay the creditor. The girl had become his wife. If the chief were a man of exceptional integrity he might give the complainant something very small as compensation; this was all he would get, and he would not dare to object.

Another instance was where a man had paid the money for a bride-price, and the owner of the *iŋɔl* had spent it. without having handed over the woman. When the case was brought before the chief, he sent out to have the defendant arrested and brought in, together with his *iŋɔl*. The man was treated with great harshness and made to pay back the money to the chief, who gave a little to the complainant, and kept the rest, together with the woman, for himself. The woman became the wife of the chief, and the two disputants lost everything.

Moreover, if a staff-chief sought a woman in marriage she was usually willing enough to accept, however old he might be, because she thought that as the wife of a chief she would have everything she wanted. And even if the girl herself tried to refuse, her people would badger her into the marriage, because with the help of the chief behind them they would gain the advantage in any dispute which they might have with their neighbours.

These were the ways in which a chief used to acquire a large number of wives. A man who before appointment had only one wife, or perhaps two, after he had been made one of the staff-chiefs of the white man had good cause to congratulate himself. Some married forty wives, some sixty, some eighty. When the number of wives was very large, some of them got little to eat. But if one in great distress ran away home, the chief would send an order to her people to bring her back the same night. She would be very severely punished, and the other wives, seeing her fate, would remain where they were perforce, however unhappy they might be. The chief had so many wives that he could not sleep with them all. But if one of them in desperation had intercourse with some other man, and the chief heard of it, she was in great trouble. The chief tied her up and whipped her to within an inch of her life, and the rest of the wives went about in constant terror. The man was also seized by the chief and made to suffer terribly. He might ransom himself and surrender his *iŋɔl*, but the chief would not be content till he had made him atone for his offence in full. The staff-chiefs amassed huge numbers of wives, and poor men remained bachelors. Council members, policemen, and messengers all collected wives in the same way as the staff-chiefs, but the chiefs were the worst.

EXTORTION

The people used to suffer much from the extortionate practices of the staff-chiefs. If any one reared a particularly fat bull, and the chief heard of it, it was as good as his. He sent a policeman to tell the owner to catch it, and bring it to him, and also to pay the cost of the oil with which to cook it. All the best of the livestock was confiscated by the staff-chiefs for their own use. If any one wished to give a dance he had to send word to the chief, together with a payment, otherwise the chief would send his policemen on the day of the dance to break up the gathering.

Every time a court member died and the white man gave instructions for a new appointment to be made, there was money to be made by the chief, the councillors, and the policemen. There might be five candidates for office in that section, and each one would give a cow to the chief, and presents to all the court members and officials, to help him to get the post. The man who gave the most would be made section head, even though he might be a complete imbecile. All the others went away empty-handed, and their bribes were appropriated by the chief and his minions. In Tiv the fools have always had everything, and the wise nothing. Sometimes, indeed, when a fool had been stripped of a large amount of his property, the Tiv[1] allowed him to hold office for a time and then took it from him to give to a man of more sense. But usually they hesitated to appoint an able man to be the white man's chief, fearing lest he should take so firm a grip on the chieftainship that they would be unable to take it away from him again; whereas a fool they could elect without a thought, trick him out of all he possessed, and as easily depose him. They then gave the office to some one else, and did the same with him. . . .

THE POLICE

When the white man first made staff-chiefs he did not give them police; they themselves appointed young men from amongst their own followers to do the work. It was Dantsofo, a District Officer living at Katsina Ala, who first gave the Tiv policemen, and clothed them in the blue-and-white striped uniforms. The word for police-man (*dogari*) is not Tiv but Hausa. . . . At first a policeman used to inspire the Tiv with the greatest fear. They called him *Zaki Dugwer*. Even a messenger did not command so much respect. The people whom the Tiv feared most were the white man, the staff-chief, and the policeman. So once a man had secured a post in the police he could do whatever he liked.

Since the post was so much coveted by the Tiv, naturally no one was ever made policeman by a chief without paying for the appointment. If the white man wanted policemen for his own purposes he used to pick out one or

[1] I.e. the electors, not the common folk.

two young men from amongst his regular carriers, whom he knew by personal acquaintance or report to be of good character, and put them into the uniform of policemen or messengers. These he kept with him, or sent on errands concerned with the administration of the country. But if he wished to appoint a policeman for the Tiv, he spoke to the staff-chief to whom he proposed to give the policeman or messenger, telling him to find a man of intelligence, and then bring him to him to be appointed. This policeman was to be attached to the chief, and serve under him in the work of administering the country for the Government. At other times he merely handed over the uniform to the chief, telling him to appoint whomsoever he pleased, and to let him know afterwards, in order that he could enter his name on the list of salaried officials. The chief then summoned the members of his council, and asked them to help him find a suitable man.

As soon as they started to look for one, the intrigue for office had begun. When they had found a man of good character and were considering him for the post, some one else would go round to the chief with a cow, and distribute presents amongst the court members. Thereupon they all left the deserving candidate whom they had been considering, and decided to give the government post to a man who was already known to be a bad character, but had given them money. As for the other, however great might be his ability and integrity, lack of funds put government service beyond his reach. He would be dismissed with ignominy, and laughed at for his failure. The chief and his councillors took the man who had bribed them, and showed him to the European as the one whom they had chosen for his sterling qualities. The white man wrote down his name, and he was given the uniform of the police. On his return to the village, things began to happen. He laid hands on people's property, saying, 'You can't play the fool with me. I was not made policeman for nothing; it cost me a cow!' In spite of his misdeeds, however, the chief would be afraid to dismiss him, lest he should complain to the European, and tell him that he had bought his post for the price of a cow. Thus the policemen and messengers became the friends of the staff-chief. Together they ate up the land, while the people cried out in distress. . . .

Perhaps the question may be asked, Since the staff-chiefs acquired so much of other people's property in addition to the pay they got from the white man, and yet did not give much for their wives whom they usually acquired by other methods, what did they do with all this money? All the sources of wealth we have described were too few for the chief's needs. First, when a chief was appointed and had taken a very large number of wives, he would give a marriage dance at which he would feast,[1] not only his own wives, but also those of his children and relations. On one day he might give five oxen for this purpose, and kill many more for the other chiefs who had come as his guests. Many oxen would be given by him for initiation to the greater *akombo*, and here also he would include his brothers and children as well as himself. He bought horses, necklaces priced at several cows, and Hausa gowns costing many pounds. . . .

The Hausa wheedled their money from the chiefs with the greatest of ease. A Hausa trader would go to a staff-chief or section head, and show him a big gown richly embroidered with cotton. He praised this article to the skies, telling the chief that the King of Wukari, or the Sultan of Sokoto, had already made an offer of five pounds for it (or six), which he had refused; but because the Tiv chief was his particular friend, he would let him have it for the same price. The chief was delighted, and called the Hausa his friend. He killed a chicken for him, telling him that he was very pleased about what he had done for him. Since he had refused to sell the gown to the Sultan of Sokoto on purpose to give it to him, he would certainly buy it. At the moment, however, he had no money. The Hausa said that it did not matter, he would come and get it at the beginning of next month. The chief expressed his admiration for the fellow's good sense. The trader would then go away and find out the day on which the chief's salary would be paid, so that he could

[1] *Nungwa*, cf. note on p. 370.

catch him as soon as possible after he had received his money. Sometimes he could not pay it all in one month. In this way some chiefs, who had bought a number of gowns or cloths from the Hausa, had to pay out the whole of their salary to this one and that as soon as the month began, and were left penniless.

Over necklaces the Hausa swindled the Tiv in the same way. If it were a horse, they would tell the chief that this was not a poor man's beast, but a mount fit only for big chiefs. It had once belonged to the Emir of Yola, but when he died his followers sold it, because none of them could ride it; so if the Tiv chief wished to buy it, let him do so, for it was a chief's horse. Some chiefs paid ten pounds for a horse, some sixteen. It might live for two months; three months was a long life for a horse. After this the chief would buy another. Hausa were to be found in every chief's village. If they were not actually settled there, they were constant visitors.

THE POSITIONS HELD BY FOREIGNERS

The oppression which the Tiv used to suffer at the hands of the staff-chiefs was much aggravated by the foreign agents employed by the white man. For during all those first years not a single Tiv was ever given the post of interpreter or messenger under the Administration; all these posts were in the hands of foreigners. Moreover, in those days administrative officers did not learn Tiv, but only Hausa, and spoke to the people through foreign interpreters. The white man could look at the Tiv, but he could not talk to them. So the staff-chiefs made friends with these agents, and gave them money to keep them in the good graces of the European. If any one came to the white man with a complaint that he had been wronged by the chief, these officials drove him away, and he never obtained access to the European. Or even if, with exceptional daring, he penetrated to the presence of the political officer, the white man could not understand what he said, and would call his foreign interpreter, who turned the man's story into something quite different. The white man, not knowing this, would be angry with the complainant, and censure him for insubordination to his chief. When the Tiv came to realize this they suppressed their grievances, and suffered the tyrannies of the staff-chiefs in silence.

CASE TALLIES

The District Officer told the staff-chiefs to keep a tally of all the cases which they tried and settled, and to send in the tally-sticks to him by a head policeman or messenger at the end of the month, so that he could see what work they had done. When they took the tallies they were to give him an account of the proceedings, together with the names of those whose cases had been adjudicated. But here, too, they acted contrary to their instructions. They did little legal work, and those who did hear a number of cases gave no decision, or, if they did, took a larger share of the money paid over than the claimant. But when the new moon appeared they gave their messengers a large number of tallies to take to the white man, as a record of the cases which they had tried. Sometimes they sent in as many as fifty or sixty sticks.

If a man wished to institute proceedings against some one, he first gave a chicken to the policeman who was to serve the summons. Even so, the policeman did not go himself, but sent one of his *ugwana* to bring in the defendant. If there was a woman in the case, the *ugwana* did not take her to the chief at once, but gave her to the policeman, who would sleep with her. Whether she was married or not was no matter to him; no one would dare to question his action. When he felt so inclined he took her to the chief, who would hear the case. Alternatively, the policeman might pronounce judgement himself. In either event it was recorded by tally.

After a time the white man introduced a new system of tallies, by substituting money in the place of sticks.[1] Every time that the chief heard a case he was to take one shilling from the man who brought the complaint, and this would serve as a record. This was even better news for the chiefs. The fee of one shilling prescribed by the

[1] I.e. court fees.

Administration they raised to four shillings, ten shillings, or even more. From the large sums thus obtained they deducted the amounts required by the European as a tally, and kept the rest. Afterwards the white man came to know about this; because in recent years he has been making careful investigations into the conduct of the chiefs, and trying to find out what they are doing. So he gave them scribes.

THE COURT SCRIBES

The court scribes were Tiv youths who were given to the staff-chiefs by the white man, to help them in their work. The scribe was to be attached to the chief, and each month, when the council met to try court cases, he was to write down the proceedings. On no account was he to have any voice in the hearing of the cases; this was not his work. He was to keep silent till the chief and his councillors had concluded their discussions, and then write down whatever verdict they dictated to him. That was what the white man said. But this was not what they did. As soon as the scribes were appointed they assumed great importance. One would say to the chief, 'I know everything about writing. If you try any tricks with me, I shall write a letter to the white man, and he will depose you at once'. So the chief, and his council members, and all the white man's officials who were with the chief, were afraid of him. When a case was heard he would say that they had not tried it properly, and he was not going to record it. He gave his own version of how it should have been conducted, saying that that was what he was going to write, and the chief and his council agreed. Sometimes, if they did not judge the case to his liking, he upbraided the court members and threatened to beat them; but they cringed before him, saying that he was the European's own man, who knew all about writing, and even spoke the white man's language. If any one stood up to him, they said, he would write to the white man, who would put him in prison. So he was able to do just as he liked. He began to look round for women, and even though he had no money the chief would find him a wife, or else he would take one for nothing, and the owner of the *iŋɔl* would be afraid to take action against the white man's scribe. Sometimes he would not deign to speak to a Tiv in his own language, but only in English. One would have an interpreter, just like a European. Another would say that he did not eat corn, but only pounded yam, and if he had no yams the chief would have to try to find some for him. Another would be given a bicycle by the chief, who hoped that he would be pleased by this, and write favourably of him to the white man.

The staff-chief and the scribe shared the court takings. If the chief imposed a fine of a pound, the scribe would enter five shillings in the register, and he and the chief divided the fifteen shillings between them. So long as they shared the proceeds between them, the two got on very well together, and the scribe was feared by all the chief's group; but if he kept the money for himself, the chief and his council conspired together and brought a complaint against him. Sometimes he was dismissed, as in the case of Gbaaŋgahar, who was of the type that played for his own hand, and was deported to Kaduna. . . .

When the staff-chiefs were first given scribes they were very pleased. Nothing that the scribe did could annoy the chief, and everything went well, till one day he seduced one of the chief's wives. This annoyed the chief intensely, and from that time he sought means to encompass his downfall. The court members, seeing this, also tried to find causes of complaint against him, and finally accused him before the white man, who dismissed him, as in the case of Ker, Mkovor's scribe in Ipav. To obtain wives was indeed the main object of the scribes. Some had two, three, or four, although they were only boys.

The present District Officer has recently done much to reduce the influence of the scribes. At the general meeting of the chiefs in 1933 he told them, 'We have given you your own Tiv boys to help you, but you let them be insolent to you, and unruly. Don't be afraid of them; they are Tiv like you. If they do wrong, beat them!' The chiefs agreed in the presence of the European, but as soon as they went outside some said, 'The white man is trying to fool us. He wants to entice us into beating the scribes, and then to depose us. Because the scribes and the white man are all one; the scribe can write, just like a European. We are not going to be so stupid as to lose our chiefdoms like this!'

THE CHIEFS' VISIT TO KADUNA

The staff-chiefs were much subdued as a result of their journey to Kaduna. When they met for one of their usual conferences at Abinsi, the District Officer told them that the administrative officers wished them to go to Kaduna, to see the world. If they approved of this idea, every staff-chief should take one of his court members, a police-man, and a messenger, and any who wished might also take with him one wife. He would take them by train, and show them things that they had never seen before. They would see many different types of people on the way, a Hausa chief, and some good farming land. Then, if any one wished to settle there, he would be given the oppor-tunity to do so. All the chiefs said they would go. The white man fixed a day, and at the appointed time all the staff-chiefs came in with their council members, police-men, and wives.[1] (Now, at that time there were three staff-chiefs whose misdeeds had already come to the ears of the white man. The District Officer had made in-quiries and found out all about this, but he and the other Europeans kept it quiet, and told none of the Tiv.) They assembled at Makurdi and boarded the train. (My father, as a councillor of the staff-chief of Shitire, was one of the party.) . . .

When they arrived at Kaduna, there was a dance[2] of soldiers for the Tiv to see, at which all the chief Euro-peans were present. . . . The Tiv also danced with much vigour. The Emir of Zaria sent 200 mats for the Tiv to sleep on, and eight oxen for them to kill and eat. The next day he came himself, with much pomp, accompanied by many of his notables and about 300 horsemen. The Tiv were very much impressed by this. In the Emir they

[1] The party amounted to about 300 people.
[2] = Parade.

saw a real ruler, and in comparison their own chiefs appeared very insignificant. When they had all sat down, the Emir greeted the Tiv, asked after their country, and said he was very glad to see them. He told them to go round and look at his land, and if they liked it to come and settle there. He would be very pleased. After this the Tiv were driven in cars all round the countryside, and shown much excellent farm-land. Finally, they stopped outside the Magistrate's office. The white man asked them, 'Do you like the country?' 'Very much indeed', they replied. 'Will you come?' he asked them, and they said, 'Yes, we will come'. But when his back was turned they said to each other, 'What sort of a fool would leave his own people to come and lead a miserable existence far away here in a foreign country? However, he seems to want us to say "Yes" '.

The chiefs stayed at Kaduna for three days and then returned to Makurdi. On the morning after their arrival they were all told to assemble outside the house of the Chief of Makurdi. The Europeans, including the Resident, came and greeted them there, wished them a good journey home, and dismissed them all with the exception of three, whom they told to remain behind as they had something to say to them. When the Tiv heard this their hearts sank. They slunk back to their homes, and only the boldest stayed behind to take leave of the white man. When the other chiefs had gone and only the three were left, the white man started to try the cases. The three were Ugba, chief of Ugondo, Moji of Kunav, and Abagi of the Farm Ishaŋgev. The charges which had been brought against them to the white man, but had not until now been disclosed by him, were as follows: Ugba had oppressed his clan, Ugondo, seized their possessions and their women, and burnt their homes; Moji had extorted property and women from his clansmen; Abagi had murdered his wife on the farm. The cases were investigated with great thoroughness. Ugba was convicted and sentenced to live at Kaduna, exiled from his people. Next came the trial of Moji. Moji was not the sort of man to give trouble to the European by denying the

accusations brought against him. Every genuine charge
of extortion he admitted at once. The white man ordered
him to pay compensation. All his wives, about ninety-
three in number, whom he had acquired without payment
after the manner of the staff-chiefs described above, were
sent back to their homes. He himself was sentenced to go
to Kaduna, but on the day before that fixed for his departure he died. Some said that he had taken poison, but
careful investigation by the white man proved that this
was not so. Moji died of a broken heart. Abagi was also
convicted after a rigorous trial, and was hanged from a
fig-tree in his own village. The tree is still standing in
this year, 1935. This was the sequel to the chiefs' visit to
Kaduna.

These happenings had a very sobering effect on the
chiefs. They no longer seized their people's possessions
and women by the violent means they had used before,
through fear of being sent to Kaduna. If a chief did
wrong, and the white man heard of it, he would ask him
whether he wanted to join Ugba at Kaduna, and this
acted as a strong deterrent. Nowadays the chiefs use guile
rather than force to deprive poor men of their possessions.

❡. The motives of the white man are deeply hidden indeed. To
the Tiv, interpreting the matter—with some justification—in the
light of after-events, the expedition to Kaduna (1926) appeared
as all part of a sinister and preconceived design. It was, so it
transpired, nothing more or less than an elaborately staged warning to miscreant chiefs. The white man, being in possession of
certain incriminating evidence, cunningly disguised his true inten-
tions under a mask of friendliness and liberality, and enticed the
unsuspecting leaders of the tribe far into a foreign country. Men
who had never been beyond the borders of their own district, and
hardly believed in the existence of any other, were taken in a train
for a night and a day, a distance of about fifteen days' journey on
foot. When they felt that they had left Tivland behind for ever,
cut off from it by the many strange, and doubtless hostile, tribes
through which they had passed on the way, they were subjected
to a military demonstration, and an even more impressive display
by a powerful foreign ruler. On their return to their own country

the white man showed his hand (actually this did not happen till a few months later), and the land of Kaduna, of which their recent unnerving experience had already given them a strong fear and dislike, was revealed in its true colours as the place to which those were to be sent who failed to do what he told them.

The matter seemed plain enough. Yet in actual fact the motives underlying the scheme for forming a settlement of Tiv in the country round Kaduna were, if possibly misguided, entirely benevolent. Kaduna itself is an artificial growth; it started as a small government station in 1910, and was taken over as the head-quarters of the Northern Provinces after the War. It stands in the middle of a fine fertile piece of country, which was almost depopulated in the last century by slave raids from Zaria on one side and Kontagora on the other. The nearest big native town is Zaria, fifty miles away. As the township grew, the lack of an indigenous population to provide labour for railway construction and other public works, and to clear the tsetse-infected areas along the banks of the river, became a serious problem. There was also the need for local markets to supply the isolated colony of European officials, with its large and increasing quota of clerks, messengers, personal servants, and dependants. A couple of hundred miles to the south lived the Tiv, a vigorous and expanding tribe of agriculturists, who were showing a tendency to overflow the bounds of their allotted territory in search for fresh farming land. These people had recently been brought to official notice in connexion with the construction of the new eastern railway, in the course of which it had been observed that Tiv labour gangs compared very favourably in industry and stamina with those recruited from the other tribes through whose territory the line passed. Regarded from the somewhat detached European standpoint, a happy solution to the problem seemed to have been found, if only a section of this tribe could be induced to settle in the rich but sparsely inhabited area round Kaduna, to get rid of the tsetse by clearing the land for cultivation, and sell their surplus produce to the wage-earning population of the township, to the mutual advantage of both parties. A visit from the chiefs was therefore arranged with the object of showing them the great possibilities of the country, and everything was done for their comfort and entertainment that could make their stay as pleasant as possible.

Unfortunately, the idea was impracticable, because it did not

take into account the strength of the ties which bind a primitive
agricultural community to the soil of its fathers. It is true that
big migrations of the Tiv have taken place in the past, but then
either the tribe moved as a whole, or clans under pressure from
without split up and changed position inside the tribal territory.
No section ever allowed itself to become completely detached
from the rest of the tribe, and the people have never, so to speak,
moved out of sight of the traditional homes of their ancestors.
To the Fulani nomad the land in which he happens to be means no
more than the quality of the pasture which it provides for his
cattle; a Hausa trader is quite content to spend his life in a small
settlement surrounded by strangers, far from his native town;
but any Tiv found living outside his own country is a social and
spiritual outcast. Whether he has wilfully cut himself off from his
people, or has been driven out by them for some good reason,
he is usually by nature an unsatisfactory member of the community, and no sooner has shaken off the shackles of tribal sanctions and dicipline than he develops into a waster or a criminal.
It was inconceivable to the elders that any self-respecting householder should take such a desperate step for no cause at all. The
whole object of the expedition was a complete mystery to them—
until afterwards, when the true explanation seemed only too clear.

The sequel to the affair has already been described. It soon
became evident that the scheme for voluntary colonization of
Kaduna district by the Tiv had failed. Then arose the question
of what to do with the unsatisfactory chiefs, and it was finally
decided to punish them by deportation to the place to which they
had refused to go of their own free will. Kaduna, having failed
in its role of El Dorado, was more cogently represented as a penal
settlement. The unfortunate Ugba was the first, and only important, settler. He was treated with great consideration by the
Kaduna authorities, and given a good piece of land outside the
township, where he lived dejectedly for some years with those of
his own family who would follow him, and a few Tiv vagabonds
who drifted in from outside. But every attempt to popularize the
scheme by providing the settlers with all their wants until they
should become self-supporting, exempting them from taxation,
and giving free railway tickets to their friends to come and visit
them, failed to induce recruits of the desired type to leave their
country, in spite of the fact that it was visited at about this time

by a severe famine. Eventually the experiment had to be accounted a failure. Ugba has now been allowed to return to his own home, where he has settled down again as a highly respected elder, and the little colony has dispersed.

METHODS OF OBTAINING MONEY EMPLOYED BY THE CHIEFS IN RECENT TIMES

WHEN exchange marriage was abolished in favour of the *kem* system, the white man prescribed the following procedure for the guidance of the chiefs: When a marriage had been arranged, and the bride-price paid, the bridegroom was to come before the chief with his bride and her owner. If the chief was satisfied that the money had been paid in full, the husband was to give his wife sixpence, and no more, to pay to the chief as the Government's fee. This he was to hand over to the court scribe, who would enter the transaction in the book. This gave an opening to the chiefs to make a profit by exacting a present of three shillings, five shillings, or more, in addition to the legal sixpence.

Bribery in the courts is another source of the chiefs' income. In the night the guilty party brings the chief a large sum of money. The next day, when the case is tried, nothing that the other man may say will satisfy the chief, however firmly he may convince every one else of the justice of his cause. His statements are rejected by the chief as a tissue of lies, and he loses his case. If he wishes to have a chance of winning he must also pay some money during the night. When the chief has accepted bribes from both parties the case is a very difficult one for him to try. He cannot deal with the facts in the natural way, and great confusion results. As soon as the council members realize the difficulties in which the chief is placed, they propose an adjournment of the case until the following month. The injured party may then in desperation appeal to the white man, though he will not dare to mention the bribe; he will only say that he brought his case a long time ago, but the chief will not take the trouble to settle it. The white man then sends his messenger to hear the case; but the messenger is well treated

D d

by the chief on his arrival, and goes over to his side. When he comes back and tells the District Officer that the Court tells quite a different story from that of the complainant, the man has no chance. He is driven away by the European as a liar, and becomes a general laughing-stock. The chief is delighted, and keeps on referring to the incident. 'So-and-so was not satisfied with my verdict', he says. 'He complained about me to the white man, who, of course, soon chased him off. The white man always agrees with what I say. We see absolutely eye to eye, and I understand him perfectly.' In consequence, those who feel themselves wronged by the decision of a chief, and would like to appeal to the European, are afraid to do so. But when that chief dies, or is deposed, and another is appointed in his place, all those whose cases have been left unfinished, but who have been afraid to do anything, bring them up again. There are people who have been bringing the same case ever since the white man first came to the country, and have not yet got it settled. For this reason the number of cases awaiting trial, both old and new, is enormous.

THE SUB-DIVISION OF THE CHIEFS' AUTHORITY

Nowadays the tribe is being split up by the white man into smaller groups, each being descended from a common father, or in some cases from a common mother. A chief is appointed for each group for the purpose of settling their disputes, and is given councillors to help him. He is told that he must never try cases except in council. These men are not now officially called staff-chiefs, but 'spokesmen', and staffs of office are no longer given to them. Nevertheless, this does not make the administration of justice any easier. Because the reason why so many court cases were left unfinished was not that there were too few chiefs for the size of the tribe, but that they were too corrupt. Whenever a District Officer goes to a chief's village, he can in one day hear and pass judgement on a large number of cases which, if tried by a Tiv chief, would go on for two months and then very likely not all be properly settled. For this reason the Tiv prefer to go to the white man for judgement rather than to their own chiefs. They say that in the European's court one does not have to pay anything, and yet a decision is given at once on a matter over which they may have been going to the chief for many years in vain.

THE EUROPEAN GOVERNMENT STAFF

To the Tiv it seems that one of the causes of all these troubles is the way in which government officers come and go. No government officer ever comes to live permanently amongst the Tiv. Each, when he comes, learns to know the Tiv by watching and listening, but as soon as he begins to be able to turn his knowledge to the good of the people, he is taken away from Tivland and sent to some other part of the country, and some new European who has never been to Tivland before is put in his place. The new man must then start to learn about the Tiv. One may try to do the same as his countryman, whom he has succeeded, and in this case progress is made, the Tiv see that the white man is doing his best for their country, they make every effort to obey the laws of the land, and there are few disturbances during that time. But at other times, when a white man who knows the Tiv goes, his successor does not follow in his footsteps, but thinks and acts differently. Then the Tiv do not know where they stand. It is as though a man were to build a house, and when it was nearly completed another were to come and knock it down, and start to build again in his own style. In this way how can the house ever be finished?

The Tiv are not the same as other races, and their customs are different. Wherefore those amongst them who have perception and understanding say this: If the Governor really wishes to help the people, they beg of him to stop changing the European staff, taking away those who know them and sending new men in their place. For in this way the affairs of the tribe can never stand on a firm foundation. Let those who know the Tiv be replaced by others who also know them and speak their language; only thus can the tribe go forward.

¶. The above criticisms of the new régime are more important as an expression of native opinion than as a record of facts. There have doubtless been many cases where chiefs and subordinate officials have abused their authority, but it must not be supposed that the Tiv have suffered more than other African tribes from the misrule and corruption of their leaders. On the contrary, since the administrative organization was always recognized as empirical, it has probably received more detailed attention from European officers, and a closer check has been kept on the behaviour of the chiefs and their subordinates, than in the case of more advanced communities which are better adapted to carrying out the principles of Indirect Rule. The difference lies in the fact that the people who live in more highly developed polities have long understood and accepted the conditions of autocratic government. Many things which appear to a Tiv as intolerable acts of oppression are accepted by the Hausa or Jukun as the rightful privileges of a chief, and cases of individual injustice are suffered without complaint as unavoidable concomitants of an institution which has the support of the community, and confers much reciprocal benefit. It is inconceivable that sentiments such as those expressed in the foregoing pages could be written by a subject of the Sultan of Sokoto or the Shehu of Bornu, however emancipated or disgruntled the author might be. The rule of the 'staff-chiefs' had not, in fact, the consent of the Tiv people. Even the very limited monarchy of the drum-chiefs did not prove acceptable to them, though originally their submission in this case was voluntary.

Although Akiga's account gives a somewhat one-sided and exaggerated impression of the administrative failings of the chiefs and their subordinates, it cannot be entirely dismissed as the testimony of an irresponsible objector to rightful tribal authority. His criticisms of the administrative system, which was introduced and maintained until recently by us, can, I believe, be taken as a fairly representative and honest expression of opinion from a member of a very outspoken race. For the Tiv people are by no means inarticulate, or disposed to 'suffer the tyrannies of the chiefs in silence'. They have no hesitation whatever in proclaiming their fancied wrongs or dissatisfaction with their leaders in open conversation, in songs, before the European, or even in the public assemblies when all the chiefs are present. So that it is probably easier to gauge the trend of popular feeling in Tiv country than in any other part of Northern Nigeria. The weaknesses in the system were fully appreciated by the British Administration, and eventually, after a fair trial, and many unsuccessful attempts to educate the chiefs to a fitting sense of their position and responsibilities, the whole idea of chieftainship was abandoned and replaced by a system better adapted to the tribal temperament and indigenous organization. It was difficult at the time to see what alternative could take the place of some form of chieftainship; speaking in the light of later knowledge, it is perhaps fair to say that the Administration was handicapped by a too narrow interpretation of the principles of Indirect Rule, based on the conditions prevalent in the Muhammadan emirates. It was not realized that these general principles could be put into practice without the aid of executive chiefs through whom to administer the people. As the Tiv had no real chiefs, in our sense of the term, it was thought necessary to make some, and this policy failed for the reasons already indicated. There were other attempts, also, to force the Tiv into a conventional administrative mould. Audu dan Afoda, a Yoruba, at one time a government political agent and afterwards head of Makurdi town, was put in charge of sections of the Iharev and Masev clans; and later, as already mentioned, a part of the tribe was cut off from the rest and included in Wukari Division. Both these experiments have now been discontinued in accordance with the present policy of self-determination.

Nevertheless, when criticizing the policy which imposed upon the Tiv a political system which was foreign to them, it should be borne in mind that at the time when the British first came into contact with them at the beginning of the present century they found a large and warlike tribe, hostile to interference and suspicious of strangers, but without any internal cohesion or apparent tribal organization, and having no leaders representative of more than a fraction of the people with whom to open negotiations. The first contacts gave little hope of an early peaceful establishment of civilized rule. In the year 1900 an attempt to construct a telegraph line from Lokoja to Ibi along the north bank of the Benue met with so much opposition from the Iharev clans that, after a considerable amount of guerrilla fighting, it was abandoned and carried further to the north, in order to avoid Tiv country altogether. In 1906 the Tiv were involved in a sanguinary battle at Abinsi, during which they annihilated the Hausa community and sacked the Niger Company's store. Both these incidents necessitated sending strong expeditions against them.

To bring order amongst these turbulent people, the invention of an administrative machinery controlled by prominent members of the tribe with executive powers was, therefore, not only an experiment, but a necessary expedient. The state in which the first British officers found them, and the efforts which they made to gain their confidence and co-operation, are described by Lord Lugard, writing in 1908: 'The most important step forward has been the inauguration of peaceful penetration and occupation in . . . the hitherto impenetrable Munshi (Tiv) country, of which about one-third has now been opened up without the use of force. By a system of patrols, by the exercise of extreme tact and patience, and by the avoidance of cause of suspicion, political touch was gained with successive units until it became possible to effect permanent occupation at Katsina Ala, some hundred miles up the Katsina River, in the heart of Munshi country. This very primitive race is divided against itself by a system of vendetta whereby the hand of every division, clan, faction, group, cluster, and even individual, is against its neighbour. Incapable of rendering justice outside their own cluster, and unable to co-operate to enforce a ruling, the Munshis are showing themselves willing to accept the arbitration of a superior force in their internal affairs. It is impossible at the present stage for the Administration to commit itself to judicial decisions in these matters. The enforcement of such decisions would result in hostility and put an end to all chance of peaceful acceptance of control. But arbitration, conducted with extreme patience, sympathy, and insight are achieving successful results and steadily conducing to the gaining of confidence.'[1]

Within a short time after this most of the clans had become so amenable to the intrusion of the strangers that British officers were able to tour the area without a police escort, and a start had already been made with tax-collection and judicial work through native authorities. By 1914 the whole district had been brought under effective administration. These facts, and the undeniable popularity of the white man which has continued to the present time, reflect great credit on the tact and moderation of the early

[1] *Annual Report*, 1908.

administrators and the essential reasonableness and tractability which underlies the independent spirit of this people. A factor which determined the development of these provisional measures was the shortage of staff due to the War. With the number of European officers available at the time, it would have been impossible to dispense with native chiefs, or to increase the number of independent units, which is implied in the system of administration recently inaugurated. The years after the War were spent in trying to make the best of a system, born of necessity, but now shown to be unsuitable as an ideal for a tribe like the Tiv, which is still in the family-group stage of development.

As Akiga's account implies, unintentionally, a criticism of the Administration, it is only right that mention should here be made of the work done in the last few years, which is in practice largely directed against the abuses of which he complains. These reforms are not confined to the Tiv, but form part of a comprehensive scheme for the investigation and reorganization of non-Moslem tribal units throughout the whole of Nigeria, which was inaugurated by Sir Donald Cameron in 1933. Particularly in the Northern Provinces it had become apparent that since the British occupation the political interests of pagans had been very much overshadowed by those of the Muhammadan peoples. 'About 1907–8 the form of native administration in Kano and Sokoto was imposed on the rest of Northern Nigeria, and the full system of District Heads and Village Heads was forced on places quite unsuited to it. The result has been that a veneer of the Moslem administrative system has been laid over a great part of the Northern Provinces and the true phenomena of local government have been obscured.'[1]

An attempt has therefore been made in many parts of Nigeria to put back the political clock, and reorganize the administration of more primitive peoples on the lines which it was following at the time of the British occupation. This was preceded by a detailed inquiry into the true organization of the various tribes before it had been overlaid by foreign institutions; in the case of those peoples who had lost their independence, it was ascertained whether the alien power had any true right, either by conquest or consent, to exercise jurisdiction over its subjects. For at a time

[1] *Memorandum on Pagan Administration*, by H.H. the Chief Commissioner, Northern Provinces, January 2nd, 1934.

when less was known of the country, powerful rulers were in many cases given authority by us to administer and exact tribute from areas over which they had never formerly possessed any effective control. Territories which they claimed as their own were in effect nothing more than slave-raiding grounds, or were bound to them by the loosest of historical ties, as in the case of the King of Wukari and the Tiv clans. Where practicable, such areas are now being made independent, and the people are being given a chance to develop on their own lines.

Moreover, where formerly an advance was considered to have been made if a number of petty chiefdoms or autonomous units could be brought under the jurisdiction of a central authority, the present policy is rather to break down such unnatural combinations into their component parts, and encourage the formation of confederacies of independent units on an equal footing. In many cases the units themselves have been found to be artificially compounded, and have been further subdivided. This is what has happened with the Tiv. It has been realized that administration of the district through a paramount chief whose authority would be recognized by the whole tribe, or, failing that, through a non-Tiv ruler, is a false ideal. The real authority in the Tiv groups does not lie with the chief at all, but with the elders. The so-called district heads were regarded as protégés of the white man, and were usually quite out of touch with the real leaders of the community; even where they had the support of their own group, their influence over other groups in the clan was only maintained by European backing. Secondly, it was found that the clans were unnatural administrative units, comprised in most cases of elements which had no interests in common, nor desire to combine.

The reorganization was carried out with great thoroughness by the administrative staff, and a great advance on previous practice was made in that it was conducted, as far as the touring officers were concerned, entirely through the medium of the Tiv language and not Hausa. In 1934 the Tiv tribe was formed into a single self-contained division, including the clans which in 1927 had been placed under Wukari, and a new government head-quarters was built at Gboko, in the centre of the tribal area. The country was divided into three touring areas, each in charge of an Assistant District Officer. The administration of every clan was then remodelled on the lines of the indigenous social organization. In each case the decision as to how the groups were to be divided was left to the people themselves. The determining factor in this decision was, as it has always been, the existence or lack of individual elders with personality and influence strong enough to bind the units together. In most cases the clans, which had originally been formed by us into administrative units each under a district head, decided that their component parts had no real interests in common and asked to split up into a number of independent groups. These groups, now numbering fifty-five in all, which for want of a better name are for the present called 'clans' or 'sub-clans', are the largest units whose leaders have ever in the past met together periodically to discuss matters affecting the common good. They correspond roughly to the groups which in the past each elected its own drum-chief, but their constitution is older than the drum-chiefs, and has outlived them.

Their interests, according to ancient custom, are now placed in the hands of a council of elders, who meet together at stated intervals for consultation and to hear cases. They elect one of their number as spokesman, whose duty it is to voice their opinions and carry out their decisions. In theory, therefore, this man is the descendant of the old spokesman whose function in the conduct of affairs is well shown by Akiga in his description of the case of witchcraft tried by the council and drum-chief (p. 373). He is not necessarily the senior elder or the most influential. The Native Authority is the council, not the spokesman or president. But the basic functioning unit is not the clan or sub-clan, but a much smaller group called 'the kindred', of which the constitution has already been explained. It is the authority of the kindred which has always had the greatest influence in regulating the ordinary matters of tribal life. The institution of the drum-chief helped to bring the sections of the sub-clan together, but the effective power has always remained in the hands of the kindred. Its affairs are conducted by a council of elders who represent its component parts, that is to say, the *akombo* groups. It deals with purely civil matters affecting its own members, and is encouraged to act as a court of arbitration, but in cases affecting other kindreds it has, now as formerly, no power to enforce its decisions. In our terminology this council is the subordinate Native Authority. The superior Native Authority is the clan council, which is, in turn, composed of elders representing its component kindreds. In pre-British days this was not a regularly constituted and functioning body, but only met when some special occasion demanded. Now it meets once a month. Finally, once a year all the clans meet together at Gboko for a general tribal council. This body has no executive powers, and the object is mainly for the different sections of the tribe to become better acquainted, to learn each other's point of view, and to discuss matters of common interest, with the idea of developing the tribal consciousness, and eventually of evolving a true tribal Native Administration.

These important administrative reforms are those to which Akiga briefly refers in his penultimate section, without in the least, however, understanding their origin or purpose. This is at present true of the tribe as a whole. Having spent many years trying to learn what is the white man's idea of chieftainship, they seem likely to take as long to forget it. The elders, whose administrative faculties have become atrophied through long subservience to the will of the chiefs, are now by no means easily roused to take a share of responsibility in the affairs of the community. They are apt to show but tepid interest in the new political theory, and to concentrate their minds on the election of the spokesman, which in the present system is obviously a matter of minor importance. These officials are still called *tor* (chief) by everybody, and even taking away the staffs of office (which made a far deeper impression than any abstract curtailment of powers) has not fully convinced them of their changed status. Some have already had to be removed for assuming the powers and following the evil practices of the old chiefs. Nevertheless, progress is being made slowly, and there is no doubt that in general the elders are now beginning to take a greater share in the administration in an advisory capacity, and that the executive officials are treating them with greater respect. With the aid of much patience and perseverance on the part of those who know them well, they may one day be brought to realize the full implications of the new, which is really the old, political ideal. It is, of course, impossible to foresee what ultimate form of administration will emerge from the present reconstruction. The main thing is that the indigenous organization should be given a fair chance to adapt itself to the new conditions in whatever way the people themselves may choose. As Miss Perham says: 'Few tribal councils, after years of bewildering disintegration, are able to rationalize about the exact administrative forms with which they will compromise between the past and the present, nor can the political officer make an arbitrary decision for them. Once the familiar forms have been restored, the people are free . . . to develop and adjust them.'[1]

It may be that the course of political change from gerontocracy to autocracy, set in motion by us, has already gone too far to be arrested, and that the old forms are no longer familiar or capable of restoration. In the year of writing (1937) the question of a paramount chief was again raised at the tribal council. The proposal was made by three or four of the old chiefs (now clan spokesmen), doubtless for very personal reasons, but it was not received with any noticeable opposition by the rest of the council or spectators. It would be wrong to conclude from this, however, that the tribe is ready for such an institution, that the people understand in the least what is the theory of executive chieftainship, or that they are any more reconciled than formerly to its practical implications. The optimist may at best see in the idea the germ of a tribal consciousness, expressed as the desire for a more permanent figure to unite the common interests than is provided by the shifting personnel of the European staff. But even for this hope there is at present not very much justification, since they have hardly yet reached the stage of conceiving even the clan as an entity represented by a single leader. It is more probable that the Tiv have accepted the idea of a chief for the same reason that they have adopted the flowing robes and turban of the Muhammadan, or the trousers and sun-helmet of the European, not because they know or care about the practical value of these things or the code which they typify, but because they recognize in them the symbols of a higher culture. We ourselves have fostered this idea, purposely by twenty years of political education based on the system found amongst their more advanced neighbours, and unconsciously by the example of graded rank and dignity in our own civil service. The demand for a chief takes this form: The Hausa and the Jukun have big chiefs, the white man has his Resident and Governor. Why not the Tiv? It was this passion for imitating the externals of foreign institutions, without appreciation of the fundamentals, which drove their fathers to Wukari in large numbers to get the insignia of the drum-chiefs in

[1] *Africa*, vol. vii, p. 329.

the past. The difficulty at present is that the Tiv, like many other Africans, are apt to look upon any attempt to preserve what is good in the indigenous institutions, whether of politics, art, language, or dress, as a deliberate attempt to retard their progress towards what appears to them to be the ideal of Western civilization.

·As regards the other salaried officials who were appointed by us to carry out the duties of administration, the truth of some of Akiga's charges against them would not, I think, be denied. But his comprehensive denunciation of all ranks is unfair to the individual members who have served their employers as faithfully as the limitations of their intelligence and upbringing would allow. A certain number of abuses were inevitable. Until it was possible to ensure a degree of continuity in the European staff, all work had to be done through interpreters. At first the men chosen were Hausa-speaking natives from other parts of the Northern Provinces who had a knowledge of the Tiv language. They were known as political agents, and the chances which the post offered for exploiting the unsophisticated pagan put a severe strain on their integrity. Later on an experiment was made with Hausa-speaking Tiv political agents, but this at first brought no better results, and for a time was abandoned. The same difficulty was experienced with the native policemen and court scribes. The fact is that there is no precedent for such officials in the indigenous constitution of the tribe, as there is in the case of the more highly developed northern states, so that their authority, and the whole reason for their existence, was derived from the white man's system of government. They were quite unused to finding themselves in such a position of power over their fellow clansmen and lost all sense of values. The awe-inspiring effect achieved by the blue and white striped uniform had an unfortunate reaction on the simple mind of the wearer, who not unnaturally took himself at the valuation of others. The same thing happened to the court scribes. These young men had been trained in the government schools. As long as they were all together under the direct discipline of a European, their education had no apparent ill effects on their character, but as soon as they were sent out on their own to take up work in the villages, they immediately became aware of the powerful impression which their ability to write made on their less gifted kinsmen and seniors, and the knowledge of this turned the heads of many. It may be added that, as Akiga points out in another chapter, they were probably not drawn from the best material in the first place, and many were sent to school because their parents found no use for them at home. This gave them an additional reason for asserting their newly discovered power in a society from which they had previously been despised outcasts.

All these initial failures could hardly have been avoided. Officers for carrying out the details of administration, law, and order are an indispensable part of any European system of government, and the only possible remedy is the gradual education of the people to an understanding of the functions of these officials, and of the men themselves to a proper sense of their position and duties. The uniform of the police and the power of pen and paper are already through familiarity losing much of their terrors. Nearly all foreign elements have now been eliminated. The whole of the Native Administration police force, and eighteen out of the twenty-two messengers attached to the headquarters staff (1937), are Tiv, and, since the initial failures, are now doing very well.

There is another closely related question, referred to by Akiga in this chapter, which will have a profound influence on the future of the tribe, that is the problem of the European government staff. Conditions of service in Nigeria make it a necessary feature of government policy that all officers should be interchangeable, and the normal period of residence in any one district does not usually exceed five or six years. Although the exigencies of the roster, and the interests both of the service and of the individual, make this almost inevitable, the impermanency of the staff falls very hardly on the people, who have not that elasticity which would enable them to transfer their loyalties, or respect for the abstract idea of office or authority as apart from the individual who holds it. With a pagan tribe such as the Tiv the case for continuity is stronger than elsewhere, in view of the language question and of the great gulf which is fixed between their culture and that of the Muhammadan peoples. This difference, already noted, can hardly be over-emphasized. It is apparent in every aspect of tribal life—language, customs, religion, social organization, temperament, and approach to the white man. The European staff, therefore, can never be truly interchangeable. An officer who had done the first part of his service amongst Muhammadans, and was then posted to Tiv Division, would be in exactly the same position, as regards his relationship to the people, as if he were setting foot in Africa for the first time. In fact, his past experience and knowledge would be a definite disadvantage, and would be apt to obscure his approach to the pagan mind. The converse is equally true, but the results are less harmful, since the culture and social structure of the Muhammadan states is relatively stable, and not likely to be seriously shaken by the mistakes of a few individual officers.

In Tiv the key to the position is the language. A man who is not a natural or keen linguist, but has with the expenditure of much labour acquired a fair knowledge of Hausa, naturally shrinks from tackling a second language, very much more difficult, when he knows that by the time he has mastered it he will almost certainly be transferred elsewhere. For the average Englishman (not the linguist) takes the best part of his five years span to acquire a thorough knowledge of the Tiv language, and thereby gain a true insight into the mind of the people. For this purpose Hausa is almost useless. First, as might be expected from the great difference in culture, all the fundamental ideas in Tiv lack words in Hausa to express them, and vice versa, so that translation from one language to the other is virtually impossible. Secondly, there is the natural antipathy which exists between peoples of such widely different outlook. The Tiv has always disliked and despised the Hausa, and he has good reason, for those who have visited his country are not the best specimens of their race. The Hausa regards the Tiv with the contempt due to an ignorant pagan. Neither makes the smallest attempt to understand the other. Thus a sympathetic translation of ideas from Tiv into Hausa or Hausa into Tiv is hardly to be expected. It makes little difference whether the interpreter is a Hausa-speaking Tiv, or a Tiv-speaking Hausa. Neither has ever gained more than a superficial knowledge of the other's language or mentality.[1] If, therefore, Hausa is used as the medium, mistakes are bound to be made, due to misinterpretation, not of words, but of concepts. The administrative progress made in recent years is largely due to the fact that touring officers have had the time and ability to

[1] To those who have always used Hausa as a linguistic medium when dealing with the non-Hausa-speaking peoples of the Northern Provinces, it may appear that I have overstressed the difference in thought between the Hausa and the Tiv, but I am confident of the support of any one who knows both peoples and languages.

learn the language and attain a true perspective of the people's mentality and social organization, thereby being in a position to advise Government as to the lines along which they have the best chance of developing.

A true permanent staff for Tiv Division cannot, of course, be expected in any government department. The best that can be hoped for is that the peculiar nature of the problems may be appreciated; that officers posted to Tiv may be chosen with a view to the special type of work to be done, and be given an assurance of sufficient permanency to encourage them to learn the language; finally, that changes in staff may be made gradually, so that there may always be a large proportion of men with a sound knowledge of local conditions, to ensure continuity of policy and to preserve the confidence of the people.

In conclusion, I give two more extracts from another part of Akiga's book, because they have a bearing on the subject dealt with in this section, and express an opinion, which, though one may not agree with it, it is only fair to record in conjunction with what has gone before. He is writing on a question of vital importance to the immediate future, the fate of the old generation and of everything for which it stands.

AND he (the District Officer) places great faith in the elders, thinking that thus good will come to the land of Tiv. But he is planting seed on land which has already yielded its crop. The older men in Tiv to-day are like members of a different race that has no understanding. . . . When he gave the power to the elders, the Tiv started again to hold communal hunts and bush drives, things which had been strictly forbidden, and though some were arrested and imprisoned for this, others did it again, and throughout the country the laws of the white man are no longer enforced. The Tiv say that their land is going back to what it was before he came, and that soon they will be fighting and drinking sasswood again. In the year 1933 war broke out between the Home Ishaŋgev and Kunav, and a number of men were killed. Thereupon the spirits of all the Tiv rose, and they said that if the District Officer did not quickly make peace there would be fighting between other clans as well. Since this little war between Ishaŋgev and Kunav the Tiv have paid small regard to the white man's laws, and the only thing which prevents them from doing what he has forbidden is the speed with which touring officers now travel round the districts. If it were not for this, the country would revert to its former state.

There are indeed a few men of ability amongst the older generation, but they are so much in the minority that as a class it must be said that Tiv elders have no understanding. The chiefs lost their power when their staffs were taken from them, and since the police were deprived of their whips no one pays much attention to them either, and little work is done. In the present weak state of the chiefs the Tiv do not know how to set their affairs in order, and because they do not know the purpose behind the white man's actions, they all say, 'He has spoilt the land! He has spoilt the land!' Wherever you go in Tivland this is the phrase which you most often hear. They cannot understand the reason for what he is doing, and so suppose that it is bad for their country. They end by saying that they will wait and see what the white man will make of the land which belongs to him. But others, the few amongst the Tiv who understand, speak in praise of the District Officer, knowing him to be a man who is determined to carry through whatever he knows to be good, even though it may not please the Tiv. If they do not understand, he does not worry; some day they will understand and be thankful. . . .

Administrative officers are doing all they can to improve the country of the Tiv, and wherever they see a chance of giving help to the people they give it. But there is one thing which impedes the progress of their reforms. They think that every Tiv custom is indigenous to the tribe, and that it cannot be abolished without doing harm to the country. This is not necessarily so. There is only one thing indigenous to the Tiv: that is exchange marriage. Everything else they have got from other tribes. For many of their customs they do not understand the reason, and only observe them because they have seen them practised by their fathers. And if they have given up exchange marriage, which was indeed their birthright, and still the country has not been ruined, what else is there that they could not give up without spoiling the land? There is nothing that the white man might forbid to the Tiv, of which the loss would do any serious harm to the country; they are only trying to frighten him.

Look well at many of the Tiv customs, and at their attitude towards them. They are like children playing with toys. Some take bits of calabash and call them bowls, or pick up sherds and pretend they are pots. Others grind sand and make believe that it is corn, or mount a palm-stem saying they have got a horse. If one day they get hold of a knife or an arrow, and an older person takes it from them, they cry bitterly. But if he puts something else into their hands in the place of what he has taken away, they stop crying, and though it may not please them as much as what they had before, afterwards they get to like it. When they grow up, they laugh at the things which they used to have. 'When we were small,' they say, 'we used to think those things tremendously important, but now that we are no longer children, but men, we do as men do.'

¶. There has been a great change in the last ten years, and it has come very rapidly. In 1926 there were half a dozen schools in Tiv country; in 1936 there were fifty-seven. But this only affects the younger generation. The old people have stood still; they cannot alter or adapt themselves to our ideas. The tide of Western culture is rising, and no barrier that we may raise can keep it back. Flowing mainly from the south, it brings with it much rubbish and undesirable surface matter, but is washing away, for good or bad, many of the old institutions. Soon there will be little to which the older generation can cling except a few barren forms and practices of which they have already begun to forget the meaning. Nevertheless, our hope of saving the tribe from complete dis-integration lies with the old men; not the very old men, for age by itself, without wisdom and *tsav*, never carried any weight with the Tiv, but men of mature judgement and experience, senior enough

E e

to command respect and to take their place on the kindred council.

The present stage is one of disruption; the elders complain that they have no control over their families, and the young people have lost their respect for the old. In the old days sons would stay with their parents, and in this way the lore and traditions of the fathers, and the spiritual life of the tribe, was carried on from one generation to the next. But young men who have been to school are not to be bothered with such old-fashioned stuff. They leave home at an early age to find employment and make money to *kem* a bride. For since the abolition of exchange marriage they are no longer dependent on their parents for a wife. The result is a cleavage, and the breakdown of tribal discipline. Therefore it is essential that we should buttress up the authority of the elders, and encourage the preservation of the sanctions on which that authority rests, at least until such time as these sanctions are replaced by the growth of Christianity. For unless this is done, the spiritual sanctions of the tribe will die out with the present generation of elders. The most important of the family cults received a severe blow from the abolition of exchange marriage in 1927; some of the public cults, like the *Ilyum* and *Iwoyaŋgegh*, had already fallen into disuse, and others, such as the *Biamegh-Poor* and *Imborivuŋgu*, were partially stamped out by the *tsav* investigation of 1929. Those which remain will probably not survive the unbelief of the rising generation. Christianity has as yet hardly touched the tribe as a whole, and until it becomes an effective force the Tiv will be left spiritually rudderless. This is a very grave danger, and the most serious aspect of it is that it is on these spiritual sanctions that the whole authority of the elders rests. If this authority is lost, the family itself will have nothing to bind its members together, and when this happens the Tiv tribe as an entity will cease to exist. Hope for the immediate future lies (*pace* Akiga) in the best of the present elders, and in the essential reasonableness and receptivity of the Tiv character, which will tide them over the dangerous period of transition.

TIV BIBLIOGRAPHY

Compiled by PAUL BOHANNAN

ABRAHAM, R. C.
    1933*a* *The Tiv People* (first edition). Lagos: Government Printer.
    1933*b* *The Grammar of Tiv.* Kaduna: Government Printer.
    1940*a* *The Tiv People* (second edition). London: Crown Agents.
    1940*b* *A Dictionary of the Tiv Language.* London: Crown Agents.
    1940*c* *The Principles of Tiv.* London: Crown Agents.
    1940*d* *Tiv Reader for European Students.* London: Crown Agents.

AKIGA (AKIGHIRGA SAI)
    n.d. MS. An original manuscript, in Tiv, of which 'Akiga, 1939'
          is a partial translation.
    1939 *Akiga's Story* (translated by Rupert East). London: Oxford
          University Press for International African Institute.
    1954 'The "Descent" of the Tiv from Ibenda Hill' (translated by
          Paul Bohannan). *Africa*, xxiv, 1954, pp. 295–310. [Valuable on the
          type of myths which are told about past and future movements
          in Tiv migration.]

ALEXANDER, BOYD
    1907 *From the Niger to the Nile.* London: Arnold. [A Hausa view
          (pp. 32–34) of the Tiv about 1905, before they were brought under
          government control, and giving the Hausa folk-etymology of
          their term for Tiv, 'Muntschi'.]

ARNOTT, D. W.
    1958*a* 'Councils and Courts among the Tiv—Traditional Concepts
          and Alien Institutions in a Non-Moslem Tribe of Northern
          Nigeria', *Journal of African Law*, ii. 1, Spring 1958, pp. 19–25.
    1958*b* 'The Classification of Verbs in Tiv', *Bulletin of the School of
          Oriental and African Studies*, 1958, xxi. 1, pp. 111–33.
    1964 'Downstep in the Tiv Verbal System', *African Language Studies*,
          v, pp. 34–51.

BAIKIE, W. R.
    1856 *Narrative of an Exploring Voyage up the Rivers Kwora and
          Binue in 1854.* London.

BALFOUR, HENRY
    1948 'Ritual and Secular Uses of Vibrating Membranes as Voice
          Disguisers', *Journal of the Royal Anthropological Institute*, lxxviii,
          parts I and II. [Fine description of the Tiv *imborivungu*.]

BETTS, T. F.
    1941 'The Tiv Plantations, 1939–41', *Farm and Forest*, ii, p. 110.

BOHANNAN, LAURA
    1952 'A Genealogical Charter', *Africa*, xxii. 4, pp. 301–15. [A de-
          tailed account of the role of genealogies.]

1956 'Miching Mallecho.' In *From the Third Program*, edited by J. Morris. Nonesuch Press.

1958 'Political Aspects of Tiv Social Organization.' In *Tribes Without Rulers*, edited by John Middleton and David Tait. London: Routledge & Kegan Paul.

1960 'The Frightened Witch.' In *The Company of Man*, edited by Joseph Casagrande. New York: Harper & Rowe.

BOHANNAN, LAURA AND PAUL

1953 *The Tiv of Central Nigeria*. London: International African Institute. (Ethnographic Survey of Africa, Western Africa, Part VIII.)

1957 'Tiv Markets', *Transactions of the New York Academy of Sciences*, New Series, xix. 7, May.

BOHANNAN, PAUL

1953 'Concepts of Time among the Tiv of Nigeria', *Southwestern Journal of Anthropology*, ix. 3.

1954a 'The Migration and Expansion of the Tiv', *Africa*, xxxiv. 3. [An analysis of one of the most important factors of Tiv social organization.]

1954b 'Circumcision among the Tiv', *Man*, iv. 2.

1954c 'Translation—a Problem in Anthropology', *The Listener*, May 13, p. 815.

1954d *Tiv Farm and Settlement*. Her Majesty's Stationery Office. [Detailed information on Tiv farming practices, labour groups, consumption and trade of food, land tenure and migration.]

1955a 'A Tiv Political and Religious Idea', *Southwestern Journal 'of Anthropology*, xi, pp. 137–49.

1955b 'Some Principles of Exchange and Investment among the Tiv', *American Anthropologist*, lvii. 1, pp. 60–70.

1956a 'On the Use of Native Language Categories in Ethnology', *American Anthropologist*, lviii. 3.

1956b 'Beauty and Scarification amongst the Tiv', *Man*, 1956, no. 129. (Reprinted in *World Digest*, May 1957.)

1957a *Justice and Judgment among the Tiv*. London: Oxford University Press for International African Institute. [Analysis and case material on Tiv law.]

1957b 'An Alternate Residence Classification', *American Anthropologist*, lix. 1, pp. 126–31.

1958 'Extra-Processual Events in Tiv Political Institutions', *American Anthropologist*, lx. 1, pp. 1–12.

1959 'The Impact of Money on an African Subsistence Economy', *American Journal of Economic History*, xix. 4, December.

1960a 'Homicide among the Tiv of Central Nigeria.' In *Homicide and Suicide in Africa*, edited by Paul Bohannan. Princeton University Press.

1960b Article on 'Tiv' in *Encyclopaedia Britannica*.

1961 'Artist and Critic in an African Society.' In Marion W. Smith (editor) *The Artist in Tribal Society*. London: Routledge & Kegan Paul.

1965 'The Tiv of Nigeria.' In James L. Gibbs, Jr. (editor) *Twelve African Tribes*. New York: Holt, Rinehart & Winston.

Tiv Economy. In preparation, for publication in the monograph series of the American Ethnological Society.

BOHANNAN, PAUL AND LAURA
1957 *Three Source Notebooks in Tiv Ethnography*. New Haven: Human Relations Area Files.

1959 'The Family in Africa.' In the second edition of *The Family*, edited by Ruth Nanda Anshen. New York: Harper & Brothers.

BOWEN, ELENORE SMITH
1955 *Return to Laughter*. New York: Harper & Brothers. Reissued in paperback, Natural History Press, 1963. [This novel, written under a pseudonym by Laura Bohannan, is about a woman anthropologist's reaction to field work. Although the tribe is not named, the ethnography is accurate for the Tiv between 1949 and 1953.]

BRIGGS, G. W. G.
1941 'Soil Deterioration in the Southern Districts of Tiv Division, Benue Province', *Farm and Forest*, ii. 1, pp. 8–12.

1944 'Crop Yields and Food Requirements in Tiv Division, Benue Province, Nigeria', *Farm and Forest*, v. 2, pp. 17–23. [Contains the only information available on crop yields by Tiv farming methods.]

BRITISH AND FOREIGN BIBLE SOCIETY
1964 *Bibilo*. (The Bible in Tiv.) [Parts of the Bible, translated by the Rev. A. S. Judd, were first printed in 1914.]

BURDO, ADOLPH
1880 *A Voyage up the Niger and Benue*. London: Richard Bentley & Son. [Like most travellers of his time, Burdo was afraid of the Tiv, and merely repeated a few stories about them.]

BURNS, SIR ALAN
1948 *History of Nigeria*, 4th edition. London: George Allen & Unwin.

CASALEGGIO, ERIC
1965 *A History of the Dutch Reformed Church Mission in Tivland* (in Afrikaans). Cape Town.

CROCKER, W. R.
1936 *Nigeria—a Critique of British Colonial Administration*. London: George Allen & Unwin.

CROWTHER, SAMUEL ADJAI
1855 *The Countries on the Banks of the Niger and Binue*. London. [Bishop Crowther, then a young man, accompanied the Hutchinson–Baikie expedition up the Benue; pp. 61, 63–65, 67, 71, and 76 contain valuable information about Tiv location at that time.]

DETZNER, H.
1913 In *Mitteilungen aus den Deutschen Schutzgebieten*, XXVI. 4, pp. 326–9.

1923 *Im Lande des Dju-dju*, pp. 229–341 and *passim*. Berlin.

422 BIBLIOGRAPHY

DEWAR, K.
1935 *Intelligence Report on the Ukan District of the Tiv Division of the Benue Province*. (Unpublished MS.).

DOWNES, R. M.
1933 *The Tiv Tribe*. Kaduna: Government Printer.

DUGGAN, E. DE C.
1932 'Notes on the Munshi Tribe', *Journal of the African Society*, xxxi, pp. 173–82.

EAST, RUPERT
1939 *Akiga's Story*. London: Oxford University Press for International African Institute.

FLEGEL, E. R.
1880 'Der Benue von Gande bis Djen.' *Petermanns G. M.*, XXVI, pp. 220–8.

FORDE, D. and SCOTT, R.
1946 *Native Economies of Nigeria*, pp. 189–90. London: Faber & Faber.

FROBENIUS, LEO
1924 'Die Muntschi, ein Urwaldvolk in der Nachbarschaft der sudanischen Kulturvölker.' Part III of *Volksdichtungen aus Oberguinea*, Atlantis, Band XI. München. [Records forty-three folk tales, and the way they are told, with a few remarks on Tiv culture.]
1913 *The Voice of Africa*. (English translation.) [An over-written description of a couple of nights spent in Tivland listening to stories while gathering material culture-objects: pp. 661 ff.]

GASKIYA CORPORATION, ZARIA, NIGERIA
1964 *Anzaakaa*, 2nd edition. [Tiv proverbs in Tiv.]

GREENBERG, J.
1949 'Studies in African Linguistic Classification: I. The Niger–Congo Family', *Southwestern Journal of Anthropology*, v. 2, pp. 79–100. 'III. The Position of Bantu', ibid., v. 4, pp. 309–17.

GUTHRIE, F.
1962 *Simplified Tiv Grammar*. Published by the Roman Catholic Diocese of Makurdi and printed by Benue Printing Venture, Makurdi.

HARRI, ALIS
1894 *Nos Africains*, (p. 212). Paris. [Not seen, but said to contain an important Tiv autobiography.]

HORNBURG, FRIEDRICH
1940 *Die Musik der Tiv. Ein Beitrag zur Erforschung der Musik Nigeriens*. Berlin (Phil.). [Summary in *Die Musikforschung*, I, 1948, pp. 47–59.]

HUTCHINSON, T. J.
1855 *Narrative of the Niger, Tschadda and Binue Explorations*. London: Longmans. [The Tiv are mentioned on pp. 90, 91, 99, and 150.]

Iyenge, Ali
    n.d.   *Tiv Grammar* (*c.* 1961). Printed at Mkar by Gar's Correspon-
            dence Service. [In Tiv; used in primary schools.]

Johnston, Sir Harry
    1919   *A Comparative Study of the Bantu and Semi-Bantu Languages.*
            Oxford: Clarendon Press.

Judd, A. S.
    1916   'Notes on the Munshi Tribe and Language', *Journal of the
            African Society*, xvi, 61, pp. 52–61; xvi, 62, pp. 143–8.

Kitson, A. E.
    1913   'Southern Nigeria: Some Considerations of its Structure,
            People, and the Natural History', *Geographical Journal*, xlvi,
            pp. 16–38.

Koelle, S. W.
    1854   *Polyglotta Africana.* London: Church Mission House. [Con-
            tains the earliest Tiv vocabulary, which Koelle got from a
            liberated slave in Sierra Leone. It is close to the speech of today
            and much better than anything collected before 1930 (Malherbe
            and Abraham).]

Kumm, Karl W.
    1910   *From Hausaland to Egypt.* London: Constable & Company.
            [Tiv are mentioned on pp. 42, 43, 244, and 251.]

Lane, M. G. M.
            'The Music of Tiv', *African Music*, 1, pp. 12–15.

Lewin, L.
    1923   *Die Pfeilgifte.* Berlin, pp. 224–9.

Lugard, Sir Frederick
    1908   Annual Report.

Lukas, J.
    1952   'Das Nomen im Tiv', *Anthropos*, XLVII. 1/2, pp. 147–76. [A
            careful study of Tiv nouns, better than Abraham or Malherbe,
            but containing no ethnographic information: is valuable for
            anyone wanting to learn Tiv.]

MacBride, D. F. H.
    MS   Notes on the Tiv Tribe.

McIntosh, D.
    1941   'The Tiv Plantations', *Farm and Forest*, ii. 1, pp. 26 ff.

Maher, H.
    1961   *Scholar's Vocabulary English–Tiv.* Zaria: Gaskiya Corporation.
            [A word-list for Roman Catholic primary school students in
            Tiv Division.]

Malcolm, L. W. G.
    1920   'Notes on the Physical Anthropology of Certain West African
            Tribes', *Man*, xx. 8, pp. 116–21.

Malherbe, W. A.
    1934   *Tiv–English Dictionary with Grammar, Notes and Index.* Lagos.

1959   *Tiv Beliefs and Practices re Death, Burial and Witchcraft*. Privately printed by Dutch Reformed Church Mission, Mkar.

MARQUARDSEN, H.
1909   *Der Niger-Benue*, pp. 54 et seq. Berlin.

MAXWELL, J. LOWRY
1953   *Half a Century of Grace*, a jubilee history of the Sudan United Mission. Sudan United Mission, 112–14 Great Portland St., London, W. 1.

MEAD, MARGARET (ed.)
1955   *Cultural Patterns and Technical Change* (pp. 96–126 *et passim*). New York: UNESCO.

MEEK, C. K.
1925   *The Northern Tribes of Nigeria*. London: Oxford University Press.

1931   *Tribal Studies in Northern Nigeria*. London: Kegan Paul.

MIGEOD, F. W. H.
1925   *Through British Cameroons*. London.

MOCKLER-FERRYMAN, A. F.
1892   *Up the Niger*, pp. 74 et seq. London.

MOSLEY, L. H.
1899   'Regions of the Benue', *Geographical Journal*, xiv, pp. 630–7. [Mosley, apparently a trader, spent several months south of Ibi, and in the south-eastern and southern corners of Tivland in 1888–9; the few comments about Tiv on pp. 634–5 are historically interesting and describe the size of villages.]

MURRAY, K. C.
1943   'Tiv Pottery', *Nigerian Field*, ii, pp. 147–55.

1949   'Tiv Pattern Dyeing', *Nigeria*, 32, pp. 41–47.

1951   'The Decorating of Calabashes by Tiv (Benue Province)', *Nigeria*, xxxvi, pp. 469–74.

NIGERIA, NORTHERN
Annual Reports for 1900–8.

ORR, C. W. J.
1911   *The Making of Northern Nigeria*. London. [One of the few published sources, at pp. 171–2, on the Tiv uprising in Abinsi in 1906.]

PASSARGE, SIEGFRIED
1895   *Adamaua*. Berlin. [A description of the Tiv from hearsay at pp. 355–62, and a description of a bush market on the banks of the Benue at p. 360.]

PERHAM, MARGERY
1937   *Native Administration in Nigeria*. London: Oxford University Press.

PRICE-WILLIAMS, D. R.
1961a   'A Study concerning Concepts of Conservation of Quantities among Primitive Children', *Acta Psychologica*, xviii, pp. 297–305.

1961b 'Analysis of an Intelligence Test Used in Rural Areas of Central Nigeria', *Oversea Education*, xxxviii, pp. 124–33.

1962a 'Abstract and Concrete Modes of Classification in a Primitive Society', *British Journal of Educational Psychology*, xxxiii, pp. 50–61.

1962b 'A Case Study of Ideas concerning Disease among the Tiv', *Africa*, xxxiii, pp. 123–31.

1962c 'New Attitudes Emerge from the Old', *International Conference on Health and Health Education: Studies and Research in Health Education*, v. pp. 554–7.

1965 'Displacement and Orality in Tiv Witchcraft', *Journal of Social Psychology*, lxv, pp. 1–15.

ROWE C. F.
1928 'Abdominal Cicatrization of the Munshi', *Man*, xxviii. 10, pp. 179–80.

STAUDINGER, P.
1889 *Im Herzen der Haussaländer*. Berlin.

SUDAN UNITED MISSION, MKAR
1961 *The Coming of the Gospel into Tivland*. [On the fiftieth anniversary of the arrival of the first missionaries in Tivland.]

1962 *Tiv Hymnal*. [Over half the book is devoted to Tiv hymns composed by Tiv Christian writers and set to Tiv music.]

1963, 1965 *Atsam Agen*, nos. 1 and 2. [Tiv hymns.]

TALBOT, P. AMAURY
1926 *The Peoples of Southern Nigeria*. London: Oxford University Press.

TEMPLE, C. L. and O.
1922 *Notes on the Tribes, Provinces, Emirates and States of the Northern Provinces of Nigeria*. Lagos: C.M.S. Bookshop.

TERPSTRA, GERARD
1959 *English–Tiv Dictionary*. (Mimeographed.) Mkar.

TERPSTRA, GERARD and IPEMA, PETER
1961 *Tiv Grammar Notes*. (Mimeographed.) Mkar.

WATERFIELD, O.
1947 'Tiv Fishing Party', *Nigeria*, 26.

WESTERMANN, DIEDRICH.
1927 *Die westlichen Sudansprachen und ihre Beziehungen zum Bantu*. Berlin.

WESTERMANN, DIEDRICH and BRYAN, M. A.
1952 *Languages of West Africa*. Part II of *Handbook of African Languages*. London: Oxford University Press for International African Institute.

WHITLOCK, G. F. A.
1910 'The Yola–Cross River Boundary Commission, Southern Nigeria', *Geographical Journal*, xxxvi, pp. 426–38.

INDEX

(Vernacular terms in italics; meanings given in the text, where shown. Names of *akombo* (supernatural agencies) in italics and with initial capital.)

Aba, chief of Shitire, 367
Abagi, chief of Ishaŋgev, 397, 398
Abaivo, 280–1
abaji, see marks, tribal
Abakwariga, 365, 382
Abaverijuwa of Ukum, 232, 233
abeer a uyia, 70
Abinsi, 162, 280, 406
abortion, for magic purposes, 227–8
abɔ̃, 366, 370, 382
Abraham, Captain, R.C., 41, 63, 181, 207, 257, 276, 289, 292, 294, 365
absolution from *akombo*, 301, 303; *see also* purging
Abul Abaŋga, chief of Ukan, 367
Abumkpekpe, 304
Acii of Mbala, 349
Adamawa, 24
Administration, the:
  policy, general, 14, 406; re witchcraft, 289–95; marriage, 99, 121–2, 162–75, 201; inheritance of wives, 314, 317; chiefs and tribal organization, 367, 383–5, 402, 404–18; police, 389–90, 412–13; interpreters, 392–3, 412; native courts, 393–6, 401, 406, 409–10; attempt to bring Tiv under Jukun rule, 364, 405; attempt to found Tiv settlement at Kaduna, 396–401
  confidence of the tribe in, 175, 496; criticisms of, 9, 402, 403, 404, 405
administrative staff, 11, 13–14, 173; and language, 392, 403, 414–15; lack of continuity, 403, 412, 413–14
adultery, *see* seduction
adze, 65, 304
Adzɔv, pl. of *Ijɔv, q.v.*
'afflictions' of the *Ijɔv*, 267
afialegh, 70, 90
afterbirth, 302, 303
Agaishuwa, 270
Agaku Akpacum, 95
Aganyi, 275–7
agase, see crops
Agashi, 87, 91, 178, 186
agbadu, 89
agbaga, 151
Agbega, 286, 287, 288
agbo, 82
age, respect for, 344, 364
  for marriage, *see* marriage
age-grades, 28, 29, 37, 40–2, 213–4, 241, 290
  age-feast, 42, 329
  age-mates, in marriage by capture,

147, 148; in *Poor* rites, 203–4; avenge death, 241, 330; help each other against kinsmen, 290; demand removal of spell, 42, 329; taunting of, 27–9, 37, 40, 41, 149, 199, 381
agegha, 54, 58
Ageraiber, 268
Agishi, 276, 284–5, 287, 289
agondo, 65
agɔm, 150
agriculture, *see* farming; crops
aguda, see hoyo
agyanku fruit, 358
Ahina, 207
ahuma bean, *see* crops
Ahumbe, 30, 31, 178
Ajaa of Tɔmbo, plate facing 177
aka, 359
Akaa, chief of Ukan, 367
Akaakase of Nɔŋgov, 232–3
Akaanya, chief of Mbajir, 142
akafi, 66
Akiga, childhood and alleged occult powers of, 1, 242–5; researches of, 2–5, 8, 181; literary style of, 5–8; extent of Christian influence on, 2, 4, 5, 231, 236, 240; frontispiece
akiki, bird of *mbatsav*, 257, 343
akombo, 176–225:
  definitions, 31, 186–7; origin of, 183–4; classification of, 180–5; nature of belief in, 31–2, 176–83, 191–4; used as protection, 35, 36, 185–6; subject to power of *mbatsav*, 63, 223, 251; offences against, 30–2, 186, 189, 206, 207, 212; precautions against, 31, 92, 178–9, 353; inheritance of, 192; control of, 31, 179, 211, *see also* 'mastery'; initiation marks social progress, 41, 213–4; loss of faith in, 224, 418
  akombo of birth, 178, 180, 183–6, 188–208; of crops, 183, 242; of hunting, 118, 178, 180, 183, 184, 190, 211–4, 276; of arrows, 181, 183, 298; of exchange marriage, 117–8, 163, 169, 183, 191–4, 418; of the grave, 311, 332; rites after death, 330–1; in farming, 78, 83, 85, 87, 90–2
  cause sickness, 165, 178, 182, 184, 191, 206, 207, 214, 325, 348; crop failure, 189, 191; delayed childbirth, 301; bad luck, 181, 184, 187, 204, 212, 214; only kill children, 251, 305

427

meni oil tree, used in magic and medicine, 37, 211, 299, 324, 336, 359, 360
menstruous women tabooed, 211, 268
messengers, 216, 291, 385, 388–93 *passim*, 401
mgbe, 258
mgena, 151
mhiandem, 66
Middleton, H. H., 292, 294
midwife, 302–3
migrations of the Tiv, 15–17, 21–4, 400
millet, *see* crops
miscarriage, 206, 311, 332; *see also* abortion
missionaries, first appearance amongst the Tiv, 1, 2, 234; compared with officials, 3, 361
mjiir, 324–5
mkamande creeper, 52
Mkɔmon, 50
Mku, 95, 211, 213
mkurum beetle, 76
Moji, chief of Kunav, 397–8
monitors, killing tabooed, 269
monkeys, as pests, 72; and witchcraft, 373–7
'monkey's head', the, 294, 376
monstrosities, 267
moral standards, clash of, 167, 170; decay of, 354–5, 377
'mosquitoes' (face-mark), 39
mother, spirit of the, 118, 178, 192
'mothers of our line', 305
mother-in-law, treatment of, 60; presents to, 111, 125–7; in marriage ceremonies, 113, 114
mother-right, 103–5, 124, 136, 191–4
mourning, 332, 335
mouse, in magic rites, 224, 227, 271; to test magic, 265, 274, 275
mtam, 188, 300, 304
mtsakombo, 202
mtselama, 201
Muan, 49
Muanawuha, 49
mud, used in magic, 30, 32, 92, 296, 297
Mue Ityɔkatyever, chief of Ukan, 163
Muhammadan peoples, contrasted with Tiv, 13–15, 68, 405, 413–14; position of women among, 170 –religion, 233, 234, 347
Muharram, custom of giving presents in, 25
mumu, 73
Munshi, change of name from, 14
murder, due to marriage disputes, 162, 165; ritual, *see* sacrifice
mutual help, between the Tiv and

Fulani, 21, 22, 24; between age-mates, 42; within the group, 54, 55
Myam, 270

'Nail', the, *see* marks, tribal
nambe, 196, 208, 370; *see also* presents
Native Authority, 411
natural causes, recognition of, 182
nature cults, 179–80, 230
nets, *see* hunting
ndovorkpoo, 353
ŋgohol, 146
ŋgɔkem, meaning, 121
nickname, 144
Nigeria, Northern Provinces of, native authors in, 5, 8; organization of, 13, 14, 407; classification of chiefs in, 384–5
Nile perch, as omen, 336
nomenclature of groups, 18, 106–11
Nɔŋgov, 44, 77, 184, 218, 232, 269, 383
nuaŋge, 82
nuŋgwa (*tor, kwase*), 370, 391
nyia Ijɔv, Igbe, 270
Nyikaan, 275–6

oath, on the forge, 63; on the *Swem*, 220–3; on the *Ijɔv*, 270–1; on the sasswood, 318, 321–2, 323, 324, 329
officials, salaried, 170, 215, 390, 412–13
oil, compared with blood, 36, 43; used in medicine, 39, 43; in cooking, 68, 87, 89, 197; in the blood-pact, 142
okra, 70, 90
old and young, split between, 290, 293, 295, 418
omens, 258, 260, 335–6
ɔnov (children), used to mean relatives on the female side, 143
oracle, *see* divination
Oralai, the case of, 284–9
ordeal, trial by, 156, 157, 158, 165, 319–22, 415; death by, not mourned, 351; by chickens, 156, 320, 323–6, 375
organization, tribal, 17, 18, 99, 100, 106–11
over-cultivation, 193
owl, bird of *mbatsav*, 245, 257, 274, -pipe, *see imborivuŋgu*
'owners', of women, meaning, 47, 158; responsibility of, 120, 156–8, 159, 161, 252, 253; rights of, 47, 115, 136, 155–7, 166, 174, 300–1, 317, 318; difficulties of, 154–5
of the kill (hunting), 97

THE LAND OF THE

Ishare

MAKURDI   ABINSI

Mbakor

Mbayion
GBOKO   Yandev

Mbaitiav   Ipe

Kpare

Uka

OTURKPO

Farm

Ishangev   Gav

THE DAM

Masev

FRENCH WEST AFRICA

Sokoto   Kano

Northern Provinces

Zaria

Kaduna

NIGERIA

Togo

Dahomey

Southern Provinces

Cameroons

Accra   Lagos

Gulf of Guinea